REGNUM STUDIES IN MISSION

The Diaconal Church

Series Preface

Regnum Studies in Mission are born from the lived experience of Christians and Christian communities in mission, especially but not solely in the fast growing churches among the poor of the world. These churches have more to tell than stories of growth. They are making significant impacts on their cultures in the cause of Christ. They are producing 'cultural products' which express the reality of Christian faith, hope and love in their societies.

Regnum Studies in Mission are the fruit often of rigorous research to the highest international standards and always of authentic Christian engagement in the transformation of people and societies. And these are for the world. The formation of Christian theology, missiology and practice in the twenty-first century will depend to a great extent on the active participation of growing churches contributing biblical and culturally appropriate expressions of Christian practice to inform World Christianity.

Series Editors

REGNUM STUDIES IN MISSION

The Diaconal Church

Edited by

Stephanie Dietrich
†Knud Jørgensen
Kari Karsrud Korslien
Kjell Nordstokke

In Memory of Knud Jørgensen

First edition published 2019 by Regnum Books International

Regnum is an imprint of the Oxford Centre for Mission Studies
St. Philip and St. James Church, Woodstock Road
Oxford, OX2 6HR, UK
www.ocms.ac.uk/regnum

09 08 07 06 05 04 03 8 7 6 5 4 3 2 1

British Library Cataloguing in Publication Data
A catalogue record for this book is available from the British Library

ISBN: 978-1-506477-08-4

Typeset by Words by Design
Cover design by Lina Nordlie, Diakonhjemmet Foundation
and Words by Design

The boat on the front cover is part of the altarpiece by artist Gunnar Torvund displayed at Diakonhjemmet Chapel in Oslo © Gunnar Torvund / BONO 2019

The publication of this volume was made possible by the
generous financial assistance of Digni

Distributed by Fortress Press in the US and Canada

Contents

This collection of essays is published in memory of our colleague and friend, **Knud Jørgensen** (1942-2018). Knud had an unusually full and productive life in media, publishing, teaching and organizational activities. During his studies at the University of Copenhagen he worked as a journalist at the Danish Radio. While working, he completed a master's degree in anthropology and a PhD degree in missiology, both at Fuller Theological Seminary in the US.

Jørgensen was 20 years old when he started in Denmark's Radio. After theology studies, he was employed by Lutheran World Federation, LWF, in Ethiopia as program director and program editor at the Gospel Voice of Ethiopia, before joining the LWF in Geneva in 1978 as Executive Secretary for Communication. From 1981 he led the International Mass Media Institute in Kristiansand for seven years before becoming principal at the mission school 'Gå Ut Senteret' with the Santal Mission. He moved on as Director of Communication in Norwegian Church Aid, before returning to Ethiopia in 1994 as dean of the Leadership Department at the Mekane Yesus seminary. In 1998, Jørgensen was appointed as Director of Areopagos, where he worked until his retirement in 2010.

In recent years, Jørgensen had been the editor of many of the 39 books in the Regnum Edinburgh Centenary Series of missionary literature, a series that followed the celebration of the 'Edinburgh 2010' mission anniversary. He had also authored and edited many other volumes, and so became a keen supporter, friend and contributor to the Regnum Publishing family. We shall miss him.

Foreword

I am glad and thankful that this book has been written. Because it is a timely and necessary publication.

First, because it so firmly and convincingly anchors *Diakonia* in the very being of the church, in its essence. When a church engages in loving service to the neighbor, it does so because of what the church is. Being and doing are deeply connected and because of this, there is an inevitability for the church to meet the oppressed and excluded and journey with them as they assert their God-given dignity. Because of what the church *is*, it can't *do* otherwise!

The specific references in this book to the sacraments in the church, Baptism and Eucharist, underline this deep connection and take us to a key insight that we can find in Scriptures: those meeting the transfigured face of our Lord are called to go down to the plains to meet the disfigured faces of the wounded and broken (Mt. 17). Because of who we are in Christ, we become who we are called to be in this world: a diaconal church.

Second, this publication doesn't only make the point of linking *Diakonia* with ecclesiology, but it constantly roots both concepts in the missiological discourse of the churches' participation in God's holistic mission. The church reaches its deepest meaning and purpose when it takes up its vocation to participate in God's mission, which encompasses proclamation, service (*Diakonia*) and advocacy (public voice). This mission, in turn, is one shaped by God's incarnation in Christ, hence by God reaching out and approaching humankind with the compassionate desire of leaving no one behind (Luke 15). That determination is one that requires to be announced in words, practiced in concrete action and defended publicly where it is being challenged. It is not one against or over the other, but these three dimensions of holistic mission influencing and enriching one another.

This leads me to the third aspect to be highlighted: the book is so timely and necessary because it reaches practitioners, theologians and teachers at a time when the concern for the suffering neighbor is increasingly questioned. It becomes, therefore, a prophetic call to resist theological or political discourses and practices that lull communities – sometimes with their churches – into an attitude of indifference toward the suffering neighbor. It is a call to remain steadfast in faith, hope and love, of which love is declared to be the greatest (1 Cor 13).

Published as the third book in a series dedicated to *Diakonia*, I recommend this book to readers in academic settings, within churches, their institutions for theological formation, and their diaconal structures. It is indeed a timely and a necessary book!

Martin Junge
General Secretary
Lutheran World Federation

Introduction
The Diaconal Church

Stephanie Dietrich, †Knud Jørgensen
Kari Karsrud Korslien and Kjell Nordstokke

This book is the third volume in a series published by Regnum presenting academic studies on *diakonia* as church-based social practice. The first volume, *Diakonia as Christian Social Practice – An Introduction*, was published in 2014. It sought to introduce *diakonia* as an academic theme, both by clarifying its normative point of departure in theology and social sciences and by presenting examples of concrete diaconal practice through case studies from different parts of the world. The second volume, *Diakonia in a Gender Perspective*, published in 2016, maintained the same interdisciplinary approach. On the one hand, it presented biblical and theological perspectives in the pursuit of engendering diaconal practice, and on the other, it pointed to experiences in different social and ecclesial contexts linked to the challenge of gender mainstreaming.

In the introduction to volume 1, the editors presented their understanding of *diakonia*, referring to recent research.[1] It mainly views *diakonia* as a biblical call to service, and as such an integral part of the nature and the mission of the church. Church of Norway has adopted this definition in its Plan for *diakonia*:

> *Diakonia* is the caring ministry of the Church. It is the Gospel in action and is expressed through loving your neighbor, creating inclusive communities, caring for creating and struggling for justice.[2]

The present volume largely follows this concept of *diakonia* when addressing its ecclesiological dimension, both as theory and practice. It roots *diakonia* in the Gospel of Jesus Christ and in his call to discipleship, thus affirming *diakonia* as constitutive for the being and the doing of the Church. In addition, it points to a broad variety of possible action areas in the pursuit of serving God and the neighbor, of defending human dignity and promoting justice, peace and the integrity of creation.

---

[1] *Diakonia as Christian Social Practice – An Introduction*, 1-4.
[2] https://kirken.no/globalassets/bispedommer/nord-halogaland/dokumenter/tema/diakoni/plan_diakoni_2010_english.pdf.

The church is both a religious and social phenomenon, which implies that ecclesiology, as academic discipline, requires both theological and sociological reflection. In particular, this is imperative in the study of *diakonia*. Its analysis of social reality must be interdisciplinary, its proposals for good diaconal practice will harvest from insights from social work, practical theology and other relevant fields of practical knowledge. Not least, it has to be critical, in the sense that insights from different knowledges (sic! – plural) inform and question one another mutually and provoke in a constructive way new approaches and methods in diaconal action.

This methodological approach affirms the empirical turn in ecclesiology, emphasizing the importance of studying the church as a social phenomenon, giving a critical account of its life and work. At the same time, it implies a constant reference to the normative basis of the church, which affirms its faith fundament and the need of theological reflection, however critically in order to avoid an idealization of the church (for instance, Christianity as the historical model that for a long time dominated in Europe and the regions of the world that were colonized by Western empires). *Diakonia*, both as practice and theory, will always wrestle with the contradiction between the ideal and the real church; it will be realistic regarding the ambiguities and shortcomings of the church as it appears in historical contexts; nevertheless, it will look for ways and opportunities of realizing the vision and values that are embedded in the vocation of the body of Christ and of participating in God's mission for the healing of the world. All authors of this book share this commitment, expressing it differently according to their background and experiences. This makes the personal, or even better, the biographical dimension of what is reflected and expressed, notable, which, according to some academic standards, may be considered questionable, but which according to our understanding is a most productive way of bringing forth insight and reflection to be used for the purpose of presenting relevant theory on *diakonia*.

According to this view, the diaconal church is a given reality, as such an expression of God's gracious love and care in a concrete historical context. To portray the diaconal church is thus both a critical learning process in relation to local experiences of being a diaconal church with the purpose of gaining insight that may inspire and enlighten diaconal practitioners in their work, and at the same time, an ongoing reflection on the normative foundation for imagining what it takes be a diaconal church. These diaconal practitioners together with students of *diakonia* are imagined as the prime readers of this book; it intends to strengthen their ability to reflect critically and constructively on their practice and to equip them with relevant and well-founded tools in the pursuit of an improved practice.

This publication reflects an understanding of the Church as the community of believers, knowing the Church universal only exists in its concrete manifestations as churches in different contexts and traditions. As such, generalized reflections about "The Church" need to be concretized in the encounter with the concrete reality of the lives of people and communities. Diaconal approaches reflect the Churches' presence in different contexts, in the public sphere, not separated from the life-world of the people.

In many ways, this book reflects developments within the study of ecclesiology since German Protestant theologian Otto Dibelius in 1927 named the 20th century *The Century of the Church.*[3] Following the example of Dibelius, this book will also develop its reflection on the church in light of burning social issues in the contemporary world, with reference to learning processes within the ecumenical movement. It will also focus on *diakonia* as a constituent element in the being and the doing of the church, and seek to explore this theme as a resource in the process of clarifying what it means to be church in times as ours.

The following statement from the World Council of Churches Assembly in Vancouver, Canada, in 1983 clearly affirms this understanding:

> *Diakonia* as the Church's ministry of sharing, healing and reconciliation is of the very nature of the Church. It demands of individuals and churches a giving, which comes not out of what they have, but what they are. *Diakonia* constantly has to challenge the frozen, static, self-centered structures of the Church and transform them into living instruments of the sharing, healing ministry of the Church. *Diakonia* cannot be confined within the institutional framework. It should transcend the established structures and boundaries of the institutional church and become the sharing and healing action of the Holy Spirit through the community of God's people in and for the world.[4]

In addition to affirming the **ecclesial dimension** of *diakonia*, this statement also points at its **holistic dimension**, which rejects the temptation to limit *diakonia* to social action performed by specialized agencies. *Diakonia* is an integral part of the church's mission, and cannot be disconnected, neither from the proclamation and teaching, nor from advocacy and public witness. It remains a demanding task on the one hand to avoid practices that reduce diaconal action to a tool for obtaining other goals, such as recruiting new church members, insisting that diaconal action in itself fully manifests the purpose of participation in God's mission for the healing of the world. On the other hand, it affirms that any diaconal action as faith-based action as a sign announces God's care and goodwill for humanity and all of creation.

Together with the growing attention given to ecclesial and holistic dimension, the ecumenical movement has also affirmed the **prophetic dimension** as fundamental in its understanding of *diakonia*. In particular,

---

[3] Otto Dibelius, *Das Jahrhundert der Kirche. Geschichte, Betrachtung, Umschau und Ziele*. Berlin, Furche-Verlag, 1927.

[4] David Gill (ed.), *Gathered for life. Official Report VI Assembly World Council of Churches, Vancouver, Canada 24 July – 10 August 1983*. Geneva, World Council of Churches, 1983, 62.

voices from the global South have raised this concern; they claim that the diaconal church cannot respond to the challenges of today's world by activities in the form of benevolent action; *diakonia* must address the root causes of injustice and be rights-based in its analysis, methodology and practice. As faith-based and rights-based practice, *diakonia* is inspired by prophets in the Old Testament, and even more by Jesus, who boldly defended human dignity and resisted practices of social and religious exclusion, setting people free and empowering them to enjoy the gifts of the community.

These dimensions will permeate the different presentations in this book, acknowledging that each context presents particular challenges in pursuing the task of manifesting the church's distinct nature and mission.

Part 1 Outlines Theological Fundamentals

Stephanie Dietrich opens this chapter with *Ecclesiology on the Move: Rethinking the Church in a Diaconal Perspective*, where she describes and discusses the recent development within theology and ecclesiology within the framework of the WCC, as reflected in the Faith and Order study on ecclesiology (*The Church towards a common vision*, TCTCV), and WCCs work under the agenda of a "Pilgrimage of Justice and Peace". TCTCV links together traditional issues of ecclesiology with an emphasis on the need to link these themes with an understanding of the Church's identity "in and for the world" (chapter 4), the Church in society. In the same way, the notion of "Pilgrimage of justice and peace" tries to link together the Church's engagement in the world, for justice and peace, with the Christian understanding of being a community "on the move", together toward unity. The author discusses critically the notion of "pilgrimage", including ambivalences and unclear aspects related to the pilgrimage terminology. Notwithstanding the author's critical approach to the pilgrimage terminology, she concludes that the recent development within the WCC represents a promising approach to a more holistic and diaconal ecclesiology.

Kjell Nordstokke deals with *Diakonia as Mark of the Church*, which reminds us that since the 4th century, Christians have confessed their faith in "one, holy, catholic and apostolic church". Known as the marks of the church (notae ecclesiae), they have been used to express what is essential in the church's being and at the same time notable to all. This chapter seeks to interpret the notae ecclesiae in a diaconal perspective. It establishes ways of reading the marks that affirm the diaconal nature of the church, and as imperative norms that urge churches and in particular church leaders to evaluate critically the commitment to unity, holiness, catholicity and apostolicity from the perspective of people who experience suffering and marginalization.

The third chapter, written by Maria Munkholt, deals with the different emphases and meanings that have been associated with *diakonia* in church history as she reflects on *Historical Perspectives on Diaconal Ecclesiology*. The chapter gives examples of sources mentioning deacons, deaconesses and *diakonia* in the early church, and shows how ideas from the early church were later taken up and refashioned in the course of church history. Several scholars have noted a shift occurring within the reformation churches of the 16th century. In these churches a "charitable diaconate" developed and replaced the former primarily liturgical diaconate. The 20th century witnessed other innovations regarding the concept of *diakonia* in the churches as *diakonia* increasingly came to be seen as a general responsibility of all church members and thus as constitutive of Church per se. This has, for instance, been the case in the ecclesiological work of the World Council of Churches.

Concepts of the Church in the New Testament by Jostein Ådna tell us that all forms of ecclesiology in the New Testament originate from a fundamental understanding of the church as a community of believers in Christ, uniting them by transcending traditional and established divisions. How such a community inter alia includes attention to basic economic-social needs is a prominent feature in Luke's description of the early church in Jerusalem (Acts 2:42–47; 4:32; 6:1–7). Therefore, the Hellenist mission church in Antioch and the network of Pauline churches saw themselves as obliged to support the believers in Jerusalem and Judea well into the fifties of the 1st century AD (Acts 11:27–30; Gal 2:10; Rom 15:25–27). The specific Pauline understanding of the church as the body of Christ has strong diaconal implications: as the body of Christ, the church is commissioned to represent and mirror creation conquered by and positioned under the reign of God and the Kyrios Christ, where – based on Jesus' example and teaching (Mark 10:42–45; John 13:12–17) – *diakonia* and equality are practiced both internally and externally (Gal 3:26–28; 1 Cor. 11:17ff.).

Nicolas Abou Mrad's focus is on *Diaconal Perspectives between the Book of Acts and the Orthodox Liturgy*. Based on the conviction that the Exodus from Egypt is a depiction and a dramatization of a liturgical act tracing the itinerary of the "People of God" from alienation and submission to the "power of man", to the worship of God that culminates in the declaration of God's law centered around "serving the other", this article offers an analysis of the occurrences of the word *diakonia* and its cognates in the book of Acts, and especially in 6:1-6, which, the author believe, taps into the Exodus tradition, and relates *diakonia* to an act of continuous Exodus toward the fulfillment of the Word of God's sovereignty over the whole earth. In this sense, and considered from the point of view of the dramatization of the preaching in Acts, Liturgy becomes, in Orthodox perspective, a continuous act rooted in the gathering of the community around the word of God and unfolded in the community's daily life as a "serving qahal – ecclesia".

Risen to a New Life in Christ: Baptismal Perspectives on Diaconal Ecclesiology is the focus of the sixth chapter written by Stephanie Dietrich.

This chapter seeks to explore how a baptismal ecclesiology can contribute to developing a diaconal ecclesiology based on a baptismal theology, emphasizing the human renewal through and toward Christ – a life of Christian growth based on baptism. This chapter focuses on the reconsideration of an ecclesiology, which gives space for the active role of the Christians and the Church in the world, binding together the Church's doctrinal identity with its place in and for the world. The gift of baptism is simultaneously the gift of God's call to Christians to *diakonia* – incorporated in Christ and the community of believers, the Church, liberated to live and act God's call to *diakonia*, and cleansed, renewed and empowered to live God's call to *diakonia* in the world. Thus, this chapter explores different aspects of how a baptismal theology underpins the development of a diaconal ecclesiology.

Rodolfo Gaede writes about *Sharing the Body of Christ: Eucharist in a Diaconal Perspective*. His article reminds the reader that the Last Supper of Jesus, in which he instituted the Eucharist, is the culminating event of a series of other suppers held by him during his ministry. This text proposes a reflection on the inseparability between the Supper and the suppers of Jesus. The argument used for this study is the diaconal element that characterizes both the Eucharist and the other table communion that Jesus practiced and which he used as a metaphor to speak of the kingdom of God. The diaconal element is in the experience of sharing. This experience has the potential to transform the world and allows us to taste the banquet of the kingdom of God beforehand.

Wanda Deifelt deals with *Ecclesiology from the Margins – the Power and Authority to Define the Church*. The word 'church' (ekklesia – the assembly of those "called out") was often misunderstood to be a community of people whom God has called *out of the world* and into a wonderful light (1 Peter 2:9), immune to the troubles and tribulations of earthly existence. Still today, segments of the church (and theology) who want to pay closer attention to issues of power and change are labeled preachers of a social gospel – but not the gospel of Jesus Christ. A closer look at Jesus' own ministry, however, shows that the gospel does not call Christians *out of the world* but precisely *into the world*, to bear the message of love and grace that restores hope, dignity and wellbeing for the entirety of creation. This paradigmatic shift is feasible when one redefines church (*ekklesia*) not from its center of power but from the margins, through the suffering of Christ. This idea is delineated, in this chapter, through an exploration of key features of the church: a call to discipleship, a time for growth, a place for reconciliation, a catalyst for reformation, and an encouragement to engage and transform the world.

Part 2 Explores the Diaconal Church Being 'Sent into the World'

Knud Jørgensen's contribution is entitled *The Church's Holistic Mission*, in which he indicates that the basic thinking of the missional church is: the church is. The church does what it is. The church organizes what it does. The ministry of the church flows out of the church's nature. This ministry is holistic, including worship, discipling, fellowship/*communio*, *diakonia*, witness/ *martyria* and stewarding. The chapter further discusses the ecclesiological implications of 'integral mission', encompassing *diakonia* and evangelism, yesterday and today.

Rose Dowsett's chapter provides reflections *on United through Action? Glimpses into the Evangelical Story from Eighteenth Century Revival to Cape Town Commitment 2010*. She notes that both the Lausanne Movement and the World Evangelical Alliance are 'wide umbrellas'. They are confessional, in that they have clear doctrinal foundations, but they are also strongly interdenominational. Individuals, local churches (and sometimes complete denominations), mission agencies, networks and institutions: all these and more identify with one or both of these movements, from all around the world. The 18th-century Evangelical Revival was born into a setting where the divisions between denominations were deep, very painful and often acrimonious; the Spirit of God brought believers from different traditions together to undertake particular tasks as well as to bridge some of those divisions. That momentum was spurred on through the founding of the Evangelical Alliance movement in 1846, and through the rise of numerous interdenominational mission agencies (both domestic and cross-cultural) ever since. Respect for different denominational convictions can combine with prayer and worship together, and supremely in joining together in shared mission and service. Today, both Lausanne and WEA contribute to enabling many parts of the global church to work and serve together in bringing the good news of Jesus Christ to the nations, and in bringing the love of God to His world. The church is not defined by denominational structures but by shared faith and service: unity through action!

Kari Karsrud Korslien has written a chapter on *The Church as a Space for Recognition*. This chapter offers a reflection on *diakonia*, emphasizing the opportunity to develop recognition between people in congregations. What is recognition, and what are the challenges when the church as a space tries to make recognition happen? How do churches cope with diversity? The author argues that recognition and diaconal engagement are closely interconnected.

In the chapter *Seeking Conviviality – A New Core Concept for the Diaconal Church*, Tony Addy introduces the concept of 'conviviality' as a core concept for *diakonia*, which is related to the specific challenges faced by local communities. It is contrasted with notions of community, which tend to exclude as well as include. Conviviality has three dimensions: it points toward a vision of society and the economy (future perspective), it is based on a relational approach that coheres with Judeo-Christian understandings of the person-in-relation, and it supports a specific approach to diaconal and social practice. The chapter outlines these aspects and then proposes 'seeking conviviality' as a process that starts close to the diverse life-worlds of people and supports diaconal congregational life.

Rudolf von Sinner writes about *The Diaconal Church in the Public Sphere*. Christian theology is a theology of life linked to the God of life seeking to contribute in society so that there may be life that is worthy of being lived by all. It is the theological and practical expression of the church's intrinsic task to serve and to advocate for not only its own members but also to witness, through its diaconal action, God's love and justice in the public sphere. On the way to such transformation, education is tantamount. In order to develop this basic thesis, it is necessary to reflect on the place and role of religion in the contemporary world. Informed by a thorough analysis of such presence, a public theology reflects on it in a constructive, critical and self-critical way, communicating with other sources of knowledge and seeking to provide orientation to the churches as to a pertinent way of being present in public. On a background of the Brazilian context, this chapter proposes a public theology focused on citizenship, grounded on theological foundations gained mainly from the Lutheran tradition, as a response to challenges to human rights, the precarity of life in many places and the need for social justice and transformation. This includes nurturing by education and capacitating for service – *diakonia* – two intrinsic dimensions of being the church.

Carlos Ham gives insight about *The Church Responding to the Agenda 2030*. He starts by introducing the United Nations 17 Sustainable Development Goals and then suggests how the faith-based organizations (FBOs) in general and the churches in particular can creatively respond to them. He argues, on the one hand, that the SDGs can provide valuable practical interdisciplinary inputs and strategies for action to enable more effectively the churches' social practice. On the other hand, he claims that the SDGs provide valuable networking for the FBOs to engage in a global effort, involving states and the civil society, in order to improve the quality of life of the people, as part of God's Creation. In the various examples he focuses on and refers to some SDGs in relation to the diaconal mission of the Latin American churches in particular.

Part 3 Provides Contextual Reflections on the Diaconal Church

In the first chapter of this section, Zo Ramiandra Rakotoarison writes about *Diakonia as Asset-based Action and the Role of the Church/Congregation*. Her article is based on various documents related to the Use Your Talents projects such as documents, reports and books. She starts the article by defining the word 'talents' in relation to the word 'asset'. Then the project Use Your Talents is presented as the church *diakonia* in comparison to other asset-based action. She then presents the role of the congregation in this asset-based diaconal action: how the congregation make the difference in its community using the talents of the congregation members and of the community.

Beatrice Juma asks the question *New Paradigms of Leadership in the Church: Leadership as Empowerment?* She notes that leadership is a crucial and widely discussed topic where change has been experienced both in the corporate world and religious circles. This article discusses change in models of leadership in the church where new models are coming into play. Empowerment is one of the three core aspects of *diakonia*, which has increasingly been discussed in the new ways of leadership. The article discusses the difference between authority and empowerment and how both are experienced in new church paradigms of leadership. The discussion refers to servant leadership as a new leadership model of empowerment. Reference is also made to research conducted in Kenya on two Methodist congregations on the topic: Use of talents: a way to transform and develop communities in Kenya through congregations. This research revealed that church leaders had a great role in either empowering church members to use their talents or the opposite, depending on the leadership approach they engaged.

Jeromy Limbani Juttah's chapter proposes a *Rethinking Ecclesiology in a Diaconal Way in the Anglican Church in Malawi.* The article is a reworking of his June 2016 master thesis under the title 'The role, identity of deacons and the practice of diaconal ministry in the Anglican Church in Malawi: How is the deacon's ministry understood and how this affects the practice of diaconal ministry in the Anglican Church in Malawi?' Among the findings was the perception the church's ecclesiology and practice had gaps in terms of linking the available theological language and the praxis with regard to the diaconal ministry of the church as well as that of the designated personnel, the deacons. This has created a need to discuss a diaconal ecclesiology within the perspectives of the Anglican Church in Malawi. In the present study the author seeks to explore the link between the ecclesiology of the church and the diaconal identity and how much of this is reflected in the history of Malawi; how does this relate to the ecclesiology of the church or conversely, and how does the ecclesiology of the Malawian church influence the action of the church. He also asks the question of how the Church's connection to colonialism and missionary work influence its present self-image and its practice of mission and ministry. The Malawian church needs to explore its self-image in light of its calling to the diaconal ministry. Ecclesiology deals with the nature, identity and purpose of the church. Fuchs (2008) argues that the very nature and being of the church is that it seeks to relate to its divine origin and realize its spiritual entity, while at the same time to live its purpose in the community of believers and the world at large. Ecclesiological identity has had a strong influence on the practice of the Church and action toward human development.

Olav Fykse Tveit's chapter is a reflection on *Diakonia: An Ecumenical Perspective*. The concept of *diakonia* – that is, the service of the churches in and for the world – has undergone significant change in the past ten years, even as the churches' work has become more vital. In this chapter the author addresses, first, the theological underpinnings of *diakonia*; second, efforts in the World Council of Churches to integrate the classic quest for Christian unity with the mandate to realize the reign of God in justice and peace; third, how the WCC understands *diakonia* in light of the programmatic focus on the Pilgrimage of Justice and Peace; fourth, the changed context for *diakonia* today, especially recent and widespread respect for the role of religion in human life and development; and finally, our fundamental commitment within the ecumenical movement to a diaconal spirituality guided by a realistic hope for the human future.

Salvation and Healing in a Diaconal Church is the focus of the chapter by Cardinal Luis Antonio Tagle. The renewal brought about by the Second Vatican Council to the Catholic Church has led to a rethinking or re-imagining of the Church as a Servant or Diaconal Church, one significant sign of which was the restoration of the permanent diaconate. This renewal was a product of many factors, among them a rediscovery of Biblical and Patristic sources, an openness to other Christian communities and non-Christian religions, and a non-belligerent view of the world. In Jesus Christ the family is called into the family of the children of God. The Church does not exist for itself but for the Kingdom of God and for the human family. In Christ the Head and in the animating Holy Spirit, the whole Christian community has a vocation to be a Servant or Diaconal Church.

The concluding reflection is written by Rudelmar Faria de Bueno, exploring *Diakonia as Public Service and Public Witness*. Historically, churches have played a prophetic role in society, in some situations even shaping national and global political agendas and highlighting values of inclusion and human dignity in the public sphere. However, over the past decades the prophetic voice of churches has been silent or not loud enough, especially in times when the people needed it the most. We are now in a change of era, which will define the future of humanity. The rapidly changing and complex state of the world requires that churches rethink their way of being church today. This chapter seeks to identify elements of the changing world and potential situations and processes for prophetic and political engagement of churches and diaconal organizations in the public realm. It also seeks to establish some principles for *diakonia* as public service and public witness.

The editors of this volume are connected to VID Specialized University, Oslo, Norway, within the framework of the Faculty for Theology, *Diakonia* and Leadership. As editors, we want to give thanks to VID for giving us space, working hours and economic support to produce this third volume of the *Diakonia* series. A special thanks to DIGNI, an umbrella organization for 20 Norwegian mission societies and churches engaged in long-term development cooperation, for their economic support; and to the two external referees for giving us substantial academic feedback on all the chapters, and which helped us to improve the publication. Finally, the editors want to give a special thanks to Arlene A. Henry, Master student on the VID "*Diakonia* and Christian Social Practice" program, who comes from Jamaica. Her exceptional administrative skills, language knowledge and huge working capacity helped us profoundly to finish this volume, especially in times of loss.

In the final phase of editing this book, our dear colleague Knud Jørgensen fell seriously ill and was hospitalized. From his laptop next to the hospital bed, he continued his tireless work of bringing the book to its conclusion, in dialogue with the authors, in securing the quality of the texts. When he passed away in December 2018, most of the work had been finished. As editors, both of this book and the two previous volumes, we have hugely benefitted from Knud's insights and skills as a theologian, communicator and practitioner, and from his vast ecumenical network of colleagues, many of whom have contributed to these books. His contribution in this volume strongly expresses this, and not least his deep personal commitment to the church's holistic mission. Without Knud, it is difficult to imagine that the project of publishing three academic books would have been possible. We recognize this with admiration and gratitude, acknowledging Knud's significant contribution in so many other areas of serving the Lord, as we dedicate this volume to Knud and in his memory.

Part 1:

Theological Fundamentals

Ecclesiology on the Move: Rethinking the Church in a Diaconal Perspective

Stephanie Dietrich

Introduction

There is a need to develop a diaconal ecclesiology, fathoming *diakonia* as Christian social practice *and* embracing both the Church's ethos and its structures, as an expression of what the Christian Church *is* by its very nature, and what it *does*. *Diakonia* is not only an activity of the Church but also belongs to the Church's being; it is a mark of the church.

This function was underlined in earlier studies on *diakonia*, like the document *Diakonia in Context* (2009) from the Lutheran World Federation.[1]

> *Diakonia* is thus an intrinsic element of being Church and cannot be reduced to an activity by certain committed persons or made necessary by external social conditions. *Diakonia* is deeply related to what the Church celebrates in its liturgy and announces in its preaching. In the same way, liturgy and proclamation relate to *diakonia*.[2]

This chapter focuses, therefore, on rethinking ecclesiology toward a dynamic and diaconal understanding of the Church, and thereby introduces this volume on "The diaconal church".

In order to pursue this goal, I will base my discourse in this chapter on documents resulting from the recent development within the framework of the World Council of Churches (WCC). Main materials for this discussion are the Commission of Faith and Order's (FaO) study document on ecclesiology (*The Church towards a common vision*, TCTCV[3]), and the WCCs work under the agenda of a "Pilgrimage of Justice and Peace". Even though these documents and programs do not elaborate extensively on *diakonia*, they offer important theological inputs and attempts to rethink ecumenical ecclesiology in a more diaconal perspective. I will discuss critically the notion of "pilgrimage",

---

[1] See http://www.diakoni.nu/wp-content/uploads/2013/12/*Diakonia*-in-context-LWF-2009.pdf, last seen August 29, 2018.

[2] Ibid., 29.

[3] See https://www.oikoumene.org/en/resources/documents/commissions/faith-and-order/i-unity-the-church-and-its-mission/the-church-towards-a-common-vision, last seen August 29, 2018.

reasoning that the recent development within the WCC represents a promising approach to a more holistic and diaconal ecclesiology, where issues of traditional ecclesiology are unfolded in interaction with an understanding of the Church as situated in the middle of people's lives. That also means that a diaconal ecclesiology gives attention to the role the whole people of God plays in the Church's presence and mission in the world – in other words, the priesthood and diaconate of all believers, The role of what is called the "laity", or all the people of God together, constituting the Church, needs to be discerned and lifted up as decisive for our understanding. Concluding, the need for a dynamic ecclesiology and a *communio* ecclesiology as the bases for rethinking the Church in a diaconal perspective will be emphasized.

The Church Towards a Common Vision (TCTCV)

The relationship between efforts toward manifesting the *unity* of the church and efforts toward common Christian *witness and service* in the world has always had an important place on the ecumenical agenda, though not always communicating with each other very well. Throughout decades of ecumenical dialogue, there have been repeated affirmations that these two efforts should be held together – and equally frequent statements, and actions, that set one against the other. The traditional texts from the Faith and Order Commission on ecclesiology have mostly focused on the first effort – the unity of the Church, based on doctrinal convergences and agreements. Nevertheless, there have been a number of studies dealing with the question of how to bring together "Faith and Order" and "Life and Work", also through theological discourses.[4]

The Church towards a common vision, TCTCV, published in 2013, represents a milestone in Faith and Order's work on ecclesiology since the famous *Baptism, Eucharist and Ministry* (Faith and Order Paper no. 111, the "Lima Text") in 1983.[5] TCTCV addresses first the Church's mission, unity, and its being in the trinitarian life of God. It then addresses the churches' growth in communion – in apostolic faith, sacramental life, and ministry – as churches called to live in and for the world. TCTCV thus links together traditional issues of ecclesiology (baptism, eucharist, authority, etc.) with an emphasis on the need to link these themes with an understanding of the Church's identity "in and for the world" (TCTCV chapter 4), the Church's missional identity, the Church in society.

---

[4] See, for example, *CHURCH AND WORLD The Unity of the Church and the Renewal of Human Community*. Faith and Order Paper No. 151 WCC Publications, Genève, 1990.

[5] See https://www.oikoumene.org/en/resources/documents/commissions/faith-and-order/i-unity-the-church-and-its-mission/baptism-eucharist-and-ministry-faith-and-order-paper-no-111-the-lima-text, last seen August 29, 2018.

Likewise, the Program of "Pilgrimage of justice and peace" tries to link together the Church's engagement in the world, for justice and peace, with the Christian understanding of being a community "on the move" together toward unity. In other words, the "Pilgrimage of justice and peace" is not only a framework for all the WCC work areas but also an attempt to bring together the earlier distinction between "Faith and order issues" and "Life and work issues" toward a more holistic understanding of what it means to be a Christian Church today.

TCTCV chapter 4 starts by underlining that "(…) service (*diakonia*) belongs to the very being of the church" (58). Chapter 4 emphasizes that God is love, and that God's primary attitude to the world is love toward every human being and the whole creation. Based on this emphasis on God's very identity as love, TCTCV 58 underlines: "The Church was intended by God, not for its own sake, but to serve the divine plan for transformation of the world." The promotion of justice and peace is thus understood as a constitutive aspect of the sharing of the good news. Chapter 4 also mentions religious pluralism and the moral challenge of the Gospel and discusses the role of the Church in society.

Chapter 4 in TCTCV represents an attempt to develop further approaches to ecclesiology known from earlier FaO studies, toward the inclusion of reflections about the actual situation and role of the Church in the world and in different contexts. By so doing, it underlines that the development of an ecclesiology that includes a reflection about the Church in the world is not just a matter of application of ecclesiological reflections on the concrete life of the Church.

This perspective, only touched upon in the TCTCV, needs to be elaborated on and explored much further. Chapter 4 of TCTCV is an interesting attempt to develop this perspective, though one might say that the chapter is the least developed chapter in TCTCV. A number of official responses to TCTCV underline both the importance of chapter 4 and the need for further work on this way of "doing ecclesiology".[6] Although the TCTCV has a clear understanding of *diakonia* as an intrinsic part of the Church's identity and mission, it does not explore the consequences for such an ecclesiology for the Church's life and practice and its mission.

Thus, it will be a decisive task in the forthcoming years to develop further a joint ecumenical ecclesiology that brings together the understanding of the Church as the godly place of Christ's presence, the perseverance of tradition and Christian community, and *at the same time* the Church as a body in the middle of societies and very different contexts, where it partakes as an actor in local communities and civil societies.

[6] At the time this contribution was written (2018), the Faith and Order Commission was studying the official responses received and plans to publish a broad discussion of TCTCVs reception in the forthcoming years.

While the Faith and Order TCTCV document tries to think afresh about ecclesiology "in and for the world", and relates this to the Church's *diakonia*, the core document from the WCC *Commission on Mission and Evangelism* almost seems to avoid the *diakonia* terminology when elaborating on the social ministry of the Church. One might have expected that the WCC document on mission and evangelism, *Together Towards Life: Mission and Evangelism in Changing Landscapes (TTL)*, prepared by the Commission on World Mission and Evangelism (CWME), would have explored the relation between mission and *diakonia* further. As Nordstokke points out, TTL "lacks a consistent view on *diakonia* as being an integral part of the church's holistic mission".[7]

TCTCV's underlining that *diakonia* belongs to the very being of the Church shows that precisely *diakonia* as Christian social practice might contribute to this act of bridge building. The documents from Faith and Order do not develop a theology of *diakonia*, nor do they point explicitly to its bridge-building potential. Since *diakonia* is deeply rooted in the Church's tradition and history and biblically grounded, and at the same time, as a practice of the Church and Christians throughout all history, is oriented toward human needs, vulnerability and precarious life-conditions in different contexts and societies, it could hold a core function in rethinking and reframing ecumenical ecclesiology in future discourse.

The former moderator of the Faith and Order Commission, Mary Tanner, expressed the need to hold the Church's doctrine and life together, by underlining "Convergence in faith and convergence in life belong together."[8] *Diakonia*, holding together what the Church proclaims and celebrates with its action in and for the world, can therefore become an important tool to develop an ecumenical ecclesiology that is widely acceptable and having credibility toward different actors both in and outside the Church.

This *diakonia* approach is clearly linked with the WCC's program of being on a "Pilgrimage of Justice and Peace", and with an understanding that seeking unity in doctrine should not compete with, but rather correlate with efforts to collaborate in service, *diakonia*. The Faith and Order Commission, at its Plenary meeting in Pretoria in 2017, underlined this understanding of the pilgrimage: "Being together on pilgrimage implies that Christian service is rooted precisely in our common faith in God's saving and renewing plan for the world. Empowered by the grace and guidance of the Holy Spirit, the people of God may respond together to Christ's invitation to "Come and see.""[9]

---

[7] Kjell Nordstokke (2014): "Ecumenical *Diakonia* Responding to the Signs of the Times" in *The Ecumenical Review* Vol. 66, nb. 3, October 2014, 268.

[8] Mary Tanner (2009): "What is Faith and Order?": https://www.oikoumene.org/en/resources/documents/commissions/faith-and-order/xii-essays/what-is-faith-and-order-mary-tanner, last seen August 29, 2018.

[9] World Council of Churches Commission on Faith and Order (2017), *Minutes of the Meeting at the eMseni Christian Centre Benoni, near Pretoria, South Africa, 15-21 June 2017*; Faith and Order Paper No.223, Geneva: World Council of Churches, 93-102.

One of the challenges with the decision to subsume the WCC's program for the forthcoming years with the term "Pilgrimage of Justice and Peace" is that the concept may become so all-encompassing and general that it does not really manage to serve the Churches as a guideline for their working together. In the following paragraph, I will look critically into some aspects of the concept in order to show how the concept may be useful in the enhancement of a "diaconal ecclesiology".

Pilgrimage of Justice and Peace

The Tenth General Assembly of the World Council of Churches chose the "Pilgrimage of Justice and Peace" as the theme to guide the Council's efforts to foster greater unity among Christians and to respond, within the context of today's religiously plural world, to the challenges facing the human family in our time.[10]

The Secretary General of the WCC, Olav Fykse Tveit, said:

> We must make decisions about all our programs in light of our understanding of this call to move together, defining and organizing them as a Pilgrimage of Justice and Peace. All projects must contribute to make this happen. All projects must be seen as serving this purpose.... The idea of pilgrimage is not something besides or beyond what we are supposed to do, nor is it simply a rhetorical device to provide programmes with a title. It is a way to speak the language of faith and hope in the complex reality of today and tomorrow.[11]

In our context here, it might be interesting to look into the term's focus on "justice and peace", clearly linked to the Church's social presence and action in the world, and its link to "pilgrimage", a clearly religiously loaded expression for a "holy journey" of believers commuting together with a common purpose.

The Commission on Faith and Order tried to look into the theological premises and discussion related to the "Pilgrimage of Justice and Peace" program, and adopted a joint text called ""Come and See": A Theological Invitation to the Pilgrimage of Justice and Peace".[12] In this statement, the Commission unfolded the concept of "pilgrimage" in the framework of the Bible and Christian tradition. The document also underlined that the pilgrimage concept has an ecclesiological dimension: "It means living in communion with other disciples of Jesus, nourished by hearing the Word of God, and celebrating

---

[10] "An Invitation to the Pilgrimage of Justice and Peace", Revised, Doc. #GEN 05 Rev, July 2014.

[11] Olav Fykse Tveit, "The Pilgrimage of Justice and Peace", *Ecumenical Review* 66.

[12] World Council of Churches Commission on Faith and Order (2017), *Minutes of the Meeting at the eMseni Christian Centre Benoni, near Pretoria, South Africa, 15-21 June 2017*; Faith and Order Paper No.223, Geneva: World Council of Churches, 93-102.

the sacraments of faith. Christian existence is a shared pilgrimage undertaken as God's people."

The pilgrimage concept is widely used in the ecumenical context. It describes many different ways of "being on the move". Traditionally, pilgrimages were trips to Holy places, and they involved spiritual concentration, repentance and other motives. Historically, pilgrimages, like the crusades, also habitually involved abuse of power, war and oppression. This historic aspect of "pilgrimage" is not widely referred to in the context of its use in the ecumenical sphere. Rather, one refers to the general concept of pilgrimage as a joint move of the churches together toward the fulfillment of the reign of God. The pilgrimage notion becomes a wide term for describing Christians' and Churches' journeys together. The idea is that journeying together on pilgrimage creates unity in difference and strengthens communion within and between the churches.

When reading ecumenical statements about the Pilgrimage of Justice and Peace, one realizes that the term becomes almost all-encompassing. It is supposed to pay respect to core aspects of Christian theology and the ecumenical strive for unity, and simultaneously lay the path for humankind's engagement for justice and peace, care for creation, human rights, and all other good purposes pursued within the framework of the churches' ecumenical cooperation. There is thus a danger that it just becomes a slogan one cannot object to, nor relate to, or find meaningful to apply in their work. It might be perceived as an exaggeration of the possibilities that lie within this concept, or even a blue-eyed presumption and concept that does not pay sufficient attention to the challenging sides of the terminology. Official WCC statements like "The search for Christian unity "so that the world may believe" and may embrace the unity of the whole cosmos as final goal of the eschatological promise of God's reign remains the main empowerment of the common journey of our ecumenical movement"[13] might overkill their good intention, though they are not per se wrong. My critique refers both to the *generalization* of concepts like "The Pilgrimage of Justice and Peace" and to their *exaggeration* and *lack of contextual applicability*.

Notwithstanding these critical remarks, it can be interesting to consider in which way the "Pilgrimage of Justice and Peace" concept carries elements of a diaconal ecclesiology, which are noteworthy to pursue in the concept of this study. The pilgrimage notion has a clear emphasis on the need to move, to develop, to walk together, to pursue a goal. It thus prevents theologians from sticking to a static and unchangeable ecclesiology. It gives a certain dynamic to the understanding of the Christian Church, which is useful when trying to develop an ecclesiology that relates to people's tradition and context.

Kjell Nordstokke, from his viewpoint of diaconal ecclesiology, gave an appreciative evaluation of the concept:

---

[13] *The Ecumenical Review*, Vol. 66, Number 3, October 2014, 384-385.

> The notion of a pilgrimage of justice and peace therefore presents a new opportunity for the WCC and all its partners, especially those engaged in diaconal work, to consider the understanding and role of *diakonia*. On the one hand, it is an opportunity to recognize the rich tradition of diaconal work and all the assets they represent – at the level of the local congregation as well as in the form of international cooperation. On the other, it is a time for reflecting together on how *diakonia* should be shaped today, according to the signs of the times and in a way that gives space to all of its potential, especially that of the margins.[14]

In the following, I want to explore the role the whole people of God plays in the Church's presence and mission in the world – in other words: the priesthood and diaconate of all believers. The role of all the people of God, together constituting the Church, needs to be discerned and lifted as decisive for our understanding.

The Church as Diaconate of all Believers

The pilgrimage concept also offers the possibility to emphasize that the Church is constituted by its members, the people of God. Modern ecclesiologies emphasize that this communal aspect of ecclesiology is of utmost importance.[15] The Church is not primarily about structures, traditions, institutions and hierarchies, but serves as a gathering of people united in their faith in the triune God, in continuity through time and space. Surprisingly, not many ecumenical dialogues seem to have focused on the role of the people of God as constitutive for the being of the Church, although the ecumenical potential lying in this very basic and biblical understanding might be beneficial. In other words, although many ecumenical documents deal with the understanding of the church, little attention seems to be given to the unifying power that lies in the fact that the Church, as Christ's body, only exists with and through its members. The Church, and the Church's *diakonia*, is carried out by its members. Against a departmentalization of *diakonia* to special agencies or specialists or ordained ministers, a renewed focus on the power and potential that lie in the work ordinary Christians and local congregations, as agents of *diakonia*, do can contribute to a fresh understanding of diaconal ecclesiology, and a renewed approach to the role of religious stakeholders, churches in community development.

Mark 10, 42-25 underlines that following Christ implies serving and "being the slave of all", because Jesus himself served and became the "slave of all". Mark 10:45 (NIV) says: "For even the Son of Man did not come to be served, but to serve, and to give his life as a ransom for many." Jesus did not come "to

---

[14] Kjell Nordstokke (2014): "Ecumenical *Diakonia* Responding to the Signs of the Times" in *The Ecumenical Review*, Vol. 66, nb. 3, October 2014, 273.
[15] See Veli-Matti Kärkkäinen (2002): *An Introduction to Ecclesiology. Ecumenical, Historical & Global Perspectives*. IVP Academic, Downers Grove, Illinois, 85-87.

be deaconed", but "to deacon", as the Greek version highlights. Unity with Christ as unity of Christ-followers in the Church thus implies a communal "diaconate of all believers" forming the basis for a diaconal ecclesiology.

The Church exists in and through the fellowship of Christians, the *koinonia* and community, with Christ and with each other. Pointing to the relation between *diakonia* and *koinonia*, the embedded nature of care and sharing and mutuality in the being of the Church underlines *diakonia's* rootedness in people's lives and communities. This became evident in the Early Church, where care for people's faith and care for their life were closely connected, and an intrinsic part of the early congregation's life. The Church could grow and spread rapidly precisely because its members cared for each other, protected each other and made sure that no one was neglected. Acts 6 is a story of the community's caretaking for all its members, both the Greek and the Hebrew-speaking widows.

Many theologians have emphasized this link between the church as the body of Christ constituted by its members and the Church's social responsibility. Among the most famous theologians to be mentioned is Dietrich Bonhoeffer, who emphasized the Church's presence in the world, in the societies, as an aspect of the Church's identity. An important part of Bonhoeffer's ecclesiology *Sanctorum Communio* talks about the Christian concept of person and what that means for the church and the individual's relationship to it:

> The concepts of person, community, and God are inseparably and essentially interrelated. A concept of God is always conceived in relation to a concept of a community of persons.... In principle, in order to arrive at the essence of the Christian concept of community, we could just as well begin with the concept of God as with that of person. And in choosing to begin with the latter, we must make constant reference to the concept of God in order to come to a well-grounded view of both God and the concept of community.[16]

The concept of Christian personhood in Bonhoeffer's ecclesiology, depending on social relations, then leads to an understanding of the Church as "Christ existing as community".

The Church does not exist in a sphere that is different from the world. There is only one world, one reality, and the Church exists in its middle, as the people forming the community of believers and realizing Christ's presence in and for the world.

---

[16] Dietrich Bonhoeffer, Sanctorum Communio: A Theological Study of the Sociology of the Church. Translated by Reinhard Krauss and Nancy Lukens. Minneapolis: Fortress Press, 2009 (1927), 34.

The empirical turn in ecclesiology[17] links to this concept of the church being a reality in the world, in different societies and contexts. Therefore, discerning theologically what the Christian Church is must always imply a reflection about its concrete reality in and for the world.

Diaconal Ecclesiology as Dynamic Ecclesiology in Changing Contexts

Diaconal ecclesiology can be understood dynamically as the ecclesial community wrestles with the tension between understanding the church as Christ's, oriented toward its ultimate truth, together with its subsistence in a specific context within the reality of people's lives. In ever-shifting contexts, it contributes to engage the concrete church in its practical, prophetic performance of witness, discipleship and *diakonia*. Such a dynamic ecclesiology supports the notion of the church as a space for critical theological analysis of the contexts in which ecclesial communities find themselves.

The Church is dynamic in that it is a part of God's mission, the *missio Dei*, empowered by God's living Spirit to transform the world. Being "Church on the move" thus also means letting oneself be challenged by ever-changing contexts and open up for empowerment and transformation. The Holy Spirit blows where she wants: "The wind blows wherever it pleases. You hear its sound, but you cannot tell where it comes from or where it is going. So it is with everyone born of the Spirit" (John 3:8, NIV). God's Spirit is never static, as is the wind, as should be the Christian Church.

This concept of ecclesiologies that develop and evolve over time, based on and challenged by different contexts and the needs of the times, is widely known within a Protestant context as "*ecclesia semper reformanda*", Latin for "the Church must always be reformed". This obligation for reformation is not an ethical demand, but rather an ontological reality, embedded in the being of the Church. Though the historical foundation of this term is not clear (it is clearly not expressed with this terminology by Martin Luther and other Protestant reformers themselves), it nevertheless serves within many Churches shaped by the Reformation era to underline that their self-understanding and historical shape are subordinated by the claim to continuously re-examine oneself, concerning both doctrine and practice. Reformed and Presbyterian churches, especially, underline that this call for continuous reform is based in the Reformation itself, demanding a continuous renewal and re-examination of one's ecclesiology in order to make it consistent with the biblical foundation and responsible in ever-shifting contexts and circumstances.

Also, within a Roman-Catholic Context, in the aftermath of the Second Vatican Council, there has been a turn toward a more dynamic ecclesiology,

---

[17] Cf. Jonas Ideström, Tone Stangeland Kaufman (eds.), *What Really Matters: Scandinavian Perspectives on Ecclesiology and Ethnography*, Church of Sweden Research Series 17, Pickwick: Oregon, 2018.

when the Church in *Lumen gentium* is defined as "the holy people of God".[18] The church is both *one* in Christ – and consists of *many* in different contexts and peoples. The Church is understood as God's people who are journeying in history as pilgrim people of God. God's reign is not incarnated in the Church, but the Church moves toward God's reign as its final goal, and as its drive toward a final goal.

Such an understanding of the Church as *dynamic* also contributes to avoiding any triumphalist tendencies, where the Church is perceived apart and separated from the world and contexts in which it exists.

The goal of *diakonia* is always the sake of humankind. Methodologically, this also implies that theorizing within the field of ecclesiology from a diaconal point of view necessarily will draw on both theological and non-theological insights. Both are important and may help the Church to live more truthfully as it acknowledges and reforms its own failures and shortcomings and engages in ever-shifting ecclesiological contexts by drawing critical theological attention back to the struggles and complexities of life.

Conclusion: Communio Ecclesiology as the Basis for Rethinking the Church in a Diaconal Perspective

The life of the Church in the world is intrinsically interwoven with the life of the Church as *communio*, in word and sacrament. God's *communio/koinonia* becomes lived and experienced within the Church that is placed within the world, within the societies and concrete contexts. If Jesus Christ, as witnessed in the New Testament, is the utmost example of God's communication with and for the world, it becomes very clear that the incarnated God communicates with humankind in a holistic way, in words and deeds and physical embodiment. Christ's encounter with humankind, according to the gospels, is always a holistic encounter, taking care of the whole human being. Through the sacraments, God communicates holistically about God's presence and grace and fellowship. God's word is spoken and lived, and involves a holistic caretaking of the whole human being. It is based on the triune God's own identity as divine love and God's plan for the transformation of the whole cosmos.

The Church is called to live its diaconal call and identity, because God has lived this call in the world through God's own son, his incarnation and service, death and resurrection. By serving the world and human people, the Church fulfils its task to bear witness to God's reconciliation, healing and transformation of the cosmos.

[18] *Lumen Gentium*, Chapter 2: http://www.vatican.va/archive/hist_councils/ii_vatican_council/documents/vat-ii_const_19641121_lumen-gentium_en.html, last seen August 30, 2018.

This chapter has focused on rethinking ecclesiology toward a dynamic and diaconal understanding of the Church. Ecclesiology today, or a "rethinking" of the Church, needs to balance an interaction between the desire to preserve the essential character of the church and the need that it roots itself within new historical situations, between a normative concept of the church and the need that it becomes enculturated in the lives of its members. Ecclesiologies focusing on a general understanding of "the Church" per se need to stand in a continuous dialogue with ecclesiologies taking their starting point in an empirical analysis of church life, congregational life, as it appears in different contexts.

This contribution is located in a long-standing scholarly conversation about how to understand the church both faithfully and realistically. The question needs to be posed how the use of doctrinal language can require inherently the language of social thought, or how a social interpretation of the Church necessarily excludes the more distinctively theological and doctrinal interpretation.

A *communio* ecclesiology with a diaconal perspective serves in holding together social and theological understandings of the church in its local reality. A diaconal ecclesiology helps to balance attempts to reduce ecclesial reality to its functions on the one hand, or ideals on the other.

Hopefully, such an approach can contribute to a more holistic vision for what the Church can yet become as a sign of Christ's life for the world. The Church happens where people journey *together* in faith in the triune God, facing and engaging with the life and the challenges of humankind both in their nearest communities, societies and countries, and globally.

Bibliography

Bonhoeffer, Dietrich,111 *Sanctorum Communio: A Theological Study of the Sociology of the Church*. Translated by Reinhard Krauss and Nancy Lukens. Minneapolis: Fortress Press, 2009 (1927).

Ideström, Jonas and Stangeland Kaufman, Tone (eds.), *What Really Matters: Scandinavian Perspectives on Ecclesiology and Ethnography*, Church of Sweden Research Series 17, Pickwick: Oregon, 2018.

Kärkkäinen, Veli-Matti, *An Introduction to Ecclesiology. Ecumenical, Historical & Global Perspectives*. IVP Academic, Downers Grove; Illinois, 2002.

LWF, *Diakonia in Context*. Geneva: Lutheran World Federation, 2009.

Nordstokke, Kjell, "Ecumenical Diakonia Responding to the Signs of the Times" in *The Ecumenical Review*, Vol. 66, nb. 3, October 2014.

Tanner, Mary, "What is Faith and Order?", Geneva: WCC, 2009: https://www. oikoumeneorg/en/resources/documents/commissions/faith-and-order/xii-essays/ what-is-faith-and-order-mary-tanner, last seen August 29, 2018.

Fykse Tveit, Olav, "The Pilgrimage of Justice and Peace," *Ecumenical Review*, 66.

WCC/Faith and Order, *The Church towards a common vision.* Geneva: WCC, 2013. See https://www.oikoumene.org/en/resources/documents/commissions/faith-and-order/i-unity-the-church-and-its-mission/the-church-towards-a-common-vision, last seen August 29, 2018.

WCC/Faith and Order, *Church and World. The Unity of the Church and the Renewal of Human Community*. Faith and Order Paper No. 151, WCC Publications, Geneva, 1990.

WCC/Faith and Order, *Baptism, Eucharist and Ministry*. Faith and Order Paper No.111, WCC Publications, Geneva, 1973: https://www.oikoumene.org/en/resources/documents/commissions/faith-and-order/i-unity-the-church-and-its-mission/baptism-eucharist-and-ministry-faith-and-order-paper-no-111-the-lima-text, last seen August 29, 2018.

WCC, "An Invitation to the Pilgrimage of Justice and Peace," Revised, Doc. #GEN 05 Rev, July 2014.

WCC/Faith and Order, *Minutes of the Meeting at the eMseni Christian Centre Benoni, near Pretoria, South Africa, 15-21 June 2017*; Faith and Order Paper No.223, Geneva: World Council of Churches, pp. 93-102.

Diakonia as Mark of the Church

Kjell Nordstokke

Since the 4th century, Christians have confessed their faith in "one, holy, catholic and apostolic church". Known as the marks of the church (notae ecclesiae), they have been used to express what is essential in the church's being and at the same time notable to all. This chapter seeks to interpret the notae ecclesiae in a diaconal perspective. It establishes ways of reading the marks that affirm the diaconal nature of the church, and as imperative norms that urge churches and in particular church leaders to evaluate critically the commitment to unity, holiness, catholicity and apostolicity from the perspective of people who experience suffering and marginalization.

Introduction

The first ecumenical Council of Constantinople in 381 confirmed the Nicene Creed and its way of confessing faith in the "one holy, catholic and apostolic church" (*unam, sanctam, catholicam et apostolicam Ecclesiam*). Since then, this formula has accompanied reflections on the being of the church. It has been used to identify the basic marks of ecclesial identity; the marks have therefore been called the *notae ecclesiae*. Their role has changed according to historical circumstances. In the time of schism and in the aftermath of the Reformation, the *notae* became a tool in the effort to discern the true church from heretical church formations, and of the hierarchy to subdue and marginalize critical voices within the church. Later, as the ecumenical movement emerged, church leaders used the *notae* to lift up common marks across denominational particularities, thereby turning them into a program for promoting unity and cooperation, for instance in the mission work, inspired by the prayer of Jesus for his disciples, "that they may all be one … so that the world may believe …" (John 17:21).[1]

While in the past, the *notae* largely were seen as a given reality, expressing the divine nature of the church, newer reflections on ecclesiology use a critical approach when referring to them, asking whether churches, as a socially embedded reality, in fact are characterized by the *notae*. Division and internal conflicts, rather than unity, mark the life of the churches, they claim. Further, church leaders do not appear to be more holy than others; the media report

[1] Hans Jörg Urban und Harald Wagner (Hg.), *Handbuch der Ökumenik, Band III/2* (Paderborn: Verlag Bonifatius-Drückerei, 1987), 71-72.

frequently about struggles for power within the church, or even worse, abuse of power. When it comes to catholicity and apostolicity, there are striking examples of uncertainty, even contradictions, regarding the church's message and mission. Danish theologian Anne Marie Aagaard describes how different theological traditions have dealt with this dilemma, admitting that the *notae* are not always recognized in the real life of the church, although they claim to be recognizable by all.[2]

Any reflection on ecclesiology must acknowledge this tension between the confessed, or ideal church and the experienced church; if not, we will either have only an idealistic presentation of the church, or, alternatively, portray it merely as a social phenomenon. The *notae* turn out to be helpful tools in dealing with this tension. On the one hand, they affirm the church as God's gift and gracious promise, and therefore a reality of faith and trust. On the other hand, they point to the core issues in the task of building Christian communities and of giving visibility to the mission of promoting God's kingdom.[3]

In this chapter, our key question is how a reflection on the *notae ecclesiae* can inform and inspire the understanding of a diaconal church. We shall start by looking at the theological (or dogmatic) reading of the *notae*, asking whether this formula confirms or questions the concept of diaconal church. Next, we shall undertake an analysis of church practices, with the purpose of exposing how to interpret the *notae* as gateways for affirming and strengthening the diaconal nature and mission of the Church.

The *Notae* as Signs of God's Grace

In the perspective of faith, the church is not a human construction, but God's gift. The English term "church" comes from Greek "*kyriake*", which means what belongs to the Lord. The Spanish word "iglesia" derives from "*ekklesia*", which refers to an assembly that is called together, in this case, called into being by God. The Holy Spirit calls persons to faith and communion. The formula of the *notae ecclesiae* therefore belongs to the third article of faith, expressing our faith in the Holy Spirit. The Spirit ignites the light of faith, both in the life of the individual Christian and in the life of the Christian congregation. In this light, unity, holiness, catholicity and apostolicity are notable as gifts; the congregation confesses the reception of these gifts when gathered in worship and thanksgiving.

---

[2] Anne Marie Aagaard, *Identifikation af Kirken* (Frederiksberg: Anis forlag, 1991), 15-53.

[3] Philip J. Hefner refers to the ambiguities of the notae, expressing both what faith tells us about the church and at the same time, what the church is called to embody. 'The Church', 203, in Carl E. Braaten & Robert W. Jenson (eds.), *Christian Dogmatics, Volume 2* (Philadelphia: Fortress Press, 1984), 179-247.

At the same time, these gifts relate to Jesus and his ministry. He called people to follow him, in the first place those at the margins of society, often condemned by the religious and social establishment. He set people free from the bondage of sin and guilt; he empowered them to be members of his new community of faith; he authorized them to be witnesses of the Kingdom that he had brought near through words and deeds. The ministry of Jesus thus remains the foundation of the church's unity, holiness, catholicity and apostolicity. Equally important, it establishes the guiding principles of how to interpret them as *notae* of the life and the mission of the church today.[4]

All reflections on the *notae ecclesiae* thus include a basic reference to God's gracious action in the middle of human reality, through Jesus and his saving and liberating ministry, and to the life-giving work of the Holy Spirit. It announces God's action as "good news to the poor", to be experienced today as "the year of the Lord's favor" (Luke 4:16-21). The *notae* proclaim the Kingdom of God as present and experienced by the people of faith, although amid contradiction; at the same time, they call God's people to wait eagerly for the Kingdom to come in its fullness – in prayer and work (*ora et labora*). In doing this, they point to the power of the Holy Spirit to renew the church, to equip its members and leaders for a ministry marked by unity, holiness, catholicity and apostolicity.

Thus, the *notae ecclesiae* are constant reminders of what the church by God's grace is given to be, and at the same time called to embody. They constantly question the life and the mission of the church and call it to critical self-examination and repentance.[5]

Unity as Diaconal Note

The prayer of Jesus for unity (John 17:21) expresses his caring love, both in relation to the disciples and to the world to which they are sent. Jesus' relation to his heavenly Father is the model of unity ("As you, Father, are in me and I am in you, may they also be in us"). It is a unity based on mutual love and recognition. It also implies a vision of bringing God's plan for healing and saving the world to fulfillment. The unity of the triune God is not a static and self-affirming reality; it implies sending, with the purpose of bringing God's living Word to the world.

---

[4] Jürgen Moltmann, *Kirche in der Kraft des Geistes. Ein Beitrag zur Messianischen Ekklesiologie* (München: Chr. Kaiser Verlag, 1975).

[5] Leonardo Boff criticizes Catholic scholars for using the notae to prove the exclusiveness of the Roman Catholic Church, and proposes to discuss them "in a society based on classes". In his view, the basic Christian communities with their rootedness in socio-political reality have a much more relevant understanding of the *notae* than the traditional institutionalized church. 'Theological characteristics of a Grassroot Church' in *The Challenge of Basic Christian Communities* (Maryknoll: Orbis, 1981), 124-144.

The disciples are included in this mission "so that the world may believe". Unity is thus vital for the being of the church as well as for its mission. To strive for church unity means to affirm the importance of caring love and mutual recognition within the church; at the same time to engage for unity in a broken and conflictive world. A church that does not live up to the vocation to be one in Christ jeopardizes its vocation to be Christ's witness and servant in the world.

The New Testament clearly expresses this concern. In Acts, Luke depicts the congregation in Jerusalem as a model of church unity, to the wellbeing of all its members: "All who believed were together and had all things in common; they would sell their possessions and goods and distribute the proceeds to all, as any had need" (Acts 2:44). This may well be an idealized picture; nevertheless, the author points to what happened when the congregation grew in number, and a vulnerable group suffered the sad experience of being ignored at the "daily *diakonia*" (Acts 6:1). Some translate this as "the daily distribution of food" (for instance, the NRSV), but more likely it means participating in the daily life of the communion, sharing its gifts, including the gifts of the table.[6] Those ignored were women; they were widows, meaning they had no one to defend their cause. They had Hellenistic origin, which implied that they could not easily communicate with those in charge. Their social status made them victims of mechanisms of exclusion. Fortunately, the apostles registered their murmuring and brought the issue before the whole congregation, proposing to establish a new leadership group with particular responsibility for the *diakonia* (or ministry) of the table (διακονειν τραπεζαις – 6:2). It is worth noting that this group of seven, perhaps the first deacons, all had Greek names, which indicates their ability to function as go-between, and to develop a pattern of inclusive practice that would contribute to the restoration of unity within the church.

Another passage that confirms this concern is 1 Corinthians 11:17-21. Here, Paul criticizes the congregation in Corinth for the way they celebrate the communion meal. The dominant group starts eating and drinking before all the members have arrived, most likely, the poorest among them together with the slaves; they are unable to attend the gathering before they had finished their work. When they finally arrive, the others have more or less finished the meal. This creates "divisions among you", Paul states (11:18-19). The right administration of the Holy Communion, a key concern of the Reformation, clearly has a social, or better, a diaconal dimension of inclusion and sharing. Therefore, Paul admonishes the Corinthians to change their practice, restoring unity: "So then, my brothers and sisters, when you come together to eat, wait for one another" (11:33).

---

[6] John N. Collins, *Diakonia. Re-interpreting the Ancient Sources* (New York / Oxford: Oxford University Press, 1990), 230-231.

In the early church, the bishop was responsible for the unity in the church; the task to include all members, in particular the sick and poor, belonged to his ministry of oversight.[7] The deacon would assist him in this task, bringing to his ears information about church members who were unable, due to illness or other circumstances, to attend the gatherings of the congregation. The bishop would then include them in the prayers during the worship and see to it that they were visited, bringing food left over from the communion table.

Here, the basic arena for promoting unity is the local congregation. It requires practices of inclusion and sharing, and at the same time, readiness to unmask attitudes and patterns of behavior that cause stigmatization, marginalization and exclusion. The term 'conviviality' expresses well this fundamental mark of being church, as internal lifestyle of mutual care and sharing, and as a way of relating to the local context, promoting practices that envisage the construction of a world in which all have a better life.[8]

The letter to the Ephesians refers to "the bond of peace" as a basic pillar and requirement in "the unity of the Spirit". It urges its readers to "lead a life worthy of the calling to which you have been called, with all humility and gentleness, with patience, bearing with one another in love" (Ephesians 4:2-4). The New Testament concept of humility (ταπεινοφροσυνης) does not correspond to the modern notion of personal modesty and shyness; rather, it refers to the social environment and a person's readiness of degrading one's own social importance for the sake of solidarity with the poor and marginalized. This is how the early Christians perceived the humility of Jesus, as assuming a ministry of self-emptying and presence among ordinary people, walking the way of the cross (Philippians 2:5-8).

The ministry of Jesus established a new and lasting "bond of peace" when it reconciled God with the world. This created a new platform for unity among people and nations that until now had lived in conflict with one another. "For he is our peace; in his flesh he has made both groups into one and has broken down the dividing wall, that is, the hostility between us", reads Ephesians 2:14, referring in the first place to the conflict between Jews and gentiles. Again, this is both a gift and a task, as clearly expressed when Paul reminds the readers in Corinth, a congregation ridden by conflicts and divisions, of the ministry of reconciliation (την διακονιαν της καταλλαγης):

> So if anyone is in Christ, there is a new creation: everything old has passed away; see, everything has become new! All this is from God, who reconciled us to himself through Christ, and has given us the ministry of reconciliation; that is, in Christ God was reconciling the world to himself, not counting their trespasses

---

[7] Lutheran World Federation, *Episcopal Ministry within the Apostolicity of the Church. The Lund Statement 2007*: https://ecumenism.net/archive/docu/2007_lwf_lund_episcopal_ministry_apostolicity_church_en.pdf.

[8] See Tony Addy's contribution "Seeking conviviality" in this book.

against them, and entrusting the message of reconciliation to us (2 Corinthians 5:17-19).

Promoting peace and reconciliation are therefore prime tasks when striving for unity in the church and in the world. The diaconal perspective reminds us that working for peace and reconciliation seldom will succeed when done from above; it requires humility and sensitivity, and courageous solidarity with the victims of conflict and hate. The quotation "not counting their trespasses" does not mean that painful experiences simply are to be set aside. That would mean to ignore the reality of injustice and guilt in broken relationships. To build unity presupposes processes of reconciliation that secure safe space for telling the truth; it includes initiatives of restoring justice. Only then can healing of relations take place and peace be established.

Shalom, the biblical word for peace, does not only mean absence of conflict. Much more, it expresses well-being because of harmonious relations to others, to God and to one's neighbors. There is no peace without justice, and no justice without peace according to the biblical witness of unity.

In some cases, the work for unity causes division in the church. When Christians committed themselves to combat racism and to support the struggle against apartheid in South Africa, other church members would accuse them of provoking conflicts within the church. It raises the question whether church unity is more important than engagement related to burning issues in the social and political arena.[9]

This question also comes from the political field. Oppressive governments often accuse the opposition for destroying the unity of the nation; they may claim that national security is more important than human rights. Clearly, this is a matter of power, and of abuse of power. It is illustrative of how power also may work within religious communities, inclusive in the life of the church.

Engagement for justice, reconciliation and peace must include a critical power analysis. Injustice in itself does not cause division, it rather points to a division that already exists and has been ignored. Who possesses the right to decide what promotes or hurts the unity within the church and society? Is it the most powerful? Should not the voice of those who carry the burden of conflict and marginalization count more? In a diaconal perspective, experiences of injustice and systemic violence are not just social-political issues; they have a profound spiritual and theological significance. Justice and peace are key concepts in the biblical message. Paul presents them as basic gifts of the Kingdom (Romans 14:17), with a clear consequence for the social behavior of the church. In the dispute with Peter about the communion at the table, Paul claimed publicly that the other's practice was not "consistently with the truth of the gospel" (Galatians 2:14). On the one hand, to accuse a church leader of

[9] The South Africa Kairos Document from 1985 reflects this dilemma: http://ujamaa.ukzn.ac.za/Libraries/manuals/The_Kairos_Documents.sflb.ashx.

hypocrisy implies a risk of conflict and division. On the other hand, the way Peter acted already institutionalized division in the life of the church, disqualifying gentiles to sit with him at the Lord's Table.

In this case, Peter seems to have acted out of fear. Also, today, fear is often a major hindrance when working for peace and reconciliation. In many situations, there are real reasons for being afraid. It also happens, however, that fear possesses people in a way that disables them from responsible action. The diaconal ministry for unity will therefore seek to create safe spaces that address experiences of fear, with the intention of overcoming conflicts and creating bonds of friendship and mutual trust.

Holiness as Diaconal Note

Paul is explicit in stating that holiness is God's gift in Christ: "He is the source of your life in Christ Jesus, who became for us wisdom from God, and righteousness and sanctification and redemption" (1 Cor. 1:30). The church is holy because God is holy (Isaiah 6:3; Leviticus 11:44-45). On this basis, God's people are called to be holy (1 Peter 1:14-16; 2:9).

Holiness is not a matter that establishes categories among the Christians, presenting some as more pious and holy than others. On the contrary, it expresses the transformative power of the Holy Spirit and God's option of choosing "what is weak in the world to shame the strong; God chose what is low and despised in the world, things that are not, to reduce to nothing things that are" (1 Corinthians 1:27-28).

Sanctification, thus being a gift that God freely gives, at the same time appears as a vocation to a lifestyle of faith, hope and love. As stated by a Faith and Order study, the church is holy because of "the holy words it proclaims and the holy acts it performs".[10] *Diakonia* or diaconal acts are clearly included in this vocation.

However, it remains clear that it is not up to the believer to mobilize the required energy to grow in holiness. As Paul reminds us in the final greeting of his first letter to the congregation in Thessalonica, the relation to God is foundational: "May the God of peace himself sanctify you entirely; and may your spirit and soul and body be kept sound and blameless at the coming of our Lord Jesus Christ" (1 Thessalonians 5:23). This echoes the prayer of Jesus for his disciples:

> "Sanctify them in the truth; your word is truth" (John 17:17).

[10] *Confessing the One Faith. An Ecumenical Explication of the Apostolic Faith as it is Confessed in the Nicene-Constantinopolitan Creed (381). Faith and Order Paper No. 153* (Geneva: World Council of Churches, 1992), 88.

Any reflection on holiness as *nota ecclesiae* must be based on this understanding, especially in a diaconal perspective. Holiness links to the being of the church as *congregatio sanctorum*, which is not the communion of people who succeed in living a holy life, but those who are sanctified while gathered around the holy gifts of Word and sacraments, gifts that transform and sanctify. This understanding of holiness implies a strong inclusive character; it turns upside down human views on dignity and worthiness; it opens an attitude of seeing the last first and the importance of what is often regarded as worthless. It always involves risk to connect holiness to the exercise of power as it may allow and even legitimize practices of stigmatization and exclusion. Jesus rejected such practices, in word and action. The narratives of Jesus affirm this; he recognized the faith of sinner and marginalized, and their contributions as examples for others (Matthew 15:21-28; Luke 7:36-50; 8:43-48; 21:1-4).

It remains an important diaconal imperative to affirm the faith and the spiritual gifts of those who are often considered as belonging to the periphery of the church. This may include questioning ruling norms of pious life, established by the religious or social elite. The understanding of holiness is not to be restricted by patterns that envisage uniformity; rather, it should be oriented by the view that the Spirit empowers to freedom. "Where the Spirit of the Lord is, there is freedom" (2 Corinthians 3:17). In the Spirit, this freedom empowers the believer to grow in faith, hope and love, in relation to God and one's neighbor; the golden commandment thus remains the guiding principle of Christian holiness.

Martin Luther emphasized this view, maintaining that the vocation to be a Christian is to be performed in the middle of human life, and not within ecclesial or religious confines.[11] He refers to the example of a shoemaker who will produce good shoes and sell for the right price; to use our competences, serving and caring for others, promoting common good – these are all expressions of living according to our vocation. In other words, they are opportunities of responding to the call to holiness, and of sanctifying spaces of human life.

According to Luther, this argument links to another of fundamental importance, the continuous simultaneity of being righteous and sinner (*simul iustus et peccator*). This counts for every Christian and constitutes another important guard against tendencies to judge some to be either righteous or sinful in relation to God. It also counts for the being of the church; the recognition of the church as simultaneously holy and sinful serves as a guiding principle for steering clear of ecclesial triumphalism on the one hand and unilateral church criticism on the other.

This does not mean resignation in relation to sin and practices of injustice. Luther accentuated the importance of penance when he published the 95 theses on indulgences: "Our Lord and Master Jesus Christ, in saying, "Repent ye,

---

[11] Martin Luther, *The Freedom of a Christian* (Minneapolis: Fortress Press, 2008).

etc.," intended that the whole life of his believers on earth should be a constant penance".[12] The word of God calls the church and all its members daily to convert. To confess sin is part of the process of sanctification, so is also taking initiatives to restore what has be broken in relation to one's neighbor. True penance implies embarking on processes of transformation, reconciliation and empowerment.

There is a long tradition in the church of regarding poverty as a sign of holiness.[13] This does not mean an idealization of poverty, which would be ignoring the just struggle to overcome its dehumanizing power. Rather, it is an invitation to a life in simplicity, to solidary with the poor and their cause, and a rejection of the kind of consumerism that threatens the sustainability of our planet, which judges well-being according to what we possess. In times of greed and irresponsible consumption, diaconal holiness may express itself through a lifestyle of simplicity, claiming in word and practice "enough is enough"![14]

Holiness is rooted in the life in Christ; it matures and takes form in discipleship. "Whoever serves (διακονη) me must follow me, and where I am, there will my servant (διακονος) be also," Jesus told his disciples (John 12:26), indicating that discipleship implies mobility and willingness to serve. This saying is placed in the middle of the gospel of John; it points back to the narratives of the signs, of the healing presence of Jesus amid human suffering, and it points forward to his death on the cross and resurrection. The call to diaconal discipleship implies both: to follow his example of lifting up signs of healing and reconciliation where we are called to live, and readiness to walk the way of the cross, if necessary assuming the vocation to martyrdom.

Catholicity as Diaconal Note

Catholic refers to the whole world, both geographically and socially, stating that no corner of human existence is outside God's caring love. The same goes for the church's caring ministry. Catholicity also refers to what is common, notable to all, indicating that the church is a public institution, rooted in everyday life.

Catholicity clearly correlates with unity, but with the intention of providing space for the wholeness of creation and human reality, acknowledging the gifts of diversity and particularities. It also correlates with holiness, announcing the

[12] Timothy J. Wengert, *Martin Luther's Ninety-Five Theses: With Introduction, Commentary, and Study Guide* (National Book Network, 2015).

[13] Gustavo Gutiérrez, *A Theology of Liberation* (Orbis: Maryknoll, 1973), 287-306.

[14] According to Hefner, the call to holiness is not only inner-churchly concern; it points to "the fulfilment of all humanity", Hefner, 'The Church', 207.

church's mandate to sanctify all dimensions of human life is "None left behind"![15]

Catholicity acknowledges diversity as an expression of God's generosity in creation; to be different is a gift, not a problem in the life of the community. It constantly challenges the church to recognize the opportunity each particular way of being represents to enrich the well-being of all, both for the church in its local context, and as a global communion.

Theologically, the image of the church as the body of Christ expresses this view on diversity and union. Paul emphasizes the diversity as a fundamental condition for being functional as a body; he warns his readers of regarding some members as being more important than others are. They should therefore care for each other, recognizing that they together share suffering as well as joy (1 Corinthians 12:12-26). This vocation to care for each other is concretely expressed in the invitation to participate in the campaign in favor of the poor in Jerusalem (2 Cor. 8-9). To be a part of this *diakonia*, as Paul calls it, affirms the bonds of grace and love in the life of the communion; it takes the form of solidarity beyond geographic, social and cultural borders.

God sent his Son to the whole world, historically as Jesus living in one particular context, eschatologically to cosmos in its totality. In Christ, so also the church is sent to the end of the world, a sending not limited by geographical or timely boundaries (Matthew 28:20). This is the eschatological determination of the church, as the church father Ignatius states: "Where Christ is, there is the catholic church."[16] The mission of Jesus thus has both a particular and a universal character. The same goes for the mission of the church; its sending is trans-contextual in the sense that it holds together diversity and particularities.[17]

An important question here is how to express this holding together. A diaconal perspective will look critically at how the church structures itself when seeking to manifest catholicity.[18] Church history presents many examples

[15] This focus on wholeness differs from the conventional association of catholicity with geographical spread. See Mark S. Burrows, 'Globalization, Pluralism, and Ecumenics: The Old Question of Catholicity in a New Cultural Horizon', *Journal of Ecumenical Studies* 29, nos. 3-4 (Summer-Fall 1992).

[16] Ignatius of Antioch, Letter to the Smyrneans, 8, in Michael W. Holmes, *The Apostolic Fathers in English, 3rd Edition* (Grand Rapids: Baker Academic, 2006), 121-125.

[17] Moltmann underscores that catholicity rather relates to Christ than to the church in itself; when related to the church, it contains a strong missiological and eschatological connotation. Moltmann, *Die Kirche*, 374-375.

[18] "The essential catholicity of the Church is undermined when cultural and other differences are allowed to develop into division. Christians are called to remove all obstacles to the embodiment of this fullness of truth and life bestowed upon the Church by the power of the Holy Spirit." World Council of Churches, *The Church: Towards a Common Vision*, 22: https://www.oikoumene.org/en/resources/documents/commissions/faith-and-order/i-unity-the-church-and-its-mission/the-church-towards-a-common-vision.

of centralist power, requiring submission and obedience to its model of being church. True catholicity recognizes the polycentric nature of the church; in addition, it considers the experiences of the margins as vital for its mission in the world. It is not power from above, but a promise of transformation from below, in accordance with the vision expressed in Mary's song of praise:

> His mercy is for those who fear him from generation to generation. He has shown strength with his arm; he has scattered the proud in the thoughts of their hearts. He has brought down the powerful from their thrones, and lifted up the lowly; he has filled the hungry with good things, and sent the rich away empty (Luke 1:50-53).

Apostolicity as Diaconal Note

Apostolicity refers to the messianic sending of Jesus that also marks the being of the church. He sent his disciples into the world with the mandate of giving continuity to his mission (John 20:21; Matthew 10:5-15). The 12 receive a unique task of keeping alive the memory of Jesus, his words and deeds. They were also responsible for instituting the life of the church, its model of sharing and mutual care, with its mandate to holistic mission.

In a diaconal perspective, apostolicity means a constant reminder of the healing and liberating dimensions of the ministry of Jesus, of his way of relating to groups considered outside the true community of faith at his time: the sick, women, children and gentiles.[19] Jesus sensed their situation, affirmed their dignity, healed them and empowered them to belong to the community. Parallel to this action, he criticized the powerful, unmasking their hypocrisy and prejudices. The memory of this practice of Jesus constitutes the apostolic foundation of diaconal action; as *nota ecclesiae* it reminds the whole church of the gift of sharing and conviviality, and the mission to heal, dignify and include.[20]

Hospitality and visitation are basic expressions of this mandate; the New Testament strongly affirms them as integral elements of the apostolic mandate of the church. 1 Timothy 3:2 states that a bishop must be hospitable; in other instances, the whole congregation is reminded of this task (Romans 12:13; Hebrews 13:2; 1 Peter 4:9). When practicing hospitality, the church gives continuity to the practice of Jesus, of inviting sinners to his Messianic table, and of establishing a table communion that would transform, reconcile and empower its guests (Luke 14:7-14; 22:14-20; 24:13-35; John 21). Diaconal initiatives, including traditional institutions that offer health and social care and contemporary responses to social challenges such as human trafficking and

---

[19] Rodolfo Gaede Neto, *A Diaconia de Jesus* (São Leopoldo: Editora Sinodal, 2001).

[20] Moltmann affirms that apostolicity is not a category of legitimacy in the first place, but of promise and assignment. Moltmann, *Die Kirche*, 385-386.

forced migration, are concrete expressions of this mandate, although not always recognized in the daily work. From the diaconal point of view, Christian hospitality is much more than a social activity. It is witness to the apostolic mandate of inviting and welcoming persons, in the first place those excluded or disqualified for the gifts of communion.

The same goes for visitation. When Jesus raised the widow's son at Nain, those who witnessed what happened exclaimed: "God has visited his people!" (Luke 7:16). His ministry can rightly be interpreted as a divine visitation, with the purpose of healing and saving, bringing the gifts of life to the world (John 3:16-17). The sending of the disciples intends to give continuity to this holistic mission: "As you go, proclaim the good news, 'The kingdom of heaven has come near.' Cure the sick, raise the dead, cleanse the lepers, cast out demons. You received without payment; give without payment" (Matthew 10:7-8). The book of Acts affirms this as the practice of the apostles (5:12-16). Visitation is also an integral part of the mission of Paul; repeatedly he expresses his care for the churches that he had founded and his wish to see them again (1 Corinthians 16:5-7; Philippians 1:5-8; 1 Thessalonians 2:17; 3:10). In today's ecumenical movement, there is a tradition of organizing pastoral visitation to churches that are suffering due to internal or external conflicts. In line with the apostolic tradition, it includes diaconal awareness and care, as well as bold advocacy defending the dignity and the rights of the marginalized.

The book of Acts gives more examples of the diaconal dimension of apostolicity. The church established on the day of Pentecost is open to people of all languages, restoring the brokenness of Babylonian confusion and scattering. In his speech that day, Peter referred to the vision of the prophet that both women and men, young people and slaves should be included and have a voice in the life of the communion. The church manifests this as a new reality, of equal dignity and participation. It is an integral part of its apostolicity. The narrative in Acts 6:1-8 witnesses to this understanding of inclusiveness and conviviality; the performance of the daily *diakonia* becomes a test of the apostolicity of the church.

The apostles received the call to follow Christ and to walk the way of the cross. This is the deepest meaning of apostolic succession.[21] That is another sign of the apostolicity of the church, risking suffering and even martyrdom for the sake of the gospel. In the view of faith, even suffering is a way of sharing and of solidarity, and of affirming the power of the Resurrected in the middle of human weakness (1 Corinthians 1:3-11).

---

[21] 'Successio apostolica' means 'successio passionis Christi'. Moltmann, *Die Kirche*, 388.

Conclusion

In this chapter, we have tried to develop an understanding of the *notae ecclesiae* related to the concept of the diaconal church. It has implied a critical perspective, affirming the importance of depicting the church as experienced from the margins, by groups that often are ignored or even stigmatized socially and in view of their faith. It has aimed at applying the *notae ecclesiae* as tools for analyzing the being and the mission of the church in a way that would identify diaconal concern and practices.

In conclusion, we affirm the relevance of the *notae ecclesiae* when developing a theology of *diakonia*, and in particular, in understanding the intrinsic nature of the diaconal church. The *notae* are helpful in presenting a comprehensive view that composes the essential being of the church, as a reality that every person is able to see and experience. As such, they belong to the public character of the church, theologically spoken as God's gift and gracious presence in human reality, sociologically spoken as empirical reality, seen and experienced by all. In this way, they help us to overcome the tendency to make a division between the visible and invisible church, which may turn out to be a strategy of not giving importance to how people experience the church in their daily life. The *notae* claim unity, holiness, catholicity and apostolicity as qualities that are notable by people, and urge the church, in particular its leadership, to promote structures and practices that bear witness to them as God's gifts and promise. In other words, they are key references when discerning what witness the true being of the church, avoiding both an idealistic or triumphalist view of the church and one-sided social criticism of its being and doing.

This is only possible by maintaining both the indicative and the imperative nature of being church. The *notae* help us to understand that the gift of belonging to the body of Christ includes a vocation to live according to this being. In addition, they help the church to set priorities in its ministry. They help us to draw insight from the life and experiences of the Early Church and at the same time recognize the need to respond to contemporary challenges when developing models of being a diaconal church.

In a world of increasing inequality between the powerful and the powerless, marked by divisions and conflict, the mandate to promote unity, working for peace and reconciliation at all levels, remains a central diaconal task.

Where people are victims of prejudices and exclusion, the church has a mandate to call people to convert themselves and change behavior and patterns of practice that defend human dignity and promote justice and peace. Diaconal practice should give visible signs to this call to holiness.

In a time when ideological trends speak in favor of building walls around individual and national interests, the church is called to speak clearly about the whole world as an arena for conviviality and care. Catholicity implies caring for creation as a just cause, and attention for groups of people that the powerful tend to ignore, or even consider dispensable. Diaconal practice must therefore have an ecumenical and ecological signature, having in mind the wholeness of creation as household of God.

In all of these commitments, the apostolic heritage, in the first place the memory of Jesus, his words and deeds, nurtures the church and empowers it to grow in maturity as a caring community engaged in diaconal practices of compassion and love. In this perspective, apostolicity means faithfulness to what the Apostles have transmitted, and its ability to interpret this heritage in view of the signs of the time. From this, it follows that Christian discipleship manifests itself in relevant diaconal action, lifting up signs that point to Christ and his Kingdom with its gifts of "righteousness and peace and joy in the Holy Spirit" (Romans 14:17).

Bibliography

Aagaard, Anne Marie, *Identifikation af kirken*. Frederiksberg: Anis forlag, 1991.

Boff, Leonardo, 'Theological characteristics of a Grassroot Church' in *The Challenge of Basic Christian Communities*, Maryknoll: Orbis, 1981, 124-144.

Burrows, Mark S., 'Globalization, Pluralism, and Ecumenics: The Old Question of Catholicity in a New Cultural Horizon', *Journal of Ecumenical Studies* 29, nos. 3-4 (Summer-Fall 1992).

Collins, John N., *Diakonia. Re-interpreting the Ancient Sources*. New York / Oxford: Oxford University Press, 1990.

Gaede Neto, Rodolfo, *A diaconia de Jesus*. São Leopoldo: Editora Sinodal, 2001.

Gutiérrez, Gustavo, *A Theology of Liberation*. Orbis: Maryknoll, 1973.

Hefner, Philip J., 'The Church' in Carl E. Braaten & Robert W. Jenson (eds.), *Christian Dogmatics, volume 2*. Philadelphia: Fortress Press, 1984, 179-247.

Holmes, Michael W., *The Apostolic Fathers in English, 3rd Edition*. Grand Rapids: Baker Academic, 2006.

Luther, Martin, *The Freedom of a Christian*. Minneapolis: Fortress Press, 2008.

Lutheran World Federation, *Episcopal Ministry within the Apostolicity of the Church. The Lund Statement 2007*: https://ecumenism.net/archive/docu/2007_lwf_lund_episcopal_ministry_apostolicity_church_en.pdf.

Moltmann, Jürgen, *Kirche in der Kraft des Geistes. Ein Beitrag zur messianischen Ekklesiologie*. München: Chr. Kaiser Verlag, 1975.

Urban, Hans Jörg und Harald Wagner (Hg.), *Handbuch der Ökumenik, Band III/2*. Paderborn: Verlag Bonifatius-Drückerei, 1987.

Wengert, Timothy J., *Martin Luther's Ninety-Five Theses: With Introduction, Commentary, and Study Guide*. National Book Network, 2015.

World Council of Churches, *Confessing the One Faith. An Ecumenical Explication of the Apostolic Faith as it is Confessed in the Nicene-Constantinopolitan Creed (381)*. Faith and Order Paper No. 153. Geneva: World Council of Churches, 1992.

World Council of Churches, *The Church: Towards a Common Vision*. Geneva: World Council of Churches, 2013.

Historical Perspectives on Diaconal Ecclesiology

Maria Munkholt Christensen[1]

Introduction

From a church historian's point of view, the semantics of *diakonia* are not clear, nor is the concept of "diaconal ecclesiology". In different periods, in different confessions and in different circumstances, *diakonia* has been understood and practiced differently. It is not always obvious what it entails to serve as a Christian in the church and in the world, or who bears the responsibility for providing the proper service. There is no historical consensus about whether *diakonia* is the responsibility of particular office holders or of all Christians, lay or clergy alike. Likewise, it is not always evident which functions are diaconal. In general, diaconal work can comprehend both social-caritative and liturgical aspects. Diaconal functions include such diverse acts as accompanying those who suffer, taking care of the poor and sick, teaching, consoling, assisting clergy in liturgy, administration, fighting for justice and communicating the Gospel.

This article will sketch out what we know about deacons, deaconesses and *diakonia* in the early church, and how ideas from the early church were later taken up and refashioned in the course of church history. Several scholars have noted a shift occurring within the reformation churches of the 16th century. In these churches a "charitable diaconate" developed and replaced the former primarily liturgical diaconate.[2] The 20th century witnessed other innovations regarding the concept of *diakonia* in the churches as *diakonia* increasingly came to be seen as a general responsibility of all church members and thus as constitutive of Church per se. This development will be traced by way of illustrative examples from church historical sources.

Before getting to the examples, I would like to mention my own point of departure. I come from Denmark, where church life is dominated by the Evangelical Lutheran Church. I currently work as a church historian at Göttingen University in central Germany. In many ways the Christian culture here is similar to Denmark: the secular and Evangelical Lutheran streams of

---

[1] I have written this article while working in the DFG – Collaborative Research Center 1136: "Education and Religion" (Subproject C 04: "Communication of Education in Late Antique Christianity: Teachers' Roles in Parish, Family and Ascetic Community").

[2] Charlotte Methuen, "Preaching the Gospel through Love of Neighbour: The Ministry of Katharina Schütz Zell", *Journal of Ecclesiastical History*, 61, 4, 2010, 707-728, 719.

thought come together quite harmoniously in society. However, Germany has a more visible and formalized diaconal culture than what I know from Denmark. Here in Germany, kindergartens, hospitals and many other institutions in local society are often run by diaconal organizations. This means that even the small trip across the Danish-German border brings one from one diaconal culture to another.

The Beginning: Diaconal Work in the Bible and the Earliest Congregations

Early Christian congregations were generally occupied with serving the sick and the poor.[3] It is a truism that Christianity from its beginnings had social appeal: "Among the rewards of belonging [to Christianity] was the help available within these Christian communities, which functioned in effect as social agencies at a time when there were none".[4] It was constitutive for Christians to serve and ideally to adhere to a strict moral code. However, if we look at the more or less institutionalized function of serving, *diakonia*, it is not easy to paint a consistent picture of what it meant in the earliest Christian communities or, for that matter, later in church history.

In the New Testament there are several occurrences of words of the διάκον-root. They are translated into modern languages with different terms, such as "service" and "ministry", or with the designation of a particular office, "deacon".[5] The διάκον-words are not a Christian invention; prior to Christianity, words of this root designated acts of service and acts conducted by intermediary agents and messengers.[6] In the New Testament, which reflects the concerns of the first Christian congregations, the διάκον-words are used in several different contexts – sometimes such words are attributed to Christ, sometimes to all believers, sometimes to particular persons in the Christian communities.[7] Several times in the Pauline letters, Paul declares himself a

---

[3] E.g. Hörnig. Thomas. "Geschichte der Diakonie – ein kritischer Zugang aus der Armutsperspektive" in ed. Eurich, Johannes and Schmidt, Heinz. *Diakonik. Grundlagen, Konzeptionen, Diskurse*. Göttingen, Vandenhoeck & Ruprecht, 2016, 77-109. p. 78: "Christlicher Glaube bildete Identität bildete sich nie ohne Armenfürsorge aus".

[4] Remus, Harold. "Persecution" in ed. Blasi, A.J./Duhaime, J./ Turcotte, A.P. *Handbook of Early Christianity. Social Science Approaches*, Oxford, Walnut Greek, CA: Altamira Press, 2002, 431-51, p. 441.

[5] The masculine form of the noun was used about both male and female deacons.

[6] John N. Collins in *Diakonia Studies: Critical Issues in Ministry*, Oxford: Oxford University Press, 2014, 57ff.

[7] For an occurrence of διάκον-, see, for example, Ephesians 4:11-13: "So Christ himself gave the apostles, the prophets, the evangelists, the pastors and teachers, to equip his people for *works of service* (εἰς ἔργον διακονίας)…". It is worth noting that Luther's translation of Ephesians 4:12 from 1545 has "office" (Ampts) instead of "service", which tells us that the development of offices was projected into the biblical texts

"servant" of the Gospel or of the word of God,[8] and it seems that according to Paul the real "service" for which he has been equipped is to proclaim the Gospel. Paul is a "servant" in the sense of a "message-bearer" or an "ambassador".

In Acts and in the pastoral letters, we see how words of the διάκον-root are used to describe particular office holders and works of service. Acts 6:2-4 is a well-known passage in this regard, although there is no consensus regarding its interpretation. It could seem that in the Christian congregation in Jerusalem it was a task of the Christian community to make distributions among the needy, i.e. "to wait (διακονεῖν) on tables". The apostles suggested that seven men should be appointed to do this charitable work, while they themselves should focus on another kind of service, i.e. the ministry (διακονίᾳ) of the word. Early on, this passage from Acts 6 was interpreted to the effect that the apostles appointed "deacons", and that this practice should be an example for other congregations to follow.[9] According to the interpretation of, for example, Kari Latvus, it is not obvious from the text if the seven were deacons, or which acts were entailed in doing ministry.[10] That the praxis of electing "deacons" established itself early on is, nonetheless, obvious from 1 Timothy, where we learn more about the expectations of those men who served as deacons[11] (1 Tim. 3:8–13), although the tasks of these deacons are not clearly outlined.

Thomas O'Meara has explained that from the outset, Christian ministry did not have the association of being 'sacral'. The offices were not holy, but attained meaning through their function. A designation such as "deacon" was part of 'a language-event' through which "the church fashioned a language that disclosed its way of life".[12] The deacon was called so exactly because he served, he acted out his title. "Serving" was without a doubt inherent to Christian ministry and life from the beginning. According to the Biblical Scriptures, both preaching the Gospel and doing social work were services expected either from all or from particular assigned members of Christian congregations. Gleaned from the New Testament, the importance of "service"

---

whereby the original flexibility of the διάκον-vocabulary was lost. See Collins 2014, 114ff.

[8] E.g. Ephesians 3:7; Colossians 4:23; and Col 1:25: "I have become its servant by the commission God gave me to present to you the word of God in its fullness."

[9] On the reception of Acts 6:2-4 in the early church, see Kari Latvus. "Diaconal Ministry in the Light of the Reception and Re-Interpretation of Acts 6. Did John Calvin Create the Social-Caritative Ministry of Diaconia?, *Diaconia*, 1, 2010, 82-102.

[10] Kari Latvus. *Diaconia as Care for the Poor? Critical Perspectives on the Development of Caritative Diaconia*, Kirkon tutkimuskeskuksen verkkojulkaisuja 53, 2017, 36-40.

[11] Female deacons are not mentioned in Timothy, but after the description of expectations to deacons, the text goes on: "Likewise women" (γυναῖκας ὡσαύτως). It could be a reference to female deacons or to the deacon's wife.

[12] Thomas O' Meara. *Theology of Ministry,* second edition, New York: Paulist Press, 1999, 75.

as a constitutive fact of Christian life is indisputable. However, it is relatively unclear how the congregations and the individual Christians should serve. However, more concrete ideas soon began to develop in a sporadic fashion.

Deacons in the Early Church

The first three centuries have been dubbed "a golden age for deacons",[13] and it is true that we regularly encounter deacons in early church orders and other early Christian texts. However, it is worth noting that the role and responsibilities of deacons were not the same everywhere – at least the remaining sources do not paint a completely uniform picture.

First, I shall mention a few occurrences of deacons in texts by the *Apostolic Fathers*. These are early non-Biblical texts, which reflect how church life and theology were under development in the first few centuries. One of these texts is the church order *Didache*, dating to the first half of the second century. *Didache* entails the recommendation: "Appoint, therefore, for yourselves, bishops and deacons worthy of the Lord" (Chapter 15).[14] This mentioning of deacons follows immediately after an injunction to gather at the Lord's Day to celebrate the Eucharist, and from this arrangement of the material, it appears that bishops and deacons should be appointed in order to celebrate the Eucharist. We can thus detect a strong link between the Eucharist as the focal point of congregational life and the essential work of the appointed ministers. Serving the congregation as a deacon is in this case primarily a matter of conducting liturgy. Also, the Letter *1. Clement* from around the year 100 mentions the appointment of bishops and deacons and argues that already Scripture testify to these offices. *1. Clement* also connects bishops and deacons with their performance of liturgical tasks and presents them as essential to the church. However, *1. Clement* is also emphasizing that everyone serves a role within the community, large or small, and everyone is dependent on the help of others. He prays: "let the rich man bestow help on the poor and let the poor give thanks to God, that he gave him one to supply his needs" (*1. Clement* 38).

Like *Didache* and *1. Clement*, bishop Ignatius, who also wrote around the year 100, saw bishops, presbyters and deacons as essential for the Church. He exclaims that "Without these the name of 'Church' is not given".[15] Ignatius urges all to "respect the deacons as Jesus Christ", just as they respect the bishop for being "a type of the Father".[16] Bishop Ignatius refers to deacons as

---

[13] James M. Barnett, *The Diaconate. A Full and Equal Order*. Rev. ed. Harrisburg: The Trinity Press, 1995, 43.

[14] *Didache* or *The Teaching of the Twelve Apostles*. Tr. Lake, Kirsopp. *The Apostolic Fathers*, II, Loeb Classical Library, London: Heinemann, 1912.

[15] Ignatius, *Letter to the Trallians* 3 in *The Apostolic Fathers*, I, Loeb Classical Library, London: Heinemann, 1912.

[16] Ibid.

his "fellow servants",[17] meaning that he and they are all working out God's will in the church. Ignatius represents an ecclesiology that is defined by the clergy as liturgical agents that secure unity. While these early texts generally emphasize the liturgical role of the deacons, there is a different focus in *The Shephard of Hermas* from the beginning of the 2nd century. This text mentions different charitable tasks when referring to deacons, such as taking care of the widows and the orphans.[18] According to Hermas, deacons are important as constitutive agents of the Church, because the Church is built up by certain people of past and present: apostles, bishops, teachers and deacons.[19]

Moving now away from the texts of the *Apostolic Fathers*, we will take a look at an illuminating church order, *Apostolic Constitutions* from the late 4th century. It addresses the laity as "the elect Church of God" and orders them to support their clergy financially. Here the Christian clergy is seen as heirs to the Israelite priestly orders, and the deacons are compared with the Levites (2.25).[20] Deacons are mentioned next to many other categories within the church: bishops, presbyters, readers, singers, porters, deaconesses, widows, virgins and orphans. The bishop is the minister of the Word, and the deacon should minister to the bishop "as Christ does to His Father" (2.26). According to the *Apostolic Constitutions*, the deacon assists the bishop in many different ways: to carry messages, to travel about, to serve, in doing home visits, minister to the sick, in celebrating Eucharist, helping at baptism and saying prayers. For instance, after the Eucharist the deacon must pray for the whole Church and the peace of the universe (2.57). Characteristically deacons are often mentioned in contexts that have to do with the unity of the Church.

Deaconesses in the Early Church

Both men and women served the church through diaconal work in the first centuries. Already in Romans 16:1, we encounter the first female deacon as Paul commends "sister Phoebe, a deacon of the church in Cenchreae" to the Roman congregation. Paul commends her with the words "she has been the benefactor of many people, including me", but we cannot know precisely what Paul here meant by "deacon". We can, however, note that many have interpreted the passage to suit later norms and expectations. For instance, in the 16th century the Italian reformer Peter Martyr Vermigli made sure to mention that Phoebe had not been teaching in public since that would not have been

---

[17] E.g. Ignatius, *Letter to the Philadelphians* 4.

[18] *The Shephard of Hermas*, Parable 9.26.2 in *The Apostolic Fathers*, II, Loeb Classical Library, London: Heinemann, 1912.

[19] *Vision* 3.5.1. *The Shephard of Hermas*, Parable 9.26.2 in *The Apostolic Fathers*, II, Loeb Classical Library, London: Heinemann, 1912.

[20] *Apostolic Constitutions*. Tr. Donaldson, J. *From Ante-Nicene Fathers*, Vol. 7. Ed. Roberts, A./ Donaldson J./ Coxe. AC. Buffalo: Christian Literature Publishing Co., 1886.

fitting for a woman: "Men think that this holy woman carried this epistle of Paul to Rome. She had been a minister in the Church of Cenchrae, not indeed in teaching publicly, but in looking after the poor."[21]

In the early church, women also served as "widows".[22] This kind of ministry seems to have established itself before the ministry of deaconesses, but held some of the same obligations. However, celibacy and virginity increasingly became prime Christian virtues, and eventually virgins in the role of deaconesses became the finest "office" for women. According to the *Apostolic Constitutions*, which likened the bishop to God the Father and the deacon to the Son, the deaconess resembles the Holy Ghost. This description serves to honor, but also limit women's agency, because the conclusion drawn from this comparison is that deaconesses should not do or say anything without the deacons, like the Holy Spirit lets Christ do the talking (Chapter 2.26). Deaconesses were necessary to perform certain acts in the church where other women were involved. Several sources mention decency as the reason for having deaconesses. It would be indecent to let men and women mingle, particularly in relation to baptism where women were partly undressed.

It has often been discussed whether women were ordained as deaconesses, and what kind of office they had.[23] In general, female deacons did not have the same public or liturgical functions as male deacons,[24] but it would be unfair to judge their office according to later formalized ideas of what ordination is and entails. There are famous examples of ordained deaconesses from late antiquity, such as Queen Radegund, the wife of the Frankish King Clothar. According to her vita, *Life of Radegund*, written by Fortunatus c. 587, she was consecrated as deaconess by a bishop: "laying his hands on her, [he] consecrated her as a deaconess".[25] Another famous deaconess is Olympias from Constantinople. She is known from several sources, including *Life of Olympias* from the 5th century. According to her *vita*, the most holy patriarch John Chrysostom ordained her as a deaconess, and the hagiographer adds that this happened "by the divine will" (Chapter 6). John Chrysostom also ordained three of her female relatives: Elisanthia, Martyria and Palladia. When

---

[21] Peter Martyr Vermigli, *In epistolam S. Pauli Apostoli ad Romanos... commentarii doctissimi Basle 1558, 640* in Charlotte Methuen, "Preaching the Gospel through Love of Neighbour: The Ministry of Katharina Schütz Zell", *Journal of Ecclesiastical History*, 61, 4, 2010, 707-728, p. 719.

[22] Susanna Elm. *'Virgins of God'. The Making of Asceticism in Late Antiquity*, Oxford: Clarendon Press, 1994, 166ff.

[23] For a description of such discussions, see Valerie A. Karras, "Female Deacons in the Byzantine Church", *Church History*, 73:2, 271-316, 2004, p. 302ff.

[24] See, e.g. Karras, 2004, 285-86; 302ff.

[25] Chapter 12, *manu superposita, consecravit diaconam. Vita Sanctae Radegundis* in Venanti Fortunati Opera pedestria, ed. Krusch, B. MGH, Auctorum antiquissimorum, 4/2 [Berlin: Weidmannos, 1885], 41; Tr. In McNamara, J.A. and Halborg, J.E. *Sainted Women of the Dark Ages*, Durham, 1992.

Olympias' good deeds are recounted in her *vita*, the following are mentioned among others: raising the orphans, shielding the elderly, looking after the weak, engaging in much catechizing of unbelieving women (Chapter 14). Olympias was not only deaconess but also abbess in a monastery, and this combination is not seldom.[26] Deaconesses are often found in monastic milieus, which might suggest that the Church's acceptance of female office holders was confined to a relatively closed environment. However, the fact that there existed female deacons and that texts were in circulation that praised them shows us that at least in certain contexts it was emphasized symbolically that gender is no obstacle in serving God. The hagiographer Fortunatus wrote about Radegund that God acted through her weakness, and thereby Fortunatus also expressed the opinion that women can serve because God enables them:

> Our Redeemer is so richly and abundantly generous that He wins mighty victories through the female sex and, despite their frail physique, He confers glory and greatness on women through strength of mind. By faith, Christ makes them strong who were born weak.[27]

At a certain point, however, the tide turned, and church orders began not only to limit the activities of deaconesses but also altogether to forbid them.[28]

The occurrences of deacons and deaconesses presented here give a broad idea about how the idea of *diakonia* was applied in the early church: the major role of deacons and deaconesses express that the Church was defined by its clergy, its internal unity and its liturgy. A major focal point of the early church was the liturgical celebrations where the servants of the church were present. The tasks performed by deacons and deaconesses were manifold and reflect the fundamental diaconal ecclesiology of the early church, which was grounded in its liturgical life and visible in its social work. It is not possible to give a clearer account of diaconal work in the early church, because there were major regional differences, the ministries developed only gradually and were in a state of continuous transformation. The role of female deacons is to some extent obscured by the normative sources that tried to do away with them. In the following centuries, diaconal work continued and changed character. Social work was increasingly taken care of by religious orders; the diaconal office became, in many instances, an intermediary state for men aspiring to priesthood; and the ministry of deaconesses slowly disappeared altogether.

---

[26] Elm, 1994, 178-80.

[27] Ibid. 1.

[28] "The ordination of deaconesses was rejected by the Council of Orange in 441 and by the Counci of Orléans ca. 533, and by the 11th century had gradually disappeared" (Latvus, K. "Deacon, Deaconess", *Encyclopedia of the Bible and its Reception*. Berlin/Boston: Walter de Gruyter, 2013).

Protestant Reception of the Early Ideals

Within the Protestant reformation the role of deacons gained some emphasis, and several reformers envisioned a revival of the diaconate according to the example of the Bible and early church. However, what they promoted was in fact an innovation and resulted in the development of a diaconate focused on doing charity. This charity, especially in the form of supporting the poor, took place either directly in the context of the church or by way of city officials.

Luther had mentioned the important role of deacons.[29] Johannes Bugenhagen referred to "deacons" in the church orders that he edited for use in Germany and the Scandinavian countries. In Strasbourg, Martin Bucer emphasized the double service of the church: the care of the needy both through the ministry of the cure of souls and through the ministry of physical care. The reformed John Calvin in Geneva made a special effort to establish a diaconate, and he wrote "deacons" into his church order *Institutes of Christian Religion*, from 1541:

> For although the term *diakonia* has a more extensive meaning, Scripture specially gives the name of deacons to those whom the Church appoints to dispense alms, and take care of the poor [...]. Such deacons as the Apostolic Church had, it becomes us to have after her example.[30]

Calvin also had a vision of incorporating women into church service by returning to the ancient practice of having "widows" work for the church: "For there was no public office which women could discharge save that of devoting themselves to the service of the poor."[31] However, this idea was not put into practice. Although the reformers in general did not let women play an influential role, there were women among the innovators of Christian theology in the 16th century. In Strasbourg, Katharina Schütz Zell, who was married to a pastor, saw her own work as complementing the work of her husband. She served the community in Strasbourg, e.g. by organizing care of refugees arriving to the city. In a letter she pointed directly to the Christian responsibility of service, as she wrote: "we ought to exercise and practice toward one another our office (commended to us by God), the ministry and office of care and love".[32] Regarding the role of women in the wider

---

[29] For several examples of the way that deacons were mentioned in writings of Protestant reformers, see Latvus, 2010, p. 93-100; also, Latvus, K. "Deacon, Deaconess", *Encyclopedia of the Bible and its Reception*. Berlin/Boston: Walter de Gruyter, 2013.

[30] John Calvin. *Institutes of the Christian Religion* 4.3.9., tr. H. Beveridge, Grand Rapids, 1964.

[31] John Calvin. *Institutes of the Christian Religion* 4.3.9., tr. H. Beveridge, Grand Rapids, 1964.

[32] Charlotte Methuen quotes *Katharina Schütz Zell, Church mother: the writings of a Protestant Reformer in sixteenth-century Germany,* ed. and trans. Elsie McKee,

reformation movement, it is worth mentioning that the Mennonites were one of the first to include both deacons and deaconesses in their communities.[33]

If we look further down the line of this Western-European diaconal trajectory, we find that *diakonia* received even more attention in the 19th century. At this point in history, the German concept of *Diakonie* developed and came to refer to acts of humbling caritative work by lay men and women. Also within this diaconal revival movement, references were made to the early church to undergird its endeavors. For instance, in 1820 the pastor Friedrich Klönne wrote a text with the telling title: *On the Revival of Deaconesses of the Old Church in the Female Associations.* [34] Klönne among others influenced Theodore Fliedner, who together with his first and second wife, Friederike Münster and Caroline Bertheau, established diaconal institutions for education and nursing. Their efforts were carried on in the inner mission movement by Johann Hinrich Wichern. This German social work was internationally acknowledged, and promoted by Florence Nightingale, who published a text about Fliedner's Institution for women, *The Institution of Kaiserswerth on the Rhine, for the Practical Training of Deaconesses.*[35] The inner mission movement promoted a form of Christianity in which social work was an essential part, and it follows that mission and diaconal work were closely related.

The contemporary scholar Anni Hentchel has pointed out that although the reformers of the 19th century idealized the diaconal work of the past and attempted to copy it, they ended up creating a whole new thing: "Judged from the perspective of biblical sciences, a number of errors of interpretation occurred. Some of these, we must say were 'productive' mistakes in that they contributed in practice to strengthening of love of neighbour."[36] In fact, the *Diakonie*-movement has to this day contributed to a well-respected social profile of many European churches. However, an ecclesiological question arises in relation to this kind of more or less professionalized diaconal work:

Chicago/London, 2006, in Methuen, C. "Preaching the Gospel through Love of Neighbour: The Ministry of Katharina Schütz Zell", *Journal of Ecclesiastical History*, 61, 4, 2010, 707-728, p. 707.

[33] Latvus, 2013.

[34] The original title is: *Über das Wiederaufleben der Diakonissen der alten Kirche in den Frauenvereinen*. It is mentioned in Leen Van Molle, *Charity and Social Welfare: The Dynamics of Religious Reform in Northern Europe, 1780-1920*, Leuven University Press, 2017, 224.

[35] Florence Nightingale. *The Institution of Kaiserswerth on the Rhine: For the Practical Training of Deaconesses, Under the Direction of the Rev. Pastor Fliedner, Under the Direction of the Rev. Pastor Fliedner, Embracing the Support and Care of a Hospital, Infant and Industrial Schools, and a Female Penitentiary*. London: London Ragged Colonial Training School, 1851.

[36] Anni Hentschel. "Diakonie in der Bibel" in ed. Kottnik, Klaus-Dieter K. and Hauschildt, Eberhard. *Diakoniefibel: Grundwissen für alle, die mit Diakonie zu tun haben* (Gütersloh: CMZ Gütersloher Verlag, 2008), 17-20; 20 (tr. Collins, 2014, 46).

how can the churches integrate and engage "ordinary" lay Christians in its diaconal ministry? This has been an issue in contemporary church history.

Diaconal Ecclesiology in the Twentieth Century

During the 20th century, attempts were made to bring *diakonia* into focus as constitutive for the Church and to reincorporate a diaconal perspective in Christian life as such. From the beginning of the century, the circumstances of churches were rapidly changing due to many factors, such as the demographic changes after the industrial revolution and the First World War of 1914-1918. In these challenging times the modern ecumenical movement played a substantial role in the rediscovery, in many parts of Christianity, of the centrality of the Church's role as an agent of service in and for the world.

The formally organized concern for the promotion of justice and peace by Christian individuals and institutions began with the Movement of Life and Work, led by clergy and lay, but not as an initiative of churches. This led to the Stockholm Universal Conference on Life and Work in 1925. However, in the early 1930s the theological dynamic pushed "Life and Work" to equate service in the world with being Church. This was expressed in the transformation of the movement into a "Universal Christian Council for Life and Work", in which the word "council" points to a prominent role assigned to the churches. This council pushed toward the establishment of the World Council of Churches, whose first general secretary, Willem Visser 't Hooft, underlined the importance of a diaconal ecclesiology. At the consultation of the Division of Interchurch Aid and Service to Refugees at Les Rasses, in Switzerland in 1956, Visser 't Hooft mentioned three aspects of the mission of the Church: *kerygma*, *koinonia* and *diakonia*: "[*Diakonia*] is the ministry, the expression of faith in Christian love and compassion and in the service of the needs of men".[37] This threefold understanding of the mission of the Church was further advanced in the World Council of Churches and developed into a theological vision of visible unity among churches. The understanding of the ecumenical way to unity thus presupposes, at least in an implicit way, a vision of the Church in which *diakonia* is a central element. With this focus from the World Council of Churches, *diakonia* rose to a prominent place in ecclesiological considerations, which also had consequences for how the concept of ministry was understood.

The ecumenical pioneer Hendrik Kraemer focused on Christ as the *Diakonos*, the servant and hence the minister, and because of that he came to the conclusion that: "The Church *is diakonia*, *is* ministry."[38] For Kraemer, this also meant that "the ministry of the laity is as constituent for the true being and

---

[37] Ans J. van der Bent, *Vital Ecumenical Concerns*, World Council of Churches, Geneva: 1986, p. 217. Cf. Visser 't Hooft, W.A. *The Pressure of Our Common Calling*, London: SCM Press, 1959.

[38] H. Kraemer. *A Theology of the Laity*, London: Lutterworth, 1958, 149.

calling of the Church as the ministry of the 'ministry' (the office-bearers or clergy)".[39] The Fourth World Conference on Faith and Order in Montreal in 1963 had acknowledged these theological and ecclesiological developments to such a degree that it promoted the role of the laity in the church, because: "ministry is the responsibility of the whole body and not only of those who were ordained. The recovery is one of the most important facts of recent church history."[40]

An idealistic approach prevailed in ecumenical circles for some decades, and in the 1960s the analysis of the structural causes of human/social problems led to an emphasis on political engagement as service. This created suspicion in relation to the role of *diakonia* as purely an "assistencialism" that did not root out systemic causes of social problems, but only nursed the suffering.[41] However, in recent years a new focus on ecumenical *diakonia* has emerged, which aims at rethinking in critical but proactive terms the Church as a community of service.

Against this historical backdrop, the recent convergence text from Faith and Order, *The Church: Towards a Common Vision* (2013; hereafter TCTCV), builds on the notion that the communion of baptized is a reflection of Trinitarian communion and exists for the sake of communion with all humans and the whole creation.[42] For this reason, the text speaks of the Church as a sign in the world of God's coming reign, as "Sign and Servant of God's Design for the World" (§ 25-27), which leads to TCTCV, chapter IV: "In and for the World". TCTCV includes several references to the importance of being church and serving those on the margins. The text thus testifies to the fact that a diaconal ecclesiology with focus on social service has been adopted across confessional boundaries.[43] In summary, John N. Collins is right in pointing to

---

[39] Ibid. 154. A similar point was formulated poignantly by e.g. Karl Barth: "Each one is called with equal seriousness, to play his part, and to do so as if everything depended on him [...]. Law and order in the community are never the particular priesthood of a few, but the universal priesthood of all believers. [...]. Even linguistically, it must avoid the fatal word 'office' and replace it by 'service', which can be applied to all Christians." (Barth, Karl. *Church Dogmatics*. Vol. 4, Part 2, Eng. Transl. Edinburgh: T&T Clark, 1958, 694.

[40] P.C. Rodger and L. Vischer (eds.), *The Fourth World Conference on Faith and Order*, Faith and Order Paper No. 42 London: SCM, 1964, 62.

[41] The notion that *diakonia* should be preoccupied with creating justice is expressed in the *Larnaca Declaration*, World Consultation on Interchurch Aid, Refugee and World Service, *Diakonia* 2000, 1986.

[42] *The Church: Towards a Common Vision*, Faith and Order Paper No. 214, WCC Publications, 2013.

[43] Benedict attributed an important role to *diakonia* in his first Encyclical Letter *Deus caritas est*:
"The Church's deepest nature is expressed in her three-fold responsibility: of proclaiming the word of God (*kerygma-martyria*), celebrating the sacraments (*leitourgia*), and exercising the ministry of charity (*diakonia*). These duties presuppose

the establishment of the World Council of Churches and the Second Vatican Council as processes that led to a renewed focus on *diakonia* with immense importance for ecclesiology in the 20th century. "From the 1960s-80s, *diakonia* contributed fundamentally to a redeveloped theology of ministry that impacted deeply upon ecclesiology," he writes.[44] However, it remains a challenge for churches to convey and practice the theological conviction that serving is an essential expression of the Church. Furthermore, the role of the ordained ministry remains a matter of divergence between confessions, which complicates easy ecumenical solutions to ecclesiological questions about *diakonia* and the diaconate.[45]

Conclusion

It goes without saying that a short article like this cannot do justice to a phenomenon as broad and multifaceted as *diakonia* and its ecclesiological significance. The history of diaconal work is still in want of more research to overcome narratives that are too easy, such as the assumption that certain periods experienced a decline of diaconal efforts or the judgement that the deaconesses were less valid than their male counterparts. This article has offered some highlights in this story, particular from the early church and the Protestant churches, and we can draw a few conclusions: obviously different periods expressed different understandings of the place of *diakonia* in ecclesiology, and what *diakonia* is in itself. There are some inherent tensions in diaconal ecclesiological visions regarding whether the authority should be with lay or ordained ministry, if the focus should be on liturgical or caritative service, or if purely caritative work fails to empower people in seeking just conditions. None of these categories – lay, ordained, liturgical, caritative, just – necessarily exclude one another. It is always an open question precisely how one should serve as a Christian in a given time and place, and to which degree Christian service is a task of ordained ministry or of all Christians. This brief investigation shows that within the Church, there has always been awareness of a responsibility of the church to serve and counter the needs of the world, both its spiritual and physical needs. There was no time in which the Church was not

---

each other and are inseparable. For the Church, charity is not a kind of welfare activity which could equally well be left to others, but is a part of her nature, an indispensable expression of her very being." (Pope Benedict, *First Encyclical Letter* "Deus Caritas est" 25, 2005).

[44] Collins, 2014, p. 32.

[45] Nordstokke gives an enlightening description of the ecumenical work done on this theme in the framework of the World Council of Churches. See Nordstokke, K. "*Diakonia* and diaconate in the World Council of Churches", *International Journal for the Study of the Christian Church*, 13, 4, 286-99. I thank the director of Faith and Order, Odair Pedroso Mateus, for giving me advice in relation to this paragraph, "V. Diaconal Ecclesiology in the Twentieth Century".

diaconal, but it is worth acknowledging that churches at different times have dealt with their diaconal responsibilities in different ways when facing rising challenges, and *that* might be the historical lesson.

Bibliography

Sources

Apostolic Constitutions, Tr. J. Donaldson. *From Ante-Nicene Fathers*, Vol. 7. Ed. Roberts, A./ Donaldson, J./Coxe, A.C. Buffalo: Christian Literature Publishing Co., 1886.

1. Clement. Tr. Lake, Kirsopp. *The Apostolic Fathers*, I, Loeb Classical Library, London: Heinemann, 1912.

Barth, Karl, *Church Dogmatics*. Vol. 4, Part 2, Edinburgh: T&T Clark, 1958.

Benedict XVI, *First Encyclical Letter "Deus Caritas est"*: http://w2.vatican.va/content/benedict-xvi/en/encyclicals/documents/hf_ben-xvi_enc_20051225_deus-caritas-est.html#_ftn17, 2005.

Calvin, John, *Institutes of the Christian Religion* 4.3.9., tr. H. Beveridge, Grand Rapids, 1964.

Didache or *The Teaching of the Twelve Apostles*. Tr. Lake, Kirsopp. *The Apostolic Fathers* II, Loeb Classical Library, London: Heinemann, 1912.

Ignatius' Letters, Tr. Lake, Kirsopp. *The Apostolic Fathers* I, Loeb Classical Library, London: Heinemann, 1912.

Larnaca Declaration, World Consultation on Interchurch Aid, Refugee and World Service, Diakonia 2000, 1986: https://www.oikoumene.org/en/resources/documents/wcc-programmes/justice-diakonia-and-responsibility-for-creation/ecumenical-solidarity/larnaca-declaration.

World Consultation on Interchurch Aid, Refugee and World Service, Diakonia 2000.

Nightingale, Florence, *The Institution of Kaiserswerth on the Rhine: For the Practical Training of Deaconesses, Under the Direction of the Rev. Pastor Fliedner, Under the Direction of the Rev. Pastor Fliedner, Embracing the Support and Care of a Hospital, Infant and Industrial Schools, and a Female Penitentiary*. London: London Ragged Colonial Training School, 1851.

The Church: Towards a Common Vision, Faith and Order Paper No. 214, WCC Publications, 2013.

The Shephard of Hermas, Parable 9.26.2 in *The Apostolic Fathers*, II, Loeb Classical Library, London: Heinemann, 1912.

Vita Olympiades, tr. in Clark, Elizabeth A. *Jerome, Chrysostom, and Friends: Essays and Translations* (Studies in Women and Religion, volume 2), New York: Mellen Press, 1979.

Vita Sanctae Radegundis, in *Venanti Fortunati Opera pedestria*, ed. Krusch, B., MGH, Auctorum antiquissimorum, 4/2 [Berlin: Weidmannos, 1885], 41; Tr. in Jo Ann McNamara and John E. Halborg, *Sainted Women of the Dark Ages*, Durham, 1992.

Literature

Barnett, James Monroe, *The Diaconate. A Full and Equal Order*. Rev. ed. Harrisburg: The Trinity Press, 1995.

Collins, John N, *Diakonia: Re-Interpreting the Ancient Sources*, Oxford University Press, 2009.

Elm, Susanna, *'Virgins of God'. The Making of Asceticism in Late Antiquity*, Oxford: Clarendon Press, 1994.

Hentschel, Anni, "Diakonie in der Bibel" in ed. Klaus-Dieter K. Kottnik and Eberhard Hauschildt, *Diakoniefibel: Grundwissen für alle, die mit Diakonie zu tun haben*, Gütersloh: CMZ Gütersloher Verlag, 2008, 17-20.

Hörnig, Thomas, "Geschichte der Diakonie – ein kritischer Zugang aus der Armutsperspektive", eds. J. Eurich and H. Schmidt: *Diakonik. Grundlagen, Konzeptionen, Diskurse*, Göttingen: Vandenhoeck & Ruprecht, 77-109, 2016.

Karras, Valerie A., "Female Deacons in the Byzantine Church", *Church History* 73:2, 271-316, 2004.

Kraemer, H., *A Theology of the Laity*, London: Lutterworth, 1958.

Latvus, Kari, "Diaconal Ministry in the Light of the Reception and Re-Interpretation of Acts 6. Did John Calvin Create the Social-Caritative Ministry of Diaconia?", *Diaconia*, 1, 82-102, 2010.

Latvus, Kari, "Deacon, Deaconess", *Encyclopedia of the Bible and its Reception*. Berlin/Boston: Walter de Gruyter, 2013.

Latvus, Kari, *Diaconia as Care for the Poor? Critical Perspectives on the Development of Caritative Diaconia*, Kirkon tutkimuskeskuksen verkkojulkaisuja 53, 2017.

Methuen, Charlotte, "Preaching the Gospel through Love of Neighbour: The Ministry of Katharina Schütz Zell", *Journal of Ecclesiastical History*, 61, 4, 707-728, 2010.

Nordstokke, K., "*Diakonia* and diaconate in the World Council of Churches", *International Journal for the Study of the Christian Church*, 13, 4, 286-99.

O'Meara, Thomas, *Theology of Ministry*, second edition, New York: Paulist Press, 1999.

Sullivan, Francis Aloysius, *From Apostles to Bishops: The Development of the Episcopacy in the Early Church*, Paulist Press, 2001.

Remus, Harold, "Persecution" in eds. Blasi, A.J./Duhaime, J./ Turcotte, A.P. *Handbook of Early Christianity. Social Science Approaches*, Oxford, Walnut Greek, CA: Altamira Press, 2002, 431-51, p. 441.

Rodger, P.C. and Vischer, L., eds., *The Fourth World Conference on Faith and Order*, Faith and Order Paper No. 42 London: SCM, 1964.

van der Bent, Ans J. *Vital Ecumenical Concerns: Sixteen Documentary Surveys*. Geneva: WCC, 1986.

van Molle, Leen, *Charity and Social Welfare: The Dynamics of Religious Reform in Northern Europe, 1780-1920*, Leuven University Press, 2017.

Visser't Hooft, W.A., *The Pressure of Our Common Calling*, London: SCM Press, 1959.

Concepts of the Church in the New Testament

Jostein Ådna

What concepts of the church with particular relevance and significance for *diakonia* do we encounter in the New Testament? In fact, essential diaconal features in the life of the early church often appear outspokenly in narrative traditions. Hence, the concepts that we look for must to a certain degree be drawn from such narrative traditions; respectively, how they are rooted in a practice reflected in these traditions will be central in our discussion.

Jesus as Example

Both explicitly and implicitly the gospels address and apply what they recount about Jesus to the recipients in the early Christian communities. They portray Jesus as the Servant of the Lord, whom the Lord has anointed with his Spirit (see quotations of Isaiah 42:1–4; 53:4; and 61:1–2; in Matthew 8:17; 12:17–21; and Luke 4:16–21). Characteristic of Jesus as the messianic Son of Man is that he, contrary to the expectations of many, 'came not to be served but to serve, and to give his life a ransom for many' (Mark 10:45; Matthew 20:28).[1] This Son of Man saying concludes a passage where Jesus teaches the 12 disciples, whom readers know to be founding apostles in the church, to serve instead of to rule:

> 42 So Jesus called them and said to them, 'You know that among the Gentiles those whom they recognize as their rulers lord it over them, and their great ones are tyrants over them. 43 But it is not so among you; but whoever wishes to become great among you must be your servant, 44 and whoever wishes to be first among you must be slave of all. (Mark 10:42–44, cf. Matt 20:25–27; Luke 22:25–27)

In the Gospel of John, Jesus washing the feet of the disciples takes up most space in the story of the last meal and stands at its center (John 13:1–17):

> 13 You call me Teacher and Lord – and you are right, for that is what I am. 14 So if I, your Lord and Teacher, have washed your feet, you also ought to wash one

---

[1] Quotations from the Bible follow the NRSV Anglicized Edition. The Greek verb translated 'to serve' is διακονέω (*diakoneō*).

another's feet. [15] For I have set you an example, that you also should do as I have done to you.

Shortly afterward, Jesus impresses the commandment to love each other into his disciples, referring to his own example:

[34] I give you a new commandment, that you love one another. Just as I have loved you, you should love one another. [35] By this everyone will know that you are my disciples, if you have love for one another. (John 13:34–35)

The apostle Paul draws on the example of Jesus in his letter to the Philippians when he includes the famous Christ hymn in Philippians 2:6–11 as a decisive motivation to care not for themselves, but for the others (see Phil 2:1–5). Also, when he urges the Christians in Corinth to contribute generously to the collection for the poor in Jerusalem, Paul refers to the example of Christ as motivation (2 Cor. 8:9, see section 3 below).

The Early Community in Jerusalem

A conspicuous feature of the description in Acts of the Apostles of the early community of believers gathered in Jerusalem during the first weeks and months after Easter is their unity. This applies already to the short period before Pentecost (Acts 1:12–14), and all the more to the community filled with the Holy Spirit (Acts 2:4, 16–18). The exemplary model for the life of the Jerusalem church in the early days is reflected in two passages in Acts 2 and 4:

Acts 2:44–47:

[44] All who believed were together and had all things in common; [45] they would sell their possessions and goods and distribute the proceeds to all, as any had need. [46] Day by day, as they spent much time together in the temple, they broke bread at home and ate their food with glad and generous hearts, [47] praising God and having the goodwill of all the people. And day by day the Lord added to their number those who were being saved.

Acts 4:32–35:

[32] Now the whole group of those who believed were of one heart and soul, and no one claimed private ownership of any possessions, but everything they owned was held in common. [33] With great power the apostles gave their testimony to the resurrection of the Lord Jesus, and great grace was upon them all. [34] There was not a needy person among them, for as many as owned lands or houses sold them and brought the proceeds of what was sold. [35] They laid it at the apostles' feet, and it was distributed to each as any had need.

The question 'to what extent the ideal of 'Christian communism' materialized in the early days of the Jerusalem community' is disputed. At any rate, it is interesting that the two most important Jewish authors contemporary to the New Testament whose works have been preserved, Philo of Alexandria and Flavius Josephus, both describe the lifestyle of the religious group called Essenes to be very similar (cf. Philo, *That Every Good Person Is Free* 76–77, 85–87, and Josephus, *Jewish War* 2 viii.3–4 [§§ 122–127]). This parallel in another Jewish community in Palestine has been confirmed by the regulations for the Essene Qumran group in the Rule of the Community (see 1QS 6.16–23), belonging to the Dead Sea Scrolls. In Acts, the described practice of selling private property and putting the proceeds at the common disposal of the community is immediately succeeded by two examples, one positive and one negative. Barnabas from Cyprus laid all the money acquired by selling a field at the apostles' feet (Acts 4:36–37). On the contrary, the couple Ananias and Sapphira held back part of the proceeds gained by selling a piece of property and lied about it; as a consequence, they fell down and died (Acts 5:1–11). The text shows that it was not regarded as wrong or illegal to own a property or to keep the proceeds of its sales; the serious offence of Ananias and Sapphira was that they pretended to have shared the whole profit with the community. Further, the first major tension or conflict in the early church in Jerusalem about which we are informed, is recounted in Acts 6. Here, we suddenly become aware that the community of believers consists of two different language groups, the Hebrew and/or Aramaic-speaking 'Hebrews' and the Greek-speaking 'Hellenists', for 'the Hellenists complained against the Hebrews because their widows were being neglected in the daily distribution of food' (Acts 6:1).[2] Obviously, the story about Ananias and Sapphira and the information about the complaint of the Greek-speaking (Jewish) believers show that the early community in Jerusalem did not succeed long in upholding an undisturbed harmonious unity. However, at the same time these deviations from the general pattern described in Acts 2:44–47 and 4:32–35 (see above) confirm that pattern as a normative ideal for the author, Luke.

According to Luke's presentation, the complaint of the 'Hellenists' against the discrimination of their widows prompted the apostles, who so far had taken responsibility and administered all matters of communal life in the early church

---

[2] 'Distribution' is a contextual rendering of the Greek noun διακονία (*diakonia*). BDAG (*Greek-English Lexicon of the New Testament and Other Early Christian Literature*, 3rd edition, 2000) classifies *diakonia* in Acts 6:1 as a 'rendering of specific assistance' to be translated '*aid, support*', and lists Acts 11:29 and 12:25 as the only other occurrences of this specific usage of *diakonia* in the New Testament.
Widows were a particularly vulnerable group. If most of the 'Hellenist' widows had come to Jerusalem from somewhere in the diaspora in order to end their days in the Holy City, they were in an especially endangered position with perhaps no relatives around them to take care of them. The lasting challenge of how to integrate widows properly in the communities and how to care for their specific needs is reflected in 1 Timothy 5:3–16.

in Jerusalem, to hand over the 'service at the tables' (cf. Acts 6:2)[3] to others in order to devote themselves exclusively to 'prayer and to serving the word' (Acts 6:4). As a consequence, a group of seven men with Stephen at their head were entrusted with the task (see Acts 6:1–6). Although they are not called διάκονοι (*diakonoi*), the formal initiation with the apostles' laying on of hands recounted in Acts 6:6 has nevertheless had the effect that this incident later has been regarded as the founding inauguration of the ministry of deacons: 'They had these men stand before the apostles, who prayed and laid their hands on them.'[4]

It is implied that the appointment of the seven to take care of the relief of the 'Hellenist' widows solved the crisis in the Jerusalem community. However, Luke does not give us sufficient information to assess how things developed in the longer term because the leader of the seven, Stephen, is soon stoned to death (Acts 6:8–7:60), and in the persecution against the church following his murder apparently all leaders of the Greek-speaking group and many of its members fled Jerusalem (cf. Acts 8:1). On one occasion around AD 45, an upcoming famine motivated the church in Antioch (see n. 4) to 'send relief to the believers living in Judea' (Acts 11:27–30). Barnabas and Paul were the bringers of this, handing it over to 'the elders' (πρεσβύτεροι [*presbyteroi*]). Because the famine affected believers all over the region of Judea, and because the seemingly best attested text of the verse telling about the completion of their mission, Acts 12:25, states that Barnabas and Paul 'returned to (εἰς [*eis*]) Jerusalem',[5] they probably traveled to different communities in Judea and distributed the aid from Antioch there before ending up in the mother church in

[3] For the puzzling phrase in Acts 6:2, διακονεῖν τραπέζαις (*diakonein trapezais*), see the discussion in BDAG διακονέω (*diakoneō*), s.v., entry 5.

[4] As is apparent from the following passage in Acts 6:8–15, the activity of the Stephen group was in no way restricted in the sense that verse 4 might have indicated. On the contrary, Stephen appears, in the encounter with the Greek synagogues in Jerusalem, as bold as the apostles Peter and John in the previous chapters of Acts; those who argued with him 'could not withstand the wisdom and the Spirit with which he spoke' (Acts 6:10). Their only way to stop him is to have him sentenced as a blasphemer and executed by stoning (see Acts 7). Next, the second man in the group of seven, Philip, in Acts 21:8 explicitly called an 'evangelist', appears as the pioneer missionary to the Samaritans (Acts 8:5–13) and to the Ethiopian eunuch (Acts 8:26–40). The 'Hellenists', who were forced to leave Jerusalem after the martyrdom of Stephen, seem to have been the most successful missionaries toward Greek-speaking Jews (see Acts 8:4), and in Antioch they founded a church (Acts 11:19–26) that played a prominent role in the mission during the first decades of the church, repeatedly referred to by Luke throughout Acts.

[5] Supported both by Codices Sinaiticus and Vaticanus and by the Majority text and clearly representing the *lectio difficilior* against the alternative prepositions ἐξ (*ex*) and ἀπό (*apo*), speaking about the return 'from Jerusalem'.

Jerusalem, from where they 'brought with them John, whose other name was Mark' back to Antioch.[6]

Paul's Collection to the Church in Jerusalem

Irrespective of whether Paul's journey to Jerusalem recounted in Galatians 2:1–10 is to be identified with the trip in Acts (11:30 and) 12:25 or with the next one, on the occasion of the meeting of the apostles and elders in Jerusalem (Acts 15:1–35), there seems to be a connection between the economic situation of the church in Jerusalem and the obligation that Paul took upon himself: 'They asked only one thing, that we remember the poor, which was actually what I was eager to do' (Gal 2:10).

From Paul's letters we know that to 'remember the poor' meant to organize a collection of money in his missionary churches that one day was to be brought to the mother church in Jerusalem. In 1 Corinthians, written AD 54 or 55,[7] Paul instructs the community in Corinth to organize the collection of money foreseen for the church in Jerusalem in the same way as he has already asked the churches in Galatia to operate:

> 1 Corinthians 16:1–4:
>
> 1 Now concerning the collection for the saints: you should follow the directions I gave to the churches of Galatia. 2 On the first day of every week, each of you is to put aside and save whatever extra you earn, so that collections need not be taken when I come. 3 And when I arrive, I will send any whom you approve with letters to take your gift to Jerusalem. 4 If it seems advisable that I should go also, they will accompany me.

Before Paul arrived in Corinth, he also sent two Corinthians to the community there. This gave him an opportunity to follow up on the topic of the collection, and he does so in chapters 8 and 9. Paul urges the church in Corinth to follow the fresh example of the churches of Macedonia that 'voluntarily gave according to their means, and even beyond their means, begging us earnestly for the privilege of sharing in this ministry to the saints' (2 Cor. 8:3–4). Although the collection originated in an obligation put upon Paul by the 'pillars' in Jerusalem, James, Cephas and John to 'remember the poor' and he gave directions in his missionary churches to implement a collection of money as the fulfillment of the obligation, we observe that he now emphasizes the voluntary commitment of the Gentile churches themselves to be included in the

---

6 The return with John Mark to Antioch is clearly presupposed in the continuation of the text. See Acts 13:1–3, 5b.

7 That is, six to ten years after Paul took upon himself the obligation at the meeting in Jerusalem, depending on whether the visit in Jerusalem in Acts (11:30 and) 12:25 or in Acts 15 is meant (see above).

'ministry to the saints'.[8] Paul's intent by telling about the attitude of the churches of Macedonia is to inspire and motivate the Corinthians to complete the collection voluntarily (2 Cor. 8:7–15) in the same way as Paul has boasted about the Corinthians to those in Macedonia (2 Cor. 9:1–5).[9]

On the background of Christ's willingness to become poor in order to make humans rich (2 Cor. 8:9; cf. Phil 2:6–8), Paul unfolds the spiritual aspects of the collection:

2 Corinthians 9:11–13:

11 You will be enriched in every way for your great generosity, which will produce thanksgiving to God through us; 12 for the rendering of this ministry not only supplies the needs of the saints but also overflows with many thanksgivings to God. 13 Through the testing of this ministry you glorify God by your obedience to the confession of the gospel of Christ and by the generosity of your sharing with them and with all others.

The last time Paul talks about the collection is in his letter to the Romans, written from Corinth in the spring of AD 56 or 57.

Romans 15:25–28:

25 At present, however, I am going to Jerusalem in a ministry[10] to the saints; 26 for Macedonia and Achaia have been pleased to share their resources with the poor among the saints at Jerusalem. 27 They were pleased to do this, and indeed they owe it to them; for if the Gentiles have come to share in their spiritual blessings, they ought also to be of service to them in material things. 28 So, when I have completed this, and have delivered to them what has been collected, I will set out by way of you to Spain.

As we can see from this passage, what Paul hoped for when he formulated 1 Corinthians 16:1–4, cited above, is about to take shape. Although the Christians in Rome are eagerly waiting for the apostle to visit them, he tells them that he

---

[8] The Greek word rendered 'ministry' is διακονία (*diakonia*). BDAG lists all four occurrences of διακονία (*diakonia*) in the passage of 2 Corinthians 8–9 (8:4; 9:1, 12, 13) that is about 'service rendered in an intermediary capacity', as '*mediation, assignment*'. Also, Rom 15:31 belongs to this entry in BDAG.

[9] 2 Cor 8:8: 'I do not say this as a command, but I am testing the genuineness of your love against the earnestness of others.' 2 Cor 9:2–3: 'I know your eagerness, which is the subject of my boasting about you to the people of Macedonia, saying that Achaia has been ready since last year; and your zeal has stirred up most of them. But I am sending the brothers in order that our boasting about you may not prove to have been empty in this case, so that you may be ready as I said you would be.'

[10] The Greek text has at this point the verb διακονέω (*diakoneō*). BDAG lists this sole occurrence in Romans in its entry 3, 'to meet an immediate need', to be translated as '*help*'. This usage of the verb corresponds to how the noun διακονία (*diakonia*) is used in Rom 15:31 and four times in 2 Corinthians 8–9 (see n. 8).

must first travel to Jerusalem to deliver the collection from his missionary churches. Whereas Paul in 1 Corinthians 16:3–4 still had left it open whether he himself would travel with the delegation of representatives of the involved churches or not, it seems that by the time of writing 2 Corinthians he had decided to travel to Jerusalem (cf. 2 Cor. 8:19–21), and now this decision has been made. Acts concurs with the information in Romans. According to Acts 19:21, Paul states toward the end of his long stay in Ephesus that he will pass through Macedonia and Achaia and then continue to Jerusalem before he goes to Rome. In Acts 20:1–6 his stay for three months in Greece, apparently most of the time in Corinth, is mentioned, and seven members of the delegation accompanying him are named in verse 4. Paul was conscious of threats lurking in Jerusalem (cf. Rom. 15:30–31; Acts 20:22–25), but his commitment to deliver the collection of his missionary churches to the church in Jerusalem was so firm and unwavering that even strong warnings from Christian communities that they visited on their way to Jerusalem did not halt him (cf. Acts 21:4, 10–14). Actually, Acts does not say anything about the collection, but tells in detail about how Paul was arrested in Jerusalem and imprisoned in Caesarea before he was brought to Rome because he had appealed his case to the emperor (Acts 21–28).

In the passage from Romans 15, quoted above, the two designations of the collection that have appeared in the texts we have consulted thus far – namely, 'to remember the poor' (Gal 2:10) and 'the collection/ministry to the saints' (1 Cor. 16:1; 2 Cor. 8:4; 9:1; Rom 15:25) – converge: the collected money shall assist and benefit 'the poor among the saints at Jerusalem' (Rom 15:26). In all these texts 'the ἅγιοι (*hagioi*)' is an honorary title for the members of the Jewish-Christian mother church in Jerusalem. The unity with Jerusalem, from where the gospel has gone out, is imperative for all Christian churches wherever they are located and whoever their founding fathers and mothers might be. When some of the Jerusalemite Christians have basic economic needs and are poor, it is appropriate that Gentile Christians support them by putting some of their own resources at the disposal of 'the saints' in Jerusalem. Having been granted a share in the spiritual blessings of the believers in Jerusalem, the Gentile Christians owe it to them to do something for them in return, and the collection takes this role. Hence, spiritual treasures and material things are not separated and divided into different spheres not communicating and interacting with each other. The mutuality of those united with each other in the church might be expressed through an exchange of services according to which the care for basic social and economic needs in no way is excluded from the spiritual sphere. Moreover, Paul seems to consider the fellowship of sharing goods with each other, characteristic of the church in Jerusalem in its earliest days, as a valid guiding principle. In his long exposition on the collection in 2 Corinthians 8–9 he states, with reference to Exodus 16:18 as scriptural warrant:

2 Corinthians 8:13–15:

[13] I do not mean that there should be relief for others and pressure on you, but it is a question of a fair balance between [14] your present abundance and their need, so that their abundance may be for your need, in order that there might be a fair balance. [15] As it is written, 'The one who had much did not have too much, and the one who had little did not have too little.'

Hence, the value of as equal social living conditions as possible and the call for solidarity to secure such equality is one aspect of Paul's argument for convincing the Corinthians to participate in the collection. At the moment, the brothers and sisters in Jerusalem are in need of relief; later, the situation might change, and if the Corinthians will no longer be the affluent but instead the needy ones, then the Jerusalemites will share their abundance for the needs of the Corinthians.[11]

The Church as the Body of Christ

There is an inherent connection between Paul's strong commitment to the completion of the collection to Jerusalem, even at the expense of his own freedom and the chance to embark immediately on his mission to Spain via Rome, and his designation of the church as τὸ σῶμα τοῦ Χριστοῦ (*to sōma tou Christou*), 'the body of Christ', and the believers as τὰ μέλη (*ta melē*), 'the members' of this body (cf. 1 Cor 12:12–31; Rom 12:4–8). The image of the Christian fellowship as members belonging to the same body is capable of expressing the mutual dependence and solidarity between the believers:

1 Corinthians 12:24b–27:

[11] In this presentation I have applied Gal 2:10 to Paul's collection to 'the poor among the saints at Jerusalem' (Rom 15:26). However, what about the other Christian communities in Judea that were among the recipients of the aid from Antioch on the earlier occasion of Acts 11:27–30 (see above)? In Paul there are only rare references to these other communities (see Gal 1:22–24 and 1 Thess 2:14), with no indication that he had visited them or emphasized his connection to them, whereas the unity with the Jerusalem church is at the heart of his ecclesiology. Although Paul acknowledges the biblical tradition of care for the poor and admonishes his communities to such care (e.g. Gal 6:9–10; 1 Thess 5:14 [supported by Acts 20:35, I take 'the weak' to mean the economically disadvantaged]; Rom 12:13), it is highly unlikely that Gal 2:10 refers to the general obligation of care for the poor. The whole scene in Gal 2:1–10 is about the Jerusalem pillars' recognition of Paul's law-free gentile mission, and a refusal on their part would have meant that Paul 'was […] running, or had […] run, in vain' (Gal 2:2). Therefore, the obligation to 'remember the poor' must be related to the issue of fellowship between the Jerusalem church and the Pauline mission. As confirmed by Paul's later statement in Rom 15:27 (in corroboration with 2 Cor 8:4, 24; 9:1–2, 12–13), through the collection Paul and his churches express and acknowledge the spiritual inheritance from and their unity with the Jerusalem mother church.

> [24] […] God has so arranged the body […], [25] that there may be no dissension within the body, but the members may have the same care for one another. [26] If one member suffers, all suffer together with it; if one member is honoured, all rejoice together with it. [27] Now you are the body of Christ and individually members of it.

The ecclesiological and diaconal implications of this theologoumenon can only be drawn by analogy from the meaning of 'body' and 'members' as anthropological concepts in Paul's theology. Because of their bodily existence, the human being is so firmly located and bound inside the world that no escape whatsoever is possible. As a 'body', the human being appears in the created and fallen world and communicates in interaction with other human beings and other entities, and this communication takes its shape through the 'members' (cf. Rom 6:12–19).[12] Applied to the church as the body of Christ and the believers as the members of this body, this means that the church appears as the site where communication between the risen Lord and our world can take place. The church is the part of the world where Christ executes his reign after his exaltation. Hence, the church is the body of Christ due to being the site of his present dominion, from where and through which he communicates with the world through word, sacraments and the sending of believers into the world. In the church Christ is obeyed already prior to his second coming and the inauguration of the kingdom. Consequently, the solidarity practice of the believers (the 'members') within the church (the 'body of Christ') and from there in the interaction with the world outside is nothing less than exercising Christ's kingly reign.

It follows from the church's commission to represent and mirror creation conquered by and positioned under the reign of God and the Lord Jesus Christ that within its community a fellowship that overcomes traditional separation and oppression ought to be practiced. In his letter to the Galatians, Paul has taken up a baptismal formula that applies the unity in Christ to traditional ethnic, social and gender oppositions:

> Galatians 3:27–28:
>
> [27] As many of you as were baptized into Christ have clothed yourselves with Christ. [28] There is no longer Jew or Greek, there is no longer slave or free, there is no longer male or female, for all of you are one in Christ Jesus.

---

[12] See in particular vv. 12–13, 19b: '[12] Therefore, do not let sin exercise in your mortal *bodies* (sg. in Greek: ἐν τῷ θνητῷ ὑμῶν σώματι [*en tō thnētō hymōn sōmati*]), to make you obey their (Greek: its) passions. [13] No longer present your members to sin as instruments of wickedness, but present yourselves to God as those who have been brought from death to life, and present your members to God as instruments of righteousness. […] [19] […] For just as you once presented your members as slaves to impurity, so now present your members as slaves to righteousness for sanctification.'

The parallel statement in 1 Corinthians 12:13 speaks about being baptized into the one body of Christ[13] and the transcending of the traditional borders between Jews and Greeks as well as between slaves and free (cf. also Col 3:11).

The passage 1 Corinthians 11:17–34 is particularly informative with regard to the consequences of the unity in Christ, respectively in the one body of Christ. To Paul, it is absolutely intolerable that the Lord's Supper is practiced in Corinth in such a way that divisions in the community between the socially and economically privileged and 'those who have nothing' (cf. v. 22: οἱ μὴ ἔχοντες [*hoi mē echontes*]) become apparent:

> 1 Corinthians 11:20–22, 33:
>
> 20 When you come together, it is not really to eat the Lord's Supper. 21 For when the time comes to eat, each of you goes ahead with your own supper, and one goes hungry and another becomes drunk. 22 What! Do you not have homes to eat and drink in? Or do you show contempt for the church of God and humiliate those who have nothing? What should I say to you? Should I commend you? In this matter I do not commend you! […] 33. So then, my brothers and sisters, when you come together to eat, wait for one another.

The Lord's supper must be organized in such a way that it clearly reflects the unity of all believers in the one body of Christ (cf. 1 Cor 10:16–17).

The Church as Community and Servant

At the very heart of the New Testament notion of the church (ἐκκλησία [*ekklēsia*]) is the recognition of the communion of all believers with God and the Lord Jesus Christ and with each other in the one body of Christ (cf. section 4). The horizontal aspect of this communion takes shape in a unity marked by mutual care and solidarity (cf. sections 2 and 3). The service for the sisters and brothers in the church and for individuals and humankind at large, following the example of Jesus (cf. section 1), is frequently expressed by the noun διακονία (*diakonia*) and its cognate verb διακονέω (*diakoneō*). Hence, there is a clearly recognizable link between the vocabulary of the New Testament and the term *diakonia* employed today as an overarching major designation for imperative fields within and aspects of theology and the church's life, as exemplified by this book and the earlier volumes in this *diakonia* series.

---

[13] '[…] we were all baptized into one body' (ἡμεῖς πάντες εἰς ἓν σῶμα ἐβαπτίσθημεν [*hēmeis pantes eis hen sōma ebatisthēmen*]). Hence, the formulation in Galatians 3:27, 'you were baptized into Christ' (εἰς Χριστὸν ἐβαπτίσθητε [*eis Christon ebatisthēte*]) can be understood as an abbreviated variant of the more explicit statement in 1 Corinthians 12:13 about the ecclesiological significance of baptism as the sacrament of bringing the baptized into the unity and community within the body of Christ.

Diaconal Perspectives between the Book of Acts and the Orthodox Liturgy

Nicolas Abou Mrad

Introduction

The expression "diaconal church" is readily linked to the usage of the term *diakonia* and its derivatives as a "service" rendered by the Church to the marginalized, needy and poor,[1] in various ways and contexts. Much ink has been spilt about its implications within the Church's life,[2] particularly in the framework of ecumenical reflections on the involvement of the churches in "diaconal" activities.[3]

The Orthodox position with regard to the nature of *diakonia* within this process of reflection was formulated in the consultation on "The Orthodox Approach to *Diakonia*" (Chania, 1978). From an Orthodox perspective, *diakonia* is understood in terms of the 'liturgy after the liturgy',[4] an extension of the Eucharist and an expression of the unity of the Church as the body of

---

[1] On *diakonia* as "loving assistance rendered to the neighbor", see H. W. Beyer, "διακονέω, διακονία, διάκονος," *Theological Dictionary of the New Testament*, ed. G. Kittel, trans. and ed. G. W. Bromiley, vol. 2 (Grand Rapids, MI: Eerdmans, 1964), pp. 81-93. This view was aptly challenged by J. N. Collins in *Diakonia: Re-interpreting the Ancient Sources* (New York: Oxford University Press, 1990). Cf. also J. N. Collins, *Diakonia Studies: Critical Issues in Ministry* (New York: Oxford University Press, 2014); A. Hentschel, *Diakonia im Neuen Testament: Studien zur Semantik unter besonderer Berücksichtigung der Rolle von Frauen* (Tübingen: Mohr Siebeck, 2007).

[2] For an overview of the different approaches and interpretations, see J. N. Collins, *Diakonia*, 5-45.

[3] The values associated with the expression *diakonia* in the World Council of Churches include: inter-church aid, transfer of power in terms of social action aimed at empowering the poor, resource-sharing systems, sharing, healing, reconciliation, prophetic solidarity with peoples in their struggles for justice and peace and human dignity, promotion of gender equity and the liberation of the marginalized, etc. See Alexander Belopopsky (ed.), *From Inter-Church Aid to Jubilee, A brief history of ecumenical diakonia in the World Council of Churches* (Geneva: 2002). On the development of the notions of *diakonia* and diaconate in the World Council of Churches cf. the critical article of Kjell Nordstokke, "*Diakonia* and Diaconate in the World Council of Churches" in *International Journal for the Study of the Christian Church*, 13/4 (2013), 286-99.

[4] This expression was first used by Ion Bria in *The Liturgy after the Liturgy: Mission and Witness from an Orthodox Perspective* (Geneva: WCC, 1996).

Christ. In this approach, the self-emptying love (*kenosis*) of Jesus Christ, "whose sacrifice was made for the salvation of all humankind", is the basis of the "liturgical *diakonia*",[5] clearly delineated as service to the whole person, the community and creation, and as a sign and foretaste of the kingdom of God.[6]

In his keynote lecture at the Chania consultation, Alexander Papaderos stressed the Eucharistic liturgy as center and origin of a particular way of life, in which there is no room for any separation between the worship of God and the service of human beings. In this sense, "the distribution of the daily bread and the gift of the Word, the bread of life, are inseparable".

The position formulated in 1978 about the intrinsic relationship between *diakonia* and the Eucharistic liturgy should, in my view, be credited with providing a counterbalance to approaches to *diakonia* based solely on effective programs and specialized ministries. Yet, I believe that revisiting and nuancing the meaning and connotation of *diakonia* in light of its usage in the New Testament could contribute to a more complete image of how *diakonia* is related to the Eucharistic breaking of bread. In this article, I shall address one of the most important and widely quoted texts for questions related to *diakonia* in the New Testament, namely the election of the Seven in Acts 6:1-6, in a quest to understand the context in which Luke uses the *diakon*-words in his second work *ad Theophilum*. I shall then revert to the Orthodox liturgy for conclusions on how the relationship between *diakonia* and Eucharist is reflected in it.

The Election of the Seven (Acts 6:1-6)

The story of the election of the Seven comes in the context of the "growth of the Word" and the increase in numbers of believers.[7] It is characterized by a fresh usage of terms, such as "disciples" for all believers (6:1, 2, 7); "the Twelve" for the apostles (6:2; only once in Acts); the pair "Hellenists and Hebrews/Jews" for believers (6:1); and the usage of *diakon*-words in relation to preaching (6:4) and "waiting at table" (6:1-2). Besides, the introductory

[5] The title of the main paper presented at the 1978 consultation by Alexandros Papaderos, "Liturgical Diaconia" in *An Orthodox Approach to Diaconia. Consultation on Church and Service. Orthodox Academy of Crete, November 1978* (Geneva: WCC, 1980).

[6] Belopopsky, *From Inter-Church Aid to Jubilee*, p. 14; *Hope in the Desert: The Churches' United Response to Human Need*, 1944-1984, ed. K. Slack (Geneva: 1986), 134; M. Opocensky, "European Theology-Other Theologies: An East European Contribution" in *European Theology Challenged by the World-Wide Church, Occasional Paper no. 8 of the Conference of European Churches* (Geneva: 1976), 94; *An Orthodox Approach to Diaconia*, 41-42.

[7] The theme of the increase in the number of the disciples forms an *inclusio* in 6:1a and 6:7a.

narrative formula "in these days", which does not attempt precise chronology,[8] marks Luke's intention to give his narrative a new course of action.[9]

In fact, the tension between Hellenist and Hebrew disciples introduced in 6:1 opens the way to multiple developments in the narrative:

1) After Stephen's martyrdom, the proclamation of the Word, limited so far to Jerusalem, crosses the city walls and opens up to the wider world;

2) The 12 apostles are no longer alone in preaching; after the election of the Seven, their role as preachers diminishes substantially, giving way to the leading role of Stephen in arguing with the authorities (chapter 7), to Philip in preaching the Samaritans (chapter 8), and to Saul/Paul and his companions among Gentiles (chapters 13–21);

3) Peter, the principal actor in Jerusalem, is depicted in a new light: he follows the lead of Philip in Samaria; his story with Cornelius is about his own conversion (chapters 10-11); with the exception of his role in the Jerusalem meeting (chapter 15), the last story about him is his imprisonment and miraculous release (12:1-19);

4) While in chapters 2–5 the community continues praying daily in the temple, after Stephen's speech the temple is no longer a friendly space for the disciples (21:30);

5) Whereas in chapters 2–5 the tension is between the believers and the religious leadership, the attention of the reader is directed in 6:1 to internal issues related to acceptance and inclusion. In the context of these developments, the story of the Seven introduces a narrative itinerary, in the course of which the story advances, characters develop and others emerge, borders are crossed and barriers are destroyed, allowing the "growth of the Word" without limits.

Diakonia and Universal Witness

The word *diakonia* occurs at important junctures in Acts. We find it twice at the outset of the apostles' mission in 1:17 and 25, where it is presented as their main function, embracing their preaching and witnessing activity "in Jerusalem, in all Judea and Samaria, and to the ends of the earth" (1:8).[10] For Luke, this apostolic *diakonia* is so essentially linked to the divine appointment that any falling away from it is harshly punished (1:18-20).

The word *diakonia* also occurs twice at the close of Paul's preaching activity. Before his martyrdom trip to Jerusalem/Rome, Paul refers in his farewell speech to his preaching activity among "Jews and Hellenes" (20:21) as *diakonia* rooted in the commission he received from the Lord to preach and to

---

[8] See, for example, C. K. Barrett, *The Acts of the Apostles* (Edinburgh: T&T Clark: 1994), pp. 3-6.

[9] The same expression begins in 1:15, the first section about preaching in Jerusalem, and in 11:27, the third section related to Paul's activity in and beyond Antioch.

[10] A similar command occurs in Luke 24:27.

suffer (see 9:16). Further, in his report to the elders in Jerusalem, *diakonia* refers to "what God has done among the Gentiles" through Paul (21:19).

On the other hand, *Diakon*-words are used in parallel in the context of food and attending at tables in the narratives of the election of the Seven (6:1-6) and the assistance sent to Jerusalem by the disciples in Antioch (11:27-30/12:24-25). These two pericopes exhibit a striking parallelism:

1) They begin with the introductory narrative formula "in these days" (two out of three occurrences in Acts);

2) The word "disciples", used for the first time in 6:1, recurs in 11:29 and is underscored in 11:26 through the narrator's remark that "the disciples were first called Christians in Antioch";

3) Antioch, the scene of 11:27-30, is mentioned in 6:5 in the information Luke provides about Nicolas, one of the Seven, as "a proselyte from Antioch";

4) Two of three occurrences of the sentence "and the Word of God grew" are found in 6:7 and 12:24 – the continuation of 11:30 – in immediate connection to the performance of *diakonia.*

Besides, these two pericopes are also marked by a contrast related to the usage of *diakonia.* The author introduces in 6:1 a tension between Hellenists and Hebrews/Jews related to "daily *diakonia*". This tension, however, is completely absent in 11:29/12:25, as *diakonia* is performed in a state of perfect harmony between Hellenists and Jews (11:19-30). Taking this contrast as a premise helps us understand the flow of the narrative, which, in my view, takes the reader on a journey from tension in 6:1-6 to its denouement in 11:19-30/12:25, in the course of which Luke introduces several constitutive elements of his plot.

A review of what is recounted in 6:1–11:30 reveals that all the stages of the witnessing program mentioned in 1:8 are covered in this section:

1) The election of the Seven triggers a wide growth of the Word and the increase in the number of the disciples "in Jerusalem" (6:7);

2) After the execution of Stephen, Philip preaches the Word in Samaria and the cities of the coastal plain (8:1-40; see also 9:31);

3) Further, the scattered disciples preach to the Jews and the Hellenists in Phoenicia, Cyprus and Antioch, where the unlimited journey of the expansion of the Word to the "ends of the earth" begins (11:19-26).

In this threefold program, the story of the Seven plays a crucial role as a unifying element; their election results in a considerable increase in the number of the disciples in Jerusalem (6:7); the martyrdom of Stephen and the ensuing persecution triggers the proclamation of the Word first in Samaria (8:1-8), then in Phoenicia, Cyprus and Antioch (11:19-26).

I shall now try to trace the main narrative developments that are noticeable between 6:1 and 11:30, by which the reader is guided to understand how the tension of 6:1 reaches its denouement in 11:27-30. This requires us to address the complex narratological strategies brought into play in this section.[11]

Hellenists and Jews between Jerusalem and Antioch

Commentators debate whether "Hellenists" in 6:1 refers to Greeks (Gentiles) or to Greek-speaking Jews. While equally strong arguments have been brought forward to support both positions,[12] I believe that historical approaches do not always do justice to the narrative value of words, places, movements and characters. The story of the Seven is followed by the dispersion of the disciples outside the walls of Jerusalem to proclaim the Word in Samaria, Galilee and Antioch. In this framework, the change of locations in the scene of *diakonia* from Jerusalem to Antioch has to be taken seriously into consideration, as an element closely related to the contrast pointed to above.

The scene of the exclusion of the Hellenist widows from "daily *diakonia*" is Jerusalem. So far, Luke has presented the city in two lights: Jerusalem is the city in which Jesus asked the apostles to remain until they receive the Spirit (1:4); in Jerusalem a growing community is established, whose life reflects ideal fellowship and unity; the temple of this Jerusalem continues to be the place where believers perform their prayers (2:46; 5:42). On the other hand, Jerusalem is also the city in which "rulers, elders, scribes and high priests" meet to judge Peter and John (4:5-6, 18), and conspire against the apostles (5:33-40). In the former Jerusalem, the Holy Spirit comes down on the apostles, people from "all nations under heaven" are gathered to hear them, and the growing community of believers is established. The latter Jerusalem kills Stephen (7:54-60), launches a severe persecution against the disciples (8:1), kills James (12:1), imprisons Peter (12:1-19), and rejects and persecutes Paul (21:27ff.).

Antioch, however, is presented as a city fully under the authority of the Word of God and His hand (11:21). It is the only city in Acts where there is no tension whatsoever in relation to preaching. There are no opponents in the scene; the disciples are free to preach, act, teach and exhort "the considerable crowd" of believers (11:21, 26). The Jews and the Hellenists who accept the Word are gathered as one community, following assiduously the unimpeded teaching and exhortation of Barnabas and Saul (11:19-26). The only tension in the story is the imminent universal famine, which is countered by the disciples

[11] The narrative relationship between the stories figuring in this section has been observed by D. Marguerat, *The First Christian Historian: Writing the 'Acts of the Apostles'*, tr. by K. McKinney, G. J. Laughery, R. Bauckham (Cambridge: Cambridge University Press, 2004), 189.

[12] C. K. Barrett, *Acts*, p. 305-6, provides examples on these two different approaches.

of Antioch through a common *diakonia* to the brethren in Judea and Jerusalem. It is noteworthy that Antioch is the only place in Acts in which it is said that "the grace of God" is seen (11:23).

Based on the above, I believe that the pair "Hellenists and Hebrews" in relation to *diakonia* in 6:1 should not be understood in a historical light, but rather as an *elliptic prolepsis*,[13] pointing forward to the continuation of the narrative rather than backward. It introduces a narrative itinerary, in which the Word will cross from "hostile" Jerusalem to Antioch, the city where the Word has its free course. As pointed out above, in 6:1 Luke diverts the attention of the reader from the tension between the believers and the religious leadership in 2-5, to internal issues related to acceptance and inclusion within the community of the disciples. In my view, the tension between the rulers and the believers in Jerusalem is projected by Luke onto the community as a tension between Hebrew and Hellenist disciples, in such a way that one could say that a "hostile" Jerusalem is somehow also at work among the disciples. Later, we will be told who this "hostile" Jerusalem is; in 11:1-2, the author mentions the brethren of the circumcision who refuse to eat with the Gentiles; in 15:1, certain persons from Judea are teaching the Gentiles that they cannot be saved if they are not circumcised; in 20:29-30, Paul mentions the "grievous wolves" who shall arise "from among you" – the elders of the Ephesian church – "speaking perverse things, to draw away the disciples after them"; finally, the elders in Jerusalem tell Paul about the "many thousands of Jews who believed and are all zealous for the law", who have been told that Paul teaches the Jews to abandon the customs of Moses (21:20-21). This is the inner tension Luke is dealing with, using the tension between the "*two Jerusalems*" as a literary mediation. His projection is brought into play on a particular practice, which he calls "daily *diakonia*", and which touches on, in my reading, a very sensitive issue in the relationship between "Jews" and "Gentiles", namely, common meals, and in particular, the Eucharistic breaking of bread.

The Daily Diakonia

The Twelve say that "it is not pleasing that we should leave the Word of God *to attend at tables*" (6:2). Through this reaction, Luke directs his reader to perceive the usage of the *diakon*-words in two different semantic fields: the word *diakonia* in 6:1 and the infinitive *diakonein* in 6:2 are linked to "waiting at tables", whereas *diakonia* in 6:4 relates to preaching and teaching the Word (1:17, 25; 20:24; 21:19). The usage of the verb *diakonein* in relation to

---

[13] A prolepsis is a narrative projection toward the future of the story. It is elliptic when it is made less clear and left for the reader to understand in the continuation of the narrative. On Luke's extensive use of elliptic prolepses see D. Marguerat, *The First Christian Historian*, 49-51; see also G. Genette, *Figures III* (Paris: Seuil, 1972), 90-115.

"attending at tables" is nowhere else to be found in Acts.[14] However, it occurs in a central text in the gospel of Luke: the narrative of the last supper.

Jesus as One "Who Attends at Table"

Luke 22:14-30 is the only passage in the New Testament that speaks expressly of Jesus as "attending at table" in the context of a meal.[15] After breaking the bread and blessing the cup, Jesus reacts to the dispute about who is greater among the disciples by inviting them to depart from the order of the "nations" and be like Him as one who "attends at table". Already in the sayings about the master who "will gird himself, have them [his servants] sit at table, come and attend [*diakonisei*]" to his watchful servants (Luke 12:37), Luke had presented "attending at table" as a function accomplished by the master toward his servants coming from the four corners of the world (Luke 13:29). In my conviction, this story is a *prolepsis* in the Gospel, pointing toward Acts, where the reader is expected to find its meaning and implications in the flow of the narrative in 6:1–11:26.

The Exclusion of the Hellenist Widows from "Daily Diakonia"

The careful reader of the double work *ad Theophilum* will not fail to link Acts 6:1-6 to the Lukan account of the last supper, for the following reasons:

- The reader has already encountered the word *diakonia* twice at the outset of Acts (1:15-26) as the main duty of the apostles.

- Further, through the close link established in 1:15-26 between *diakonia* and the number 12 of the apostles, which, for its importance, had to be restored after the falling away of Judas, the reader is guided to connect its usage here to Luke 22:14-30, where the number 12 forms an *inclusio* to the scene of the last supper (22:14 and 30).

As the reader proceeds through the following narratives, they gather information on the exemplary life of the community established in Jerusalem (2:42-47; 4:32-37). The daily breaking of bread and common meals are emphasized as a central and characteristic practice of this community (mentioned twice in 2:42-47 and alluded to in 5:42), alongside the prayers in the temple and the teaching of the apostles.

---

[14] The participle "*diakonounton*" in 19:22 in reference to Timothy and Erastus, translated usually as "those ministering" to Paul, might well be a reference to their preaching activity among the Gentiles "on behalf" of Paul, rather than to the mere act of attending to his needs.

[15] The verb *diakoneo* occurs in the gospel mainly in the sense of attending at table, or serving food (Lk. 4:39; 8:3; 10:40 and 17:8).

Given these hints, with the expression "daily *diakonia*" Luke stimulates his reader to think of nothing else than "breaking the bread and common meals",[16] that is the specific Eucharistic gathering of the Church in Jerusalem. In fact, the expression "every day/daily" is used twice in connection to prayer and breaking the bread (in 2:46 and 5:42). What Luke is referring to, therefore, is the attitude of the "Hebrew" disciples, who refuse to share the "Eucharistic bread" with the Hellenist widows and to admit them to the common meals.

The issue at stake, then, is fundamental and vital in the life of the community; the exclusion of the Hellenist widows from the Eucharistic breaking of bread and common meals not only undoes the work of the Holy Spirit but also endangers the nature of the breaking of bread as an implementation and concretization of the communion. Moreover, it violates the central teaching of Jesus related to *diakonia* at the last supper, namely, that it should be addressed first and foremost to the "lesser ones" (Luke 22:26-27). The widows represent the vulnerable groups of human beings that Jesus has accepted, taught, healed and fed (Luke 9:10-17) and who figure at the center of the community of the believers and its practices (2:45; 4:34-35).

As with the issue of circumcision (15), the seriousness of the misbehavior vis-à-vis the Hellenist widows necessitates a meeting of "all disciples". For this tension to be resolved, the imposed barriers between clean and unclean have to be abolished. However, this cannot happen without a change in mindset, that is, without a true understanding of the biblical story. This is precisely where the narrative of the election of the Seven fulfills its central function. The stories of Stephen and Philip produce major changes in attitudes, worldviews and places that are clearly echoed in the stories of Paul and Peter.

Stephen and the Exodus to the Wilderness: A Pattern

While the reader of Acts 6:1-6 expects the Seven to be completely dedicated to "attending at tables", nothing is subsequently mentioned about any activity involving food. Rather, the author describes an unequally successful preaching activity (6:7) and a detailed report on Stephen's speech and martyrdom (6:8 – 7:60) and Philip's preaching outside Jerusalem (8:1-40).

---

[16] For J. N. Collins, *Diakonia Studies*, 152-61, the "daily *diakonia*" is the daily preaching of the Word, which the widows "as speakers of Greek" were not free to attend for social and linguistic reasons. Accordingly, the disciples appointed Greek-speaking preachers to teach them at home. A slightly different opinion is formulated by A. Hentschel, *Diakonia im Neuen Testament*, 318-46: Luke divides the dual responsibility of the Twelve for "Word" and "deed" into separate responsibilities for the Twelve and the Seven respectively. The fact that nothing is mentioned about the activity of the Seven in "deed" suggests to Hentschel that 6:1-6 is a Lukan fiction disguising a pre-existent ministry of the "Word" carried out by the Seven among the Hellenists. In my view, neither position does justice to the narrative richness of the story and its continuation, nor to the flow of the story.

Stephen, "a man full of the Holy Spirit and wisdom" (6:3, 5, 10 and 7:55), makes the longest speech in the book of Acts, expounding the Scriptures to the religious leaders of Jerusalem, from the call of Abraham to the Exile. Dealing with the question where God must be worshipped, his speech comes as a response to allegations about slandering the temple and the law (6:13-14). In this exposition the theme of exodus occupies a central place. The story of Abraham begins with an exodus: the first order given by "the God of glory" to Abraham was "*exelthe*" – go out – "from your land and your kindred to the land which I will show you" (7:3-4). Yet, the land remained a promise awaiting "the time" of its fulfillment (7:17), which necessitated a second exodus of "the seed" of Abraham from Egypt. In the lengthy recapitulation of the story of the exodus (7:20-43), the following points are underlined: 1) the sole purpose of exodus is the worship of God (7:7); 2) the exodus was fully accomplished (7:35-36); 3) however, the house of Israel "returned in their hearts to Egypt" by refusing to obey the "living words" and worshipping the idols (7:39; 43); 4) the exile to Babylon implies that a new exodus is needed.[17]

All of the above means that the land remains a promise, due to the failure of Israel to comply with the "living words" revealed in the wilderness. That this failure continues in the presence of the addressees of Stephen's speech is shown in the conclusion, where he rebukes the leaders for their "uncircumcised ears and hearts", that is, for their unfaithfulness and for not "hearing" the Scriptures and obeying *Torah* (7:51-53).

Accordingly, exodus should not be understood as a mere geographical movement from one place (Egypt) to another (Jerusalem), but as a journey toward the "living words" of God in the wilderness. This is a divine directive. The Lord who is speaking through Stephen is the Lord who turned the wilderness into a "*ge agia*" (7:33), the place where the Church should be (7:38). The true and faithful worship of God is realized, therefore, in an exodus from a world controlled by a hostile authority (Pharaonic Egypt, Babylon, Jerusalem ruled by the oppressive religious authority) to the world in the center of which the living Word of God is received and obeyed.

From Stephen's speech one may deduce that, for the author of Acts, if the Church is to exist, it has to be permanently in a state of exodus, as a movement toward the Word of God, for the Lord and His words are to be found only "outside" the realm in which humans rule and exercise egocentric, oppressive authority. Against this background, Luke will adopt exodus as a pattern, applying it throughout Acts. After Stephen's martyrdom, the Church makes its exodus from the oppressive city to spread the Word outside its walls (8:1; 11:19-26). The reader observes a recurrence of the exodus pattern in Saul's exodus from Damascus (9:25) and from Jerusalem (9:29-30), and Peter's exodus from the prison in Jerusalem to Caesarea (12:1-19). The same pattern is

[17] See Paul N. Tarazi, *The New Testament – Introduction, Luke and Acts* (St. Vladimir's Seminary Press: Crestwood NY, 2001), 207-216.

applied also in the Pauline section: Paul leaves Antioch of Pisidia because of the oppression of Jews and Hellenes (13:50) and "goes out / *makes his exodus*" from Iconium (14:5-7), Lystra (14:19-29), Philippi (16:39-40), Thessalonica (17:13-15), Athens (17:33) and Ephesus (20:1) for the same reason.

In this sense, Stephen's speech is constitutive, in that it posits the lexicon as well as the premises for the subsequent narratives. The exodus pattern will be brought into play by Luke in the following narratives to guide the reader from the rejection in 6:1 to the inclusion in 11:19-30. The deconstruction of the centrality of Jerusalem and the temple will be concretized in the conversion of the "outsiders" and, through them, the conversion of the "insiders" from the centrism of "Jerusalem and the temple" to the vastness of the earth created by God.

Philip: The Exodus of the Church

Jerusalem kills Stephen and launches a severe persecution against the disciples (8:1). However, instead of quenching the Word, this persecution gave it a renewed impetus. The disciples who left the oppressive Jerusalem started preaching the Word on a large scale. Philip succeeded in teaching the Samaritans (8:4-8). Peter and John came to Samaria to acknowledge that the Spirit is free to be anywhere and that the Samaritans too, the people with whom Jews do not mingle for reasons related to "the law", receive the Holy Spirit that cannot be appropriated, nor can anyone lay hand on it or purchase it (8:14-24).

The story of the eunuch is of the utmost importance in this context. It is worth highlighting the usage of the word "wilderness" at its outset (8:26). The mentions of the "angel of the Lord", Gaza and the wilderness are reminiscent of the terminology of Genesis, as well as of Stephen's speech. The angel of the Lord speaks to Philip, as He spoke to the Fathers, and orders him to follow a path leading from Jerusalem to Gaza, which is described as "wilderness". The eunuch is following the same path. He had come to worship in Jerusalem. However, despite being in Jerusalem and at the temple, no one was able to make him understand the Scriptures (8:31).[18] He had to wait until he came to the wilderness to hear from a stranger walking down the same way that the text from Isaiah talks about the sufferings of Jesus. There he understood, believed and was baptized.

The stories of the Samaritans and the eunuch, the "outsiders" *par excellence*, converge in that neither needs Jerusalem to believe: the Samaritans receive the Holy Spirit outside Jerusalem, and the eunuch, the true knowledge and understanding of Scriptures after he leaves the city and its temple. In this sense, the stories of Stephen and Philip constitute a diptych: the first, with divine authority, deconstructs the centrality of the temple and Jerusalem by

---

[18] P. N. Tarazi, *The New Testament – Introduction, Luke and*, p. 219.

underscoring the exodus as the way of the Lord, and the second implements this deconstruction through the preaching of the Samaritans and the eunuch.

The premise that readers should keep in mind is that Stephen and Philip were elected to "attend at tables" in order to remedy the exclusion of the "Hellenist widows". From this perspective, Luke recounts their stories. Unless one takes seriously this premise, one is bound to mishear what Luke is narrating. Given that the issue of the "daily *diakonia*" is internal, the lesson about the exodus from Jerusalem has to be heard primarily by the "insiders", that is, by those who reject any mingling with "outsiders" on the basis that they are not "like them". The stories of Saul and Peter confirm this.

Saul: The Exodus of the Oppressive Jerusalem

Saul's reference in persecuting the communities of believers is Jerusalem and its high priest. He was in charge of bringing the believers bound to Jerusalem (9:2) to destroy them (9:21). He had consented to the execution of Stephen, the Lord's messenger (8:1). However, this very Saul is converted by the Lord Himself to the faith he was seeking to destroy. Even more, he is commissioned to carry the name of Jesus Christ to nations, kings and to the children of Israel (9:15). The conversion of the staunch persecutor of the disciples takes place, like that of the eunuch, outside Jerusalem, on the road to Damascus.

Luke introduces in the story of the conversion of Saul interesting details.[19] Saul's conversion faces two parallel obstacles. On one hand, resistance to his call comes from Ananias (9:13-19) and the community of the disciples (9:26-27). However, the reader was already informed that the animosity of Saul was brought down on the road to Damascus, and that the action of Christ anticipated the reaction of Ananias, whose opposition was overcome[20] in the Lord's order to him: "Go, for he is a chosen vessel unto me" (9:15). Further, the objection of the disciples in Jerusalem to accept Saul as one of them was overcome by the intervention of Barnabas, who explained to the apostles that the Lord Himself spoke to Saul in a vision (9:27).

On the other hand, Saul was also rejected in Damascus by the "Jews" (11:23) and in Jerusalem by the "Hellenists" (9:29). However, this refusal was dealt with differently; whereas in the case of Ananias and the disciples the Lord intervened to change the attitude of his own with regard to the new identity of Saul as the agent of the universal *diakonia*, in the case of the Jews and the

---

[19] A rich narrative analysis of the conversion of Paul is provided by Marguerat in *The First Christian Historian*, 179-204.

[20] D. Marguerat, *The First Christian Historian*, p. 194; see also J. Calloud, 'Sur le chemin de Damas. Quelques lumières sur l'organisation discursive d'un texte, Actes des apôtres 9, 1-19', *Sémiotique et Bible* 37, 1985, 3-29; 38, 1985, 40-53; 40, 1985, 21-42; 42, 1986, 1-19; D. Marguerat and Y. Bourquin, *How to Read Bible Stories. An Introduction to Narrative Criticism* (London: SCM Press, 1999), 71-2.

Hellenists, the intervention was through the disciples who helped Saul exit both cities (9:25, 30). In the first case the result is inclusion, and in the second an exodus. This parallelism between inclusion and exodus is what Luke is highlighting for his readers. *There can be no inclusion if there is no exodus.* Ananias' attitude in Damascus and that of the disciples in Jerusalem would not have been very different from that of the Jews and Hellenists, had the Lord not intervened. To Ananias and the disciples who might have doubts as to whether "the oppressive Jerusalem" can convert, the Lord has shown in the case of Saul not only that it does but also that it is called to preach the Word to the whole world. In the conversion of Saul, the oppressive Jerusalem makes its exodus from itself to join the persecuted community of disciples, and the disciples make their exodus from refusing that this can happen into acknowledging that the action of the Lord has the upper hand.

Peter: The Exodus to the House of Cornelius

Parallel to the conversion of Saul, a conversion in the opposite direction takes place in the story of Peter and Cornelius (10:1–11:18), namely the conversion of Peter from a "Jew who does not mingle with those of other nations" (10:28) to someone who "eats with the uncircumcised" (11:2). Usually considered a story of Peter converting a Gentile, this story and the way it is narrated reveal that it is not so much about the conversion of Cornelius as it is about the conversion of Peter himself.[21] In fact, the intervention of God guiding all the details of the events, turning points and characters of this story obliges Peter to leave the house of Simon the Tanner (10:19-23) to go to the house of the Italian Cornelius. Peter here does not appear as a self-confident preacher who preaches openly and does signs and wonders, but as someone who is fully unaware of what is happening, unable to understand a vision repeated three times (10:17), and utterly ignorant of why he was brought to Cornelius's house (10:29). It was Cornelius who told him that the aim of his visit was to speak to them about "what God had commanded you" (10:33). However, God "who shows no partiality" (10:34) pours the Holy Spirit on Cornelius and his house in a Pentecost-like manner (10:44-46). The same Spirit that gave the apostles in Jerusalem the gift of speaking about the great deeds of God in tongues has given the Gentile Cornelius and his house the same gifts. Yet this happens simultaneously with a radical change in Peter himself: "God has shown me that I should not call anyone profane or unclean" (10:28). Peter, who so far is reluctant to "eat with those of another nation", who prefers to stay several days

---

[21] Expression used by D. Marguerat, *The First Christian Historian*, p. 55; see also L. Marin, 'Essai d'analyse structurale d'Actes 10,1–11,18' in R. Barthes et al (eds.), *Exégèse et Herméneutique* (Paris, Seuil, 1971), 213-38.

in the house of someone of his nation, carrying the same name,[22] in order not to be defiled by "outsiders", is now converted to someone who not only eats with the Gentiles but also defends this practice before those who are in Jerusalem as the irresistible will of God (11:17). Through his conversion, the brethren in Jerusalem were converted too, and the opponents of common meals with the Gentiles "became silent", and glorified God because "He granted to the Gentiles repentance unto life" (11:18).

The Seven and the "Daily Diakonia"

How did the Seven then "attend at tables" for the Hellenist widows? Before answering this question, let us recap the main ideas related to the usage of *diakonia* in the context presented above. Luke roots the *diakonic* commission of the apostles to preach the Word universally in the teaching about the last supper. In Jesus' saying about "attending at table" as a sign of true greatness, the author links *diakonein* to the breaking of bread as "remembrance" of Jesus' death and resurrection. Given that Luke has prepared the readers, in the gospel, to view *diakonein*, in the first place, as "waiting at table", an act that expresses high esteem for those who are attended to, the *kerygma* with which Jesus entrusted His disciples (Luke 24:47) is not only a proclamation of the Word but also an embodiment of the teaching about Jesus' death and resurrection as the fulfillment of the totality of Scriptures (Luke 24:44-46) in the life, acts and worldview of the disciples. Since the *kerygma* is to "all the nations starting from Jerusalem", Jesus' command about "attending at table" in the last supper is a universal command, an invitation to His disciples to introduce in the world a new order, emanating from the meaning of His death and resurrection. In Acts, Luke underscores the fundamental character of this teaching by calling the mission of the apostles "*diakonia*", which has two facets: the *kerygma* to "all nations" and the *table fellowship* open to "all nations" and expressing the fact that "Jesus' breaking of bread" is a universal event in which all are invited to participate without exception.

In order to give the universal character of *diakonia* its course, Luke resorts to the exodus pattern presented in Stephen's speech. The animosity of the nations to one another and the egocentricity of humans do not allow a common participation in table fellowship. Taking the "oppressive Jerusalem" as an example and literary mediation, Luke invites the true disciples to make their exodus from oppressive human authority, exclusiveness, rejection and animosity toward the Word of God that took flesh in His "suffering servant".

[22] Note the use of the expression "Simon, whose surname was Peter", used only here in the book of Acts, always in association with the name of his host "Simon, the tanner" in 10:5-6, 17-18 and 32, to create an assonance between the two names in order to draw the attention of the reader that Simon stayed, and therefore ate, at the house of a Jew, in order not to eat anything unclean (10:14).

Without an exodus there can be no real encounter. Following the prototype of the "suffering Christ", Luke emphasizes that the way of exodus follows the path of Jesus toward His death in Jerusalem, which culminates in the resurrection. It is worth noting in this context that Luke refers twice to Jesus' death as an exodus: once in the pericope of the transfiguration (Luke 9:31), and once in the statement of Peter in Acts 1:21. Originally an exodus from oppressive slavery in Egypt toward the "worship" of the Lord in the vastness of the wilderness, the exodus in Acts is toward the concretization of the worship in self-denial, communion and inclusion in "all the earth" created by God.

Back to the question Luke kept pending so the reader may discover the answer in the continuation of the narrative: the Seven "attended" to the Hellenist widows, through Stephen who died like the Lord for deconstructing the exclusivity of the temple and unveiling the ignorance of the *Torah*, and through Philip who showed that the Holy Spirit can be received regardless of ethnic origin, status, race and location. In Antioch, which functions as wilderness and ultimately as the "whole earth", the harmony and the unity of all was re-established after the "opponents" of the divine will were converted to "helpers", through the common meal gathering Hellenists, Jews and the impoverished brethren of Judea and Jerusalem as the ultimate expression of the *diakonia* "in Christ".

Diaconal Church and Eucharistic Liturgy: Perspectives

The inseparability between the proclamation of the Word and the Eucharistic table, as shown in Acts, is a major foundation in the Orthodox understanding of Liturgy. The "liturgy of the word" and the "liturgy of communion" are not two juxtaposed units, but constitute one and the same gathering in which the community hears the Word of God in the readings from the Bible and the sermon and partakes in the Eucharistic communion. There is no room in this article to embark on a detailed and comprehensive exposition of the Orthodox liturgical service. I would like, however, to point to some elements that are of importance in the context of our exposition.

The Eucharistic liturgy is viewed as an "exodus" and "entrance" in the biblical sense of these words. The liturgy of the word proper begins with a procession headed by the deacons carrying the Bible. Originally, this procession, called "the entrance", was the movement of all believers from outside into the church. The elements of this "entrance" suggest a *mimesis* of the exodus to the wilderness: the golden Bible adorned with figures of the Cherubim stands for the Ark of the Covenant (Ex. 37:1-9); the table in the middle of the "holy of holies" stands for the table in the center of the tabernacle (Ex. 37:10-16); the veil usually covering the table is reminiscent of the tabernacle itself; the priestly garments mimic the garments of Aaron and his sons (Ex. 39); the light, the incense and the covers are all elements pertaining to the exodus scenery. "Blessed is the entrance of your saints" is the sentence uttered by the celebrant, reflecting the understanding of this movement, not only as procession into the church but also as movement toward the presence of the Lord in His Word in the Bible as the "Ark of the Covenant". The "entrance" culminates in the Lord's ceremonial appearance in the readings from the Bible, preceded by the *trisagion* (three times holy) chanted in the book of Isaiah to the Lord who appeared in His glory in the temple (Is. 6:1-4), as He appeared on Mount Horeb, allowing only those who are purified to approach it (Ex. 19; Is. 6:5-7). The prayer preceding the readings in the Orthodox liturgy[23] echoes this understanding:

> Shine within our hearts, loving Master, the pure light of Your divine knowledge and open the eyes of our minds that we may comprehend the message of Your Gospel. Instill in us, also, reverence for Your blessed commandments, so that having conquered sinful desires, we may pursue a spiritual life, thinking and doing all those things that are pleasing to You.

According to this prayer, the believers are invited to stand before the proclamation of the Word in the readings like the people gathered around Mount Horeb to receive the living words of God.

Called an "entrance", this movement toward the proclamation of the Word is understood as the final goal of an exodus. The theme of exodus is developed in the *anaphora*, or the Eucharistic prayer, which, in the liturgy of Saint Basil the Great, recaps the Biblical story from creation to the last supper. Starting with the fall of the man God "*honored with His own image*" through the disobedience of the commandments, the theme of exodus is brought up in the following sentence:

> Releasing us from the delusions of idolatry, He guided us to the sure knowledge of You, the true God and Father. He acquired us for Himself, as His chosen people, a royal priesthood, a holy nation.

The place from which the celebrants are released is "the delusions of idolatry". Further, Basil refers to this place as "*death in which we were held captive, sold under sin*". In his abridged version of the much longer *anaphora* of the Apostolic Constitutions,[24] Basil omits the detailed mention of the exodus from Egypt in order to highlight the universal bondage of all nations under the sin, expressed in the form of "delusions of idolatry". Not only Israel but also "the whole lost race of the men" broke "the natural law"[25] and, through this, suffered its captivity. Besides the universal character of the exodus, Basil

---

[23] In the two commonly used liturgies of Saint John Chrysostom and Saint Basil the Great.

[24] R. H. Cresswell (tr. and ed.), *The Liturgy of the Eighth Book of the Apostolic Constitutions* (New York: SPCK, 1900).

[25] R. H. Cresswell, *Liturgy of the Apostolic Constitutions*, 61.

stresses that it was the act of Jesus, who "released us" and "guided us", pointing to the ultimate act of salvation, namely the death and resurrection. The place toward which the path of exodus leads is "the knowledge of God". There, the people consisting of "all nations" are sanctified, and appointed as "a royal priesthood and a holy nation" (Ex. 19:6), precisely in the gathering around the presence of the Lord in His Word.

The act of exodus reaches its culmination in the last supper, the table at which Jesus offers his flesh and blood as food for "all" those who were guided by Him, as the ultimate expression of the knowledge of God. Hence, the cross becomes the final goal of the biblical story and the "location" to which the exodus path leads. There the Lord appears in His glory and reveals His commandment that all be "*united to one another in partaking of the one bread and the one cup in the communion of the Holy Spirit*" (epiclesis). What is worth pointing to, in this context, is that the *anaphora* ends with an *anamnesis* (remembrance) of a long list of "suffering" groups of human beings: the sick, travelers, widows, orphans, captives, exiled, prisoners, afflicted, needy, distressed, etc. Lest anyone be left out, the text reads,

> Remember, O God, all those whom we have not remembered through ignorance, forgetfulness or because of their multitude since You know the name and age of each, even from their mother's womb. For You, Lord, are the helper of the helpless, the hope of the hopeless, the savior of the afflicted, the haven of the voyager, and the physician of the sick. Be all things to all, You who know each person, his requests, his household, and his need.

The exhaustive remembrance of all categories of the afflicted plays a crucial role in the *anaphora*. Their remembrance between the cross and the breaking of bread concretizes the knowledge of God the people were guided to through the cross. There can be no passage from cross to "table fellowship" without "remembering" the afflicted and the needy, that is, without the full awareness of the church that standing before the cross as the ultimate knowledge of God entails carrying the cross of others, so that the table fellowship be completed. At precisely this point in the liturgy, where the community offers to the Lord "*what is His*", the collection is taken up to be sent "in *diakonia*" to the needy brethren. The offering to God of "what belongs to Him" is concretized in the offering presented to the needy. This is the way to the full communion in the breaking of bread at the table offered by the Lord, served by the Lord, and on which the Lord Himself is served.

From Glory to the Cross: Diakonia of the Church

The feast of the Transfiguration of the Lord in the Orthodox Church (celebrated on August 6) and the feast of the Holy Cross (celebrated on September 14) are separated by 40 days. Focusing on themes related to exodus and the appearance of the Lord on Mount Horeb/Sinai, the liturgical texts of the feast of Transfiguration are rooted in the Lukan narrative of the transfiguration and clear reference is made to the exodus of Christ on the cross. The glory witnessed by the three disciples on Mount Hermon, which they could not look at, is revealed, seen and understood on the cross. Thus, the transfiguration is the first step in a journey of 40 days toward the feast of the Cross, which is celebrated as a defeat of the hostile powers. The 40 days are the journey in the wilderness, and the cross is the final phase in that journey. Through this, the church is invited to understand the glory of God from the perspective of the Cross and to walk on the same path. Luke calls this path *diakonia*. In so doing, he puts the "breaking of bread" at the center of the Church's life. The Church, which learns in the Eucharistic gathering the meaning of exodus, commits itself to do "the pleasing deeds", and remembers all humanity, particularly the suffering ones, is a *diaconal* Church that lives its liturgical Eucharist in the love it learned from the divine words and makes its way from glory to Cross. *Diakonia*, which is primarily the Word reaching out to all human beings, is also the responsibility of all to attend to all in meekness, humility, self-denial and self-emptying love, as a concretization of the commitment to the Word. It is a responsibility and a divine call, and the genuine path toward the communion and fellowship to which we are summoned.

Bibliography

Belopopsky A. (ed.), *From Inter-Church Aid to Jubilee, A brief history of ecumenical diakonia in the World Council of Churches* (Geneva: 2002).

Beyer H. W., "διακονέω, διακονία, διάκονος," *Theological Dictionary of the New Testament*, ed. G. Kittel, trans. and ed. G. W. Bromiley, vol. 2 (Grand Rapids, MI: Eerdmans, 1964), pp. 81-93.

Bria I., *The Liturgy after the Liturgy: Mission and Witness from an Orthodox Perspective* (Geneva: WCC, 1996).

Calloud J., 'Sur le chemin de Damas. Quelques lumières sur l'organisation discursive d'un texte, Actes des apôtres 9, 1-19', *Sémiotique et Bible* 37, 1985, pp. 3-29; 38, 1985, pp. 40-53; 40, 1985, pp. 21-42; 42, 1986, pp. 1-19.

Collins J. N., *Diakonia: Re-interpreting the Ancient Sources* (New York: Oxford University Press, 1990).

Collins J. N., *Diakonia Studies: Critical Issues in Ministry* (New York: Oxford University Press, 2014).

Cresswell R. H. (tr. and ed.), The Liturgy of the Eighth Book of the Apostolic Constitutions (New York: SPCK, 1900).

Genette G., *Figures III* (Paris: Seuil, 1972).

A. Hentschel, *Diakonia im Neuen Testament: Studien zur Semantik unter besonderer Berücksichtigung der Rolle von Frauen* (Tübingen: Mohr Siebeck, 2007).

Marguerat D., *The First Christian Historian: Writing the 'Acts of the Apostles'*, tr. by K. McKinney, G. J. Laughery, R. Bauckham (Cambridge: Cambridge University Press, 2004), p. 189.

Marguerat D. and Y. Bourquin, How to Read Bible Stories. An Introduction to Narrative Criticism (London: SCM Press, 1999), pp. 71-2.

Marin L., 'Essai d'analyse structurale d'Actes 10,1–11,18' in R. Barthes et al., eds., *Exégèse et herméneutique* (Paris, Seuil, 1971), pp. 213-38.

Nordstokke K., "*Diakonia* and Diaconate in the World Council of Churches" in *International Journal for the Study of the Christian Church*, 13/4 (2013), pp. 286-99.

Opocensky M., "European Theology-Other Theologies: An East European Contribution" in *European Theology Challenged by the World-Wide Church, Occasional Paper no. 8 of the Conference of European Churches* (Geneva: 1976).

Papaderos A., "Liturgical Diaconia" in *An Orthodox Approach to Diaconia. Consultation on Church and Service. Orthodox Academy of Crete, November 1978* (Geneva: WCC, 1980).

Slack K. (ed.), *Hope in the Desert: The Churches' United Response to Human Need*, 1944-1984 (Geneva: 1986).

Tarazi P. N., *The New Testament – Introduction, Luke and Acts* (St. Vladimir's Seminary Press: Crestwood NY, 2001).

Risen to New Life in Christ: Baptismal Perspectives on Diaconal Ecclesiology

Stephanie Dietrich

Introduction

Water is essential for all life. Without water, we die. We can survive for a while without food, but not without water. Water nourishes and cleans, and water is decisive for the growth of plants and all nutrition. As much as water is life giving, it is also life threatening, where natural disasters, droughts or floods hit communities, where water is polluted or wasted, or where it is unjustly distributed.

Not surprisingly, water rituals play an important role in most religions, so also in Christianity. Jesus calls himself the source of life-giving water, thus allowing his followers to become sources of life-giving water as well (John 7: 37-38):

> On the last and most important day of the festival, Jesus stood up and shouted, "If you are thirsty, come to me and drink! Have faith in me, and you will have life-giving water flowing from deep inside you, just as the Scriptures say."

One of Christianity's core rituals, an act of initiation into the Christian community and widely referred to in the New Testament, is a water ritual: baptism. Baptism was an integrated practice from the time of Early Christianity. Becoming a Christian included from the beginning being baptized and being taught the core doctrine of Christian faith – that Jesus Christ is *kyrios*, Lord. Confessing Jesus Christ as the Lord was not only the condition for being baptized but also included the risk of persecution and martyrdom in the first centuries of Christianity. The New Testament witnesses about the central role of baptism for Christians' self-understanding. Baptism is more than a mere ritual of initiation; it incorporates the Christian into Christ and Christ's body, which is the Church. The baptized partakes in Christ's death and resurrection, and thus receives forgiveness of sins and eternal life. Romans 6: 3-5 underlines:

> Or don't you know that all of us who were baptized into Christ Jesus were baptized into his death? We were therefore buried with him through baptism into death in order that, just as Christ was raised from the dead through the glory of the Father, we too may live a new life.

The core role of baptism in New Testament theology and the practice of the Church throughout all history is indisputable. In my own, the Lutheran tradition of Church of Norway, we underline that Baptism in the name of the triune God, with water, is the only criterion for membership. Based on the Lutheran Confessions, Confessio Augustana IX, we emphasize: "Concerning baptism it is taught that it is necessary, that grace is offered through it, and that one should also baptize children, who through such baptism are entrusted to God and become pleasing him."[1]

In this article, I want to look into how baptismal theology can contribute to a rethinking of ecclesiology, with a specific emphasis on the impact baptism has on the life of the baptized, both as an individual and as the community of baptized. Thus, I do not only want to elaborate on a baptismal ecclesiology but also on baptismal ecclesiology as related to *diakonia* as an indispensable aspect, the DNA of the Christian church, Christian life. When discussing Christian life, this connects directly to *diakonia*, understood as Christian service for and with others. This service connects the being of the church with its diaconal identity.

When exploring baptismal perspectives on diaconal ecclesiology, this article focuses on a selected number of aspects of the theology of baptism.

First, the gift of incorporation into Christ as *incorporation in Christ's community*, the Church as a serving community; and second, the *liberating and empowering dimension of baptism*, enabling the Christian to do *diakonia*. All these aspects play a specific role in a rethinking of the Church's *diaconal* identity in the light of baptismal theology. Methodologically, this chapter is based on the analysis of theological documents from the ecumenical context, thereby raising the question how these ecumenical texts deal with the understanding of baptism as a source for the development of a diaconal ecclesiology. These texts are mainly developed within the framework of multilateral ecumenical discourse, both globally, from the World Council of Churches' context, and nationally.

When exploring a *diaconal* ecclesiology, I want to show how an approach starting in baptismal theology can shape and renew modern ecclesiology emphasizing *diakonia* as a mark of the Church.[2] Baptismal theology emphasizes humankind's recreation through baptism, as participation in Jesus' death and resurrection and the beginning of a believer's life-long journey of growth in Christ toward a new life – already now and yet to be reached. Baptismal theology emphasizes the equal dignity and vocation of all human beings baptized in the name of the triune God, and thus a call to solidarity and joint service.

Through this endeavor, I want to contribute to a reconsideration of an ecclesiology, which gives space for the active role of the Christians and the Church in the world, binding together the Church's doctrinal identity with its

---

[1] Robert Kolb and Timothy J. Wengert (eds.), *The Book of Concord: The Confessions of the Evangelical-Lutheran Church.* (Minneapolis: Fortress Press: 2000), 42.

[2] See Nordstokke's contribution, chapter 5.

place in and for the world. The gift of baptism is simultaneously the gift of God's call to every Christian person to *diakonia* – being incorporated in Christ, and at the same time, into the community of believers, the Church. Through baptism, humankind becomes liberated to live and act God's call to *diakonia*, and cleansed, renewed and empowered to live God's call to *diakonia* in the world. Thus, this chapter will explore different aspects of how a baptismal theology underpins the development of a diaconal ecclesiology.

Combining Eucharistic Ecclesiology with Baptismal Ecclesiology

The Faith and Order document *Baptism, Eucharist and Ministry* (WCC 1982) represented a decisive step for ecumenical bi- and multilateral dialogues. All ecumenical dialogues since 1982 refer to this agreement, either explicitly or implicitly, as a reference document. The BEM document suggested avenues seeking further convergence on what remained some of the most difficult and unresolved issues: the relation between children's and adult/believers' baptism; who may be baptized; the understanding of humankind's sinfulness from birth, or its falling into sin, in relation to the grace bestowed through baptism; and the mutual recognition of baptism between the different traditions and churches. Within a Northern European context of Lutheran majority churches, the emphasis on taking seriously the need for instruction (*catechesis*) became an important reminder, which many of our churches have taken seriously and tried to follow up. In their responses to BEM,[3] churches generally affirmed an impressive degree of agreement and convergence on baptism, while there was a stronger disagreement on the Eucharist and Ministry parts of BEM.

Unitatis redintegratio, a core text for the ecumenical renewal of the Roman-Catholic church from the Second Vatican Council, underlines that baptism is commonly mutually acknowledged, and thus establishes "a sacramental bond of unity which links all who have been reborn by it".[4] Though remaining differences in the understanding of the sacrament of baptism are underlined frequently, it is a striking fact that traditions which normally are rather resistant to recognize other churches' true ecclesiality tend to be much more positive in recognizing baptismal practices in other churches and traditions, if performed in the name of the Triune God, and including the use of water.[5]

---

[3] Cf. *Baptism, Eucharist and Ministry*, 1982-1990: *Report on the Process and Responses*, Geneva, WCC, 1990.

[4] Ibid., Ch. II, 22.

[5] Cf. BEM Baptism C.15: "Mutual recognition of baptism is acknowledged as an important sign and means of expressing the baptismal unity given in Christ. Wherever possible, mutual recognition should be expressed explicitly by the churches." (https://www.oikoumene.org/en/resources/documents/commissions/faith-and-order/i-unity-the-church-and-its-mission/baptism-eucharist-and-ministry-faith-and-order-paper-no-111-the-lima-text, last seen August 21, 2018).

This positive attitude toward mutual recognition of baptism can be seen in many ecumenical discourses. Thus, the recognition of baptism experienced between many churches and traditions today might also be understood as a certain recognition of other Churches' ecclesiality. Recognizing one's baptism implies recognizing that you have become a part of the body of Christ, which is the Church.

Though differences in theology and practice remain, baptism has become the sacrament where a large degree of theological convergence has been achieved, partly based on the inspiration in the aftermath of the discussion on the BEM document, when many churches responded positively to the notion that there is a growing agreement in the mutual understanding of and recognition of each other's baptism. BEM became groundbreaking for further work on a joint understanding of baptism.

It is therefore worthwhile to explore further how baptismal theology can inspire wider parts of the work on ecclesiology, also what in our context here is called "diaconal ecclesiology". As BEM affirmed: "Through baptism, Christians are brought into union with Christ, with each other and with the Church of every time and space."[6] This union with Christ and with each other is not only a spiritual union but also encompasses the whole Christian life, and Christian witness and ministry to the world, i.e. *diakonia*.

Ecumenical ecclesiology widely draws on communion ecclesiology, closely related to eucharistic theology, and an emphasis on the Holy Communion as the core event, which is shaping the Church's communal identity (McPartlan, 1995).

Inspired by specific strains within orthodox theology, ecumenical theology has largely adopted that ecclesiology should be developed in the light of Eucharistic theology – emphasizing communion/*koinonia* as decisive aspects of being Church. Although Eucharistic ecclesiology clearly adds decisive moments to the development of a common and largely agreed ecclesiological approach, the question is left open how this relates to the fact that the sacrament of the Eucharist remains the most significant symbol of the *division* between Christians and Churches. A significant number of Christian Churches still cannot share the Eucharistic table with each other, or practice Eucharistic hospitality. Church traditions, like the Roman Catholic Church and the Orthodox Church, underline that Eucharistic communion is the final *goal* for all ecumenical encounter, never a means or instrument to achieve unity, and can only be celebrated when the Churches have overcome all their divisions. This was underlined in the ecumenical core documents of the Second Vatican Council, *Unitatis Redintegratio* (UR), and still forms an important aspect of the Roman Catholic approach to other Churches, or "ecclesial communities":

[6] BEM, D.6: Incorporation into the Body of Christ.

> When the obstacles to perfect ecclesiastical communion have been gradually overcome, all Christians will at last, in a common celebration of the Eucharist, be gathered into the one and only Church in that unity which Christ bestowed on his Church from the beginning. We believe that this unity subsists in the Catholic Church as something she can never lose, and we hope that it will continue to increase until the end of time.[7]

Also, in literature from the field of diaconal studies, much emphasis has been given to the Eucharist as an event of communion between humankind and God, and among humankind; the sharing of Christ's body and blood as a resemblance of God's call to sharing the goods of God's creation with everyone. Many theologians, and theorists on *diakonia*, have underlined the close link between the sacrament of Eucharist and *diakonia*.[8] Eucharistic theology underlines how communion with Christ also shapes the communion and community of humankind. The sharing of bread and wine reminds of the sharing of God's gifts of creation with all those who are in need. The very material dimension of the Eucharist, bread and wine, reminds us of the gifts of creation, and the suffering of creation threatened by climate change, pollution and global exploitation. All of this is at the heart of diaconal studies.

In our context of diaconal ecclesiology, it is interesting to explore how a baptismal ecclesiology can contribute to bringing the churches closer to each other in witness and service. This comprises developing a diaconal ecclesiology based on a baptismal theology, which emphasizes the human renewal through and toward Christ – a life of Christian growth based on baptism.

The Gift of Incorporation into Christ as Incorporation in Christ's Community as Diaconal Community

In 2007, 11 member churches of the Council of Christian Churches in Germany achieved a consensus[9] on the mutual recognition of baptism. The German

---

[7] Unitatis redintegratio (1964), Ch. 1,4 (http://www.vatican.va/archive/hist_councils/ii_vatican_council/documents/vat-ii_decree_19641121_unitatis-redintegratio_en.html, last seen May 11, 2018).

[8] Cf. Rodolfo Gaedes contribution in this book.

[9] See https://www.ekd.de/en/Mutual-Recognition-291.htm (entered April 7, 2018): "Jesus Christ is our salvation. Through him, God has overcome the distance of sinners from God (Romans 5:10) to make us God's sons and daughters. As a sharing in the mystery of Christ's death and resurrection, baptism signifies our new birth in Jesus Christ. Those who receive this sacrament, and in faith confess God's love, are united with Christ and at the same time with his people of all ages and places. As a sign of the unity of all Christians, baptism unites them with Jesus Christ, who is the foundation of that unity. Despite differences in our understanding of the Church, a common understanding on baptism exists between us. Therefore, obedient to the command of Jesus, we all recognize baptism administered with water, in the name of the Father, the

multilateral agreement, like most other ecumenical discourses and agreements on baptism, refers to the BEM statement as a basis for its argumentation:

> With the Lima Text, we confess that "our one baptism into Christ constitutes a call to the churches to overcome their divisions and visibly manifest their fellowship" (Baptism, Eucharist and Ministry, Baptism, para. 6).

Baptism implies "visible manifestation of fellowship", and is therefore a call to community. Through baptism, humankind is not only becoming united with Christ but also united with the Christian community. In many traditions, this is made visible in the liturgical act, when the newly baptized is presented to the congregation, and the congregation is asked to look at them as a full member of the Christian communion, both locally and worldwide, to take care of them, and to pray for them. Many Lutheran churches emphasize that baptism is the utmost and only condition for full church membership. That does not imply that one forgets about the necessity to grow in faith and life, and to become an active member of the Christian community. But, the incorporation in Christ and in the Church through baptism is a sign of God's unconditional grace.

Creating inclusive, healthy communities is at the heart of the diaconal church. The baptismal rite is a reminder to the Christian community that it is called to unity, to mutual respect and care, and to support each other. Different ecumenical dialogues on baptism have pointed to that aspect of baptismal theology. Being baptized into the same Christ, into the Christian Church, implies becoming a part of the Christian community locally and globally. Unity with Christ implies unity with all Christians. Unity is not a mere ideological construct. Unity is not only about an agreement in doctrine or faith. Unity also means being responsible for one another and caring for one another. This became obvious in the Christian congregations as described in Acts 6: You cannot be united as Christians, in Christ, when people in the congregation are suffering. The sacraments can only be celebrated rightly when the Christian congregation also takes care of the practical needs of the people attending. Acts 6 thus becomes a witness of the early church's emphasis on holistic ministry. Being included into the body of Christ, the Church, through baptism, means being included in a community of mutual service in word and deed, in mutual accountability. In this way, a baptismal ecclesiology can become a powerful reminder of the call to visible unity in witness and service.

The WCC Faith and Order Commission has continued to work on the themes raised in the famous BEM document referred to earlier. One of these follow-up documents, *One Baptism: Towards mutual recognition* (WCC 2011),

---

Son and the Holy Spirit, in the symbolic act of immersion or affusion, and we rejoice at the baptism of every person so baptized. This mutual recognition of baptism is an expression of our bond of unity in Jesus Christ (Ephesians 4:4-6). Baptism thus administered is once-for-all and unrepeatable."

emphasizes that agreement on baptismal theology is closely related to the biblical vision of Christian unity. Christians who through baptism are brought into union with Christ, are also brought into union with each other and with the Church of every time and space. The Church's division witnesses to its brokenness, and thereby also to the division of Christians and their witness to the world.

From the perspective of diaconal ecclesiology, the call to unity is also a call to solidarity with all humankind. Baptized into the same Christ, with the same calling and empowered through the same Holy Spirit to stand in solidarity with one another, baptism also becomes a call to stand together and jointly act as God's messengers in word and deed.

The baptismal call into communion with God and with one another implies the gift of community. The act of baptism incorporates a person into Christ, Christ's church, and into the sending into the world. It is not only a salvific act related to eternal life but it also has concrete consequences both for the individual and the community one is received into.

The Liberating and Empowering Dimension of Baptism

As a symbol and pattern of the new life in Christ, baptism becomes important in relation to diaconal ecclesiology: in Christ, and through Christ, Christians are called to share their faith and life with others. A new life in Christ implies growth in words and deeds, implies standing together for human dignity, for peace and justice and the integrity of creation. Neglecting this call to *diakonia* means neglecting God's gift and calling.

Becoming a Christian: The Ecumenical Implications of our Common Baptism (WCC 1999) is the result of a study process linked to the WCC Faith and Order Commission. The document reflects a move in the ecumenical theological discourse, emphasizing worship and liturgy as decisive aspects in the theology of baptism. It allocates Christian baptism in the framework of Christian initiation, where faith and baptism belong together, while the order of faith and baptism can vary in different traditions, and baptism should be seen as a life-long process.

Becoming a Christian also points to the fact that baptism has an ethical dimension, since it has implications for both personal and social life, life in community (88-89). This ethical dimension should be explored further when developing a diaconal ecclesiology. Baptism both represents the beginning of the Christian life for the individual, and a call to grow and mature in faith as a follower and disciple of Christ. Both discipleship and stewardship are Christian answers to the call and gift one has received through baptism. Baptism is an initiation into the community of believers, and a life-long process of growth in Christian identity and discernment. It serves as a rite of initiation, not only into a life of faithfulness but also into a life of continuous growth in faith and discipleship.

Several biblical texts underline the call, which lies in baptism, to reconcile with God and with one another. Being baptized into Christ means being "clothed with Christ", and thus eliminating the differences that usually divide human beings and often contribute to devaluating one before the other. Galatians 3:27-28 gives one of the clearest descriptions of how Christian anthropology as baptismal anthropology has consequences for the whole understanding of humankind, and how we relate to each other: "for all of you who were baptized into Christ have clothed yourselves with Christ. There is neither Jew nor Gentile, neither slave nor free, nor is there male and female, for you are all one in Christ Jesus."

Baptism thus also has a *critical* ethical dimension, when addressing that all human beings are equal, have the same value and the same God-given dignity, because of their baptism in the One Christ. The basic Christian assumption that all human beings are created in the image and likeness of God, and thus deserve the same respect and dignity and have the same value, is decisive for the Church's diaconal self-understanding.

Thus, baptism is of utmost importance when spelling out what the Christian Church is called to be: the Church does not exist for itself, but exists for humankind, as a place where the presence of the living Christ can be experienced and lived in community, for the sake of the community and the world. This baptismal call to life in community is also a call to *diakonia*: Christians are called to be Christ-followers and to live according to this call in their societies and different contexts. Baptism visualizes God's active call to service/*diakonia*, and God's cleansing and empowering gift, visualized and experienced through the waters of Baptism and God's performative word and blessing imparted in the baptismal liturgy.

Baptism and Life-long Growth into Christ

Baptism is a call to a life-long process of becoming more Christ-like in faith, word and deeds.

Therefore, baptism is both an event and a process. Within the Lutheran tradition, much emphasis has been put on the first aspect, the salvific and gracious event. Nevertheless, also Luther himself and the Lutheran tradition underscore that baptism has a processual character, as "daily garment that they are to wear all the time. Every day they should be found in faith and with its fruits, suppressing the old creature and growing up in the new. If we want to be Christians, we must practice the work that makes us Christians, and let those who fall away return to it."[10] This "daily garment" of baptism, which we are to wear all the time, is closely linked to a Lutheran ethics of call, emphasizing that

[10] Martin Luther, *Large Catechism*, IV: 8486; *The Book of Concord: The Confessions of the Evangelical Lutheran Church*, eds. Kolb and Wengert, Fortress Press: Minneapolis 2000, 466-467.

every Christian in whatever they do is valuable – there is no difference in value before God's eyes between the vocation of a king, bishop, farmer, priest, housewife – all of them are baptized into the same Christ, and called to serve God according to their vocation.

Baptismal ecclesiology can help to underline the priesthood of all Christians. Being incorporated into Christ through baptism, Christians attain a share in Christ's priesthood. They are called to be the presence of Christ in the world and to serve the world in witness and service. According to 1 Peter 2:9, the baptized become part of the "royal priesthood" and are called to exercise their priestly ministry in the societies and in the world in which they live.

Within the global ecumenical movement, this aspect has been embraced and expressed through terms like "pilgrimage of justice and peace".[11] Baptism expresses the start of a lifelong journey, which includes the continuous need for growth in human relation to God, ourselves, each other and the whole creation.

This understanding is shared between many different Christian traditions, and the Roman Catholic Church. Baptism, according to the Second Vatican Council's *Unitatio redintegrato (UR)*, leads to an incorporation into Christ, rebirth "to a sharing of the divine life", and unites "all who have been reborn by it".[12] Interestingly enough, this unity in Baptism is given notwithstanding the ecclesial tradition Baptism is performed within. UR underlines that the final goal is ecclesial communion, including the sharing of the Eucharist, which can only happen when the Church is fully united. Nevertheless, it talks about unity of Christians given per se through the Christian's incorporation into Christ in their baptism.

One might therefore say that baptism can be understood as a call to a growing life as Christ-followers, in all aspects of life, also in *diakonia*. Since this call is common to all Christians, and baptism to a large degree is mutually recognized, the common call to *diakonia*, which lies in baptism, is also a common call to act together with all people of good will.

Within the field of *diakonia*, Christians in many different contexts manage to cooperate widely. Often, it is underlined that they do so, as people of good will, even though there is no agreement on doctrinal issues. However, the foundation of the WCC in 1937 was based on a merger of the Faith and Order Movement and the Life and Work Movement, with the goal of "seeking unity, a common witness and Christian service"; the distinction between these strands has continued.

The reference to baptism as the common ground of Christian cooperation, both in life and witness, can be a fruitful starting point for further exploration, since baptismal theology incorporates both the aspect of faith and incorporation into Christ, and into the Church as Christ's body on earth, *and* the implicit call

---

[11] Cf. The WCC website offering material on this pilgrimage: https://www.oikoumene.org/en/what-we-do/pilgrimage-of-justice-and-peace/, last seen April 24, 2019.

[12] UR II, 22.

to live according to God's commandment, as followers of Christ in our daily life.

All Christian traditions emphasize the importance of growth in faith and life. In some traditions, this is described as sanctification, in others as *theosis*, deification or "life-long growth into Christ" (*One Baptism*, D. §§41-55). All these terms, situated in different traditions and ecclesiologies, subsume the aspect of Christian life growing out of baptism, being in continuous development. Though baptism in most traditions is an unrepeatable liturgical event, it is indispensably connected with the catechumenate and the processes of nature and growth based on the baptismal event. This life-long growth includes formation in faith individually and participation in the life of the Christian community. Baptism thus is the decisive point in the journey of Christian initiation. Baptism becomes an expression of God's total acceptance of the person, a basis for growth that one can always return to and is called to build one's life on.

Baptism in a Lutheran Tradition

In a Lutheran tradition, Baptism is understood as an event where God's gracious gift, through the work of the Holy Spirit, is given to the baptized. Sacraments for Luther were not mere signs pointing to grace, but the necessary efficacious instruments of God who is present in them. The Christians are called to return to their baptism daily. In this sense, baptism is an inauguration of a Christian life that is open-ended, even though the sacrament in itself is complete. When celebrating rituals of the remembrance of baptism, one not only remembers the act of God's salvific action but also the call to live out baptism in daily life, in witness and service, *diakonia*. Luther underlines that Baptism shapes the whole life and existence of Christians as their "daily garment", connected to both faith and the fruits of faith, "the work that makes us Christians". Baptism always lies there as a foundation and a call, a refuge and a treasure.

As Christ, the mercy seat, does not withdraw from us or forbid us to return to him even though we sin, so all his treasures and gifts remain. As we have once obtained forgiveness of sins in baptism, so forgiveness remains day by day as long as we live, that is, as long as we carry the old creature about our necks.[13]

Thus, Baptism becomes the source and reference point for Christian life and the utmost expression of God's first and continuous call to follow Christ in faith and life, every day. This call to life-long growth is also a call to lifelong *diakonia* as a part of Christian life.

Lutheran theology has sometimes been accused of being pacifying. The strong emphasis on "grace alone", and salvation through faith alone – not by

---

[13] Luther, *Large Catechism*, IV: 84-86; BC, 466-67.

deeds – has been understood as a hinder for including the Christians' duty to live their lives in continuous growth and doing good deeds. This common misunderstanding of Lutheran theology has also been related to Lutheran baptismal theology, underlining that all the baptized are saved, notwithstanding their personal faith.

In the context of the Reformation anniversary and commemoration in 2017, the Lutheran World Federation, LWF, has underlined the close connection between the message of "justification by faith alone" and its implications for humankind and creation. Salvation by grace alone implies that neither humankind nor creation are for sale. As justified sinners, we are freed by God's grace to do justice. *Diakonia* is not a human deed to obtain salvation, but a necessary and non- negotiable consequence and part of our being saved in Christ, by faith alone.[14]

In many Western churches, like the Lutheran majority churches in Northern Europe, the percentage of baptisms is much higher than the percentage of active churchgoers. Does that mean that everyone is saved, just through a single act, without any kind of personal involvement with Christian faith during their life? For the Lutheran majority Churches in many of these countries, it is important to emphasize that Baptism as a gift and call from God, and an entry into the community of Christ, which is the Church, is always valid. When Luther talks about "seeking one's refuge in one's own baptism", this underlines that Baptism as a decisive act and confirmation of God's total acceptance of the individual is always remaining, and a place of comfort to rely on or turn back to. At the same time, Luther and Lutheran theology make clear that Baptism also includes a life-long call of becoming more Christ-like in our lives, a call for sanctification, growth and good deeds. Not as basis for salvation, but as an implicit aspect and consequence of being saved, as a contribution to our common creation. Justification and sanctification are both indispensable parts of a Christian's life, remaining "day by day as long as we live".[15]

A Lutheran understanding of Baptism therefore leads to a diaconal understanding of baptism, because baptism, as gift and source, empowers humankind and calls and sends the Christians for service, into a life of growth in faith. This faith is lived out in word and deeds, in proclamation and service. This service is a service to the world, for the sake of all humankind and creation, not for the sake of the Church.

Baptism as Foundation for Life-long Growth and Theosis

Many Christian traditions underscore this life-long growth, based on baptism. In the Orthodox tradition, this life-long growth is called *Theosis* ("deification",

[14] See the documents from the LWF Assembly 2017 in Windhoek on these themes, https://www.lwfassembly.org/en/liberated-gods-grace. last seen April 27, 2019.
[15] Ibid.

"divinization") and describes the process of a worshiper being gradually united with God, beginning in this life, and later consummated in bodily resurrection. Based on 2.Pet. 1:4, *theosis* is understood as "participation in divine nature", which is lived through loving God and your fellow humans. Orthodox theologians often refer to Church Fathers like St. Athanasius of Alexandria, who underlined that "The Son of God became man, that we might become god."[16] This is also named divinization or deification. Hippolytus of Rome links *theosis* to baptism, when he states "If, therefore, man has become immortal, he will also be God. And if he is made God by water and the Holy Spirit after the regeneration of the laver he is found to be also joint-heir with Christ after the resurrection from the dead."[17]

In March 2018, the WCC's World Mission Conference in Arusha pointed to *theosis* as an area of convergence in the mission of the Christian Church.

> Discipleship is both a gift and a calling to be active collaborators with God for the transforming of the world (1Thessalonians 3:2). In what the church's early theologians called "theosis" or deification, we share God's grace by sharing God's mission. This journey of discipleship leads us to share and live out God's love in Jesus Christ by seeking justice and peace in ways that are different from the world (John 14:27). Thus, we are responding to Jesus' call to follow him from the margins of our world (Luke 4:16-19).[18]

Arusha also underlined the connection between the call that lies in our baptism "to transforming discipleship: a Christ-connected way of life in a world where many face despair, rejection, loneliness, and worthlessness". Baptism implies both a call to transforming discipleship, and an empowerment to do so, through the gift of the Holy Spirit.

Baptism: Death-Dealing and Life-Giving

Water cleanses and rescues but it also threatens and kills people. In his letter to the Romans, the apostle Paul describes the act of baptism as being killed and risen with Christ (Rom: 6:1-10). The act of baptism puts the Christian into lifelong communion with Christ in an eschatological perspective. Unity with

---

[16] "Αὐτὸς γὰρ ἐνηνθρώπισεν, ἵνα ἡμεῖς θεοποιηθῶμεν" (*Migne, Patrologia Graeca, 25, 192 B De incarnatione Verbi*, 54: literally, "…that we might become…". Grammatically, the verb θεοποιηθῶμεν could be translated as "be made God" himself or "be made gods".

[17] Hippolytus of Rome: *The Discourse on the Holy Theophany* (http://www.ccel.org/ccel/schaff/anf05.iii.iv.ii.vi.html, accessed May 24, 2018).

[18] March 13, 2018. World Council of Churches' Conference on World Mission and Evangelism, 'Moving in the Spirit: Called to Transforming Discipleship: The Arusha Call to Discipleship' (https://www.oikoumene.org/en/resources/documents/commissions/mission-and-evangelism/the-arusha-call-to-discipleship, accessed June 7, 2018),

Christ also means striving to live the right life together with Christ. BEM underlines: "Through baptism, Christians are brought into union with Christ." This union with Christ is related both to Christ's death – as Paul put it in Romans 6 – "buried with Christ" – and to Christ's resurrection. Christ's death as an act of atonement, solidarity with all who are suffering and as a victory over the powers of death, is directly linked to the Christian's burial and resurrection experienced in Baptism.

Thus, baptism is a performative act and at the same time a sign of God's call to faithful life in words and deeds. The waters of baptism are the utmost expression of this salvific event, where humankind is drowned and rescued simultaneously. To be buried and risen with Christ implies the call to a new life, and thus a call for the Church as communion of baptized to live this life as diaconal Churches.

"Death-dealing" also implies dealing with the powers of death in our world, with injustice and oppression, violent conflicts and gender-related abuse. Being "drowned with Christ" is therefore a sign and witness of the call to fight the powers of evil in our world. "Life-giving" points to the fact that God empowers the Christians to work for transformation, promote human dignity, justice and peace – all of which are at the heart of diaconal action.

Conclusion: The Baptismal Call to Unity as a Diaconal Call to Solidarity

Through baptism, Christians are brought into union with each other and with the Church of every time and space, and her mission to work for a better world.[19] This is not only related to unity in faith and the need to work for growth in agreement on faith issues but it also means unity in life; unity in the Christian Church's common effort to serve each other and the whole creation.

By God's grace and power, the baptized person is incorporated into Christ's body. Most churches would agree that baptism is enabled and enacted by the triune God, in the unity of the Father, Son and Holy Spirit. Thus, as Christ is undivided, also baptism into the one Christ, through the work of the one, triune God, represents a call to the churches to overcome their divisions and live their fellowship and communion in Christ and with each other. As God is one, and Christ is one, and humankind is baptized into the one Christ, baptism also implies a call to strive for unity and against division. Being baptized into the one Christ implies being baptized into the one humanity. Being baptized into the one Christ implies a quest for respect for all human beings.

Summing up the reflections on a baptismal ecclesiology, I want to conclude by underlining the core aspects of baptismal theology, which are closely interrelated with an understanding of the Church and Christian life focusing on *diakonia* as a mark of the Church.

---

[19] F. BEM.

Baptism *liberates* the believer to *diakonia.* As a gift and calling by God, baptism lies as a foundation of all Christian life, which one can return to and rely on, notwithstanding one's own life experiences. Thus, the baptized becomes free, becomes liberated, to "go and serve the Lord", because God has confirmed them as a fully accepted, saved and freed person in baptism.

Baptism serves as a *call to solidarity*, since all the baptized are baptized into the one body of Christ and called to support and minister to each other. The act of baptism visualizes the equality and equal value of all human beings, and thereby lies an important value basis for the Church's *diakonia.*

Baptized into Christ's death and resurrection, humankind shares the experiences of the powers of death and life, the powers of suffering and God's rescuing and uprising power. Thus, baptism partakes in the empowerment of humankind to partake in God's *diakonia.* As a gift from God, baptism also becomes a sign of the given-ness of life, and the given-ness of humankind to each other, which is at the very heart of all diaconal action. The waters of baptism are an efficacious sign of God's empowering act of salvation, and thus a call to *diakonia.*

Bibliography

Kolb, Robert and Wengert, Timothy J. (eds.), *The Book of Concord: The Confessions of the Evangelical-Lutheran Church.* (Minneapolis: Fortress Press: 2000).

Luther, Martin, Large Catechism, in *The Book of Concord: The Confessions of the Evangelical Lutheran Church*, eds., Kolb and Wengert, (Fortress Press: Minneapolis 2000).

McPartlan, Paul, *Sacrament of Salvation: An Introduction to Eucharistic Ecclesiology* (Edinburgh: T&T Clark, 1995).

The Roman Catholic Church, *Unitatis redintegratio* (Rome: 2. Vatican Council, 1964): (http://www.vatican.va/archive/hist_councils/ii_vatican_council/documents/vat-ii_decree_19641121_unitatis-redintegratio_en.html).

WCC/Faith and Order Commission, *Baptism, Eucharist and Ministry*: (https://www.oikoumene.org/en/resources/documents/commissions/faith-and-order/i-unity-the-church-and-its-mission/baptism-eucharist-and-ministry-faith-and-order-paper-no-111-the-lima-text).

WCC/Faith and Order, *Baptism, Eucharist and Ministry, 1982-1990: Report on the Process and Responses* (Geneva: WCC, 1990).

WCC/Faith and Order, *Becoming a Christian: The Ecumenical Implications of our Common Baptism* (WCC 1999).

WCC/Faith and Order, *One Baptism: Towards Mutual Recognition* (Geneva: WCC 2011).

WCC/CCME, *Moving in the Spirit: Called to Transforming Discipleship: The Arusha Call to Discipleship.* World Council of Churches' Conference on World Mission and Evangelism, 13 March 2018: (https://www.oikoumene.org/en/resources/documents/commissions/mission-and-evangelism/the-arusha-call-to-discipleship).

Sharing the Body of Christ: Eucharist in a Diaconal Perspective[1]

Rodolfo Gaede Neto

Introduction

The Last Supper, in which the Eucharist is instituted (Matthew 26:26-30; Mark 14:22-26; Luke 22:14-20), is the culminating event in a series of other suppers of Jesus during his ministry. This means one cannot isolate the Last Supper from the preceding history and from the context in which Jesus of Nazareth was acting.[2] The importance of these suppers is attested by the Gospels.[3] Their importance must be duly recognized in all of Jesus' further activities. Norman Perrin even states that "in this table communion we can witness the main ministry of Jesus".[4] The same importance is recognized by John Dominic Crossan when he states that it is "the essence of Jesus's original movement".[5]

Among the various facts that highlight the importance of Jesus' table communion, we must highlight the fact that the conflicts that he had with the religious authorities were because of commensality[6] with 'publicans and sinners' (Mark 2: 15-17), i.e. because the open and inclusive community suppers were one of the main factors leading to the cross.[7] 'There must have been something in this that caused serious offense to the contemporaries of Jesus,' says Norman Perrin.[8]

In this study we try to present subsidies that help understanding the relationship between the daily suppers of Jesus with the people, and the Holy Supper. The study of this relationship will open the access to the diaconal dimension of the Eucharist and its relevance to ecclesiology.

---

[1] Original text written in Portuguese and references are in Portuguese and German

[2] a) Brunner, Peter. Zur Lehre vom Gottesdienst der im Namen Jesu versammelten Gemeinde. In: Müller, K. F.; Blankenburg, W. (Hrsg.). *Leiturgia*: Handbuch des Evangelischen Gottesdienstes. (Kassel: Johannes Stauda, 1954, v. 1). 224; b) Bolyki, János. *Jesu Tischgemeinschaften*. (Tübingen: Mohr Siebeck, 1998). 7; c) Martini, Romeu Ruben. *Eucaristia e conflitos comunitários*. (São Leopoldo: Sinodal, 2003). 45.

[3] Bolyki, *Jesu Tischgemeinschaften*, 1.

[4] Norman Perin, *O que ensinou Jesus realmente* (São Leopoldo: Sinodal, 1977). 133.

[5] John Dominic Crossan, *O Jesus Histórico*: a vida de um camponês judeu do Mediterrâneo (Rio de Janeiro: Imago, 1994). 378.

[6] Commensality is the act of eating meals together around the table. In this text, we will refer to the activity of Jesus in which he often ate meals in the company of different people.

[7] Bolyki, *Jesu Tischgemeinschaften*, 1.

[8] Perin, *O que ensinou Jesus realmente*, 127.

As to the structure of this text, we will begin with a study of Jesus' commensal practice and his use of the image of supper as a metaphor for the Kingdom of God. Second, we will approach the Last Supper (institution of the Eucharist) and its relationship with the other suppers of Jesus. Third, we will reflect on the diaconal perspective of the Eucharist in connection with the communions at Jesus' table. Finally, we will present a brief conclusion.

My contribution comes from the Brazilian and Latin American context. Here, we have been reflecting on *diakonia* taking into consideration the suffering of a large part of the population. That suffering is the result of a political, economic, social, legal and religious situation that creates and maintains structures of exclusion. As a result, we face poverty, unemployment, and deterioration of public systems of health, education, safety, social security, housing and transportation. We practice Bible reading and theological reflection about *diakonia* from what Assmann calls "logic of exclusion".[9]

The Table Communions of Jesus: Practice and Teaching

The Practice of Commensality

When Jesus characterizes his ministry by saying 'among you I am as one who serves' (Luke 22:27; Mark 10:45), he is referring to his intense activity around the tables at different times, with different groups of people.[10] The communions in which Jesus is the protagonist are to be understood within the whole of his ministry, whose mission is to offer visible signs of the outbreak of the Kingdom of God.[11] Jesus acts driven by the hope of the Kingdom, one form of the presence of the Kingdom being the experience of communion, of inclusion, of sharing, of gratuitousness; in short, the experience of God's unconditional love toward his creatures. In the examples of commensality that follow, it is possible to perceive signs of the new time being inaugurated by Jesus.

1. Table communion in the house of the Pharisee Simon (Luke 7: 36-50). There, the anointing of Jesus' feet is done by a woman considered sinful. She entered this house uninvited, not having been welcomed. For a Pharisee it would be morally unsustainable to open his house to a prostitute.[12] Therefore, Jesus assumes the role and risk of being a host in the house of Simon, by giving attention to the pain of this woman, welcoming her as a worthy human person and by wishing her *shalom*, that is, peace in its deeper meaning, which is the

---

[9] Assmann, Hugo. *Crítica à lógica da exclusão*: ensaios sobre economia e teologia. São Paulo: Paulus, 1994, 19.

[10] Perrin, *O que ensinou Jesus realmente*, 127-133.

[11] Bolyki, *Jesu Tischgemeinschaften*, 229.

[12] Wiefel, Wolfgang. *Das Evangelium nach Lukas*. (Berlin: Evangelische Verlagsanstalt GmbH, 1988). 154.

peace of the Kingdom of God.[13] For this reason, Wiefel argues that in this episode it was an act of healing, that is, a diaconal attitude.[14]

2. Table Communion in the house of Levi, where Jesus eats with publicans and people considered sinners (Mark 2: 15-17). This gesture deeply questions a religious system that, from a legalistic and fundamentalist position, excludes and condemns people.[15]

3. Table Communion with the multitude (Mark 6: 30-44). When, under the rule of Herod, the people are hungry and disoriented like sheep without a shepherd, in the company of Jesus "all have eaten and had their fill" (v.42), including those who "came from afar" – a reference to the Gentiles[16] – (Mark 8.3).[17] While Herod's government is characterized by the concentration of income in the hands of an elite (Mark 6.21), generating poverty for the majority, Jesus is guided by the paradigm of sharing.[18] Even the disciples had to learn that access to bread must not depend on whether one possesses money or not.[19] The challenge of the Kingdom of God is to promote table fellowships in which 'all may eat and be satisfied'.

4. Table communion in Zacchaeus the publican's house (Luke 19: 1-10). Zacchaeus sought Jesus (verse 3), but instead was found by him (verse 10). The meritorious effort to seek Jesus is considered unnecessary, since Jesus' attitude toward the Kingdom of God is characterized by gratuitousness. The table communions of Jesus are a gift. This gift is made possible despite the limitations of the guests; these are people invited without imposing

---

[13] Wiefel, *Das Evangelium nach Lukas*, 154-156.

[14] Wiefel, *Das Evangelium nach Lukas*, 156.

[15] a) Wegner, Uwe. *Exegese do novo Testamento*. (Manual de Metodologia. São Leopoldo: Sinodal, 1998). 280ss.; b) Schottroff, Luise; Stegemann, Wolfgang. *Jesus von Nazareth – Hoffnung der Armen*. 3. Aufl. (Stuttgart; Berlin; Köln: Kohlhammer, 1990). 17s.; c). Bolyki, *Jesu Tischgemeinschaften*, 109; d) Becker, Jürgen. *Jesus von Nazareth*. (Berlin, New York: de Gruyter, 1996). 204.

[16] Myers, Ched. *O Evangelho de São Marcos*. (São Paulo: Paulinas, 1992). 255-258.

[17] The reference to the inclusion of the Gentiles in the table communion of Jesus wants to point, in our view, to the dimension of the universality of the Kingdom of God, that is, a place for which, in the understanding of the Evangelist Mark, all peoples are invited, indistinctly. It is not intended, therefore, to insinuate or substantiate, for example, the participation of persons not baptized in the celebration of the Supper of the Lord.

[18] a) Bolyki, *Jesu Tischgemeinschaften*, 89-102; b) Wegner, Uwe. Jesus e Economia no Evangelho de Marcos. *Reflexos da Brisa Leve.* (Belo Horizonte: CEBI, 1991). 98ss; c) Dri, Ruben. *A utopia de Jesus*. (São Paulo: Ícone, 1986). 154s.; d) Kollmann, Bernd. *Ursprung und Gestalten der frühchristlichen Mahlfeier*. (Göttingen: Vandenhoeck & Ruprecht, 1990). 205; e) Gnilka Joachim. *Jesus de Nazaré*: mensagem e história. (Petrópolis: Vozes, 2000, parte 2). 9s.

[19] Dri, Rúben. *A utopia de Jesus*, 154. Afirma o autor: "Quem acumulou riqueza, quem tem dinheiro, pode comer. Os demais estão condenados a pedir esmolas ou a se converter em assaltantes" (Whoever has accumulated wealth, who has Money, can eat. The others are condemned to ask for alms or to become robbers).

preconditions. As a gift, communion always breaks and transcends every kind of barrier the human condition imposes on people invited as well as found. The change in the life of Zacchaeus did not come about because of a prior conversion requirement, but as a consequence of Jesus' anticipated confidence in proposing table fellowship with him, even though he was 'a big shot publican and rich man' (v. 2). Jesus' invitation brought him down from his high level of power to put himself on the level of his host, who chose to 'come down' from his incarnation (Philippians 2: 5-11). Jesus demonstrates that God descends into the abyss of isolated and stigmatized people, sees them, remembers them, finds them, becomes their neighbor, gives them back the citizenship of his people, offers them free communion.[20]

5. Table Communion in the marriage of Cana of Galilee (John 2: 1-11). In this narrative, the mentioned jars allow us to perceive two opposing situations: a) while used for the traditional rites of purification with water before meals (v. 6), they may be referring to the precepts demanded by religious leaders; these had become a burden to the population, given the rigid surveillance by the authorities; legalism had separated the people into pure and impure; the rulers of the nation, to avoid contact with the 'unclean', were kept separate not only from the Gentiles but also from most of their people; the precepts of purification had become a system of segregation; b) these same carvings were used by Jesus to shelter the wine; in this way, they came to represent instruments in the service of joy, celebration, abundance and freedom of a people; replacing the wine meant that the jars were considered instruments for continuing the feast, which, according to tradition, lasted a whole week. The people who went through this liberating experience realized something the prophets had proclaimed, for whom wine is the sign of eschatological joy and abundance, an announcement of the Messianic time of salvation, where wine of extraordinary quality and great abundance will be offered (cf. Amos 9:13, Jeremiah 31:12, Hosea 14:7). Messianic days resemble a marriage (Isaiah 42: 4ff). The people present at the marriage at Cana realized that with Jesus began the time of *gámos* (marriage) in which God begins to create a new world of abundance; therefore, they may have supper and feast with joy.[21]

---

[20] a) Bolyki, *Jesu Tischgemeinschaften*, 109-114; b) Jeremias, Joachim. *Neutestamentliche Theologie*. (Gütersloh: Gütersloher Verlagshaus Gerd Mohn, 1971, t. 1). 214s. c) Droogers, André. Lucas 19.1-10. *Proclamar Libertação*: Auxílios Homiléticos. (São Leopoldo: Sinodal, v. 8, p. 219-227, 1982). 221-225; d) Baeske, Albérico. Lucas 19.1-10. *Proclamar Libertação*: Auxílios Homiléticos. (São Leopoldo: Sinodal, 1977. v. 2, p. 112-122). 115-120.

[21] a) Wegner, *Exegese do novo Testamento*, 193 (nota 334); b) Bolyki, *Jesu Tischgemeinschaften*, 103-106; c) Veloso, Mário. *Comentário do Evangelho de João*. (Santo André: Casa Publicadora Brasileira, 1984). 7, 72, 73, 75; d) Schneider, Johannes. *Das Evangelium nach Johannes*. 2. Aufl. (Berlin: Evangelische Verlagsanstalt, 1978). 83.

6. Table Communion in the house of Martha and Mary (Luke 10: 38-42). Jesus' visit to Martha and Mary is in the context of his journey to Jerusalem, that is, the prospect is the cross.[22] Therefore, he is not any ordinary visitor, but the one with whom the Kingdom of God is to irrupt into this world. For this reason, any opportunity to hear him should not be missed. Mary was moved by this understanding.[23] This does not mean that Martha's attitude is being criticized in this narrative. She took on her responsibility as the 'lady' of the house (this is the meaning of her name), performing what the text calls "*diakonein*" (v. 40) and what the previous pericope recommends doing: acting as the Good Samaritan (Luke 10.25-37).[24] She was moved by the need for good hospitality and this makes a lot of sense. The intention of the text, which is found in the context of Jesus' table fellowships, is to draw attention to the fact that in the Kingdom of God, whose banquet can be tasted beforehand in communion, the host is Jesus. It is he who serves at the table (Luke 22:27). Before him, it is fitting to stand empty-handed and allow him to fill your hands with his grace and his love.[25] Thus, we become guests in our own house, just like Zacchaeus. So, yes, we can say to Martha: action must not become independent of listening. When this happens, we commit the error of unreflective activism, detached from the teaching of Jesus and not based on the cross of Christ.[26] However, we must point to another no less important fact in this pericope: it introduces two women. They are characters who reveal limits and possibilities of the feminine universe in the patriarchal context of Jesus' time. Martha's role denounces the reality of women's imprisonment in household tasks. That of Mary announces the correctness of her experience of liberation; and Jesus is her accomplice in her daring to break the barrier of gender discrimination and to become a disciple.

We could continue the study in relation to other activities of Jesus connected with table fellowship, mentioning, for example, the supper in which Jesus washes the disciples' feet (John 13: 1-11); the supper of Jesus with the fearful disciples after the crucifixion (Luke 24: 36-43); the supper of Jesus with the disciples of Emmaus (Luke 24: 28-35); or the supper by the sea, where the resurrected eats with the disciples (John 21: 1-14). However, we deem the cases mentioned above as sufficient to highlight the elements that characterize the commensality of Jesus, namely: the inclusion of discriminated persons; the denunciation of systems (religious, political, economic, social or cultural) that

---

[22] Grundmann, Walter. *Das Evangelium nach Lukas*. 7. Aufl. (Berlin: Evangelische Verlagsanstalt, 1974). 198.

[23] Schmithals, Walter. *Das Evangelium nach Lukas*. (Zürich: Theologischer Verlag, 1980). 129.

[24] a) Grundmann, *Das Evangelium nach Lukas*, 226. b) Bolyki, *Jesu Tischgemeinschaften*, 116-118.

[25] Dreher, Carlos Arthur. Lucas 10.38-42. *Proclamar Libertação*: Auxílios Homiléticos. (São Leopoldo: Sinodal, 1980, v. 6). 127.

[26] Dreher, *Proclamar Libertação*, 128s.

exclude people; sharing bread and overcoming hunger; gratuitousness; experiences of anticipation of the Kingdom of God (irruption of the new aeon)[27]; overcoming unreflective activism; the experience of a spirituality in which Jesus is host and we are guests in our own home; the experience of a spirituality in which, empty-handed, we let ourselves be served by Jesus; the experience of table fellowship with guests different from us; and experience of communion as complicity with discriminated individuals and groups.

Communion as a Metaphor in the Teaching of Jesus

In addition to the practice of commensality, in his teachings Jesus repeatedly uses the concepts of supper, banquet and weddings as metaphors to illustrate what the Kingdom of God is.[28] Here are some texts.

1. Matthew 8:11 and Luke 13:29: The Kingdom of God is like a table at which people from all over the Earth will have a seat together with Abraham, Isaac and Jacob.[29]

2. Matthew 22: 1-14 and Luke 14:21: The Kingdom of God is like the feast to which the people are invited who are at the crossroads, in the streets and alleyways; the poor, crippled, blind and lame, good and wretched.[30]

3. Luke 16: 19-31: The Kingdom of God is like a table in which the sharing of food happens, where the poor Lazaruses receive deserved hospitality and can satisfy their hunger; on the contrary, the Kingdom of God is not characterized by concentration of wealth, accumulation of goods, by avarice and selfish enjoyment of riches.[31]

4. Luke 15: 11-32: The Kingdom of God is like that table served with the fattened calf to celebrate the gratuitous inclusion of the person considered unworthy (as was the case of the Prodigal Son); on the contrary, the Kingdom of God is not characterized by the exclusion of people due to fundamentalism and religious legalism (attitude displayed by the Prodigal Son's older brother).[32]

5. Luke 14: 7-14: The Kingdom of God is like the table that opens to the poor, crippled, lame and blind people, that is, those who are not able to reciprocate the invitation of wealthy, closed groups around their large tables. The inclusion of these people implies a new concept of economic relations,

---

[27] Brandt, Wilhelm. O serviço de Jesus. In: Nordstokke, Kjell (org.). *A diaconia em perspectiva bíblica e histórica.* (São Leopoldo: Sinodal, 2003). 11.

[28] Bolyki, *Jesu Tischgemeinschaften*, 76 e 229.

[29] a) Jeremias, *Neutestamentliche Theologie*, 134, 236; b) Bolyki, *Jesu Tischgemeinschaften*, 69.

[30] Bolyki, *Jesu Tischgemeinschaften*, p. 8 e 76.

[31] Moxnes, Halvor. *A economia do reino*: conflito social e relações econômicas no Evangelho de Lucas. (São Paulo: Paulus, 1995), 90s.

[32] Arguments in favor of this interpretation are found in Krüger, René. Lucas 15. 1-3, 11-32. *Proclamar Libertação*: Auxílios Homiléticos. (São Leopoldo: Sinodal, 1991. v. 17). 88-93.

built on the paradigm of sharing between people and economically unequal groups.[33]

We consider that the texts mentioned above bring together the main theological elements of Jesus' teaching concerning table fellowship. Table communion is an experience of anticipating the Kingdom of God. As such, it is characterized by openness to all people (universal dimension), free and unconditional inclusion of excluded people, sharing and just distribution of bread, overcoming the accumulation of goods and thus overcoming the abyss between social classes; by overcoming the fundamentalist and legalistic system that excludes people from the communion of God's people; and by building new economic relations conceived on the paradigm of sharing.

The Last Supper or the Institution of the Eucharist

The Presence of Jesus in Sharing the Bread and the Chalice (Mark 14: 22-26, Matthew 26: 26-30, Luke 22: 19-23)

As in all the commensalities, also in his Last Supper, Jesus shares a meal. The difference is that on this occasion he establishes a relationship between the meal being shared and his future presence among those who belong to him: "this is my body" […], "this is my blood" (Mark 14:22, 24). (Mark 14:22, 24).[34]

It is necessary to pay attention to the fact that it is not simply the 'bread' and the "chalice" that Jesus refers to, but the 'broken bread given' and the "chalice distributed" (Mark 14:22, 23). Therefore, the fact that Jesus has chosen exactly the shared bread and the chalice to signal his presence among us can no longer be considered accidental.[35]

Therefore, as Jesus confronts the disciples with the reality of his absence, he assures them of their presence in the shared meal. His body from now on will be the shared meal. It will be present in the act of sharing the meal. This is the foundation of the Christian religion: the presence of divinity among humans is inseparably linked to the sharing of a meal. Here is also to be found the link between the Eucharist and ecclesiology: the body of Christ, that is, the Church of Christ, is defined by the sharing of a meal.[36]

It is revealing that, of the four evangelists, three relate the presence of the risen Christ to table fellowships (Mark 16:14, Luke 24: 13-35, Luke 24: 41-43 and John 21: 1-14). In the testimonies of Luke and John, the risen Lord is

---

[33] Bolyki, *Jesu Tischgemeinschaften*, 88.

[34] Brakemeier, Gottfried. A Santa Ceia do Novo Testamento e na Prática Atual. *Estudos teológicos*. (São Leopoldo, v. 26, n. 3, 1986). 247-275.

[35] Wegner, *Exegese do novo Testamento*, 103.

[36] a) Veloso, Reginaldo. Fome e eucaristia nos escritos do Novo Testamento. *Estudos Bíblicos*. (Petrópolis, v. 46, 1995). 52-62; b) Crossan, *O Jesus Histórico*, 436; c) Perrin, *O que ensinou Jesus realmente*, 130.

recognized in the act of sharing the bread (Luke 24: 13-35, 24: 41-43, John 21: 1-14). In Matthew, the Christ of the Last Judgment is present in this world through those people whose hunger and thirst claims for the sharing of a meal (Matthew 25: 31-46).

This understanding is also clearly reflected in the testimony given by the Acts of the Apostles concerning the life of the first Christian communities: the presence of Jesus takes place in the breaking of bread (Acts 2:42) and to meet the basic needs of the people (Atos 4, 32ff). Celebrating the presence of Jesus in breaking the bread and to meet the human needs meant the establishment of new social relations, which eliminated class relations in the ecclesial space.[37]

In this context, it is inevitable to briefly refer to the Pauline understanding of the Eucharist, clearly present in the text of 1 Corinthians 11: 17-34. This text presents a vehement criticism by the apostle against distorting the meaning of the Eucharist, to the detriment of the sharing of the meal with poor people.[38]

The community of Corinth met daily for the communal meals (agapes), where the Eucharist was celebrated. The practice that should be of sharing among all the people present became a reason for dividing the community: the wealthier people, who arrived earlier, ate and drank until full and even intoxicated, while the poor, who could not arrive early because of work, could bring little or nothing, and when they arrived, they could no longer find food, and were ashamed of their hunger and thirst.[39]

Hence, it can be said that a meal in which one does not share what each one has brought, where each one selfishly eats his own meal, cannot serve as context for the celebration of the Lord's Supper.[40]

Therefore, also in the understanding of the apostle Paul, the body of Christ is present where the meal is shared without discrimination.

Table Communion in Eschatological Perspective (Mark 14:25, Matthew 26:29, Luke 22:18)

In their accounts of Jesus' Last Supper, all three synoptics include the eschatological significance of this event.

In the context of the Last Supper, Jesus understands that his death represents the connection between the table communions of the present time and the great and final banquet in the coming Kingdom. The communion between Jesus, his followers and their followers, experienced at the Last Supper and all previous ones, may again be experienced at the table of the Kingdom of God, because of

---

[37] Belo, Fernando. *Uma leitura política do Evangelho*. [s.l., s.d.]. (mimeo), 87, 89.

[38] Beozzo, José Oscar. Evangelho e Escravidão na Teologia Latino Americana. In: RICHARD, Pablo (Org.). *Raízes da teologia latino-americana*. (São Paulo: Paulinas, 1988). 85.

[39] Schneider, Nélio. Pecado e sacrifício na Ceia do Senhor: "Por isso há entre vós muitos fracos e doentes e vários já dormiram (1Co 11.30). *Estudos Teológicos*. (São Leopoldo, v. 36, n. 2, 1996). 119-128.

[40] Veloso, *Fome e eucaristia nos escritos do Novo Testamento*, 57ss.

the death of Jesus. This is not, therefore, a passive death, but the presupposition for the saving eschatological supper of which Jesus is the initiator.[41] The eyes of Jesus are able to cross the dark night of death and, beyond it, see the fullness. Among all the table fellowships of Jesus, it is at the Last Supper that the eschatological hope presents itself more sharply, certainly because the cross and death are immediately ahead. He takes upon himself the cross moved by the hope that there will be continuity of the feast of the Passover, that is, there will be continuation of table fellowship in the consummate Kingdom of God. The death of Jesus becomes the bridge to the Kingdom banquet, prepared for all people.[42]

In the text of Luke 22: 24-30, more specifically in v. 27, Jesus understands his service at the table, in communion with his disciples, as being *diakonéo*. He understands not only that particular moment but also his whole life and work as being in service (Mark 10:45), thus establishing the connection between a communion that began here and will be complete in the coming Kingdom.[43]

The "institution" of the Lord''s Supper is part of the table fellowship of the Last Supper (Mark 14: 22-26 and parallel texts). In this context, it is especially worth considering the inclusive character of this event: the *hypér pollôn* in Mark (14.24) or the *perí pollôn* in Matthew (26.28) both point, based on Isaiah 53.11, to beyond the 12 disciples or the 12 tribes of Israel, therefore, also to the peoples, to the Gentiles. So, we must state that also in this context of the Last Supper the openness, inclusiveness and universality of the table fellowship of Jesus is affirmed with great force.[44]

In conclusion, it remains to be said that, when he understands his death as a bridge between the Last Supper and the great supper of the Kingdom of God, Jesus places all the table fellows of his ministry in the same perspective of continuity: that historical experiences (sharing practices occurring despite the current reality) permeate and transcend history itself. It thus gives each of the experiences of table fellowship the dignity of being moments of anticipation of the consummated Kingdom, experiences in which Jesus himself is present.

The Diaconal Perspective of the Lord's Supper

Considering the studies carried out on Jesus' table communions and the Last Supper, and considering the relation of continuity between these activities, we formulate the following thesis, with the purpose of gathering elements that

[41] Bolyki, *Jesu Tischgemeinschaften*, 122 e 124.

[42] a) Gnilka, Joachim. *Jesus de Nazaré*: mensagem e história. (Petrópolis: Vozes, 2000). 261 (258-266). b) Bolyki, *Jesu Tischgemeinschaften*, 124.

[43] Bolyki, *Jesu Tischgemeinschaften*, 122 e 124.

[44] a) Bolyki, *Jesu Tischgemeinschaften*, 149s; b) Brakemeier, *Estudos teológicos*, 263; b) Brandt, Wilhelm. O serviço de Jesus. In: Nordstokke, Kjell (org.). *A diaconia em perspectiva bíblica e histórica*. (São Leopoldo: Sinodal, 2003). 17. We also recall the clarification made in note n. 15.

point to the diaconal perspective of the Lord's Supper and its implications for the existence of the Church.

The Eucharist and God's Diakonia

The diaconal perspective of the Eucharist lies maximally in the fact that in it (in the Eucharist) *God's diakonia* takes place. God serves the human community maximally through the saving work done in Christ, celebrated in the Lord's Supper. In the Eucharist, God gives himself totally and gratuitously through Christ, for the good of humanity, retaining nothing for himself.[45] Thus, the greatest depth of the Eucharist lies in divine self-giving. Whoever receives the Eucharist receives as a donation all the divine goods achieved by Christ.[46] That is why in the Eucharist we are guests who, with empty hands, allow ourselves to be served by God. Christian *diakonia* can have no other foundation than the *diakonia* of God himself (1John 4:19). Before performing services of love for one's neighbor, one must open oneself to receive the love of God, otherwise what one has to offer others will become very poor, superficial and inconstant.[47]

The Eucharist and its Eschatological Dimension

The diaconal perspective of the Eucharist lies in its eschatological dimension,[48] that is, in the anticipated celebration of the Kingdom of God, just as it happened in each table communion during the ministry of Jesus and as it may happen in every diaconal action that has the Kingdom banquet as perspective. As Jesus understood himself as the one who serves at the table, he established the idea of continuity between the table communion we practice in our time and that of the Kingdom that will come. Thus, no experience of fellowship will be lost. If *diakonia* does not hope for the Kingdom as a driving force, it may not have sufficient endurance and perseverance in the face of obstacles.[49]

The Eucharist and Gratuitousness

The diaconal perspective of the Eucharist lies in gratuitousness. The Eucharist is the ultimate expression of the grace of God, made real in the self-giving of Christ from the unconditional love of God. In his table fellowships, Jesus insisted on giving and gratuitousness as proper values of the Kingdom of God (Luke 14:12, 15:11-32). Gratuitousness identifies *diakonia* and distinguishes it from any initiative whose motivation is to take personal advantage in relation

---

[45] Lutero, Martim. Catecismo Maior. *Livro de Concórdia*. (São Leopoldo: Sinodal; Porto Alegre: Concórdia, 1980). 450.

[46] Lutero. Martim. Um sermão sobre o Venerabilíssimo Sacramento do Santo e Verdadeiro Corpo de Cristo e sobre as Irmandades. *Obras Selecionadas*. (São Leopoldo: Sinodal; Porto Alegre: Concórdia, 1987, v. 1). 429.

[47] Dreher, *Proclamar Libertação*, 128s.

[48] Bolyki, *Jesu Tischgemeinschaften*, 193.

[49] Brandt, *A diaconia em perspectiva bíblica e histórica*, 13s.

to the neighbor.[50] In *diakonia*, human relations are built on the principle of well-being of the person who is in a situation of vulnerability. This principle is based on the self-giving of God, which we experience in the Eucharist. God holds nothing back to himself so that the empty hands of people can be abundantly filled.[51]

The Eucharist and Sharing

The diaconal perspective of the Eucharist lies in sharing the bread and the chalice (*distribution*[52]). Just as during his ministry, also in the institution of the Eucharist, Jesus distributed the meal. The Kingdom of God, which Jesus likened to a great supper, is characterized by the sharing of a meal. His own presence lies in the sharing of a meal. The body of Christ, that is, the Church of Christ, is defined by sharing the meal.

The communions of Jesus' table were already practices of sharing (Mark 6: 30-44) and Jesus criticized the man who accumulated goods only for his own benefit (Luke 16: 19-31), warned those who held excluding tables (Luke 14: 7-14) and rejoiced with Zacchaeus when he decided to share some of the goods (Luke 19: 1-10). Therefore, there is no compatibility between the church of Christ, made of communicants, and the systems that maintain hunger in the world. The diaconal challenge of sharing, which stems from the Eucharist, continues to be formidable and urgent in today's world.

The Eucharist and Inclusion

The diaconal perspective of the Eucharist lies in the inclusion of people. Jesus' table communions were open and inclusive (Matthew 8:11, Luke 7:36, Mark 2: 15-17, Matthew 22: 1-14), just as at the Last Supper even Judas was included in the fellowship (Mark 14:18).[53] Biblical writings, in general, insist on the inclusion of orphans, widows and strangers (Deuteronomy 14:20; 16:11; 24:21; etc.). Jesus adds to this list other categories of people in situations of vulnerability, such as women (Mark 7:24-30; Luke 13:10-17; John 8:1-11; Luke 7:36-50; etc.), children (Mark 10: 13-16), people with leprosy (Luke 17:11-19), the poor (Luke 16:19-31) and the disabled (Luke 14:7-14); in short, all who are victims of discriminatory systems. Attitudes of exclusion as well as the indifference toward attitudes of exclusion are incompatible with the Body of Christ, in which, if one member suffers, all suffer with it (1 Corinthians 12.26).

---

[50] Dri, *A utopia de Jesus*, 154s.

[51] Lutero, *Livro de Concórdia*, 450.

[52] Bolyki, *Jesu Tischgemeinschaften*, 46.

[53] Bolyki, *Jesu Tischgemeinschaften*, 8, 13s, 102.

The Eucharist and the Transformation

The diaconal perspective of the Eucharist lies in transforming that reality which is opposed to the Kingdom of God. Jesus, in his table fellowships, questioned the systems that excluded people for the most different reasons, in the most different areas of life. He proposed paradigms consistent with the Kingdom of God for the political (Mark 6: 30-44), economic (Luke 14: 7-14), social (Luke 16: 19-31), cultural (Mark 7: 24-30) and religious areas (Luke 15: 11-32). Therefore, the evangelical message has a transforming character. The experience of transformation takes place in each authentic celebration of the Eucharist, at which time the tasting of the feast of the new aeon inaugurated by Jesus is performed. Thus, every action taken in the perspective of the Kingdom is profoundly transformative and carries with it the identity of Christian *diakonia*.[54]

The Eucharist and Reconciliation

A project of universal reconciliation, imbued with hope for the Kingdom of God, is clearly discernible throughout Jesus' table fellowships.[55] In the view of the evangelists, Jesus was concerned about the grave fragmentation of God's people for a variety of reasons.

In the parable of the rich man and the poor, Lazarus (Luke 16:19-31), the reason was social and the proposal was to deconstruct the abyss of classes they represent so that there would be reconciliation at the social level.

In the parable of the Prodigal Son (Luke 15:11-32), the reason was religious. There is a tension in the text because of the discordant positions between the two brothers. Among other interpretations, it is possible to perceive in the figure of the older brother the position of the Scribes and Pharisees, who felt it their duty to maintain and enforce the religious norms. The rigidity of this position is known, characterizing itself as legalistic and excluding. On the other side is the younger brother, who failed to comply with the main religious norms and, therefore, deserved excommunication. His situation refers us to a contingent of people of the time, excluded from their community for religious reasons. The father's proposal was to reconcile the two children (the one who had been excluded and the one who excluded himself), bringing them to the table of communion.[56]

In the history of the multiplication of the loaves (Mark 6: 30-44), the reason was political, since under the rule of Herod, representing the Roman Empire, people were hungry and disoriented like sheep without a shepherd. The

---

[54] Federação Luterana Mundial, *Diakonia in Context: transformation, reconciliation, empowerment*. (Genebra, 2009). 43s.

[55] Bolyki, *Jesu Tischgemeinschaften*, 11.

[56] KRÜGER, René. Lucas 15. 1-3,11-32. *Proclamar Libertação*: Auxílios Homiléticos. São Leopoldo: Sinodal, 1991. v. 17, p. 88-93.

proposal was to organize the crowd into groups and share the food so that everyone ate and had enough (also those who had no money).

At the supper by the Pharisee's house (Luke 14:7-14), the division of the people perceived by Jesus was of economic importance: wealthy people from the village gathered in closed groups to dine; meanwhile, the *poor, crippled, lame, and blind* were excluded. Jesus' proposal is to invite people who do not have to requite the invitation to the table, that is, to propose a new economic paradigm based on sharing. This means a society reconciled on the basis of a solidary economy.

Also, for other reasons of exclusion, such as ethno-cultural (Mark 7: 24-30) or moral (Luke 7:36-50), we always find in the context of Jesus' table communions the clear message of reconciliation of the human community at all levels. The Eucharist is the reconciliation of the community with God and of the communing people. Therefore, *diakonia*, which has its roots in the Eucharist, promotes table fellowship as an activity that opens the way to reconciliation. Around the table, people meet, sit face to face, look each other in the eyes, deepen mutual knowledge, take notice of others' suffering, engage in dialogue, deconstruct prejudices, forgive each other, make friendships and enter complicity, and experience communion. Finally, the *diakonia*, anchored in the Eucharist, builds bridges to reconstitute broken human relations.[57]

The Eucharist and Empowerment

The Eucharist means free access to communion with God and the community that makes up the Body of Christ. To the table of the Eucharist we may come empty-handed or take all our anguish and pain, our limits and personal failures, and receive in return all the divine benefits that Christ has earned.[58] We can experience a foretaste of the feast of the Kingdom of God, a real experience of what is the reason for our hope. This experience is restorative and empowering. The experience of participating in the communion of the Kingdom's feast generates encouragement, strength and courage to continue planting seeds of this Kingdom of justice and peace. In this sense, the Eucharist is a remedy that heals and empowers.[59] We can also say that the Eucharist is energy food: at the table of communion we are energized: energized to overcome fear, low self-esteem and pessimism to become subjects and citizens of the Kingdom of God already in this world.[60] Jesus' table fellowships certainly energized Zacchaeus,

---

[57] a) Gaede Neto, Rodolfo. *Diaconia no contexto afro-brasileiro: um estudo baseado nas comunhões de mesa de Jesus*. (São Leopoldo: Sinodal/EST, 2014). 220-226. b) Gaede Neto, Rodolfo. A reconciliação universal como projeto diaconal das comunhões de mesa de Jesus. In: Federación Luterana Mundial. Diaconía – La transformación em las manos de Dios. (Suiza, 2017). 55-63.

[58] Lutero, *Obras Selecionadas*, 429.

[59] Lutero, *Livro de Concórdia*, 493.

[60] a) Lutero, *Obras Selecionadas*, 429s; b) Federação Luterana Mundial, *Diakonia in Context*, 45.

Levi, Mary and Martha, the prostitute who anointed Jesus' feet, the crowds who ate and had their fill, the people invited to the marriage at Cana, the disciples at Emmaus, etc. In addition, the communion the Eucharist generates with the community making up the Body of Christ means the creation of solidary relationships, where the members of the body energize each other (1 Corinthians 12:25-26).

Conclusion

We conclude that the *diakonia* anchored in the Eucharist is the ministry that promotes spaces of empowerment of the weakened people; builds bridges to restore healthy human relationships; leads profoundly transforming actions in the perspective of the Kingdom of God; is characterized by inclusion and negates systems promoting the exclusion of people; fosters spaces for meal sharing and challenges the accumulation of goods causing famine in the world; is based on the consummation of the Kingdom of God; and, above all, as a guest in one's own home humbly submits to God-host, thus enjoying his loving hospitality and all the richness of his grace.

Bibliography

Assmann, Hugo, *Crítica à lógica da exclusão*: ensaios sobre economia eteologia. São Paulo: Paulus, 1994.

Baeske, Albérico, Lucas 19.1-10. *Proclamar Libertação*: Auxílios Homiléticos. São Leopoldo: Sinodal, v. 2, 1977, p. 112-122.

Becker, Jürgen, *Jesus von Nazaret*. Berlin-New York: Gruyter, 1996.

Belo, Fernando, *Uma leitura política do Evangelho*. [s.l., s.d.]. (mimeo), p. 87, 89.

Beozzo, José Oscar, Evangelho e Escravidão na Teologia Latino Americana. In: RICHARD, Pablo (Org.). *Raízes da teologia latino-americana*. São Paulo: Paulinas, 1988.

Bolyki, János, *Jesu Tischgemeinschaften*. Tübingen: Mohr Siebeck, 1998.

Brandt, Wilhelm, O serviço de Jesus. In: NORDSTOKKE, Kjell (org.). *A diaconia em perspectiva bíblica e histórica*. São Leopoldo: Sinodal, 2003.

Brakemeier, Gottfried, A Santa Ceia do Novo Testamento e na Prática Atual. *Estudos Teológicos*. São Leopoldo, v. 26, n. 3, 1986, p. 247-275.

Brunner, Peter, Zur Lehre vom Gottesdienst der im Namen Jesuversammelten Gemeinde. In: MÜLLER, K. F.; Blankenburg, W. (Hrsg.), *Leiturgia*: Handbuch des Evangelischen Gottesdienstes. Kassel: Johannes Stauda, v. 1, 1954, p. 83-364.

Crossan, John D., *O Jesus Histórico*: a vida de um camponês judeu do Mediderrâneo. Rio de Janeiro: Imago, 1994.

Dreher, Carlos Arthur, Lucas 10.38-42. *Proclamar Libertação*: Auxílios Homiléticos. São Leopoldo: Sinodal, v. 6, 1980, p. 124-132.

Dri, Ruben, *A utopia de Jesus*. São Paulo: Ícone, 1986.

Droogers, André, Lucas 19.1-10. *Proclamar Libertação*: Auxílios Homiléticos. São Leopoldo: Sinodal, v. 8, p. 219-227, 1982.

Federação Luterana Mundial, *Diaconia em contexto: transformação, reconciliação, empoderamento*. Genebra: Federação Luterana Mundial, 2009.

Gaede Neto, Rodolfo A reconciliação universal como projeto diaconal das comunhões de mesa de Jesus. In: Federación Luterana Mundial, Diaconía – La transformación em las manos de Dios. Suiza, 2017, p. 55-63.

Gaede Neto, Rodolfo, *Diaconia no contexto afro-brasileiro: um estudo baseado nas comunhões de mesa de Jesus*. São Leopoldo: Sinodal/EST, 2014.

Gnilka, Joachim, *Jesus de Nazaré*: mensagem e história. Petrópolis: Vozes, 2000.

Grundmann, Walter, *Das Evangelium nach Lukas*. 7. Aufl. Berlin: Evangelische Verlagsanstalt, 1974.

Jeremias, Joachim, *Neutestamentliche Theologie*. Gütersloh: Gütersloher Verlagshaus Gerd Mohn, t. 1, 1971.

Krüger, René, Lucas 15. 1-3,11-32. *Proclamar Libertação*: Auxílios Homiléticos. São Leopoldo: Sinodal, 1991. v. 17, p. 88-93.

Kollmann, Bernd, *Ursprung und Gestalten der frühchristlichen Mahlfeier*. Göttingen: Vandenhoeck & Ruprecht, 1990.

Lutero, Martim, Catecismo Maior. *Livro de Concórdia*. São Leopoldo: Sinodal; Porto Alegre: Concórdia, 1980, p. 450.

Lutero, Martim, Um sermão sobre o Venerabilíssimo Sacramento do Santo e Verdadeiro Corpo de Cristo e sobre as Irmandades. *Obras Selecionadas*, São Leopoldo: Sinodal; Porto Alegre: Concórdia, 1987, v. 1, p. 429.

Martini, R. R., *Eucaristia e conflitos comunitários*. São Leopoldo: Sinodal, 2003.

Myers, Ched, *O Evangelho de São Marcos*. São Paulo: Paulinas, 1992.

Moxnes, Halvor, *A economia do reino*: conflito social e relações econômicas no Evangelho de Lucas. São Paulo: Paulus, 1995.

Perrin, Norman, *O que ensinou Jesus realmente?* São Leopoldo: Sinodal, 1977.

Schmithals, Walter, *Das Evangelium nach Lukas*. Zürich: Theologischer Verlag, 1980.

Schneider, Johannes, *Das Evangelium nach Johannes*. 2. Aufl. Berlin: Evangelische Verlagsanstalt, 1978.

Schneider, Nélio, Pecado e sacrifício na Ceia do Senhor: "Por isso há entre vós muitos fracos e doentes e vários já dormiram (1Co 11.30). *Estudos Teológicos*. São Leopoldo, v. 36, n. 2, p. 119-128, 1996.

Schottroff, Luise; Stegemann, Wolfgang, *Jesus von Nazareth – Hoffnung der Armen*. 3. Aufl. Stuttgart; Berlin; Köln: Kohlhammer, 1990.

Veloso, Reginaldo, Fome e eucaristia nos escritos do Novo Testamento. *Estudos Bíblicos*. Petrópolis, v. 46, p. 52-62, 1995.

Veloso, Mário, *Comentário do Evangelho de João*. Santo André: Casa Publicadora Brasileira, 1984.

Wegner, Uwe, "Jesus e Economia no Evangelho de Marcos", in: Dreher, Carlos A. (org.). *Reflexos da brisa leve*. Belo Horizonte: CEBI, 1991.

Wegner, Uwe, *Exegese do novo Testamento*. Manual de Metodologia. São Leopoldo: Sinodal, 1998.

Wiefel, Wolfgang, *Das Evangelium nach Lukas*. Berlin: Evangelische Verlagsanstalt GmbH, 1988.

Ecclesiology from the Margins: The Power and Authority to Define the Church's Identity

Wanda Deifelt

"Jesus proclaimed the Reign of God, and what resulted was the Church," said Alfred Loisy.[1] This statement has often been misinterpreted, placing the church and the reign of God at odds with each other. The church is not the reign of God, but it is the place where one learns about and rehearses it. When Christianity began, people were moved by Jesus' message and eager to proclaim his death and resurrection. Disciples and followers believed that Jesus would return soon, so they did not hasten to create a new religious structure. Eventually, Christians realized that Jesus would not return immediately, and they needed a structure to support their beliefs and carry out the ministry that Jesus had taught them. Thus, over a period of roughly four centuries, Christians selected a canon of sacred texts, developed creeds, and established a hierarchy of officials to carry out the ministry of word and sacrament.[2] The church was necessary to keep the faith alive: preaching, teaching, baptizing, breaking bread and consoling those in need. Through its service, the church carried out its call to announce the Reign of God and witness the good news of Jesus.

As often happens, however, when a movement becomes an institution it may lose its prophetic edge. Gradually, the models of discipleship instituted by Jesus and the ministry he extended to the socially and politically outcast were overshadowed by alliances made between ruling powers and ecclesial leaders, concerned with theological disputes and accusations of heresy.[3] The need for leadership in the congregations led to the creation of offices, such as that of priest, bishop and pope. Sometimes, the egalitarian ideals of discipleship were replaced by a hierarchical model that limited the input of lay people and prevented women from ordination, for instance. There was also an increased concern with the salvation of souls, giving the church's mission a stronger spiritual undertone while weakening (albeit not eradicating) its diaconal emphasis of feeding the hungry and caring for the sick and poor.

---

[1] Alfred Loisy, *L'Évangile et l'Église* (Paris, 1902), 111. English translation: *The Gospel and the Church*, ed. Bernard B. Scott (Philadelphia, 1976).

[2] William C. Placher (ed.), *Essentials of Christian Theology* (Louisville: Westminster John Knox Press, 2003), 222-223.

[3] This is a reference to Constantine's (306-337) conversion to Christianity, when Christianity began to transition to become the dominant religion of the Roman Empire.

This tension between the church, as a beacon of hope and an institution aligned with hierarchical powers, was always visible in Latin America, the context from which the reflections in this chapter stem. The alliance between the Roman Catholic Church and colonial rulers had a deadly effect for indigenous and African peoples, since colonial theology justified slavery and the pillaging of the land. Through the Vatican II council and the emergence of liberation theologies, the Roman Catholic Church became more ecumenical and attuned to socio-political challenges. In the past century, the presence of Protestant and, more recently, Pentecostal and neo-Pentecostal denominations added to the religious landscape of the continent. The ongoing struggle is how the Church – as the body of Christ that is shaped by ecumenical diversity – can be a witness of love instead of discrimination, cooperation instead of proselytism, and life in abundance for all.

Is Church Still Relevant?

Many churches in Europe and North America (Canada and the United States) have experienced a steady decline in membership and attendance.[4] According to the Pew Foundation, fewer people identify with a particular religion and see less of a need to attend religious services. Christian denominations are currently facing the challenge of losing active church members and finding ways to keep people engaged. Mainline churches in particular have witnessed a decrease in attendance. Western Europe, for instance, has become one of the most secular regions in the world, with rising sectors identifying their religion as atheist, agnostic or "nothing in particular" (none).[5]

While in the United States there is a rising number of people who identify themselves as spiritual but not religious, in many Western European nations half or more of the population identify themselves as neither religious nor spiritual. Also, Christians have begun spending less time at church throughout the year, leading to the nomenclature "non-practicing Christians". This concept of claiming to be Christians, while distancing themselves from the church, is a relatively new phenomenon in Christian history.[6] Interestingly, however, even if people lose connection with the church and question whether worship attendance is worth their time, there nevertheless seems to be an expectation that the values espoused by Christianity be carried out in the social realm, particularly those pertaining to social justice. The majority of non-practicing

---

[4] http://www.pewforum.org/2015/11/03/u-s-public-becoming-less-religiSous/pf-2015-11-03_rls_ii-84/, accessed June 6, 2018.

[5] http://www.pewforum.org/2018/05/29/being-christian-in-western-europe/, accessed June 5, 2018.

[6] Placher, 221.

Christians in Western Europe say that the church and other religious institutions play an important role in helping the poor and needy.[7]

In the Global South, on the other hand, there is an increase not only in church attendance but also in the proliferation of new congregations found primarily among non-denominational, charismatic, and Pentecostal or neo-Pentecostal churches.[8] Countries such as Nigeria and Brazil, for example, have now reversed the traditional North-South pattern of missionary work by sending pastors and evangelists to the Northern hemisphere. These initiatives are carried out primarily but not exclusively through preachers identified with charismatic and praise type of worship, with incursions into healing services and expelling of demons. An additional feature is the dissemination of prosperity theology, that is, the belief that God will grant good health, relief from sickness and material prosperity to those who have enough faith.[9]

Interestingly, a common theme both in the Northern and the Southern hemispheres is a concern with the wellbeing of the poor:

> In every country [researched by the Pew Foundation], strong majorities of both pentecostals and charismatics believe that if enough people were brought to Christ, social ills would take care of themselves, a view that also is common among other Christians. However, renewalists also see it as their duty to work for justice for the poor. Indeed, very few people in the countries surveyed reject the notion that Christians and other religious people have a responsibility to work for justice for the poor.[10]

It is both striking and uplifting that the majority of people surveyed support the idea that Christianity has a responsibility to address social ills, particularly poverty. Indeed, the concern for the poor and outcast is a key feature of Jesus' ministry and continues to be on the theological agenda. In spite of structural and theological differences revealed among Christian denominations – ranging from liberationist, conservative, charismatic, evangelical, Pentecostal, Roman Catholic or orthodox – there is a call to work for justice for the poor. Whether the structure of a church is congregational or episcopal, if its theology leans toward biblical inerrancy or contextual reading, or the style of worship requires complex liturgies or praise bands, there is a common denominator: the concern for the poor and outcast. Different denominations may vary in their approach to

---

[7] See http://www.pewforum.org/2018/05/29/being-christian-in-western-europe/, accessed June 6, 2018. Interestingly, according to the same survey, both non-practicing and churchgoing Christians are more likely than the unaffiliated to hold negative views toward immigrants, Muslims and Jews.

[8] http://www.pewforum.org/2011/12/19/global-christianity-movements-and-denominations/, accessed June 6, 2018.

[9] http://assets.pewresearch.org/wp-content/uploads/sites/11/2006/10/pentecostals-08.pdf, 30. Accessed June 6, 2018.

[10] Ibid, 31.

carry out this mission, but they share a common concern. The church is the body of Christ and, as such, is commissioned to proclaim the good news. This is so because of the identity of the church. The church is a call to discipleship, a time for growth, a place for reconciliation, a catalyst for reformation, and an encouragement to engage and transform the world.

The Church as a Call to Discipleship

In spite of its shortcomings, the church is the community of people who received Christ's message and took it to heart. What was this message that brought women, children, widows, sick people and socially outcast to seek after Jesus? Liberation was and continues to be the gospel's message. This is a message of acceptance, inclusion and forgiveness. The church functions as a mouthpiece for this good news, proclaiming it to the world. It is impossible to receive the good news of freedom and keep it to ourselves. For this reason, it is the church's task to preach the gospel of liberation revealed through Jesus Christ. This is consistent with the biblical church. In Matthew 28:19-20, Jesus tells his disciples to "Go and make disciples of all nations." Therefore, the church's call – its vocation – is to preach the good news of the gospel of liberation. It is both the church's duty and inherent desire.

It is not possible to follow this call, be a Christian, without also tackling injustice and abuse. A Christian cannot avoid helping those in need, who are suffering and vulnerable, because that is at the core of Jesus' teachings. This attitude emulates the ministry of Jesus Christ and, in this discipleship, furthers the works of love modeled by him. In fact, Jesus' ministry was to provide solace to the suffering and liberation to the oppressed. In all of Scripture, Jesus is most often found helping the poor, sick and outcasts of society. He does what others (namely religious and political leaders) were not willing to do: to reach out to those who could not give anything back. In doing so, Jesus became one with the oppressed. He could have been born in a palace, but he chose to be born in a stable. His work could yield him political prestige and power, but he chose to minister to the poor and underprivileged. Jesus is God becoming one with those who are disenfranchised in order to reach humanity in its vulnerability. This is also the discipleship Jesus calls for, to move people out of despair and into hope.[11]

James Cone summarizes this vocation of the church through its threefold tasks: it proclaims the reality of divine liberation, it shares in the liberation struggle, and its fellowship is a visible manifestation that the gospel is a reality.[12] The church's vocation is to live Christ in community and, as

---

[11] See Walter Bruegemann (ed.), *Hope for the World: Mission in a Global Context* (Louisville: Westminster John Knox Press, 2001).

[12] James Cone, *A Black Theology of Liberation*: 20th Anniversary Edition (Maryknoll: Orbis, 1990), 130-132.

community, witness Christ to the world. The church is the community that receives the Holy Spirit and is called to live out the gospel. "Because they have experienced what that means for humanity, they cannot accept the world as it is."[13] Thus, the church actively participates in the liberation of the oppressed because they are a community of believers who do not conform to the injustices and oppression of this world. Similar to Cone, other contextual theologies (liberation, feminist, indigenous, queer, etc.) have denounced the church's passivity and sometimes even compliance vis-à-vis social injustices, but they have also emphasized the church's potential and engagement in uplifting those who are disenfranchised.

As the people of God, the church is made up of many different members who comprise the body of Christ. Christians are called to live in community, to mutually support and empower each other, to carry each other's burdens. To be part of the body of Christ is to be reassured that, even if society stigmatizes and discriminates, the church does not abide by these rules. After all, to be baptized in Christ is to put on Christ, so "there is neither Jew nor Greek, there is neither slave nor free, there is no male and female, for you are all one in Christ Jesus" (Galatians 3:27-28). Each member of the church is part of the community, and as such the body of Christ. The diversity among the people allows the church to be equally diverse and use everyone's spiritual gifts in a variety of ministries.

The Church as a Time for Growth

The Nicene Creed identifies four characteristics of the church: that it is "one, holy, catholic, and apostolic". To be one means that the church is united in Christ. Jesus said that "I in them and you in me, that they may become completely one" (John 17:22-23). All people become one through Christ, but unity does not denote uniformity. The church is made holy through baptism in Christ, and through Christ those who are baptized become holy people. Baptism does not mean that Christians are immune from missing the mark and perform wrongdoings, but that daily they repent, wash away their sins and commit themselves to God's grace. To be catholic signifies that the church is universal while communities are also local and rooted in time and place. The church continues to uphold the historic faith as it has been handed down and passes it on to younger generations. Finally, it is apostolic, seeking to include all people in the world.

To be one, holy, catholic and apostolic is not a stagnant definition but rather a blueprint for growth. The Nicene Creed's definition of the church as "one, holy, catholic, and apostolic" is a sign, constantly reminding the church of what it ought to strive for. Individuals and communities placed under the signs of unity, holiness, catholicity and apostolicity recognize the movement engendered by the Holy Spirit, through word and sacrament, and for the

---

[13] Cone, *A Black Theology*, 130.

wellbeing of the world. To claim unity does not mean that all Christians are already unified. The church longs for unity, to live the reality of being the body of Christ, but sometimes it falls short. The ecumenical movement has made strides in building bridges for better understanding and cooperation, but unity also has an eschatological dimension.[14]

Similarly, the holiness of the church and its members does not imply perfection. Rather, it is a commitment to growth. Because society often rejects people who seem different based on race, class, sex, age or wealth, the holiness of the church includes accepting all people into its body, not excluding anyone. Letty Russell explains this by saying: "The gift of holiness in the church should lead to a spirituality of connection to our whole selves, to a community of faith and justice, and to those on the margin of society."[15] The catholicity of the church requires that the church reach out not only to different denominations but also make time to grow in its own self-understanding as part of the entirety of God's creation.

The question about growth in the church usually comes associated with its number of members and financial contributions. Hughes O. Old, for instance, claims that the church today is struggling to retain members and keep people interested because it has stopped its evangelizing effort. Old states that "the worst of all our problems with being a true church is our awkwardness in preaching the Word. We have forgotten how to do it."[16] If evangelism is for the purpose of increased membership and contributions, however, then the church has missed its mark. These are secondary indicators for what the church ought to be. The church's mission is not self-aggrandizement; it is service. Its function is not to replicate business models but be a prophetic voice. This is the radical message that Jesus taught. While the visible church requires budgets and policies, its mission runs deeper than that. Evangelism is concerned with the proclamation of the gospel, the good news of grace that comes from God's forgiveness, and the teachings of love toward one's neighbor.

The measure for growth is the ministry carried out with the last, the least and the lost. The apostolic aspect of the church includes sending people out to share their experiences with Christ in a suffering world, to participate in our common life, being in solidarity with those in pain.[17] Each of the four signs of the church come from an understanding of Christ's presence in the church, as an impetus to grow in justice, mercy and faith. Thus, the church's success

---

[14] See, for instance, the work done by the bilateral Roman Catholic and Lutheran committee, *From Conflict to Communion: Lutheran-catholic Common Commemoration of the Reformation in 2017*. Leipzig: Evangelische Verlagsanstalt GmbH, 2013.

[15] Letty M. Russell, "Why Bother with Church?" in William C. Placher, ed. *Essentials of Christian Theology*. (Louisville: Westminster John Knox Press, 2003), 245.

[16] Hughes O. Old, "Why Bother with Church?" in William C. Placher (ed.), *Essentials of Christian Theology* (Louisville: Westminster John Knox Press, 2003), 240.

[17] See Jürgen Moltmann, *The Living God and the Fullness of Life* (Louisville: Westminster John Knox Press, 2015), 142-152.

cannot be measured by quantifiable data. Its success is that of emptying itself, becoming a servant and carrying out its mission, not seeking honor and glory but integrity, fellowship, affirmation of dignity, peace and love.

The church must remain a manifestation of the divine reality, a light in the darkness. By affirming Christ, the church separates itself from the world and becomes a visible representation of the good news of hope. It cannot become complacent, accepting oppression as inevitable or labeling injustices as God's will. Rather, the church finds its true identity by actively participating in the daily struggles of the people, being in solidarity with those who suffer and advocating on behalf of the marginalized. Christians are called (vocationed) to live out their faith in love for others, caring for the neighbor in need. They fight for liberation not because it is their duty, but because it is inherently their desire to share Christ's love with all human beings. A Christian vocation is to strive for growth in compassion and love.

The Church as Place for Reconciliation

Often, in social and political discourse, calls for peace are not an invitation to reconciliation but mechanisms to curb revolutionary movements, in an attempt to subsume processes of change. However, at the core of Christianity – as in every religious tradition – there is a call for transformation. John Hick calls this a call from being self-centered to being reality-centered, that is, moving from an individualistic to a holistic approach to life.[18] This goes beyond tolerance toward those who are different or who have different views than ours. It is, in fact, a change of mind and heart, as exemplified by the Greek term *metanoia*.

A *metanoia* is a conversion, a radical change of path and way of life. This can be exemplified with a change of heart and mind toward other people and cultures. For instance, in Scripture, Moabites were not allowed to enter the assembly of God's people (Deuteronomy 23:3), but Ruth, a Moabite, challenges this assumption and ends up becoming part of Jesus' genealogy (Matthew 1:5). Similarly, the people from Uz were at first described as "cursed" (Jeremiah 25:29), but from their rank came Job, who was the "most blameless man on earth" (Job 1:8). In the New Testament, the story of Acts 8 has discredited the view that eunuchs are lesser human beings. While Deuteronomy 23 states that foreigners and eunuchs were not allowed to worship in the temple (Deuteronomy 23:1), the Holy Spirit directs Philip to meet the Ethiopian eunuch so that he may be baptized into the body of Christ.

Change happens not because human beings can do it on their own, but because they are moved to change through God's own power. This is at the heart of reconciliation: restoring relations. The message of the gospel is clear. If human contentions lead to resentment and hatred, Christ's practice is of

---

[18] John Hick, *A Christian Theology of Religions* (Louisville: Westminster John Knox Press, 1995).

welcome and embrace. When there is prejudice and discrimination, Jesus reminds his followers to act with justice. In light of animosity and fear, Christian discipleship proclaims openness and affirmation. God's people are moved toward acceptance and inclusion and, in doing so, become a sign of hope.

Reconciliation begins with respect to the other, to the different, to the outcast. The root of the word *respect* is an indication of the power it coveys: re-spect, from the Latin (*re*=back + *specere*=look at), means to take a second look, to look back at, or to regard. Thus, reconciliation does not mean passive acceptance, tacit acquiescence or mere tolerance, but a willingness to keep engaged and to prevent breakdown of dialogue. The church can be the place where reconciliation is rehearsed and modled for the world at large because, in Christ, humanity was reconciled with God and with each other. In living out respectful relationships, the church leads by example.

The Church as a Catalyst for Reformation

The church is a community of word and sacrament. Letty Russell uses the metaphor of the church as a round table. She envisions its future as partnership and sharing for all members around a common table of hospitality.[19] She argues that the marks of word and sacrament point to the heart of what the church is called to do, while the signs of the church – to be one, holy, catholic and apostolic – indicate the way in which the presence of Christ shapes its life. The church, however, has often fallen short of the goal of being one, holy, catholic and apostolic. Historically, the church has many sins to atone for – financing crusades, justifying the decimation of indigenous populations, condoning slavery, or being silent in light of violence and abuse. Similar to individuals who fall short and miss the mark, the church is also in need of repentance. While the church passes down the core values of the gospel and invites humanity to constantly be transformed by God's grace, the church also needs to be willing to change.

The important thing that comes out of tradition is for the church to teach its congregation how to live their lives in a Christly manner. One of the ways Christian communities live transformative hospitality is by welcoming people into the church and sharing the love of God with them. Through word and sacrament, the church continues to live out the traditions that have been handed down. However, the church too needs to be transformed and renewed. It needs to undergo constant reformation (*ecclesia semper reformanda*) to be able to preach, teach and live the gospel anew.[20] As an institution, it does not always

---

[19] Letty Russell, *Church in the Round: Feminist Interpretation of the Church* (Louisville: Westminster John Knox Press, 2003), 245.

[20] Although the Latin quote is widely used in Protestant circles to signify the relevance of the 16th-century reformation movement spearheaded by Martin Luther, Ulrich

live according to its mission. When the church preaches love, justice and peace, it lives according to this message. Even if the church changes, its foundation – to be and become the community of Christ – remains the same.

The challenge for the church is to model respect for each other in all our differences and affirm the value of diversity in community (which includes confronting and dealing with the church's own implicit biases). In order to be inclusive, the church must be willing to expand its own views and challenge traditions that might not be in conformity to the good news of the gospel. For instance, by using inclusive and expansive language in worship. Mary Daly was among the first to illustrate the power of androcentric language in keeping women hidden and silent. An inclusive language to address God is not only possible but also necessary. She states that God-language is damaging and "compatible with sexism if it encourages detachment from the reality of the human struggle against oppression in its concrete manifestations".[21] Her solution is to address God not as a noun, but a verb.

But the church's inclusivity cannot be restrained to worship. The church also has the responsibility of breaking the barriers of stigmas that plague the world at large and announce the gospel of God's unconditional love. Liberation, feminist, queer, black, womanist, post-colonial, mujerista, dalit and minjung theologies (among others) have already trailed this path, pointing out the connection between Jesus' liberating message and current social and political struggles. A current example of this is the ecumenical theological endeavors addressing the HIV and Aids pandemic. There is a comparison between the marginalized people in Jesus' time and those who are discriminated today due to the color of their skin, social class, sex or gender identity, age, capacity for physical mobility and cognition, or because they carry the HIV virus.[22]

Although the church is not always perfect, it is continually striving to live by the message of God's reign. The church moves forward because of the promises received from God about the future of the people of Christ. This includes Jesus' promise to be present in the witness to the gospel and in the gathered community. When this promise is translated into an affirmation of dignity for all, the revolutionary dimension of the gospel extrapolates the walls of the church and becomes good news to all.[23] This promise identifies the

---

Zwingli and John Calvin, the concept of ongoing reformation is vastly ecumenical. The concept of reformation can be used to describe the changes engendered by the Second Vatican Council, for instance. See Leonardo and Clodovis BOFF, *Introducing Liberation Theology*. Maryknoll: Orbis, 2005.

[21] Mary Daly, *Beyond God the Father* (Boston: Beacon Press, 1973), 20.

[22] See Wanda Deifelt, "The AIDS pandemic and the vulnerability of God" in Valburga S. Streck (ed.), *Theology and HIV & AIDS in Latin America* (São Leopoldo: OIKOS, 2013), 19-26.

[23] An example of this comes from China, as recounted by Pirkko Lehtio: "The women's movement, with its demands for equality of men and women, is not new among Chinese

presence of Christ among the poor and marginalized, giving the church hope for the future and motivating people to keep moving forward.

The Church as an Encouragement to Engage and Transform the World

A common misunderstanding about the nature of the church is that it should not get involved in worldly affairs. The gospel, however, does not call Christians *out of the world* but *into the world*, to bear witness to God's grace and share Christ's love with it. Quite often the church has been more concerned with death and the afterlife instead of life in the here and now, causing the untimely demise of many innocent people. The silence of the church proved to be deadly. If, in the past, the church condoned the lynching of blacks, the slaughter of Jews and the massacre of indigenous people, it cannot fail to speak against genocides today. If it celebrated its own financial rewards through colonial enterprises, it needs to repent for preaching and teaching a false gospel. Even if the church was complacent with violence and war, it has also raised voices of protest that defied the church to return to its first love, to position itself at the margin, along with those Jesus cared for.

Black theology was among the first articulated voices protesting the travesty of using the gospel to justify atrocities. James Cone, for example, denounced that the emphasis on heaven in the church has served as a distraction to make blacks accept their oppressed existence. Black theology rejects the idea of an abstract, distant heaven having no relation to the present condition of the oppressed. As Cone points out, if "Christ's work is finished, then there is nothing to do but wait for the Second Coming."[24] To reduce the gospel to the afterlife denies the revelation of Christ as a promise of freedom for all. Black theology affirms the existence of life after death, but it warns not to focus solely on it, to the detriment of the struggles facing humanity. This is a trap that should be avoided.

What, then, is the role of the church in the world? The church lives the dialectic between hope and sorrow, joy and pain. The church can neither retreat from the world, nor can it embrace it. To retreat from the world would mean a denial of the revelation of Christ who demands worldly involvement on behalf of the oppressed. On the other hand, embracing the world and its values would be a compromise to the good news of the gospel. After all, the world is where the brutal reality of inhumanity makes its ungodly appearance. Jesus

---

Christians. Christian women have raised their voices for equal opportunities for women already at the beginning of this century [20th century]. Chinese women asked for equality in the church at the same time they asked why the women missionaries did not have the same rights as their male partners even though they had spoken about equality among Christians." Viggo Mortensen (ed.), *The Situation of Women in the Church of China* (Geneva: LWF, 1997), 181.

[24] Cone, *Black Theology*, 139.

proclaimed the reign of God and not the reign of empire, and his message was probably perceived as "sacred anarchy."[25] In this reign, the last are first and the first are last, the hungry are fed and the powerful are sent away empty-handed, and prostitutes and tax collectors precede the righteous into the reign of God.

The church's commitment is to preach the gospel to the world and participate in the struggle for liberation. It cannot stand by the sidelines when exclusionary systems label human beings as superfluous and place capital over the wellbeing of creation. The church in Latin America has a long tradition of denouncing these unjust systems and pointing out the exploitation of small farmers, indigenous populations, *quilombolas* (communities of former runaway slaves), homeless and landless people. Different denominations have called for economic literacy as well as biblical and theological reflections on labor, economy and the environment in order to be better stewards of God's creation. There is an ongoing plea that the church join civil society and, along with other social movements and organizations, bring about changes that contemplate human dignity and environmental consciousness.[26]

Engaging and transforming the world requires advocacy. As humans, we may think of freedom as the lack of burdens and concerns for others, to be trouble free. But as Christians, freedom liberates us from our own petty concerns to seek the wellbeing of others as well. To turn a blind eye to racism, sexism, xenophobia and homophobia not only perpetuates injustice but also condones it. It adds to the problem instead of solving it. After all, no one is free until all are free.

Contemplating the role of the church in the world also requires a change in the way we perceive and describe sin. Usually sin is understood as missing the mark, doing something wrong, and, in doing so, not paying attention to structural sin and our part in maintaining structures of inequality. This exempts us from the urgency of any social or political involvement, for the gospel, the good news of life in abundance, is privatized and spiritualized. But when we understand sin also as the good that is left undone, that is, the opportunities of correcting wrongs and establishing peace, we not only address the structural dimensions of sin but also the broader/structural dimensions of the gospel.[27]

Thus, the church and its members have the responsibility and opportunity to fight against injustice and oppression in all forms. A privatized and spiritualized representation of the gospel leads to a selfish attitude: "it is not my problem" or "if it is not happening to me, it does not happen at all". This

---

[25] John D. Caputo, "Spectral Hermeneutics: On the Weakness of God and the Theology of the Event" in Jeffrey W. Robbins, ed. *After the Death of God* (New York: Columbia University Press, 2007), 61.

[26] See, for instance, René Krüger (ed.), *Life in All Fullness: Latin American Protestant Churches Facing Neoliberal Globalization* (Geneva: LWF, 2007).

[27] See Wanda Deifelt (ed.), *Market and Margins: Lutheran Perspectives* (Minneapolis: Lutheran University Press, 2014).

mindset is highly problematic. Besides inaccurate, it is dangerous because it reduces the gospel to one's own worldview and not to the other, to the neighbor in need. Jesus knew this when he affirmed that the greatest commandment was to love God with all our hearts and minds and our neighbors as we love ourselves.

Conclusion

People feel separated from the church and might not see its relevance in light of the advancements in society or forget that they are always welcomed in the church in the context of discrimination and stigmatization. The church continues to have the prophetic mission to denounce what is wrong and uplift what is life-giving. When Jesus gathered disciples and ministered to the poor and outcast, he left a model for the church to follow. Jesus called disciples from different walks of life and accepted followers no matter who they were. The same hospitality is still felt in the church today, from its pews to its outreach activities, from the pulpit to its street ministries, from the Sunday school to the hospitals and soup kitchens.

Even if people feel disconnected from the church or see no need to participate in its fellowship, the church continues to carry out its mission: to be the salt of the earth (Matthew 5:13). It does so precisely by carrying out the ministry of Jesus, without expecting compensation or recognition. The church's consistent presence is similar to salt – it gives flavor, it can be tasted, and once it has done its job it "disappears". Its authenticity is in serving. The church's story is rooted in God's action in the life, death and resurrection of Jesus Christ. This story is not only worth telling but also above all being lived through the compassion, resilience and justice that positions it at the margins of society. The Christ event is an event of liberation. To know Christ is to encounter him in the history of the weak and disenfranchised, those who are at the margin. There is no knowledge of Christ independent of the struggle of the oppressed, and this is the place the church also finds itself.

Part 2

Sent into the World

The Church's Holistic Mission

Knud Jørgensen[1]

Christians often dispute whether what leads to salvation is good action or faith in Christ. In my view it is like asking which blade in a pair of scissors is most necessary. Is it not so that only obedience brings me to Christ, and only faith in Christ saves me from despair? Only the obedient finds faith, and only the faithful is obedient. And out of that faith springs good deeds – inevitably.

I shall in the following give an overview of the missional church and its understanding of *diakonia*. Following that, I shall discuss *diakonia* and proclamation from a biblical perspective.

The Missional Church as a Holistic Church[2]

Emil Brunner is often quoted about the nature of the church: 'The church exists by mission as a fire exists by burning.'[3] The Spirit of Christ who empowers the church in mission is also the life of the church. Jesus breathed the Holy Spirit into the church at the same time as he sent the church (John 20:19ff). Ergo: *the church is missionary by its very nature*.[4] Missionary activity is not so much the work of the church as simply the church at work.

The American missiologist Van Gelder writes:

> …the church, as the people of God in the world, is inherently a missionary church. It is to participate fully in the Son's redemptive work as the Spirit creates, leads, and teaches the church to live as the distinctive people of God … *The church is. The church does what it is. The church organizes what it does.* The nature of the Church is based on God's presence through the Spirit. The ministry

---

[1] Knud Jørgensen passed away in December 2018. This chapter may be considered his last contribution from his hand, expressing his personal commitment to the Church's holistic mission. It has been slightly revised by Kjell Nordstokke as part of the final editing of this book.

[2] See Knud Jørgensen, "Biblical and Theological Foundations: The Triune God and the Missional Church" in John Gibaut and Knud Jørgensen, *Called to Unity for the Sake of Mission* (Oxford: Regnum Books International, 2014), 40-44.

[3] Emil Brunner, *The Word and the World* (London: Student Mission Movement Press, 1931), 108.

[4] David Bosch, *Transforming Mission. Paradigm Shifts in Theology of Mission* (Maryknoll, N.Y: Orbis Books, 1991), 372.

of the church flows out of the church's nature. The organization of the church is designed to support the ministry of the church.[5]

The word 'missionary' refers to the specific mission activities of the church, whereas the word 'missional' is related to the nature of the church, as being sent by God to the world. To many of us, it began with Leslie Newbigin, who differentiated between the church's missionary *dimension* and its missionary *intention.*[6] It was the same Newbigin who, after having served as a missionary in South India for several decades before returning to Birmingham in the 1970s, commenced writing books about the church in the West. Not only did he castigate the rationalistic modernism of the West but he also claimed that the Western, modern culture was the least receptive to the Gospel:

> There is a cold contempt for the Gospel which is harder to face than opposition... England is a very pagan society and the development of a truly missionary encounter with this very tough form of paganism is the greatest intellectual and practical task facing the Church.[7]

Reading Newbigin helped me realize that my own experiences as a young missionary in Ethiopia and with the East African revival – and later from the growing church in China – were experiences of *how the church was meant to be*. Not only were these churches following in the footsteps of the Acts of the Apostles with regard to the power and presence of the Holy Spirit but they also represented a living people of God, in praise and weeping, people who gave priority to walking in the light, and who in their lives demonstrated God's renewing, healing and diaconal power in their contexts.

The understanding of 'missional church' is based on different streams from Orthodox, Roman Catholic, Ecumenical and Evangelical theology and practice, and represents in that way a joint Ecumenical concern that often has been running parallel and been intertwined with the concern for *missio Dei*. The term itself came out of The Gospel and Our Culture network, which was initially established in England in 1989, and soon exported to North America and elsewhere. The network was inspired by Leslie Newbigin and his early books *The Open Secret* (1978), *Foolishness to the Greeks* (1986) and *The Gospel in a Pluralist Society* (1991).[8]

---

[5] Craig Van Gelder, *The Essence of the Church* (Grand Rapids, Mi.: Baker Books, 2000), 31 and 37.

[6] Leslie Newbigin, *One Body, One Gospel, One World* (London & New York: International Missionary Council, 1958), 21, 43.

[7] Leslie Newbigin, *Unfinished Agenda: An Autobiography* (Grand Rapids: Eerdmans, 1985).

[8] The influence of Newbigin's theology of cultural plurality on these missiological streams has been well documented by George R. Hunsberger in *Bearing the Witness of the Spirit* (Grand Rapids: Eerdmans 1998). The American version of the network also pays tribute to Newbigin; at the same time, it is very preoccupied with its own North

It was the American Gospel and Our Culture Network that created the term *missional church.*[9] Darrell L. Guder, who was a key figure in the network, raises the issue of the *conversion of the church* in his book *The Continuing Conversion of the Church* (Grand Rapids: Eerdmans, 2000). This conversion is related to rethinking theology, evangelization, worship, leadership and structures. Most importantly, it demands undertaking measures against what is seen as "the gospel reductionism" within the church: the early church went from movement to becoming an institution; Constantine's church replaced the understanding of the gospel as an event with the formulation of a defined faith system consisting of truths; the Kingdom of God was conceived as the eternity that awaits a Christian after death; salvation was handed out to the individual by the church, in particular through the sacraments. On the basis of these "gospel reductions", the organizational structure of the church was transformed into state religion and the administrator of religious meaning in society. Likewise, the reformation and pietism have reduced the gospel to a matter of salvation for the individual: "The benefits of salvation are separated from the reason for which we receive God's grace in Christ: to empower us as God's people to become Christ's witnesses. This fundamental dichotomy between the benefits of the gospel and the mission of the gospel constitutes the most profound reductionism of the gospel".[10]

David Bosch described how we experience a shift from the modern Enlightenment paradigm in the history of Christendom toward a post-modern, ecumenical paradigm.[11] *Corpus Christianum* – the idea of a unity made up of state, religion and culture as the canopy for the church's work – no longer functions. The West is witnessing the end of the era that has lasted from the Constantine state church and church tradition in the 4th century. This calls for a dramatic readjustment process. The idea of Corpus Christianum symbolized

---

American context. This is illustrated by the fact that all the books on the topic mention North America in the titles, for example *The Church between Gospel and Culture. The Emerging Mission in North America* (Hunsberger & Van Gelder 1996), *Missional Church. A Vision for the Sending of the Church in North America* (Guder 1998) and *Confident Witness – Changing World. Rediscovering the Gospel in North America* (Van Gelder 1999). The focus on context is a common feature within the missional church thinking: What does our mission context require in terms of calling, tasks and witness? And what kind of leadership does this context call for?

[9] Darrell Guder (ed.), *Missional Church. A Vision for the Sending of the Church in North America* (Grand Rapids: Eerdmans, 1998). This book was the result of a three-year study project aiming at analyzing the situation of the American church and at defining its challenges within a mission context. Here, missional is defined to underline "the essential nature and vocation of the church as God's called and sent people". Further, it is emphasized that missional ecclesiology should be biblical, historical, contextual, eschatological and practicable.

[10] Darrell Guder, *The Continuing Conversion of the Church* (Grand Rapids: Eerdmans, 2000), 120.

[11] Bosch, *Transforming Mission. Paradigm Shifts in Theology of Mission*, 349ff.

wedlock between the church and the holders of power, which, in different ways, turned a missionary church into a pastoral institution. As the state religion of Rome, the Christian faith became the civil religion and the society's administrator of religious meaning. The church's structure adopted the shape of the society's structure, with parochial churches, and a clear division between *clerici* (priests) and *idiotes* (lay people). Faith was practiced by taking part in the arrangements of the church, and evangelization was replaced with "Christianization". Breaking with the Constantine tradition and its access to power and influence is not easy. In other parts of the world a break with the Constantine church has already taken place, or it has never been present in the first place. To Westerners in Northern Europe it has in some cases become an obstacle to mission because it conceals the fact that we are situated in a mission context.

The vision to be a missional church is born out of a critique of the Western concept of church and of mission as primarily to reach the unengaged/unreached, even when admitting the critique requires some nuances, acknowledging the multiform presence of the church throughout history. The response to the West finding itself in a mission situation is not to initiate efforts to "communicate with modern man", but to ask what is wrong with today's church since the gospel appears so irrelevant to so many and since many still are preoccupied with mission 'from the West to the rest'. The features of the Constantine church are similar to a Lutheran/Protestant conception of the church as the place for preaching the gospel and administering the sacraments. A missional church is where the people of God participate in God's mission through being, word and deed in their daily lives. The symbols of the Constantine church are the place, the temple, the Word, the sacred, whereas the symbols of the missional church are the way, discipleship, wholeness, common witness and everyday life. Likewise, one can distinguish between the custodians of the Constantine church – a clerical hierarchy of static institutions – and the custodians of the missional church – lay people, who dynamically live out their faith in everyday situations. This does not rule out the ordained ministry, but sees its role in equipping God's people for service (Eph. 4:11ff).

In the middle of this paradigm shift, the question is: How to be God's church in our time? This question in turn leads to a number of new questions – about everything we are and do as Christians and as church. This is not a matter of new methods or models. The shift that we experience today raises questions about the theology, missiology and spirituality. We are forced to reread the Scriptures about what it means to be God's people in the world, and about being signs of the Kingdom of God through who we are, what we do and what we say. In light of such reorientation, one may ask how many of our churches in the West for decades have made the traditional church structure an integral part of the gospel. How have they carried out a determined reduction of the gospel (from making disciples to a preoccupation with the personal salvation of the individual)? A reduction of what it means to be church – from the one, holy, catholic and apostolic church to a church that defines itself only by what it does (the proclamation of the gospel and the administration of baptism and communion).[12] The Reformers in a way shifted the attention away from what the church *is* to what the church *does*. Through this focus on sermon and sacraments, the church service became the primary task of the church.

The missional church concept captures the old truth that mission is part of the church's *esse* (its being). Without mission, there is no church. It lies in the genes of the church to be missional, and any ecclesiological discussion without this point of departure will necessarily derail and end up speaking of something else than the church. Therefore, mission should not be reduced to a task or a program; it is primarily the nature of the church – a nature that grows out of God's nature. In the middle of the crisis that the established church of the West experiences, what will remain is a missional communion of people who live by and demonstrate the gospel of the Kingdom of God in a holistic manner through being, expressed in word and deed, in mutual relationships of giving and receiving. Such was the ecclesiological paradigm of the early church and such should a new paradigm be. This is a matter of finding the right balance between the nature of the church (what the church is), its tasks (ministry; what the church does) and its structure (how the church organizes itself).

The task is not to invent a number of mission programs to attract new churchgoers. Instead, we are challenged to be what the church has always been: people of flesh and blood carrying the reality of the gospel within them, communicating it through missional being and action. For that reason, it is likely that the famous but seldom realized priesthood of all believers will become the basic church and mission structure. Together with this structure one could hope for a rediscovery of the gifts of the Spirit, in a broad biblical perspective, as that which equips the missionary congregation in a postmodern reality. A missional church will therefore often emphasize meditation, spirituality, presence, genuineness, *diakonia* and lifestyle. Modeled on our brothers and sisters in the South and East, we may in a new way become personal carriers of the spiritual reality the world longs for.

And when going out, our primary task is *to be witnesses*. The church's missional call, according to the NT, is to be witnesses. Mission is witness. *Marturia is the sum of kerygma, koinonia, leitourgia and diakonia* – all four of which constitute important dimensions of the witness for which the church is called and sent: "We are using a missiological hermeneutic when we read the New Testament as the testimony (witness) of witnesses, equipping other witnesses for the common mission of the church".[13] Thus, testimony becomes a demonstration through the lives and actions of God's people to the fact that the Kingdom of God becomes present in the disciples of Jesus Christ. In this way, although often fragile and vulnerable, the testimony of the gospel defines the

---

[12] Van Gelder, *The Essence of the Church*, 53ff.

[13] Guder, *The Continuing Conversion of the Church*, 53-55.

identity, activities and communication that the church has been called to since Pentecost.

Action as Sacrament: Diakonia and Proclamation

Holistic implies a vital relationship between proclamation and good works/*diakonia*. Churches deal differently with this; some emphasize the former and train their people primarily in evangelistic outreach, while other churches are led by the saying of Saint Francis: "Preach the gospel at all times and if necessary use words."

The concept of missional church impresses the need for a contextualized proclamation of the Gospel. Such proclamation will have no impact if it does not issue from a loving, hospitable, generous community. Good works cannot save, true; but godly action has *a sacramental effect.*[14] This also has to do with a messianic or Hebrew spirituality that hallows the everyday as essential to life and to the missional church – because it is here in the everyday that we exist.

> …we need to be able to redeem both the primacy and the value of the deed done in the furtherance of God's cause in the world. Our spirituality must move from primarily a passive/receptive mode to an *actional* mode…The church must rediscover the ability and inclination to find God in the place of action so that others might find him there as well.[15]

This implies, according to Frost and Hirsch, that diaconal action in itself is a sacrament of grace. They even call it the primary sacrament of the missional church. The church is to exemplify an activist understanding of being church. Just as the Lord's Supper and baptism are sacraments through which God's grace is made apparent, so is *diakonia* – because God is near in the performed action. What we are talking about here is a Hebraic mode of thinking as it comes to expression in such scripture verses as:

> In the same way, let your light shine before men, that they may see your good deeds and praise your Father in heaven (Matt 5:16).

> Live such good lives among the pagans that, though they accuse you of doing wrong, they may see your good deeds and glorify God on the day he visits us (1 Pet 2:12).

The sacred deed is full of God's glory. It is both sacramental and revelatory. God is active in the streets, at work, in the marketplaces, at play. Spirituality results in good works, in the same way as truth must issue forth in diaconal

[14] Michael Frost and Alan Hirsch, *The Shaping of Things to Come* (Massachusetts: Hendrickson, 2005), 135f.
[15] Frost & Hirsh, 135.

action. The good deed both leads to Christ and issues forth from a relationship to Christ. So, the goal is truth as deed. The missional church here advocates an active spirituality, more inspired by Hebrew thinking than Western piety.

Biblical Perspectives on Kerygma and Diakonia[16]

Kerygma (from the Greek word κήρυγμα kérugma) is used in the New Testament for "preaching" (see Luke 4:18-19, Romans 10:14, Matthew 3:1). It is related to the verb κηρύσσω/kērússō, meaning "to cry or proclaim as a herald" and used in the sense of "to proclaim, announce, and preach".

According to the New Testament (Luke 4:17-21), Jesus launched his public ministry when he entered the synagogue in Nazareth, read from the scroll of Isaiah and identified himself as the subject of Isaiah 61. The text is a programmatic statement of Jesus' ministry to preach or proclaim – *kerygma* – good news to the poor, the blind and the captive. The key term that encapsulates Jesus' message and the message about Jesus is *gospel* as we find it both in Jesus' proclamation of the kingdom (Mark 1:14-15) and in the Apostles' preaching of the crucified and risen Jesus. When Paul summarizes this message (e.g. Rom 1:3-4), he views it also as a message of transforming power to those who believe: "It is the power of God for salvation to everyone who has faith…" (Rom 1:16).[17]

Christopher Wright suggests that 'gospel' and 'evangelism' actually have their roots in the Old Testament, specifically in the book of Isaiah. The gospel goes back to the good news that came to the exiles in Babylon. In Isaiah 40-55 we hear about 'good news' four times (40:9; 41:27; 52:7; 61:1). The Hebrew word is *basar*, which in three cases in the Septuagint is translated with *euangelizomai* – the same word used in the New Testament about Jesus' preaching.[18] *Basar* means to bring or announce good news and the messenger of good news is called *mal'ak*. This is the word used in Isaiah 52:7 about the one who brings good news – news of a victory: "It is peace!" We are saved. Your God reigns. This reign of God means 'shalom', peace, the end of brokenness. God will bring wholeness and fullness when we are at peace with God, ourselves and with the world. This will be good news for all creation and all humanity. It will bring deliverance – from the captivity of the Israelite exiles. The reign of God breaks the chains of evil, sin and Satan. God is returning to God's city, bringing back with him his own people. This means

---

[16] See Knud Jørgensen, "Biblical Perspectives on Kerygma and *Diakonia*" in Rose Dowsett, Isabel Phiri, Doug Birdsall, Dawit Olika Terfassa, Hwa Yung and Knud Jørgensen, *Evangelism and Diakonia in Context* (Oxford: Regnum Books, 2016), 8-12.

[17] Harald Hegstad, *The Real Church. An Ecclesiology of the Visible* (Eugene, Oregon: Pickwick Publications, 2013), 50.

[18] Christopher J.H. Wright, *The Mission of God's People. A Biblical Theology of the Church's Mission* (Grand Rapids: Zondervan, 2010), 180ff.

comfort and redemption (Isaiah 40; 52:9-10) – comfort to those who have suffered great loss and payment of the cost needed to set the captives free. This is accomplished by 'the arm of the Lord' (see Isaiah 40:10-11; 51:9; and 53:1). In the last Servant Song, the arm of the Lord is identified with the suffering servant who would live a life of rejection and die a death of injustice, but eventually be vindicated and glorified by God.[19] This is 'good news' – for the entire world:

> The good news of the kingdom of God that is to go out to the ends of the earth, to bring comfort and joy to all nations, is the good news of the living God who reigns, who returns to his rightful inheritance, and who redeems the whole world. And all of these things God will accomplish through his mighty arm – his Arm (Servant), outstretched in gentle compassion, outstretched in suffering love, and outstretched in cosmic victory.[20]

The understanding of Jesus as 'good news' is directly linked to the songs of the suffering servant: *Jesus is God reigning*, the reign of God is beginning with his arrival (Mark 1:14-15). Here is the *mal'ak*, the anointed preacher of good news: "The Spirit of the Lord is on me, because he has anointed me to proclaim good news to the poor" (Luke 4:16f). God was reigning in and through Jesus, through his words and his works. The reign of God is found among those who make peace, do good and proclaim God's salvation. *Jesus was God returning*: with Jesus the day of the Lord has arrived; the king was coming home, riding on a donkey. And the same Jesus will come back "in the same way you have seen him go into heaven" (Acts 1:11). *Jesus was God redeeming*: here is the one who was going to redeem Israel (Luke 24:21), in spite of or because of the 'defeat' on the cross. On the cross, God's arm was stretched out for the redemption of the world. And the defeat turned out to be the victory of the God whose power is hidden under its contradiction – powerlessness and vulnerability (Col 2:14ff).

Here is the core message of the *kerygma*, "that Christ died for our sins according to the Scriptures, that he was buried, that he was raised on the third day according to the Scriptures…" (1 Cor. 15:3-5). According to Paul, Christ died for us so that we might live with him (1 Thess. 4:14, 5:10). The *kerygma* is an account of the events of Jesus' death and resurrection, understood in light of the scriptures. The reign of God has now come through the person and work of Jesus the Messiah. This good news is for all the nations – 'in Christ Jesus you (gentiles) who once were far away have been brought near by the blood of Christ' (Eph. 2:13f). The dividing wall has been set aside and the good news of reconciliation is valid for all, through him who 'preached peace' (lit. 'evangelised peace' – Is 52:7). Thus, peace-making is at the heart of the gospel

[19] Wright, *The Mission of God's People*, 185.
[20] Wright, *The Mission of God's People*, 186.

itself. The creation of a new humanity is the good news that Christ came to accomplish.

The Early Church confessed Jesus as Lord. They concluded that if Jesus is indeed Lord of all, this reality has to be proclaimed.

Diakonia is the call to participate in God's caring and liberating action for the poor, marginalized and oppressed. The terms 'deacon'/'deaconess' and 'diaconate' also come from the same root, which refers to the emphasis on service within those vocations. *Diakonia* is used in the Bible with different meanings. Sometimes, it refers to the specific kind to help any people in need. At other times, it means to serve at the tables. And still others, it refers to the distribution of financial resources. Also, in contemporary theology the word *diakonia* presents a variety of connotations and representations.

Throughout the Old Testament, God's righteous character is exemplified through his care for the poor, the weak and the powerless. Justice (*mishpat*), kindness/faithfulness (*hesed*) and compassion (*rahamin*) are listed as qualities that exemplify a healthy community. Special attention is given to widows, orphans, immigrants and the poor (the marginalized). Yahweh is "a father to the fatherless, a defender of widows" (Psalm 68:5), and his covenant people is called to be like him: "Do no wrong or violence to the alien, the fatherless or the widow" (Jeremiah 22:3). When the people are sent into exile, one of the reasons is because of their disregard for the poor and needy in their midst: hence a woe is said on those who 'deprive the poor of their rights and withhold justice from the oppressed of my people, making widows their prey and robbing the fatherless' (Isaiah 10:2).

Stephanie Dietrich calls attention to the theology of creation and humankind's inherent dignity in the Old Testament. It affirms the need for companionship, the communal aspects of responsibility in society, and the covenant between God and mankind: 'The concept of covenant is important for our understanding of *diakonia*, because it links mankind's life to its mission and sending by God and shows that God has a clear will and intention for his creation, namely, to follow God's call and to be faithful to God under all conditions.'[21]

To this should be added a prophetic *diakonia* that addresses and takes a stand against injustice. Those who oppress the innocent and take bribes and deprive the poor of justice are criticized. The cultic practice is criticized. There can be no true worship of God without service to humankind. Diaconal action should include the task of unmasking injustice and promoting justice.

---

[21] Stephanie Dietrich, "'Mercy and Truth Are Met Together; Righteousness and Peace Have Kissed Each Other' (Psalm 85:10): Biblical and Systematic Theological Perspectives on *Diakonia* as Advocacy and Fight for Justice" in Stephanie Dietrich, Jørgensen, Korslien and Nordstokke, *Diakonia as Christian Social Practice* (Oxford: Regnum Books International, 2014), 34.

The starting point for Jesus' holistic ministry is the Great Command of loving the Lord and your neighbor as yourself. Holistic ministry implies that Jesus tells people what is right and takes care of them by healing their diseases, offering forgiveness and inclusion into his fellowship with sinners. Acts 10:38 tells how Jesus 'went around doing good and healing all who were under the power of the devil, because God was with him.'

Luke has a particular interest in the poor and other marginalized groups. He portrays Jesus as 'the hope of the poor', concerned with all that deprive women, men and children of dignity, of selfhood, of sight and voice and bread. The major entry point is the programmatic statement in the synagogue in Nazareth (Luke 4:18ff). Here, Jesus talks about good news for the poor and about letting the oppressed go free, and he proclaims "a year of the Lord's favour", a Jubilee, but with no vengeance (see Isaiah 61:2, which also talks about defeating their enemies; the verse is not part of Jesus' reading in Nazareth).

Jesus' ministry is the model for today's understanding of *diakonia*. The church's *diakonia* should be understood in continuity with Jesus' healing ministry. *Diakonia* is not just an outworking of creation and the law but *the gospel in action*. The healing of the sick was from the beginning a regular part of both Jesus' own messianic activity and the mission of the apostles. The good deeds are a sign and foretaste of the coming kingdom. Redemption is the renewal of creation. *Diakonia* is done in Jesus' name; therefore, *diakonia* and the gospel cannot be separated from each other:

> It does *not* mean that *diakonia* is nothing more than a tool for preaching the gospel or witness of the gospel, and it also does not mean that the gospel must be taught explicitly in every given situation where diaconal work is in operation. Diaconal works are still *diakonia* even when the gospel is not explicitly preached. However, the connection to the gospel must always be present. Just as mission is part of the essence of being church, so *diakonia* is part of the very nature of the church and should therefore permeate and affect the whole of church life. The church witnesses to God's kingdom through its works. It is not enough to speak of God's kingdom.[22]

Diakonia is not neutral. It grows out of the sacrificial life of Christ. It is therefore this Christ-centeredness that makes *diakonia* Christian and gives it motivation and power. Otherwise, we might leave humanitarian concerns to other bodies, such as the Red Cross.

As Christians we are sent into the world, like Jesus, to serve. For this is the natural expression of loving for our neighbors. We love. We go. We serve. In this we have (or should have) no ulterior motive. True, the gospel lacks visibility if we merely preach it, and lacks credibility if we who preach it are interested only in souls and have no concern about the welfare of people's

[22] John Stott, *Christian Mission in the Modern World* (London: Falcon, 1975).

bodies, situations and communities. Yet the reason for our acceptance of social responsibility is not primarily in order to give the gospel either a visibility or a credibility it would otherwise lack, but rather simple, uncomplicated compassion. Love has no need to justify itself. It merely expresses itself in service whenever it sees need.

The interpretation of *diakonia* as 'humble service' and 'charity' has been opposed and revised. It is particularly the Australian theologian John Collins who has documented the view that this Greek word does not mean humble service, but rather an important task that is given to somebody by an important authority. In the New Testament, it often refers to ministry or leadership, including Jesus' messianic mission, and it includes the understanding of the deacon as a go-between, particularly in relation to the poor and marginalized.[23]

When the missional church people describe the community of the Spirit,[24] the focus is on the open invitation to a common table (= hospitality), on the hungry, on reconciliation and forgiven-ness, and cultivating communities of peace – all of this depicting a diaconal church. Continuing the work of Jesus in a missional context means sharing the work of Jesus, healing, and announcing the reign of God.

Rather than the traditional 'dual mandate', the focus is on *the nature of the church*: the nature of the church is holistic in relating redemption to all of life; the church exists as a social community that is both spiritual and human.[25] This community is serving – through lifestyle, witness and the demonstration of grace that unmasks the powers.

Conclusion

Holistic mission implies to walk 'worthily with the Lord' (1 Thess. 2:10-12), says Darrell Guder.[26] It demonstrates that the message and its demonstration (*diakonia*) cannot be separated and that the two emphasize the public character of the community's life. An essential part of this public demonstration is the *lay apostolate* (as advocated by the Catholic Church), which is how the church functions sixth-sevenths of the time. 'Walk worthily' has to do with being a diaconal, missional community, and it has to do with the life and conduct of the community and its understanding of 'vocation' as its defining center. Vocation is a central Christian concept, emphasized both in confessional and ecumenical traditions. It admonishes that we start every day by touching our head and say,

---

[23] John N. Collins, *Diakonia. Re-interpreting the Ancient Sources* (New York/Oxford: OUP 1990). See also Lutheran World Federation, *Diakonia in Context* (Geneva: Lutheran World Federation, 2009), 81.

[24] Darrell Guder (ed.), *Missional Church. A Vision for the Sending of the Church in North America* (Grand Rapids: Eerdmans, 1998), 163ff.

[25] Van Gelder, *Ministry of the Church*, 128.

[26] Darrell Guder, *Called to Witness. Doing Missional Theology* (Grand Rapids: Eerdmans, 2015), 129ff.

"I am baptized", then continue with Jesus' Easter announcement, "As my father sent me, so I send you." From here we enter into the world under the command, "You shall be my witnesses" – whether being prince or shoemaker.

United Through Action? Glimpses into the Evangelical Story from Eighteenth-Century Revival to Cape Town Commitment 2010

Rose Dowsett

From the Beginning...

Church history could, sadly, be read as the record of how professing Christians have fallen out with one another. From the early years of the Church, disagreements over doctrine and praxis bubbled up, exacerbated by personality conflicts. Within decades of Christ's death and resurrection, arguments swirled over the nature of Christ, the nature of the Trinity, which documents to affirm for inclusion in the canon, and how to organize the Church, locally and more widely. Who should be denounced as a heretic? How should disagreements be settled?[1]

The 16th-century Protestant Reformation accelerated the process of division, not only setting Protestant against Roman Catholic but also Baptist against Anglican, Calvinist against Lutheran, Presbyterian against Congregationalist.... Many of the same arguments that had haunted the earlier centuries were still raging. Issues of ecclesiology were constantly acrimonious: how should the Church be organized? How should the sacraments be administered (and how many were there anyway)? Where did final authority lie? What should be the relationship between Church and State?

The Lord had prayed that his followers should be 'one as I and my Father are one'.[2] The track record showed how painfully far short of that the Church had fallen.

---

[1] Some of the New Testament Epistles, e.g. 1 Corinthians, indicate disagreements from very early on; for further information from early years/centuries, see J Stevenson, ed., *Creeds, Councils and Controversies* (London: SPCK, 1966), or a general church history such as Tim Dowley, Organising Editor, *Lion Handbook: The History of Christianity* (Oxford: Lion Publishing, 1977), which also expands on much of the early part of this essay.

[2] John 17:11.

The Eighteenth-Century Revival in Britain, and its Consequences

One constant conundrum for almost all streams of the Church was that so many people who were theoretically members through baptism continued to behave in ways completely incompatible with their supposed faith. Just as the Lord had insisted that circumcision was no guarantee of acceptance by God, so baptism did not always lead to genuine spiritual life. From time to time, renewal movements challenged nominalism and urged a deeper and more authentic discipleship.

The 18th-century Evangelical Revival was one such renewal movement. In Britain it was largely the fruit of the ministry of brothers John and Charles Wesley, and of George Whitefield. The intention was not to create a new denomination but to breathe new life into Anglicanism in particular, and especially to reach out to those marginalized from the Church as a result of the social upheavals associated with the emerging industrial revolution – a renewal movement rather than a schism. An immediate result of the Wesleys' ministry in particular was that groups awakened to faith, but still regarded with suspicion by the established churches, became literate in order to study the Bible for themselves, lived more healthily as they broke with alcohol, collected funds to support those unable to work through sickness or injury or old age, and cared for widows and orphans. Many of those things were supposed to happen through the established churches, but rarely reached the newly urban or industrialized poor. Further, what came to be known as Methodism, when the renewal movement was resisted by much of the national church in particular, mobilized all its church members to serve, empowered women as well as men to take responsibility in church and community, and reduced the distance between the leaders and those led. Evangelism, proclamation and service were firmly tied together, and all members encouraged to engage fully in them all.

By the start of the 19th century, the impact of the Revival had spread across denominational divides, and 'Evangelicals' within a variety of denominations began to recognize that there were significant areas where they could serve together while still retaining distinctive convictions about how the Church should be structured, and even about how the sacraments should be administered. It was not that ecclesiology was no longer important, but that Christians could respect one another's differences in understanding what they believed the Bible to be teaching in some areas and yet focus on what could be done together, inside and beyond the structures of the denominations. The church was seen as the body of all those with deep personal faith in the Lord Jesus, rather than as tied to any particular ecclesiastical structure. It transcended denominations. This has been the evangelical story ever since.

In particular, it was recognized that there were many instances where joint action could achieve what no single denomination or local church was either able or willing to commit to, or where duplication would be just foolish. Like-minded people, with or without the support of their congregation, could band together – and pray together, act together – for specific purposes, and still in the name of Christ. So, among the earliest shared endeavors were Bible Societies to produce Scriptures and disseminate them, initially in English (or another language where evangelicals in other language contexts shared the same vision). Later, Bible Societies served those engaged in Bible translation as the missionary movement expanded to new corners of the world. There were numerous initiatives to care for the poor, to encourage literacy, to fight the scourges of prostitution or alcoholism, and many more. There were big issues of justice, with evangelicals doggedly working together to abolish British involvement in the iniquitous slave trade, and a little later in the equally iniquitous opium trade, which was causing such terrible suffering in China in particular. All these actions, British evangelicals believed, were part and parcel of the gospel, and without them neither the church nor its message had real credibility. It was a short step from here for the emergence of interdenominational missionary societies and faith missions, which became increasingly significant in taking the gospel of Jesus Christ far beyond its traditional heartlands.

British English does not use the term '*diakonia*' (although many churches have 'deacons' as an office within their structures), but what evangelicals were practicing together was indeed the service embodied in the term. Proclamation and loving service must go hand in hand for the gospel to be authentic.[3]

The Formation of the Evangelical Alliance Movement, 1846

In 1846, a group of evangelicals from a number of different denominations, and from several countries, met together and formed the Evangelical Alliance.[4] It was hoped that from inception it would be what later became the World Evangelical Alliance, but the American delegation found it impossible at that time to tie themselves to a proposed clause that would exclude slave holders. They argued that there were committed evangelical believers in America on both sides of that debate, and they were not willing to alienate those in the southern states who still had slaves working on their plantations, even though other American Christians were deeply opposed to the practice. It was an indication of just how seriously many evangelicals, not just in Europe, regarded the issue as a fundamental one of justice and gospel righteousness, as with

[3] For further reading, see John Wolffe, ed., *Evangelical Faith and Public Zeal: Evangelicals and Society in Britain 1780-1980* (London: SPCK, 1995).

[4] For the story of the Evangelical Alliance, see Ian Randall & David Hilborn, *One Body in Christ: The History and Significance of the Evangelical Alliance* (Carlisle: EA & Paternoster Press, 2001); for the wider World Evangelical Alliance story, see Brian Stiller, Todd Johnson, Karen Stiller, Mark Hutchinson, *Evangelicals Around the World* (Nashville: Nelson, 2015); or David Bebbington & Mark Noll (eds.), *A History of Evangelicalism: Vols 1-5* (Nottingham: IVP, 2005ff).

great regret the gathering decided that it was not possible at that juncture to establish a thoroughly international Alliance.

But a number of national Alliances were established and would much later become the World Evangelical Alliance (formally established in 1951). They worked together wherever possible, even praying for one another in times of war when their respective nations were enemies, and resuming joint initiatives as soon as possible afterward. They shared a common basis of faith, and common beliefs about the mission of God's people. In this, the movement was strongly confessional, even if not operating on quite the same confessional grounds used by each denomination separately.

It is important to understand this story as the background against which the Lausanne Movement emerged. The Lausanne Covenant, the Manila Manifesto and the Cape Town Commitment are all strong confessional statements, but also documents where historic biblical doctrine is married to practical application, as it is, for instance, in the New Testament Epistles. Creed and action come together. Within the Lausanne Movement, as within the World Evangelical Alliance, the emphasis is on that which unites rather than on that which divides, and on *doing*, not just *intellectually believing*. This enables the national Evangelical Alliances to bring together many local churches and numerous agencies so that they can work together both locally and also further afield, and for the World Evangelical Alliance to do that on a global scale. It enables the Lausanne Movement, whose concern has always been to bring the whole gospel to the whole world, with a strong emphasis on cross-cultural mission, to provide the context for fostering international partnerships and shared action, especially in those communities so far largely or wholly marginalized from Christian faith.

Mark Knoll, in his book, *The Rise of Evangelicalism*, suggests:[5]

> 'Many efforts have been made to summarize these convictions and attitudes. One of the most effective is offered by David Bebbington, who has identified four key ingredients of evangelicalism:
>
> - conversion, or 'the belief that lives need to be changed';
> - the Bible, or 'the belief that all spiritual truth is to be found in its pages';
> - activism, or the dedication of all believers, including laypeople, to lives of service for God, especially as manifest in evangelism (spreading the good news) and mission (taking the gospel to other societies);
> - crucicentrism, or the conviction that Christ's death was the crucial matter in providing atonement for sin (that is, providing reconciliation between a holy God and sinful humans).'

---

[5] *The Rise of Evangelicalism* (Leicester: Apollos/IVP, 2004), 16.

Both the World Evangelical Alliance and the Lausanne Movement have these beliefs and convictions at their core. It is these that make it possible for Christians who share them, from many denominations and from all over the world, to work together.

Local and Global: Some Examples from the World Evangelical Alliance

The United Kingdom Evangelical Alliance, today (2018) itself a union of movements in the four nations, brings together local churches, some complete denominations, a wide range of agencies and some networks, as well as individuals, within its membership. That basic pattern is replicated in national Alliances in many countries. The EA-UK supports its members in a host of ways: through literature, events, strengthening networks, advocacy, engagement with Parliament and the media, enabling clear voices and action in the public square, and more. In a context where British culture is increasingly dominated by the secular humanist narrative, this brings encouragement, advice and help in fulfilling the whole mission of the church, in the whole of society.

While faithfully undergirded by commitment to biblical foundations as expressed in the statement of faith to which all members subscribe, working it out in practice is crucial, whether in terms of proclamation, apologetics, or local and national action. Much of the social welfare operating in the UK, especially among the poor, the lonely and the vulnerable, comes from the churches (though secularist lobbies would prefer to ignore or deny this), with evangelicals deeply involved. It is impossible to compute accurately the aggregate time and money supplied by local congregations and volunteers as a direct outworking of their faith, and committed Christians are also disproportionately represented in the caring and service professions. This story could be replicated in numerous countries around the world, with national evangelical alliances often being significant catalysts.

It was this pattern of conviction and application that led, for instance, in 1968 to the formation of The Evangelical Alliance Relief Fund. Now called Tearfund, and legally separate from the EA-UK, but still with largely overlapping constituencies, this organization is now one of the largest charities in the UK, serving the poor and needy in some 50 countries, and working through churches and agencies on the ground. In the financial year 2016/17, Tearfund spent £26.4 million on disaster relief, £22.3 million in developing communities, £7.8 million envisioning churches, and £5.4 million in influencing policy change. This money is raised by British evangelicals, sharing the love of God with a hurting world. That is *diakonia* in action. Tearfund's conviction is that 'Together we can change the world'.

At a global level, the World Evangelical Alliance has a number of Commissions with specific briefs, for instance, the Theology Commission and the Mission Commission, but also several commissions and networks working very directly to alleviate human suffering. Among the latter are the Religious

Liberty Commission, Advocates for the Persecuted Church, Global Human Trafficking Network, Creation Care Network, and the Refugees Network. All of these, and more besides, seek to multiply effectiveness through shared action, and draw together Christians from many parts of the global church. The WEA demonstrates that it is possible to have extensive ethnic, cultural and denominational/ecclesiastical diversity within core shared beliefs and convictions. The commissions and networks are all fully international, and over the years have all made significant contributions to the cause of the gospel and the demonstration of the love of God. They strengthen friendships across the world, and foster the kind of unity for which the Lord Jesus prayed.

The Lausanne Story

In the summer of 1974, 2,700 evangelical leaders met in Lausanne, Switzerland, for a consultation that was the vision of Dr Billy Graham, the American evangelist, and the Rev Dr John Stott, Rector of All Souls Church, London. Friends since 1954, when Billy Graham conducted his first British campaign in London, both Graham and Stott were passionate evangelists with a heart for the whole world, and with extensive networks of Christian leader friends in many countries. Graham's campaign in several continents drew Christians together, and cemented many interdenominational relationships. Stott, in addition to pastoring his central London international congregation, was in great demand as a speaker at university student missions associated with the International Fellowship of Evangelical Students, again in many countries. Both men were therefore well adapted to working interdenominationally as well as internationally, and were fully convinced of the gains through united action. But each was also convinced that united action must be built on firm biblical foundations. Truth is crucial.

That first Lausanne gathering gave birth to the Movement that continues today. There have been three major Congresses – Lausanne 1974, Manila 1989 and Cape Town 2010 – and many smaller consultations in between. Each Congress has produced a significant statement: *The Lausanne Covenant*, *The Manila Manifesto*, *The Cape Town Commitment*[6]; these each crystallize both doctrinal contours and the agreed outworking flowing from them, and have influenced evangelical praxis over the decades. As with the World Evangelical Alliance, Lausanne has developed a number of networks and working groups, bringing together people serving in, and focused on, specific areas of the Church's overall mission. Lausanne does not have an official membership system, and comprises almost entirely agencies and individuals rather than local congregations or denominations. This should not be taken to mean that

[6] These documents may all be found on the Lausanne website, www.lausanne.org; they are available in many languages; see also JEM Cameron, ed., *The Lausanne Legacy: Landmarks in Global Mission* (Peabody, Mass.: Hendrickson, 2016).

Lausanne is uninterested in ecclesiology or is somehow downgrading the importance of the Church. On the contrary, each Congress statement has extensive reference to the nature and role of the Church.

The Lausanne Movement, like the WEA, builds *relationships*, *trust*, and *friendship*. These are vital for developing co-operative action and service. It is, of course, possible to produce documents that are not acted upon, but the Lausanne story has been happily different; Michael Oh, current Executive Director of Lausanne, writes 'The Second Lausanne Congress on World Evangelization, from which the Manila Manifesto issued, was to bear fruit in some 300 new mission networks and initiatives, many in the global south.'[7] Because of the commitment of Lausanne since 1974 to what has come to be called 'integral mission' or 'holistic mission', especially strongly embraced in the global south, gospel proclamation and gospel service are most often held together.

How do Covenant, Manifesto and Commitment Express This?

At the first Lausanne Congress, there were some evangelicals who were uneasy about the emphasis on holistic/integral mission. Some believed that the Lord would be returning very soon, and that the turbulent state of the world presaged this; the most urgent thing for Christians to do, they said, was to tell the story of Jesus to as many people as possible in the shortest time possible, and focus all resources on that. Others again, especially those for whom the separation of church and state was very important, saw mission as being restricted to proclamation, with many areas of service being the responsibility of the state, not of the church; church history, of course, including evangelical history, was firmly against such a view, as from the very beginning of the church after Pentecost, Christians were reaching out in loving service alongside bold teaching about Jesus.

However, the Covenant makes it very clear that we cannot separate evangelism from social action and service, nor careful biblical theology from consequent action, without distorting the gospel, and with very few exceptions the delegates chose to affirm it. It is true that for some this was a moment of recovery of something they had temporarily lost sight of, during some of the difficult years of reaction against theological liberalism, and the loss of a robust theology of integral mission. For some it seemed as if that might be more a thinly veneered humanism rather than Christian faith. The pendulum had swung too far, and especially with the help of some Latin American evangelicals like Rene Padilla and Samuel Escobar, they recovered what had been wrongly mislaid. Proclamation and service must go together. That, of course must work in both directions: service without proclamation and explanation is not complete mission, either.

---

[7] Cameron, *Legacy*, 174.

By the time of the second Congress in 1989 in Manila, many churches and agencies had been re-energized by the Covenant, and evangelicals were growing numerically especially in Africa, parts of Asia, and in Latin America. For Christians in these regions, with the great majority of the world's poor and marginalized in their midst, it was unthinkable that one could simply 'talk the gospel' without loving service of those around them. In the summary form of the 21 affirmations,[8] we find the following:

> 8. We affirm that we must demonstrate God's love visibly by caring for those who are deprived of justice, dignity, food and shelter.
>
> 9. We affirm that the proclamation of God's Kingdom of justice and peace demands the denunciation of all injustice and oppression, both personal and structural; we will not shrink from this prophetic witness.
>
> 16. We affirm that every Christian congregation must turn itself outward to its local community in evangelistic witness and compassionate service.
>
> 17. We affirm the urgent need for churches, mission agencies and other Christian organizations to co-operate in evangelism and social action, repudiating competition and avoiding duplication.

The Cape Town Commitment, encapsulating the extensive discussion both before and following the third Lausanne Congress, also brings together thoughtful, profound theological foundations and a wide range of out-workings – how that theology must inform every dimension of life. This includes concern for unity between believers being a missional imperative: just as divisions discredit the church in the eyes of the world, so loving relationships within God's family, across the divides of ethnicity, economic status, gender, and all the other things that fragment our world, are a powerful embodiment of gospel reconciliation. The Congress brought together some 4,200 evangelical leaders from 198 countries:[9] there can be few gatherings that achieve that diversity – and for those who were there, the experience of friendship, respect and co-operation was impossible to miss. To many delegates, the closing service of Holy Communion seemed like a foretaste of heaven: a multi-racial community of worshipping men and women, themselves fully committed both to God himself and to being witnesses in every nook and cranny of his world, agents of his love and grace.[10]

The *Commitment* is presented in two parts: first *The Confession of Faith*, and second *The Call to Action*. It is evangelical conviction that these belong absolutely together. Without strong biblical foundations, our actions will be vulnerable to every wind of fashion. Without robust consequent action, our

---

[8] Cameron, *Legacy*, 67-8.

[9] Cameron, *Legacy*, 102.

[10] The full text of the liturgy used, and of the final address, can be found in Cameron, *Legacy*, 162-172, 177-195.

convictions will remain theoretical concepts only. Thousands of people poured in their concerns before and during the Congress, and the resultant document can fairly be said to be as representative of contemporary evangelicalism as any document could be. It is difficult to assess how many of the numerous actions to be addressed have actually been tackled so far, though anecdotally it seems co-operative efforts have been birthed in many parts of the world. Certainly, to this author's knowledge, many mission agencies, networks and groups of churches have established new co-operative group actions to address issues in fresh and more effective ways. There is in many circles renewed impetus to find ways of working together rather than independently or competitively, although at the same time some parts of the evangelical spectrum have fragmented rather than moved closer together.

The Lausanne Movement does not have the kind of permanent structure that makes it easy to track exactly what its practical impact has been or is. It is after all a movement, not an organization in the usually accepted sense of that word, though it regularly brings together particular groups in conferences (such as younger leaders), and through its website, for instance the conference for younger leaders held in 2017. But its documents from the three Congresses, plus publications from a number of smaller consultations, remain influential, and have both inspired and informed many Christian communities in numerous countries. It has fostered relationships and co-operation and the resultant action and service that flow from that.

...And Finally

It would be untrue to claim that evangelicals are all united, or always united: they are not. But national Evangelical Alliances, the World Evangelical Alliance and the Lausanne Movement all bring huge numbers of Christians together in a large range of ways, from united prayer, local churches (and individuals and agencies) working together for outreach and service to their community, to working for social change and the welfare of others, cross-cultural mission, and much more. In that sense, there is interdenominational unity that is precious – and practical. In broad terms there is doctrinal consensus, with most disagreements regarded as of secondary importance, and, again in general terms, the willingness to respect differences while focusing on the many things that unite us.

Tracing the story from the 18th-century Evangelical Revival to the present day, it is clear that the norm has been for evangelism and service to be intertwined, despite moments of aberration when they sometimes drifted apart. 'Unity through action?' Yes, but also unity through shared convictions as to what the gospel is, what God asks his people to be and do, and our calling to be his witnesses by speech, life and character, wherever he places us. So, unity through action, but also unity through foundations of faith and belief. That is the will of God. May we be faithful to God as representatives of his Kingdom.

The Church as a Space for Recognition

Kari Karsrud Korslien

Introduction

The purpose of this chapter is to create reflection on *diakonia* and the opportunity to develop recognition between people in congregations, as well as to develop the church as a space for recognition to happen. 'Space' indicates the possibilities for recognition in congregations. However, in this chapter, I also refer to 'space' as the concrete place where people gather and create fellowship. The Church consists of local fellowships that represent a large arena for recognition. Recognition appears to be one of the core elements in describing the diaconal church. I define recognition as the action or process of recognizing or being recognized. Recognition can also be understood as an act of seeing someone or something in a new perspective. Recognizing, distinguishing or consolidating and strengthening someone are core elements in the content of recognition.[1] There are many participants in the discussion concerning recognition as theory. Axel Honneth has contributed to this discussion by focusing on love, rights and solidarity, and Nancy Fraser has contributed by focusing on recognition, participation and redistribution. This chapter is not primarily concerned with the theoretical discussion, but the purpose is to create reflection on *diakonia* and the opportunity to develop recognition between people in congregations. First, we should admit that *diakonia* can be realized in many ways. Second, it is also necessary to argue that being a church and being a diaconal church may look different from place to place even though they are built on the same core elements. Third, recognition is important for the quality of the church. This chapter investigates the connection between *diakonia* and recognition and combines the findings with elements of traditional and contextual theology.

Seven Signs of the Church

In this reflection we need to create an understanding of what we see as the church. In what ways is church a reality? Martin Luther argues that there are

---

[1] Anne-Lise Schibbye, *Relasjoner: et dialektisk perspektiv på eksistensiell og psykodynamisk psykoterapi* (Oslo: Universitetsforlaget, 2009), 256–261.

seven signs for being a church.[2] The church is the place where the gospel about Jesus is proclaimed. It is based on relations and therefore the church is a part of a broader society (1). In church both baptism (2) and the Holy Communion (3) are practiced. People can be forgiven (4) and start a new life. Further, the church has ministries to serve the people (5). We share experiences when people are gathered in worship and prayer (6). The sign of the theology of the cross (7) is not only a sign of being a church but also a sign of being a diaconal church. The church recognizes suffering, people's pain and misery. As Christians, we will always have a vocation to serve among people in need. But as such, we realize that we are people in need. Often, we are so vulnerable because we also may forget how to serve and practice *diakonia* in our life together, and also because we are dependent on each other, with our talents and shortcomings. Our deepest need is that we all share the need of God's salvation and recognition. But where there is forgiveness of sins, Luther explains, there are also life and salvation now in this present moment.[3] In this way, the church is special as a space for recognition, because we already are recognized by God. We are recognized and loved just the way we are.

Challenges

We have different functions as the body of Christ. The whole community therefore needs to learn the language of recognition. It can be explained like this: congregations are learning communities. Everyone has their own experiences. In a diaconal church, sharing is a part of the culture. And while sharing, we develop common understanding. As we know, recognition is also a question of respect for diversity. The learning community may disagree, but as a diaconal church, we should recognize our different talents and motivate each other to use our different gifts. When we realize our shortcomings, we also need to recognize our mistakes and help to understand ourselves as human and vulnerable beings. The body metaphor is often interpreted as the perfect body and does not reflect our disagreements and vulnerability. But suffering and needs are a part of human life. Weakness should therefore be recognized, even while being aware of the strength and power we share in our fellowship. We must be able to recognize the church as both vulnerable and in a position of strength. In addition, 'Diaconal action must be able to interpret reality and processes of social change in a holistic manner.'[4] That is a huge challenge.

---

[2] W. Robert Godfray (2016): https://www.ligonier.org/blog/martin-luthers-7-characteristics-church/.

[3] Paul Althaus, *The Theology of Martin Luther* (Philadelphia: Fortress Press, 1970), 404.

[4] *Diakonia in Context*, 87.

Practice

Instead of building bridges between different points of view, it seems to be a lot easier to disagree with some sort of diaconal practice. The discussions often turn into right or wrong, innovative or old fashioned, equal or hierarchical. For instance, in Norway, I often hear the view that to prepare and serve coffee and work among elderly people is old fashioned. However, it depends. If people nowadays have an emptiness in the human heart and they miss core elements of human happiness – as faith, family, community – we need to resolve these deeper social, cultural, religious and psychological problems. We should try to rediscover a new meaning among people who take part in local communities and congregations for different reasons. The activity in church kitchen and in the church hall do both have possibilities for mutual recognition and possibilities to create contact and meaningful relationship.

Struggle for Recognition: Two Examples

These two examples are from Germany. The churches in Germany failed during the Second World War. Churches were vulnerable because the war had transformed them in many ways, and they partly failed to stand up against the regime's dehumanizing ideology. The German pastor Dietrich Bonhoeffer held Jesus to be the ultimate ideal for Christians at this time when the church failed in so many ways. In 1931, Dietrich Bonhoeffer became the vicar of the Protestant Zionskirche in Berlin Mitte, at the age of 25. He was an outspoken critic of Nazism in his parish, being driven by faith and his sense of justice. He was also a part of the anti-Nazi Protestant 'Confessing Church'. He was put in jail, and later, he was hanged, during the last days of the war (April 9, 1945). His letters from prison and his sermons in Zionskirche encouraged people to fight together with others of good will for the benefit of their fellow human beings. To fight for humanity was a way of true resistance for Bonhoeffer. He found strength in community with other believers, but it was risky to know whom to trust. He kept the faith in Jesus as the greatest and most important inspiration of faith and life. He found the answers to the doubt that arose in the wartime situation in people who cared for each other and who helped each other in difficult times, recognizing that the world is hard to understand, that war hurts, but that we can still be fellow human beings who help and support each other.

Some years ago (in 2014), I visited Zionskirche, where Dietrich Bonhoeffer was a pastor. The church still had war marks from attacks. It was dilapidated, and the paint had fallen off the walls. I was disappointed that they did not care more for this place. Why, I asked myself? From the perspective of recognition, I had to look once more. In the church, they had an exhibition, they had music, there were people praying, and they invited people to church on Sundays and during the week. Young people came and reflected together on different subjects concerning their faith and everyday life. The church had developed the tradition of creating meaning further, into the present context.

At the same time, they had not wiped out their own story. This was, in my opinion, a kind of a diaconal church. They recognized:

- the value of inviting people to an open church.
- a unity in diversity through invitations to various events.
- peoples' need of creating meaning by bringing people together.
- the practice of trust, involvement and dialogue.
- the vulnerable story of the church's past and present.

These key points can be addressed as technical matters. But the purpose of my example is to show that recognition affects practice in many ways. Recognition has both normative and psychological dimensions, and in *diakonia* recognition has practical challenges that indicate questions about engagement, influence and participation. As a part of their diaconal practice they act as one diverse community.

The other example is from the neighborhood near to Zionskirche. There was and still is another church, Kaiser Wilhelm Gedächtniskirche, which was built in 1891. The church was destroyed during the Second World War and rebuilt between 1959 and 1961. In the ruin a new church was built and one of the towers from the old church was included as part of the new one. Here there is both a memory hall and a nice blue chapel. The life in the new congregation seems to me to be both cultural and diaconal. When I visited the church in 2014 it had become an important historical tourist spot, where people could take part in short ceremonies, and people dropping in could light candles in the chapel and listen to concerts. But the congregation also tried to reach out to homeless people in the city of Berlin. In this congregation they recognized the value of inviting people to an open church, they were open-minded and they kept open doors to the city. They offered a varied program and it seemed to be interesting for a lot of tourists. They also recognized poor people in the city as a group they wanted to bring together in meaningful gatherings. However, the congregation struggled to recognize itself as one congregation in action; for example, the poor people and the tourists used different doors to enter the church. The fellowship had differences that divided them more than it created an inclusive fellowship. Common involvement and open dialogue seemed to be difficult to build at the time I visited.

In this case the congregation recognized the vulnerable story of the war. In many ways, the place was a memorial, more than fellowship as in a congregation. They struggled to recognize and include the vulnerable stories of people as a part of being a congregation. They succeeded more when they went out on the streets and combined care for others with solidarity work. They recognized both the value of inviting people to an open church, and a unity in diversity through invitations to various events. They recognized people's need of creating meaning by bringing people together, and recognized the practice of involvement and dialogue. Furthermore, they recognized the vulnerable story of the past and present, but they struggled to bring the different people together. They struggled because the combination of being both a memorial place and a congregation seemed to be too hard. It seems they had some challenges in reaching out in a diaconal way to the poor at the same place where the affluent tourists were looking for cultural activities. Sharing in this case was challenging. They tried to bring people in through different doors, and keep them apart, but still it seemed to me that it created more of a wall between people than fellowship. It also reminded me of the phenomenon of a 'poor door' as a separate entrance for people in a multi-unit housing development for those living in less expensive apartments. The local news site West Side Rag coined the term 'poor door' in August 2013.[5] It was used to describe a new development on the Upper West Side of Manhattan that had separate entrances. People from the less expensive apartments had no right to use the main entrance and the facilities such as "gyms, spas, elevators, rooftop gardens, storage areas, and playrooms".

Things may have changed at Kaiser Wilhelm Gedächtniskirche, but the practice lacked a deeper reflection on engagement, influence and participation. This part of recognition is crucial to a diaconal church. This example can show us some dilemmas in the development of recognition. People of goodwill in congregations need to involve others and talk together about what recognition means to them.

Theology and Consequences

The two examples from Germany revealed some important challenges, and we also briefly looked into Luther's description of the church. In everyday practice, churches in different present-day contexts have large challenges and some are rather new. The change from being a majority church to being a minority church is one such challenge faced in many European contexts. The situation is different around the world. In Africa, and for the churches in Latin America and perhaps Oceania, Christians may make up the majority of the population. However, Christians are and will now continue to be in the minority in parts of Asia, Europe, North America, New Zealand and Australia. Often, we experience that churches have turned into places of great diversity, and more often than before it is a poor church.[6] Sometimes people in churches are persecuted, and they struggle for reaching out in a relevant way to people and especially young people.

The Catholic theologian Stephan Bevans outlines the new situation of the church in the 21st-century in many places as diverse, global, diaspora, multicultural, persecuted and poor. He describes contextual theology as a

---

[5] www.westsiderag.com.

[6] Stephen B Bevans, *Contextual Theology for the Twenty-First Century* (Cambridge: James Clark & Co 2012).

mutually critical dialogue between the present (personal, communal, culture, location, change) and the past (scripture and tradition). He talks about new agendas, methods, voices and dialogue that can be helpful in renewing being a church of today. In the book *Liberating Diakonia*, Kjell Nordstokke writes about renewing diaconal practice where new methods help to identify mechanisms of inclusion, to point at possible opportunities of diaconal practice, and to develop methods that express the new role, new authority, new language and a new logic for *diakonia.*[7] In the book *Diakonia as Christian Social Practice – an Introduction* (2014), I wrote about *diakonia* as action, and I wrote that transforming *diakonia* to action is an ongoing process. In my opinion the theological points of view are not real before they are put into action. In a way, this is to 'walk the diaconal talk'. When contextual theology focuses on the importance of the context, it is the understanding of people's situation and their own questions in life that matter. But the church has, at the same time, some themes that they offer people. It is important to sustain the dialogue between people and the understanding of what is going on in the diverse local contexts because there are continuous changes and the church must learn to tune in to people. Therefore, there is also urgency for the church as a community to reflect on their own interests for engagement, influence and participation. As a diaconal church, we should always seek to develop our competence and practice, evaluate whether this really is a renewed *diakonia* where people are taking part and are able to share each other's life-worlds.[8] That includes a reflection on the quality of our own engagement in people's life.

Perspectives and Methods

In *Diakonia as Christian Social Practice – an Introduction* (2014), I explain how to meet each other as subjects. It means to meet the other as a fellow-subject who concerns me as one on an equal footing with myself, in the things we are both concerned with in our common world. The Norwegian philosopher Hans Skjervheim warned us of the need to understand intersubjectivity 'as perfect mutual understanding, such as we might imagine to be realized among heavenly philosophers. 'Lack of understanding' is as much a modus of intersubjectivity as 'perfect understanding'."[9] Furthermore, he explains that only a being that potentially can understand something can lack understanding of it. In his famous essay *Participation and Spectator*, he states that we cannot

[7] Kjell Nordstokke, *Liberating Diakonia* (Trondheim: Tapir Akademisk Forlag, 2011).

[8] Kari Karsrud Korslien, "*Diakonia* as action" in Stephanie Dietrich, Knud Jørgensen, Kari Karsrud Korslien & Kjell Nordstokke, *Diakonia as Christian Social Practice – an Introduction* (Oxford: Regnum 2014), 210-211.

[9] Hans Skjervheim, *Selected Essays* (University of Bergen: Department of philosophy, 1996).

choose to be engaged; since we happen to be in the world, we are all engaged in something or other. Engagement is a fundamental structure of human life, but he adds that we can choose what to be engaged in. In this case, in building a diaconal church, it is not the point to share the same opinions, but rather to get involved, creating broader understanding. Recognition and engagement are connected.

Some key points can help to improve the opportunities for better understanding in these contextual situations. Let us try to work out some possible elements in a diaconal practice that include the inductive diaconal 'see, reflect and act' method.[10] Is there an active way of seeing and acting that reflects recognition as a core element in the diaconal church? The Finnish author Tove Jansson (1914-2001) wrote in tales from Moomin Valley about '*The invisible child*' (1962) and showed us how the mother in Moomin Valley, through her kind understanding and way of seeing, opened a door for a hidden child to become herself. The invisible child had been criticized for so long that she was invisible and the cure was to spend time recognizing her and to bring hope. The time you and your colleagues spend with people locally provides opportunities to understand communication that is not loud and clear and which is, in a way, invisible. What kind of hints and invitations do you get in conversations with people? Do you and your congregation react on the hints and invitations? Invitations can be more formal than hints. They can, if they are explored, be an introduction to dialogue and cooperation inside and outside the church. This is a kind of knowledge that is possible to develop using the CABLE approach.[11]

Asking and listening are important elements in developing an atmosphere of trust and recognition. Coffee time may offer possibilities for building trust. To be able to bear each other's burdens depends on trust and recognition (Gal 6: 2). Often when stories about misrecognition are told, people feel vulnerable and hurt. We need to develop a tolerance for listening and supporting the person who shares their personal story. If people in the congregation wish to be helpful, being part of a healing act in such situations, they must listen, be patient, and be open to the other's life and reality. It is important to be patient, listen to the whole story and confirm it when possible without jumping to the end, and start reflecting before the story is finished. Our recognition is not important as such, but a way of living our life in Christ is through strengthening the person's own ability of coping with difficult situations and taking part in the community.

---

[10] Lutheran World Federation, *Diakonia in context, Transformation, Reconciliation, Empowerment* (Geneva: Lutheran World Federation 2009), 59.

[11] CABLE approach means Community Action Based Learning for Empowerment. Addy, Tony, 'New approaches to community based work, social service and Diaconia Challenges from the CABLE approach' in '*Diaconia, Journal for the Study of Christian Social Practice*', Göttingen, Vandenhoeck & Ruprecht, Vol. 4, Issue 2, 2013.

When people talk about what they really did to cope within specific situations, recognition and change is possible. To tell their story may also open for a change when life inevitably must go on. Listening, telling and sharing are ways of learning our strengths and planning for our future life. The stories may be vulnerable, but from the theological tradition we learn that God will be together with us, He loves us forever and needs us in His mission for the world.

In a way, we practice active listening in a safe atmosphere, where understanding, acceptance and tolerance are developed. Practicing recognition is a way of acting, and a way of living. On the theological level, Jesus creates a way to the loving and forgiving God. This is an ultimate kind of recognition. We are possible members of God's mission. On the theoretical level, we know about the importance of recognition, and on the practical level, it is in action when we all create a real space for recognition among people.

In the diaconal church, we work for freedom and a connection between people. Recognition should therefore be a help to self-help, strengthened by the congregation and fellowship among people in the local community and in church. To confirm means to give authority to people's need for recognition. A challenge in the diaconal church is to develop a learning community where we all try to recognize each other.

The congregational life should reflect the complexity of modern life. As a diaconal church we should also be a home for the homeless (concretely and metaphorically). This is a challenge for dialogue. Some people do not know what to do in church. Many feel they do not fit in, because they do not have the skills to read the social codes. People in such situations are not comfortable in these unfamiliar situations. How could we manage to help in such situations? In *diakonia,* we often talk about convivial life, but as majority members of the church, we do not have knowledge about being unfamiliar. We need to develop dialogues with the members. Even though doors may be wide open, people are passing. The church tries to invite others through 'doors for the poor'. But the majority don't care or understand. Small caring projects can be developed by trying to let more people come in. In any case, the church cannot exist without the people and the church has one door, that is Jesus Christ. As St. Augustine wrote: 'Ecclesia verbo Dei generatur, alitur, nutritur, roboratur'. The dialogue indicates that the basic approach is to ask people what they expect from the church. When people are not usually seen as a resource, but more like a target group, we need to talk with people about how we could make it more trustful to be together in church activities. Then our fellowship could be a space for growth for all of us. The interest for local communities and everyday life should be in focus. In my opinion the church should be more aware that the local congregation could be a common space for people to develop spiritual and social skills.

But recognition is not just an individual kind of recognition. It is also God's recognition of our world and us. Recognition is important, but not enough. Congregations also have a responsibility for the local community. Deacons, social workers and pastors should love their neighbors, but it is also necessary for us to love our neighborhood. The doors should therefore be used as a possibility to go out and see people outside the church, get into dialogue, listening and building trust and fellowshipping together. This vulnerable necessity is needed in every church. The context is important but flourishing as a Christian fellowship indicates one more relation: the relation to God, keeping close to the word of God. This is a kind of process that can transform communities, people and relations between us all.

Conclusion

In the vision of LWF we are 'Liberated by God's grace, a communion in Christ, living and working together for a just, peaceful, and reconciled world' (LWF strategy 2012-2017).[12] The report of the LWF youth pre-assembly 2017 inspires because they practice a kind of recognition through the working processes and they show how sharing stories is a way to see each other, reflect together and act in new ways. In addition, we have a responsibility to bring new voices into the dialogue. This is a challenge to churches and we need to develop our skills to talk with people about their challenges and listen to their experiences. And even more, let people talk on behalf of themselves. This song created by the young people may show us a way of developing recognition in the congregations through the love of God:

'Our communion needs'

Revive our church, its unified work
Let's build upon the existing church
Come together now.

We're created, we're created
Created in God's image, created in God's image
Where's the equality? We want the same rights
Equality right now.

Education, education
Not for sale, not for sale
It's our right to learn and excel.
Free education now.

Chorus:
To be fed by Gods love to change the world
Our communion needs equality, revival, education
Believing God is at our side.

---

[12] Lutheran World Federation, *Report of the LWF youth pre- assembly 2017* (Geneva: Lutheran World Federation 2017).

This little lyric shows us the ideas the youths at this assembly found interesting for what 'Our communion needs'. The revival of churches, equality and education are their priorities. In all these steps, there are possibilities to strengthen each other. Maybe we share a Bonhoeffer moment today? The same rights and the right to learn are also political struggles. Standing up for your neighbor and your neighborhood includes the prophetic voices where the rights-based sense of *diakonia* combines love and inclusive fellowship with Jesus as the Lord of faith and mercy. In this struggle, we may ask, as did Bonhoeffer, 'Who is Christ for us today?' Is the center for the Church still Christ or has it turned into something else? If Christ, then recognition is something holistic we share and which we are responsible to develop as a part of the past, at this moment and as a vision of hope and joy in the future.

Bibliography

Addy, Tony, 'New approaches to community based work, social service and Diaconia Challenges from the CABLE approach' in '*Diaconia, Journal for the Study of Christian Social Practice*', Göttingen, Vandenhoeck & Ruprecht, Vol. 4, Issue 2, 2013.

Althaus, Paul, *The Theology of Martin Luther*, Philadelphia: Fortress Press, 1970.

Bevans, Stephen B, *Contextual theology for the Twenty-First Century*, Cambridge: James Clark & Co. 2012.

Godfray, W. Robert, https://www.ligonier.org/blog/martin-luthers-7-characteristics-church/2016.

Jansson, Tove, Det usynlige barnet og andre fortellinger (*The Invisible Child and Other Stories*), 1963, Oslo: Aschehoug.

Korslien, Kari Karsrud, '*Diakonia* as action' in Stephanie Dietrich, Knud Jørgensen, Kari Karsrud Korslien & Kjell Nordstokke, *Diakonia as Christian Social Practice – an Introduction*, Oxford: Regnum, 2014.

Nordstokke, Kjell, *Liberating Diakonia*, Trondheim: Tapir Akademisk Forlag, 2011.

Lutheran World Federation, *Diakonia in Context, Transformation, Reconciliation, Empowerment*, Geneva: Lutheran World Federation 2009.

Lutheran World Federation, *Report of the LWF youth pre-assembly 2017*, Geneva: Lutheran World Federation 2017.

Lutheran World Federation, *Strategy 2012-2017*.

Schibbye, Anne-Lise, *Relasjoner: et dialektisk perspektiv på eksistensiell og psykodynamisk psykoterapi*, Oslo: Universitetsforlaget, 2009.

Skjervheim, Hans, *Selected Essays, In honour of Hans Skjervheim's 70th Birthday*, Bergen: Department of Philosophy, 1996.

Seeking Conviviality: A New Core Concept for the Diaconal Church

Tony Addy

Introduction

The fact that the concepts, understanding and practice of *diakonia* have changed according to context and confession encourages critical reflection on the central or core concept of *diakonia* in the present day. This is particularly necessary when we face rapid and often disruptive contextual change. The view one takes on this is necessarily situated and furthermore, different diaconal actors in the same context face related but varied challenges. These may be related to the need to rethink local or congregational *diakonia* in the face of new issues and demands or to address the growing influence of market-based thinking on service provision, social and health care, because in some countries *diakonia* takes the form of large-scale service provision in an increasingly competitive marketplace. Related challenges face *diakonia* in terms of models of and financing for 'development work', which affects the practice of the churches and church-related agencies. Nevertheless, *diakonia* as an essential aspect of the church has to be expressed first in local congregations and contexts and then on a wider level, structurally, organizationally and politically.

My starting point for rethinking the core concept for *diakonia* is rooted in my work in Central and Eastern Europe, where there is the issue of living together in diversity and in situations of disruptive change and ambiguity. Some of the conventional words in use seemed not to capture the main issues in a creative way.[1] These reflections were extended more widely because I have been involved long term in local *diakonia* in local, national and international work. In many European contexts there is an ongoing process of discussion about community or congregational *diakonia*. The focus, as in every case, is on the present-day challenges and pressing issues, but this led to the key underlying question, which again and again returns to the underlying issue of 'how can we live together?'. Hence in these processes the concept of 'conviviality', or better the process of 'seeking conviviality' became inspirational. This chapter provides an overview of the key issues and raises some of the implications of using 'seeking conviviality' as a central idea for

[1] For ten years I have been the Head of Education for interdiac – The International Academy for Diaconia and Christian Social Action – based in the Czech Republic, and more recently involved as a resource person in the process 'Seeking Conviviality – the re-formation of community *diakonia* in Europe' of the Lutheran World Federation.

motivating diaconal practice. 'Seeking conviviality' underpins a critique, provides a future orientation and proposes working methods. It is a 'work in progress' and invites collaboration.

Present-day Challenges to Diaconal Practice

In the process of reflection on models for local or community diaconal practice, and in discussions in different European and national groups concerned with local *diakonia*, participants identified a number of critical issues. These converge in their impact on people and localities and require a new vision and approach to *diakonia* and church, and society work. In this section, I will not aim to cover every issue that could be mentioned, but I will highlight five key developments in this convergence:

1. Challenges related to diversity and difference including the new salience of borders, which so easily divide people in different regions of Europe. A further issue is the flow of migrants and refugees, which has also increased in more recent years. Alongside this, the long-standing marginalization of minority groups continues to mark many contexts. The best-known example is the treatment of Roma minorities in several countries. These are critical issues for everyday life in Europe and are mentioned as the priority in many cases.

2. The problematic developments, in society, related to the generalized feeling that people have of being under threat. One symbol of the alarm this causes is the growth of a concern with border control and the restrictions on the free movement of people, not to mention the correlated hostility to uprooted people. In present-day Europe, we are also experiencing boundary disputes, which have led to civil conflict and militarization. Furthermore, new questions of identity are raised by rapid cultural changes and growing diversity, which have been labeled by some as 'super-diversity'. This refers not only to increasing migration flows but also to the fact that at the local level, there are many cross-cutting relationships between people from different backgrounds and that new relationship patterns emerge in society. Super-diversity also signals the fact that ethnic identity may not be the most important issue to focus on in analysis and practice.[2] Other approaches are needed that do not 'essentialise' one personal characteristic over others.

3. The growth of nationalist and populist parties is a consequence of people's experience that mainstream politics has lost much of its capacity to engage with their everyday problems. The rise of a new generation of leaders in 'traditional' political parties and other representative organizations such as trade unions that seem unable to connect with the life-world of people most negatively affected by growing poverty, inequality and the other perceived threats. Other developments that have had a similar impact include

[2] Fran Meissner & Steven Vertovec (eds.), *Comparing Super-Diversities* (Abingdon: Routledge, 2017).

dissatisfaction with progress after the system change in Eastern Europe and the growth of corruption among political leaders in some countries.

4. The reality that political leaders, while on the one hand extolling the virtues of liberalism and rightly addressing political issues of identity – of recognizing the 'subject' (for example, related to gender and sexual identity) – have at the same time been reversing re-distributional gains that marked the post-war settlement in Europe. Furthermore, in many European countries, there has been a growth in the detailed control of the everyday life of people who live on the margins of the economy or receive social benefits. This partly explains the 'disconnect' of many people from what is broadly called 'politics' and their distance from 'elites'.

5. The growth of pollution in many contexts and accelerating environmental catastrophes as well as the increasing risk of industrialized systems to, for example, the sustainable production of healthy food give rise to concerns that need to be addressed. A related issue is the rising volume of food waste at a time when people are going hungry.

These five phenomena lie behind the rapid rise of populist politics, which plays into people's anxiety and fears, but at the same time increases them. These developments push those of us who are concerned for the future of society and for a sustainable economy, embedded in society, to reflect not only on relevant analysis but also on relevant concepts for diaconal work grounded in local congregational life. There is a need for an approach that does not exacerbate the marginalization of people already under threat, but which rather actively connects with peoples' diverse life worlds, builds relationships of trust and supports an alternative political approach.

Conviviality – A Vision of Living Together

The relevance of 'conviviality' as a core concept for *diakonia* first appeared in critical discussions among local diaconal actors in Central and Eastern Europe concerning current developments and the position of the diaconal church.[3] The second forum for developing these discussions is the on-going European project of the European member churches of the Lutheran World Federation, 'Seeking Conviviality – Re-forming Community *Diakonia* in Europe', which entered the third phase in 2018. This process also brings together local diaconal actors from diverse European contexts.[4]

In these processes and in many other discussions, one key question coming from various corners is, as mentioned, 'How can we live together?' ('con-vivere'). This leads to the questions 'How can *diakonia* contribute to people

[3] Tony Addy, *Seeking Conviviality – The Art and Practice of Living Together* (Český Těšín, interdiac, 2017).

[4] See the website www.luthernworld.org for the reports on this process. The main reports are listed in the Bibliography to this chapter.

living a good life together?' and 'What kind of economic and social policies support living together?' The starting point is not therefore in 'service delivery' but rather life together. This does not, of course, deny the fact that appropriate and accessible social and health care services are needed. These services can contribute greatly to seeking conviviality! In practice, working out the diaconal concept of conviviality also has implications for diaconal organizations and services, as well as for the church itself! However, seeking conviviality is not a 'project' and nor is it mainly about professional practice, although it may be supported by both projects and by people working professionally as deacons or in other roles. It is a developing concept that informs and supports new practice in congregational life and *diakonia* (including organizational *diakonia* and the wider church). Conviviality is grounded in everyday life in church and society.

The present use of the concept in relation to diaconal practice can be illuminated in dialogue with three different but inter-related background meanings, which also developed in different historical contexts. Each sheds light on the ways in which conviviality can be developed as a concept related to *diakonia* and living together. In the processes mentioned above, participants have not been seeking to develop a normative concept but to use 'seeking conviviality' as a heuristic approach toward the development of a vision and of a practice to realize the vision. In the following paragraphs I will elaborate on these three different strands.

The word 'conviviality' has its roots in the language and context of Spanish history (convivencia). It relates to the period when, in the Iberian Peninsula, Moslems, Jews and Catholics lived together in relative peace for about 500 years. I say 'relative peace' because it is romantic to think that there was no conflict prior to the 'reconquest', but certainly there were periods in different regions, sometimes lasting for at least two centuries, where there was no fundamental conflict. The study of convivencia has been given impetus by the need to understand how different religious, ethnic and cultural groups come to live peacefully together.[5] The word is also used in many Spanish-speaking contexts and is mobilized in a number of discussions about everyday life in the present day in European cities.[6]

The second use of the word conviviality refers to the sociable pleasure of people coming together and enjoying conversation and discussion in a relaxed manner, not under any constraints, for example by sharing a meal. Conviviality therefore relates to friendly dealings and also to relationships unconstrained by

---

[5] For example, the Max Planck Institute for European Legal History and the Max Planck Institute for Social Anthropology are researching the understanding of 'convivenicia' historically and in relation to present-day contexts and issues. See www.rg.mpg.de/research/convivencia and www.eth.mpg.de/4215941/convivencia for details of the projects.

[6] For example, Paul Gilroy, *Postcolonial Melancholy* (New York: Columbia University Press, 2003).

organizations or technology.[7] The roots of this understanding are to be found in Paris in the early 19th century. This aspect of the history of the word is reflected in the present day, when conviviality can be taken to describe situations of sociability and the sharing of food and drink. Not surprisingly, in diaconal and other engagement with migrants and refugees as well as with marginalized groups, the joint preparation and sharing of food is very often a feature. Maybe this also has a bearing on our understanding of the Eucharist, as it seems that the early Christians often ate and drank together and very often their celebration took the form of a 'bread and fish Eucharist'.[8]

The third discussion of the word conviviality stems from the work of Ivan Illich, a Croatian born in Vienna of Catholic and Jewish parents and who became a Catholic priest. He was a firm critic of economic growth and the misapplication of technology. His work in Latin America followed a period engaged with people in one of the poorest neighborhoods in New York. These experiences led him to produce a seminal volume, *Tools for Conviviality*, which stands in the tradition of Erich Fromm, who emphasized 'being' over 'having'.[9] Illich described a society that limits the use of technology (tools) so that it is not used to exploit people and the environment. Illich considered conviviality to be freedom realized in interdependence and as such, an intrinsic ethical value.[10] As we develop this stream of the discussion of the concept of conviviality, we are coming close to the present-day discussions that are critical of the dominant economy and economic growth and the search for 'buen vivir' ('good living').[11] It is no surprise, therefore, that the European Lutheran group chose to focus on work and economy for the second period of its collaborative work.[12]

A Convivial Vision for Church and Society

These three background themes can each be developed in relation to a contextual understanding of *diakonia*.

---

[7] Frank Adloff, 'Wrong Life Can be Rightly Lived' in *Convivialist Manifesto – A Declaration of Interdependence* (Duisburg, Kate Hamburger College/Centre for Global Co-operation Research, Global Dialogues 3, 2014).

[8] Elizabeth Saxon, 'Art and the Eucharist: Early Christian to ca. 800' in Ian Christopher Levy, Gary Macy and Kristen van Ausdall, *A Companion to the Eucharist in the Middle Ages* (Leiden, Brill, 2012) p. 103-105.

[9] Erich Fromm, *To Have or to Be* (London: Bloomsbury Academic, 2013 edition).

[10] Ivan Illich, *Tools for Conviviality* (New York: Harper & Row, 1973).

[11] Alberto Acosta, *Buen Vivir: Vom Recht auf ein gutes Leben* (Munich: oekom, 2015).

[12] Tony Addy, *Towards a Convivial Economy* (Geneva: Lutheran World Federation, 2017).

Conviviality and Diversity

The processes and discussions related to 'conviviality' referred to above are focused on local *diakonia*, *diakonia* of the local church, diaconal congregations and organizations at the local level. If we reflect on local situations, very often the question of diversity has to be newly addressed for a number of reasons that are well known, such as the growth of migration and the increasing numbers of uprooted people. Many neighborhoods and villages have for the first time experienced new migration and, of course, the other side of the coin is that migration often means that younger and better-educated people leave one locality for another. Second, many communities have been living for generations with diversity and the present migration-related discussion seems to bypass their concerns. Third, we also have long-standing minorities in different localities that continue for generations to be excluded from mainstream society. In our reflection, we have also had to think about the situation of churches, which are also for different reasons in a minority position and on the other hand the changing position of majority churches in society. It increasingly seems to be the case that the congregation or parish is a minority among minorities. On top of these concerns there are other aspects of identity and practice, which increase our understanding of diversity such as gender and sexual orientation.

The question of physical borders in Europe has also become a big issue in many situations, often related to reassertion of cultural identity and a variety of reasons. Convivial thinking and practice has implications for the work of churches and *diakonia* especially but not only when faith and identity are intertwined. In border-conflict situations, convivial thinking implies that we work for peace and reconciliation, recognizing the diversity and seeking to restore trust and conviviality.

In these different contexts, when we focus on local participatory approaches we face a number of practical and conceptual difficulties. First, we often assume that each person has a rather fixed identity – we could say 'habitus' – and that each community also has a fixed identity. This understanding is a barrier to working with diverse and diversifying societies. A community may be a very comfortable space that reinforces the members' identity and the same may be true of a congregation or church community. A community defines its boundaries of inclusion and exclusion – the word carries descriptive, sociological connotations, but also often implies a normative dimension. If we talk about community building, community development or participatory working, it means we are aiming for what has been called 'being in common'[13] and we need to ask more deeply what we mean when we speak about creating community, especially when the local congregation is sometimes socially, culturally and economically rather distinct from many people living locally.

---

[13] Sarah Neal, et al, 'Community and Conviviality? Informal Life in Multicultural Places' in *Sociology*, London, Sage Journals, Vol. 52, Nr.2, 2018.

On top of this, the resurgence of nationalism in various contexts has also tried to harness the symbolism of the national church, which represents the religion of the country as a support for exclusionary policies. In multi-faith localities this poses a further challenge to living and working together. Religion has become an important factor and it has a different meaning and significance for long-term inhabitants of a place than it does for migrants and especially uprooted people.

Reflecting further on the present context in relation to the original meaning of conviviality (convivencia) supports a practice, which encourages a wide engagement with the everyday life of people.

Conviviality and Relationships

If community is a difficult word that is regularly used in a Christian context as well as in social practice, hospitality is also a word, which has positive connotations and is often used in discussions about the need to be open to welcome immigrants and especially refugees. We also notice that it is used in relation to all people who are 'other' in terms of culture, identity or belief. There is, however, a long Christian tradition of hospitality, which also has its roots in the Old Testament.

However, if we think about this through the concept of conviviality, we can detect some of its limitations. The idea of hospitality assumes that the 'stranger' is only present for a short time and will go away. It also leaves the question of decision-making and power in the hands of the one who offers hospitality. Nevertheless, this concept of treating the stranger well lies at the basis of a good deal of positive thinking and practice in the Judeo-Christian tradition. Perhaps hospitality can be a step toward conviviality, but it may also prevent conviviality by supporting a non-participatory, patronizing approach. A further point is that if a guest stays for a long time, they may become 'like' the host population and in that sense 'disappear', or they may stay and live their life as they always did and thus be eventually excluded. Jacques Derrida published a well-known book, in dialogue with Anne Duforumantelle, on this conceptual and practical issue as long ago as 1997.[14] If we are hospitable, we can welcome the stranger and maybe learn something; it may change us or not. If we work for conviviality, we do not reckon with the 'other' leaving and therefore we have to work out how to live together.

In addition, the convivial approach forces us to look at the actual diversity of every locality and focus on how we live together. This means learning how to cross 'boundaries', for example of religion or imagined cultural or national difference. It also has implications for working with people across the 'borders' of gender or sexual identity.

[14] English translation: Jacques Derrida & Anne Duforumantelle, *Of Hospitality*, Stanford: Stanford University Press, 2000.

Seeking conviviality as an approach implies that we have to find out how to cross the boundaries between two or more worlds. Furthermore, the most important boundary may not be the most obvious one (to us). It means the communication has to be built on trust and has to be 'eye to eye'. To build conviviality, we have to learn how to cross from one world and its identity to another world and its identity, from one person to another. We can liken this to crossing a threshold and the threshold is a 'liminal' space where things are not clear and where meanings are open for conversation and change. The consequence may not be agreement on everything, but trust will be built and the finding of things in common creates a platform for good living and for action to change the situation.

The second strand of thinking about conviviality described above refers to sharing a meal and creating a climate for the exchange of ideas, hopes and dreams as well as difficult parts of life. It speaks of a kind of dialogue in which both sides are open to change. It is not surprising that this dialogue is pictured as taking place around a table with food and wine.

It is important to distinguish the 'seeking conviviality' approach from the usual idea of learning tolerance for other people's differences, or even of valuing difference for economic reasons! Arising from the trust building and the mutual respect that may ensue, people can develop a new sense of their own possibilities to act for change with others because the process builds positive identities, which create solidarity on the basis of shared experience and learning.[15]

In a convivial society people not only tolerate differences but also accept others in mutual respect. When every day is shared with others, it is possible to learn from each other. If people are able to expose their identity to other identities, they are able to build mutual relationships with other people different from them. This may partly be learnt informally over time, but seeking conviviality is not easy because it does not remain on a superficial or instrumental level. It may be that there are differences that cannot be reconciled, but these will be reflected on and understood.

Conviviality, Economy and the Environment

In every context, we can see that the concrete developments of work and economy are creating growing inequality and injustice. These changes, in conjunction with other societal and political changes, negate the dignity of the person, especially those on the margins or who are unable to integrate into the formal labor market. Indeed, the structure of the formal labor market seems to become more unjust, and often, work conditions do not recognize the dignity of the person. Actually, we can also notice that workplace conditions are now becoming a main source of mental ill health. The former idea that work is a

---

[15] Ulla Siirto, 'Conviviality – a diaconal core value' in Anna Burghardt (ed.), *Human Beings – Not for Sale*, Geneva, Lutheran World Federation, 2015.

step to social integration becomes less and less of a reality as the content of working life becomes over-regulated and the experience of work life increasingly fragmented. On top of that, more and more people earn their poverty and cannot survive unless they work excessive hours or have two or more jobs! The present economic paradigm (neo-liberalism) as it affects work, welfare, health and education actually undermines conviviality. It is this aspect of the way an economy that is financially and practically disembedded from localities and is operating on a global scale to which Illich was pointing in his critique more than 40 years ago. His understanding that the market economy would destroy the vocation to work for the common good for many people and that it would result in dehumanized working conditions is what we are bearing witness to nowadays.

On top of this, the present economic order creates huge environmental costs. The immediate impact of industrialization is to create unsustainable pollution in the ground and atmosphere. The impact on climate change, especially when transport is taken into account, is leading in a catastrophic direction. The human costs of this are met by marginalized communities in both the global north and south. From a European perspective, it is dangerous because Europe is shielded from many of the environmental costs and consequences of the production of cheap consumer goods. The products used in everyday life mostly depend on work that is done in conditions that are hazardous for health and the environment such as the extractive industries or the electronics manufacturing industry.

There are many other dimensions to this issue related to the different sectors such as agriculture and food production, and the 'leisure industries' that are rapidly expanding. If we begin to look at this issue through the lens of creating a convivial economy, we see that there are many negative effects on people, communities and the environment.

On the other hand, taking the approach through conviviality, we can reach positive ideas for reorganizing work and economy focused on vocation, dignity and sustainability. Furthermore, there are many examples of initiatives that are founded to meet local needs using resources, including skills as well as concrete assets, to create new forms of local economic initiative. These were documented in the report on work toward a convivial economy prepared as part of the Lutheran World Federation project previously mentioned.[16]

A Convivial and Diaconal Church

So far, we have explored the link between various understandings of conviviality and three key issues of diversity, creating relationships and

---

[16] Tony Addy, 'Towards a Convivial Economy', Geneva, Lutheran World Federation 2017.

creation, the environment and the economy. Now we turn to the question of practice and the implications for the church.

Choosing conviviality as the core concept through which we are developing diaconal thinking and strategy stresses the importance of building relationships in the congregation and with the wider society as a springboard for diaconal action. It already brings in ideas that are critical of the dominant individualistic view of the person and emphasizes the importance of empathy and relationships. As the 'art and practice of living together', conviviality provides an approach to *diakonia* grounded in everyday life. This should also affect the liturgy, opening it to concerns of and participation by marginalized people and groups, where this is appropriate. The emphasis on 'living together' implies a change of service model toward activities that are reciprocal and where all are 'givers and receivers' at different moments. It implies a 'horizontal' rather than 'top-down' model of communication where all can contribute ideas and practical action according to their possibilities, skills and strengths.

Local *diakonia* should be based on working approaches that build in participation and empowerment from the start. This means local *diakonia* is grounded in a long-term process rather than short-term projects. Therefore, *diakonia* in localities needs creative people and a readiness to begin to act without having all the structures clearly in place. The reason is the basis of local diaconal work is an inductive approach that does not start with preconceptions of the definition of the problem or the solution. It is clear that the development of local *diakonia* that is empowering and transformative needs to be grounded in a leadership model that combines the ability to take the initiative with an ability to listen to and reflect with people.

The understanding of *diakonia* approached through the concept of conviviality supports the concept of a diaconal church or the creation of open church meeting points. It starts with 'presence in the everyday life-world' of people. The whole group may become active in working for change and in this situation the distinction between the traditional volunteer role and that of an activist working for change is blurred. People may be in different roles at different times because the activities are rooted in everyday life and voluntary workers may take on many different roles. On the basis of the work of such local diaconal centers or engaged local churches, the connection between mutual aid and social or political action is easier to make because of the trust relations that are built up over time. A critical role for diaconal workers involves supporting learning processes during which participants can clarify their own identity and their position in relation to 'others' and their locality.[17] During the same process, they may also discover their capacity for action and the possibilities to work for change. Such training processes help to make

---

[17] Titus Schlatmann & Rob van Waarde, *That's the Name of the Game – on empowerment and community, an account of practical research*, Tubbergen, Van der Ros Verlag.

connections between different groups and interests and build solidarity.[18] This approach to diaconal work also implies a strong emphasis on networking and bridging with other institutions and organizations in the field. This perspective on diaconal practice also supports active ecumenical and interfaith working in practice. However, *diakonia* has a special concern with marginalized groups and it is important not only to focus on relationships in the locality and the support of new practice with people but also on the vocation of *diakonia* to secure justice in participation with excluded groups.

It is important to create diaconal service models where the members of different groups, for example those with a migrant background, can develop their own activities in relation with each other and those who are the traditional residents. In some cases, such church-based initiatives are the only source for many services that are denied to some groups of people, and also provide a focal point where the skills and expertise of different groups can be enhanced and shared.

Working out the idea of conviviality extends *diakonia* from the making and sharing of food to the sharing of culture and to the development of local economic activities using people's skills and interests. It can lead to innovation and it can also lead to action to influence or change political decisions at local or wider levels. However, to build on conviviality also demands reflection on the use of time, because it cannot be constrained within 'office hours' or 'normal places' and it requires an open and affirming inductive attitude. It is very different to the 'service model' that tends to dominate traditional diaconal thinking. The whole congregation can be a diaconal actor in the expression of its life together.

When we begin our practical engagement based on the concept of conviviality, we move firmly away from the concept of working *for* other people, or of the church *for* others, to working *with* other people and the church *with* others. We move away from simply well-meaning, predefined actions for other needy people toward sharing life, based on empathy, reciprocity and presence. There is a clear link here with the thinking of Paulo Freire, in that diaconal conviviality stresses the understanding that we are all co-learners.[19] This approach emphasizes that we work in dialogue with others, not that they become like 'us' but that we learn together how to change. Seeking conviviality implies that openness to the 'other' is a condition for our faithful Christian living as persons or as congregations. The people of God are those who can work with others without wanting to dominate or fight them. Part of the faithful logic behind this is grounded in the understanding that in

---

[18] Jouko Porkka & Marja Pentikäinen (eds.), *Community of the Future – challenges and new approaches to community based social work and diakonia from the CABLE approach*, Helsinki, Diak, 2013.

[19] Paulo Freire, *Pedagogy of the Oppressed*, Harmondsworth, Penguin Books, 1972.

encountering the other we encounter Christ, and in that sense, we need the other for our own Christian identity and faithful living.

Conclusion

Conviviality is based on the recognition that every neighborhood is diverse in one way or another and living together must be based on respect for difference and also on developing the 'art and practice of living together'. Toleration is not enough; mutual respect is the necessary basis when we live everyday life together. The question of the depth of relationship becomes important because most often people cultivate strong relationships with those most like themselves. They may tolerate others, but it goes no further. Seeking conviviality works when people develop those relationships where they can profoundly learn from each other and also share the deeper aspects of identity including spirituality. When every day is shared with others, it is possible to learn from each other. If people are able to expose their identity to other identities, they are able to build mutual relationships with other people different from them. This leads to trust and to an ability to appreciate the resources and strengths that people bring to common life and common projects.

In the light of these considerations we can recognize that if we want to create a diaconal church, we have to first look inside the congregational life and discover how far we share the characteristics of conviviality already. Diaconal conviviality should be a mark of church life and then it will naturally lead 'outward'. These characteristics reflect the way in which the church as the body of Christ is seeking to be 'in the midst of people' as Jesus was, especially people suffering from injustice, marginalization or worse, as well as with those who are sick or in prison. Diaconal conviviality cannot be expressed simply in a project because it exists as a way to be in relation, to be present. It is not a way to collect prestige or power, or to raise the profile of the church, but to be connected to the 'life world' of people. This model of being present and in relationship leads to a valuing of everyone's contribution and can also be a contribution to sustainable living together. As such, it calls into question the standard developmental project models and offers a fresh way forward in a time of political and economic uncertainty.

Bibliography

On Conviviality and Diakonia

Addy, Tony, *Seeking Conviviality. Re-forming Community Diakonia in Europe*, (Geneva: Lutheran World Federation, 2014).

Addy, Tony, *Seeking Conviviality – the art and practice of living together* (Český Těšín: interdiac, 2017).

Addy, Tony, *Towards a Convivial Economy* (Geneva, Lutheran World Federation 2017).

Addy, Tony (ed.), *Seeking Conviviality, Evaluation and Commentary from the European Solidarity Group* (Geneva: Lutheran World Federation, 2017).

Glitzenhirn, Dirk, 'Gemeinwesendiakonie als Verwirklichung von Konvivenz' in epd Dokumentation 39, *Kirche in der Mitte der Gesellschaft* (Berlin: epd 2011), Download from: http://www.eaberlin.de/nachlese/dokumentationen/2011-39-kirche-in-der-mitte-der-gesellschaft/epd-2011-39.pdf.

Glitzenhirn, Dirk, 'Conviviality – Facets of a Concept and Theological Framework for Community Based Diaconia' in *Diaconia, Journal for the Study of Christian Social Practice* (Göttingen: Vandenhoeck & Ruprecht Vol. 5, Issue 2, 2014).

Haugen, Hans Morten, 'Approaches to Inclusive and Equitable Societies' in *Diaconia, Journal for the Study of Christian Social Practice* (Göttingen: Vandenhoeck & Ruprecht, Vol. 6, Issue 2, 2015).

Illich, Ivan, *Tools for Conviviality* (New York, Harper and Row 1973).

Siirto, Ulla, 'Conviviality: A Core Value of *Diakonia*' in Burghardt, Anne (ed.), *LWF guide material to the themes of the 500th anniversary of the Reformation: Human Beings – not for sale.* (Geneva: Lutheran World Federation, 2015).

Sundermeier, Theo, 'Konvivenz als Grundstruktur ökumenischer Existenz Heute' in V. Küster (ed.), *Missionswissenschaftliche Forschungen, Neue Folge, Band 3* (Erlangen: Verlag der Ev.-Luth. Mission, 1995).

Background Literature

Acosta, Alberto, *Buen Vivir: Vom Recht auf ein gutes Leben* (Munich: oekom, 2015).

Derrida, Jacques & Duforumantelle, Anne, *Of Hospitality* (Stanford: Stanford University Press, 2000).

Adloff, Frank, 'Wrong Life Can be Rightly Lived' in *Convivialist Manifesto – A declaration of interdependence* (Duisburg, Kate Hamburger College/Centre for Global Co-operation Research, Global Dialogues 3, 2014).

Freire, Paulo, *Pedagogy of the Oppressed* (Harmondsworth, Penguin Books, 1972).

Gilroy, Paul, 2006, 'Colonial Crimes and Convivial Cultures', downloaded from: http://www.rethinking-nordic-colonialism.org/files/pdf/ACT2/ESSAYS/Gilroy.pdf.

Gilroy, Paul, *After Empire: post-colonial melancholia or convivial culture* (London, Routledge, 2004).

Le Bord de L'Eau, *Manifeste Convivialiste, Déclaration d'interdépendance* (Paris, Editions Le Bord de L'eau, 2013).

English translation: *Convivialist Manifesto, a declaration of interdependence*, downloaded from: www.gcr21.org/publications/global-dialogues/2198-0403-gd-3/.

Neal, Sarah, et al, 'Community and Conviviality? Informal Life in Multicultural Places' in *Sociology* (London: Sage Journals, Vol. 52, Nr.2, 2018).

Porkka, Jouko & Pentikäinen, Marja (eds.), *Community of the Future – challenges and new approaches to community based social work and diakonia from the CABLE approach* (Helsinki: Diak, 2013).

Sakrani, R. R, *Convivencia: Reflections about its 'Kulturbedeutung' and Rereading the Normative Histories of Living Together* (Frankfurt, Max Planck Institute for European Legal History, 2016).

Saxon, Elizabeth, 'Art and the Eucharist: Early Christian to ca. 800' in Ian Christopher Levy, Gary Macy and Kristen van Ausdall, *A Companion to the Eucharist in the Middle Ages* (Leiden, Brill, 2012).

Schlatmann, Titus & Rob van Waarde, *That's the Name of the Game – on empowerment and community, an account of practical research* (Tubbergen, Van der Ros Verlag).

The Diaconal Church in the Public Sphere

Rudolf von Sinner

'Theology is a game that is played when life is at stake'[1]

Christian theology is a theology of life linked to the God of life seeking to contribute in society so that there may be life that is worthy of being lived by all. It is the theological and practical expression of the church's intrinsic task to serve and to advocate for not only its own members but also to witness, through its diaconal action, God's love and justice in the public sphere. On the way to such transformation, education is tantamount. This is the basic thesis of this chapter. To this end, it is necessary to reflect on the place and role of religion in the contemporary world. Informed by a thorough analysis of such presence, a public theology reflects on it in a constructive, critical and self-critical way, communicating with other sources of knowledge and seeking to provide orientation to the churches as to a pertinent way of being present in the public.[2]

In present-day Brazil, which is the main context informing this contribution, a highly ambiguous mixture of politics and religion is in place that calls for a more humble, yet courageous and well-conceived presence. In 2018, many Christians voted for former army captain Jair Messias Bolsonaro to become president, and especially some *evangélico*[3] leaders are very close to the new government and have even occupied important government posts. In a video circulated on social media, a group of 'believers' (*crentes*, as *evangélicos* are also called and can call themselves) is shown in the river Jordan – where

---

[1] Iuri Andréas Reblin, 'Waves of Liberation Theology: God non-science since Rubem Alves', *Protestantismo em Revista*, 27 (January-April 2012), 2-8, 5.

[2] For an introduction to and overview of public theology, see Katie Day and Sebastian Kim (eds.), *Companion to Public Theology* (Leiden: Brill, 2017).

[3] *Évangelico* means, literally, 'evangelical', but the connotations of this term in English do not cover its meaning in the Brazilian context. There, in its common present-day usage, the term usually points to members of Pentecostal and Neopentecostal churches. In earlier times, Lutherans were called and called themselves *evangélicos*, and subsequently other Protestant churches. In this chapter I use it, without hiding its ambiguity, for all Non-Catholic and Non-Orthodox Christian churches in Brazil, be they of immigration origin (like Anglicans and Lutherans); of missionary origin (like Baptists, Methodists and Presbyterians); or originated in Brazil (like most Pentecostal and Neopentecostal churches).

Bolsonaro, although a Catholic baptized as a child, had been baptized again by an *evangélico* minister – forming number 17 (Bolsonaro's voting number) and shouting "Bol-so-na-ro" when being asked: "What's the name of our leader"?[4] While in some contexts there might be a lack of religious and, specifically, church presence in the public sphere, here we clearly have an excess that backfires considerably and dangerously on the image of *evangélico* churches, churches that seek to be moved by the *Evangelho*, the Gospel. After a panoramic introduction on the presence of religion in the public sphere (1), I shall argue for the need and pertinence of discourse and rational argument (2), for a thorough contribution of churches practicing *diakonia* not least through education toward solidarity (3) and point to specifically Lutheran contributions toward a theology of citizenship (4), all in the perspective of a diaconal church, a church that participates in God's mission, nurtures discipleship in the world and develops faith-based and rights-based relief, solidarity and advocacy.[5]

Religion in the Public Sphere – Positive, Ambiguous, Nefarious

There can be no doubt that religion is present in the public sphere – in a positive way, in an ambiguous way, in a nefarious way.[6] Regarding the positive role of religion, there is the example of the *contribution to citizenship* in many places – let us just remember the fundamental role of wide sectors of the Catholic Church in Brazil in the resistance, both practical and theological, to oppression, and in the construction of civil society during the period of the military regime.[7] In the Brazilian context, citizenship does not primarily refer to nationality or possessing a specific passport; rather, it is, as defined by Brazilian lawyer Darcísio Corrêa, "the democratic realization of a society, shared by all the individuals to the point that all have their access to the public space and conditions of a dignified survival guaranteed, having as its basic

---

[4] See https://www.youtube.com/watch?v=dPjg6IN7Le8, accessed March 25, 2019.

[5] See the draft paper on 'Called to Transformative Action: Ecumenical Diaconia', revised as of April 17, 2018. I thank Kjell Nordstokke for having shared this draft with me.

[6] See Judith Butler, Jürgen Habermas, Charles Taylor and Cornel West, *The Power of Religion in the Public Sphere* (New York: Columbia University Press, 2011).

[7] For an in-depth analysis see Rudolf von Sinner, *The Churches and Democracy in Brazil: Towards a Public Theology Focused on Citizenship* (Eugene, Or.: Wipf & Stock, 2012), and 'Public Theology as a Theology of Citizenship' in Katie Day and Sebastian Kim (eds.), *Companion to Public Theology* (Leiden: Brill, 2017), 231-50. Previous versions of this chapter have been presented as lectures on November 20, 2015, within the Twin Consultation on 'Reformation – Education – Transformation' in São Leopoldo, Brazil (available at: www.r-e-t.net) and on March 23, 2018, at the joint seminar on 'Precious and Precarious: Precarious Life, Fragile Democracy, and the Role of Religiosity and the Churches' between Faculdades EST and MF Norwegian School of Theology at Oslo.

value the fullness of life".[8] It is usually very positively connotated and has, so far, not been stained by signs of a xenophobic nationalism as is the case in other contexts – although there are signs that this might change.[9]

As far as *ambiguity* is concerned, there are more than a few examples of churches being present on both sides of the divide, as was the case in both the defence and defiance of the apartheid system in South Africa, especially by Reformed churches.[10] It is important to remember the ambiguity that exists in Brazil, from where I speak after having lived and worked in this country for 18 years, but also elsewhere, between conservative religious moral attitudes and progressive social attitudes, a conflict that is often also present within the same churches. It has even created hate speech, in line with the general polarized mood over corruption, violence and the need for political renewal in the country that was reinforced by the electoral campaign in 2018. It is also important to remember the significant social contribution of churches, on the one hand, and the existence of a self-interested religious lobby on the other.[11] One of the most visible symbols in the search for power, ever more publicly articulated, is the self-acclaimed replica of Solomon's Temple, constructed by the neo-Pentecostal and multinational Universal Church of the Kingdom of God (*Igreja Universal do Reino de Deus* – IURD), inaugurated on July 31, 2014 with a significant presence by the political authorities from Brazil, and intended to position the IURD as the Christian church *par excellence*.[12]

There is also the *nefarious role* of religion. There are conflicts with religious overtones, alongside political, economic and social ones – in Mali, in Syria, in Iraq, in Afghanistan, or in Nigeria, to mention only a few examples of places where every day, many people die, having the same, or a different, religion as the aggressors. This is a scandal both religious and secular. Religions, as much as they may declare that they are of peace, and act as though they are the proprietors of ethics, cannot, it seems, effectively restrain such violence. Even

---

[8] Darcísio Corrêa, *A construção da cidadania: reflexões histórico-políticas* (Ijui: Unijui, 2006), 217.

[9] The motto of the present government under president Jair Messias Bolsonaro is 'Brazil above everything, God above all' (*Brasil acima de tudo, Deus acima de todos*) and, as it appears on all government websites and letterheads, 'Beloved Fatherland Brazil' (*pátria amada Brasil*), part of the national anthem.

[10] John De Gruchy and Steve De Gruchy, *The Church Struggle in South Africa. 25th Anniversary Edition* (London: SCM, 2004).

[11] See Paul Freston, *Evangelicals and Politics in Asia, Africa and Latin America* (Cambridge: Cambridge University Press, 2001).

[12] The inauguration ceremony can be found at: https://www.youtube.com/watch?v=eYprcb5Jg3U&t=9333s, last accessed March 24, 2018; see also Andreas Heuser (ed.), *Pastures of Plenty: Tracing Religio-Scapes of Prosperity Gospel in Africa and Beyond* (Frankfurt: Peter Lang, 2015).

worse, there are situations where they support, even if not openly, violence and death as the solution of conflicts.[13]

With or without religious connotations, there are strong tendencies to think it is the task, and the sole task, of the military, the police and the intelligence agencies to resolve the problem of violence. Violence is to be resolved by violence. There is, in many places, widespread support from the population for such measures. This might all too easily turn into the idea that there is a certain group that bears all the guilt for the situation – be it the Islamic State, drug traffickers, bandits or migrants – and that the only way for a solution is to destroy them. This dangerous attitude is not mitigated by the fact that such groups might themselves share such solution as their conviction. A precarization of the attitude toward the precocity of the human being is affecting the democratic, constitutional State. At the same time, it is not by mere appeal that religions shall contribute to the overcoming of violence. Rational argument is an important element for a relevant contribution toward public discourse and the finding of ways to, together with other religious and secular communities, foster the common good. This is the basic thesis of the next section.

Discourse, Dialogue, Rational Argument as Emancipation

Violent actions like 11/13 in Paris (2015) and 9/11 in New York (2001) have religious implications, not only on the side of the attackers. I recall the initial invocation of 'infinite justice' by then US President George W. Bush, later moderated to 'enduring freedom'.[14] In contrast, I am helpfully reminded of the well-known address by Jürgen Habermas on 'Faith and Knowledge', given when he received the peace prize of the German publishers on October 14, 2001, shortly after 9/11. Since then, we can see in Habermas a search for understanding what happened as a consequence of the force of a destructive religious imperative, bringing to the fore the influence of a religious dimension all too easily overlooked by secular minds. At the same time, Habermas has come to recognize the important role religion can also play in motivating morality and providing a fertile ground for solidarity. While the secular, liberal state should not succumb to either an absolutistic religion or a naturalist science, he should not exclude either contribution. Among others, Habermas states: 'the search for reasons that aspire to general acceptance need not lead to an unfair exclusion of religion from public life, and secular society, for its part, need not cut itself off from the important resources of spiritual explanations, if

[13] For the Brazilian context see Rudolf von Sinner and Euler R. Westphal, 'Lethal Violence, the Lack of Resonance and the Challenge of Forgiveness in Brazil', *International Journal of Public Theology* 12.1 (March 2018), 38-55.

[14] See 'Infinite Justice out – Enduring Freedom, on BBC website, posted September 25, 2001, http://news.bbc.co.uk/2/hi/americas/1563722.stm, last accessed March 24, 2018.

only the secular side were to retain a feeling for the articulative power of religious discourse.'[15] There has been, since long before 9/11, in Habermas' writings a continuous search for dialogue based on communication by argument, and not by decree, still less, of course, by the language of weapons.[16] In this, it seems to me that Habermas rightly calls attention to the need for communication, discourse, and not least rational argument that can be tested and contested. In contexts where rule by decree and authoritarianism reigns – and such is the case also in a good number of *evangélico* churches – rational argument has a true emancipatory power.[17] Religious fundamentalism, on the other hand, based on the idea that it is undertaking a literal and the only true interpretation of its doctrine, demonstrates it has a very particular and, indeed, selective understanding of religious truth. It tends to shun rational argument as alien and dangerous to such truth.[18]

Speaking from within a Christian fold, instead of truly listening to the Spirit's voice, fundamentalism silences it, understanding doctrine in an extreme one-sided, allegedly literal way. It is urgent to overcome an absolutism that prevents from recognizing God's love and instead focuses nearly exclusively on the anger and exigencies of a demanding and wrathful God.[19] According to Luther, believers are related to God, the God of love and mercy, by faith, and related to their neighbor by love.[20] Jon Sobrino, a well-known theologian of

---

[15] Jürgen Habermas, *Faith and Knowledge. Peace Prize of the German Book Trade 2001 – Acceptance Speech*, available at: https://www.friedenspreis-des-deutschen-buchhandels.de/sixcms/media.php/1290/2001%20Acceptance%20Speech%20Juergen%20Habermas.pdf, accessed March 26, 2019; see also his *The Future of Human Nature* (Cambridge and Malden: Polity, 2003) and *Religion and Rationality: Essays on Reason, God, and Morality* (Cambridge, Mass.: MIT Press, 2002).

[16] The classic is Jürgen Habermas, *The Theory of Communicative Action* (two volumes, Boston, Mass.: Beacon Press, 1985).

[17] See Eneida Jacobsen, *Theologie und politische Theorie. Kritische Annäherungen zwischen zeitgenössischen theologischen Strömungen und dem politischen Denken von Jürgen Habermas*. Translated by Bruno Kern (Berlin: Peter Lang, 2018); also her 'Deliberative public sphere: The rereading of Habermas's theory in Brazil and its significance for a public theology', *Missionalia* 43:5, 493–512.

[18] See, for instance, Martin N. Dreher, 'Fundamentalismus tötet' in Franz Gmainer-Pranzl and Eneida Jacobsen (eds.), Deslocamentos – *Verschiebungen theologischer Erkenntnis. Ein ökumenisches und interkulturelles Projekt* (Innsbruck/Wien: Tyrolia, 2016), 195-233.

[19] For a comprehensive account of images and concepts of God from the perspective of a Biblical Theology, see Reinhard Feldmeier and Hermann Spieckermann, *God of the Living: a Biblical Theology*, trans. Mark E. Biddle (Waco, Tx.: Baylor University Press, 2011).

[20] Martin Luther, 'On the Freedom of a Christian', *Luther's Works,* vol. 31, ed. Helmut T. Lehmann (Philadelphia, Pa.: Muhlenberg Press, 1962), 343–77; see also the Sermon on the Third Sunday after Epiphany, quoted in Cynthia Moe-Lobeda, *Public Church: For the Life of the World* (Minneapolis, Minn.: Augsburg Fortress, 2004), 52, 88 n. 14:

liberation, defined the center of liberation as love: 'The theology of liberation is before anything else an *intellectus amoris*, intelligence of fulfilment of the historical love to the poor of this world and of the love that makes us related to the reality of the revealed God, that definitely consists in showing love to the human beings.'[21] A concrete, diaconal example of fostering love, listening to the Spirit and promoting liberating emancipation is the training of women leaders by the Ecumenical Centre for Capacity Training and Consultancy (CECA) in São Leopoldo, Rio Grande do Sul, Brazil, to become "popular attorneys" who help women who suffered violence – mostly domestic violence from their husbands or family members that do not admit a woman's autonomy and self-affirmation – to get the legal, medical and social assistance they are entitled to, but often cannot effectively access.[22] One story I was personally told is that a child, while being examined by the public health service doctor, vomited and splashed it on the doctor's apron. The latter then told the mother to take her daughter away. By coincidence, one of the popular attorneys had followed the scene and reminded the doctor of her lawful duty to examine the child. The doctor then asked: "Who are you?" in a way to suggest that this "Ms. Nobody" had no right to question the person in charge, who held a degree, was State employed, and entitled to the status of a doctor. Lawyers and physicians are commonly called *doutor* – although they generally do not hold a doctoral degree – and spoken to in the formal way, while they address clients and patients the informal way, indicating a clear hierarchical asymmetry. But the popular attorney, well aware of her own and the patient's rights and thus confident, just cited the law, and the doctor gave in to such confidence and examined the child. A conquest of citizenship from below, speaking 'truth to power'!

Love does not exclude truth. On the contrary, it is indeed necessary to speak 'truth to power' as the biblical prophets did and today's prophetic voices still do. But they did so out of love for God that implies love for the neighbor, not in a fundamentalist, destructive way. A one-sided emphasis on truth, understood as being clear and unique, prepared to see as enemies those who do not agree, is prone to enhance hate speech and foster violence, as was visible in

---

'By faith we receive blessings from above, from God; through love we give them out below, to our neighbor.'

[21] Jon Sobrino, 'Teología em um Mundo Sufriente: la Teología de la Liberación como Intellectus Amoris', *Revista Latinoamericana de Teología* 5:15 (1988), 243–266, here 259.

[22] CECA was founded in 1973 by Fr. Orestes Stragliotto as a catechetical institute in Caxias do Sul and later moved with him to São Leopoldo, where it became an ecumenical, diaconal institution in the early 1980s; see José Carlos Stoffel, *Ecumenismo de justiça: reflexão e prática. CECA – uma entidade a serviço do movimento ecumênico* (São Lepoldo: FAAP/CECA/Oikos, 2006); Mara Sandra Parlow, 'Fruto maduro não volta a verde: Promotoras Legais Populares – um estudo de caso', unpublished Master's Thesis (São Leopoldo: EST, 2000).

many manifestations during the electoral campaign in 2018. Where there is no love, such 'truth' becomes absolute and violent. The indispensable and urgent task of the churches and of theological education is to stimulate love, dialogue, forgiveness and reconciliation. By doing this, they serve, they minister and they practice *diakonia*. Only on the basis of precisely such 'fundamentals' – love, dialogue, forgiveness and reconciliation – can there be a debate about truth. The churches have a teaching ministry through which they transmit such 'fundamentals' and foster the practice of *diakonia*. This is of special importance in a country like Brazil where public education is frail and churches are providing not only formal – and as such secular – education through their confessional schools and universities but also through preaching, catechesis, counseling and many other ways of relating to people even in the poorest and more remote areas in which they are present, often as the only kind of institution. It is, therefore, tantamount in what way they exercise such ministry, which is the content of the next section.

Three Positions of the Church Related to Education – Traditional, Modernizing and Prophetic

As I elaborate on the churches' educational dimension, by which they nourish faith and diaconal service, I first recur to a text written by the great Brazilian educator Paulo Freire (1921-1997), a Catholic and an important reference for education – including training for *diakonia* – worldwide and also for Liberation Theology.[23] While working in the World Council of Churches in Geneva to where he had to flee from the military regime in Brazil, Freire wrote a seminal text in 1972 entitled 'The educative role of the churches in Latin America.'[24] He made a distinction between three positions related to the church's role in education. Although he, of course, used the terminology of his time, I believe that the tendencies he indicated are still helpful for a church's reflection and positioning. Freire first refers to the position of a *traditionalist church*, whose position is based on a dichotomy between the world and transcendence, searching to live in a supposed purity in contradiction to the world seen as dirty. These churches serve, according to Freire, as 'balm' to the 'existential tiredness' of the oppressed. At the same time, they confirm an already strong 'culture of silence' about oppression, without explicit – however, potentially with implicit – questioning. Freire acknowledges the importance of such silent posture as a form of tacit resistance, rejecting a world dominated by the lords.

---

[23] His classic is the 1968 *Pedagogy of the Oppressed*. 50th Anniversary Edition. Translated by Myra Bergman Ramos (New York: Bloomsbury, 2018).

[24] Paulo Freire, 'O papel educativo das Igrejas na América Latina' in *Ação cultural para a liberdade e outros escritos* (14th rev. ed., Rio de Janeiro: Paz e Terra, 2011), 169–211; English version: Paulo Freire, *Cultural Action for Freedom* (Cambridge, Mass.: Harvard Educational Review, 2000).

At the same time, he considers it a 'salvation without liberation', resulting in a 'quietist' and 'alienated' church.[25] Another church position Freire describes as *modernizing*, reformist, obeying the 'ideology of development'[26] then in vogue, which sought to use technical and professional education to overcome the perceived backwardness of Latin America. Such a modernizing attitude is an advance and it raises the efficiency of the church's action, but, for Freire, it does not produce real liberation, and this position is compromised by aligning itself with the elite rather than the oppressed. The third line or church position is the *prophetic*, 'as old as Christianity itself, without being traditional, as new as it, without being modernizing',[27] seeking to perceive and put in practice true liberation amid the contradictions of history. Being prophetic, as Freire says, is 'to be utopian and hopeful'; it is 'to denounce and announce', something that requires a scientific knowledge of reality.[28] Like Christ, the prophetic church should be a 'wanderer, constant traveller, dying always and always rising'[29] – we hear resonate the *semper reformanda*, the Reformation principle of seeing the church in need of constant renewal – exposing itself to the risk of participating in the dramatic struggles of reality. It is not possible to be prophetic without risk. In this view, education must be, in fact, transforming, 'in service of the permanent liberation of human beings'.[30] We find similar church types in the South African Kairos tradition.[31]

If, thus, the church is to be a prophetic church, announcing God's word on this world and denouncing injustice, serving while seeking liberation and transformation, the issue comes up how this is best done in today's context. As for Brazil and Latin America, let me cite another seminal text, published 22 years later than Freire's, by Hugo Assmann, a Brazilian Catholic theologian who migrated from the properly theological field to education. His text is entitled 'Theology of solidarity and citizenship, or else: continuing the Theology of Liberation', and was written in a context that has been clearly transformed.[32] Having been one of the most articulate theologians of liberation, he now made a scathing critique of this theology. Among other things, he wanted to better perceive, within the concrete, daily and always ambiguous real life, the poor people with their genuine desires and aspirations. Thus, he advocated 'a theology of the right to dream, pleasure, *fraternura* [tender

---

[25] Freire, 'O papel educativo', 190.
[26] Ibid., 191.
[27] Ibid., 199.
[28] Ibid., 201.
[29] Ibid., 202.
[30] Ibid., 204.
[31] Clint Le Bruyns, 'The Rebirth of Kairos Theology and its Implications for Public Theology and Citizenship in South Africa', *Missionalia* 43:3 (December 2015), 460-77.
[32] Hugo Assmann, 'Teologia da Solidariedade e da Cidadania, ou seja: continuando a Teologia da Libertação' in *Crítica à lógica da exclusão* (São Paulo: Paulus, 1994), 13-36.

fraternity], *creativiver* [creative living], happiness', summed up in the concept of embodiment or corporeity.[33] As the poor became, so to speak, 'disposable' for the dominating capitalism of the neoliberal market, they only became visible for people 'converted to solidarity'. It is for this reason that Assmann insists on the need of educating for solidarity. As Assmann says in another text: 'Over the background of the appearance of a society of learners, characterized by a market economy and changing forms of employability, there is no doubt that educating is to fight against exclusion. In this context, educating really means saving lives.'[34] He also insists that it is necessary 'to conjugate values of solidarity with effective rights of *cidadania* [citizenship]'.[35]

Following Assmann, theologically I see today the necessity of elaborating this within the perspective of a public theology, a public theology for transformation through the struggle for *cidadania* by, among other aspects, educating for solidarity, seeking to practice, mindful of Freire, a prophetic *diakonia*. As a concrete example of diaconal practice in this line, let me cite again the 'popular attorneys', in my view one of the most effective projects to foster citizenship through education serving the mostly poor population. A rights-based initiative started in 1998, it received support by a faith-based ecumenical NGO and international faith-based agencies. After 20 years, much of the project that once provided the initial and continuous training has been assumed by the 'attorneys' themselves.[36]

A Lutheran Public Theology of Citizenship

As indicated above, *cidadania*, citizenship, has become a key concept of democracy in Brazil since the 1990s. It denotes more a conceptual field than a clearly defined concept, and goes far beyond the definition of citizenship in legislation or national documents. Instead, it refers to an arena of the constant struggle of all people in a particular territory for their rights and for the well-being of the society as a whole, whether its members are nationals or not. Its effectiveness requires the profound transformation of people, society and institutions. It is clear that the definition given by Corrêa transcends the issue of rights (and duties) as foreseen by law, instead introducing a utopian, even eschatological, dimension, when speaking of the 'fullness of life', recalling John 10:10, often quoted by Christian movements and Non-Governmental Organizations: 'I have come that they may have life, and have it abundantly.'

33 Assmann, 'Teologia da Solidariedade', 30–31. *Fraternura* and *creativiver* are neologisms created by Leonardo Boff and Hugo Assmann, respectively.

34 Hugo Assmann, 'Por uma teologia humanamente saudável: fragmentos de memória pessoal' in Luiz Carlos Susin (ed.), *O mar se abriu: trinta anos de teologia na América Latina* (São Paulo: Loyola, 2000), 115-30, 130.

35 Ibid., 33.

36 Much of this is unfortunately still undocumented; I had the privilege to serve on the board of directors of CECA from 2008-18.

Christians know that our earthly citizenship is always precarious, transitory, in view of our future citizenship in the kingdom of God. This is not a reason to flee the construction of the earthly city, however. Instead, it underlines the necessity, inspired by the values of the kingdom, of contributing as Christians in this struggle for citizenship, with *parrhesia* (speaking candidly) and *kenosis* (renunciation), boldness and humility at the same time.

Here, I now wish to present five elements that I consider central to an effective contribution to the struggle for citizenship. They are an answer to specific issues, which here I can only touch upon, and, at the same time, they take up central aspects of theology from the perspective of the Reformation, especially in its Lutheran branch of which I partake, without, however, making any claims to exclusivity; on the contrary, my hope is that this will lead to many forms of convergence with theologians of other confessions. I believe that these elements are central to the being of the church in the world and, thus, of the public presence of a diaconal church as outlined in this book.

(a) It is not possible to be a citizen, to feel part of a community governed by justice and seeking the well-being of all, without being able to feel one's own value as a person. In society, value is attributed, in general, asymmetrically, depending on the importance of the family, the possession of economic goods, the formal level of educational, skin color and gender, among other characteristics. However, where should people who do not meet the expected standard in these categories find their dignity? Many people feel too humiliated to see themselves as citizens, and do not think of themselves as being part of society. Lutheran theology insists on justification by grace through faith *extra nos* (outside us), received as gift, freely given. Moreover, the theology of creation focuses on human beings being made in the image and likeness of God as a basis of citizenship. Thus, a person is a citizen not through their specific characteristics or merits, but simply by being a human being with intrinsically attributed dignity. The theology of the Reformation has a rich tradition of seeing individuals as being unconditionally accepted by a merciful God. But we have to recognize here in Brazil that it is the Pentecostal churches that have been most efficient in transmitting a real feeling of dignity and self-respect to people in situations of precarity and vulnerability.[37] Ironically, in Brazil, such people are often colloquially referred to as 'citizens' (*cidadão*), which would, in principle, denote people with their full rights guaranteed – but, in fact, these are people without rights, without roots, without recognition, not even called by their name but, anonymously, by 'citizen'. For an effective citizenship, in the first place, there is the need *to be* a citizen and to feel and understand oneself as such.

(b) A second step is to be able to live as a citizen as part of a society made possible by solidarity based on bonds of trust. It is trust, however, that seems to

---

[37] See Rudolf von Sinner, 'Pentecostalism and Citizenship in Brazil: Between Escapism and Dominance', *International Journal of Public Theology* 6:1 (March 2012), 99-117.

be most lacking in this country. Only 7 percent of Brazilian respondents in a continental survey responded positively when asked if they trust other people. The average in Latin America is 14 percent, while in Norway it is as high as 74 percent.[38] It is not that there is no trust all, but it is bound to people in the family, in one's immediate surroundings and people one knows personally. In general, it is distrust that reigns, reinforced by a constant narrative and news of scams, corruption, deception and violence. At the same time, the churches are among the institutions considered most reliable, which gives them a high potential responsibility. The fact that faith, in Greek *pistis*, in Latin *fiducia*, means trust in God transcends the trust required for the building of citizenship needed for democracy to function, but it can strengthen and renew it. Trust in God can, in an extreme situation of distrust, make possible the risk of forgiveness, of reconciliation and of construction or reconstruction of the bonds of trust between human beings.

(c) The third issue is how to deal with violence, scams, corruption, the fact that some take advantage of others, or the fact that there are a thousand reasons to distrust? To live in this world means to live in an ambiguous situation. The Bible itself is full of examples of life's ambiguity, of the mixture of good and evil, and of the impossibility of remaining with clean hands in such situations. Dietrich Bonhoeffer (1906-45), the famous German Lutheran theologian, spoke of our existence in the penultimate, even if oriented toward the ultimate word of justification through grace and faith. He took upon himself the ultimate consequences in this situation, which recognized the penultimate, supporting the July 1944 attempt to kill Hitler and suffering the consequences of its failure through his death at the gallows.[39] Everyday life is, in Brazil as anywhere, characterized by the coexistence of good and evil. Some people attempt to avoid dealing with such ambiguity by running away from it. One way of doing this is to point to Christ as being the only one able to bring about change on his return. In this case, the whole world is considered evil, a standpoint present in many conservative and millenarian churches.

Another way is to promise an all-encompassing solution through a fulfilled eschatology, as preached by the churches that hold to the gospel of prosperity. A moralistic legalism can also be seen as an attempt to resolve ambiguity. Instead of such attempts to escape ambiguity, it seems to be possible to see ourselves and others as being *simul iusti et peccatores* (both justified and sinners), being justified *in spe*, in hope, and being sinners *in re*, in reality, as

---

[38] See Corporación Latinobarómetro, *Informe 2017* (Buenos Aires: Latinobarómetro, 2017), available at: http://www.latinobarometro.org/latNewsShow.jsp, accessed June 1, 2018; on Norway, see the table at: https://ourworldindata.org/trust, last accessed March 25, 2018.

[39] Dietrich Bonhoeffer, *Ethics* (London: SCM, 1955).

Luther said.[40] I do not think this is a pessimistic vision, as some might think, but rather realistic. This also means that trust, as discussed above, cannot be a naïve trust, as if evil did not exist and the world were completely harmonious. For Christians, there is always the mistrust before human beings, as much of ourselves as of others, given our awareness of the power of sin. Knowing this, but not falling into despair because of our trust in God, we are able to endure ambiguity, a lack of clarity, constantly seeking the right path as an intrinsic part of life. This is why we as citizens are able to persevere.

(d) We also need to highlight the motivation for citizenship, something that is not limited to people's rights or even their duties. Such motivation, which for Christians has a specifically theological foundation, is neither autonomy misunderstood as mere individual interest, nor heteronomy as blind subservience, but is based on seeking free service in freedom. Through justification by faith, Christians become new creatures, free from the captivity of evil, in a position to serve amid sin and evil. In his treaty on Christian freedom, Luther clearly shows that such freedom is not simply freedom of choice, but of service; being, at the same, a 'free lord' and 'subject to all', through our own will, not by coercion. Thus, we can see citizenship as service.

(e) Finally, it is important to highlight that some Christian people and churches have a tendency to separate religion and politics, church and State, in a way to free themselves, incorrectly, of their responsibilities in relation to society as a whole. Others tend to confuse the two spheres and to impose their faith and church on others. Both tendencies need to be overcome by Christian citizens who see themselves as serving God under two distinct, but not separate, regimes. For Luther, living in the era of Christendom, it was clear that God would reign through the two regimes. This cannot be our starting point today, given religious pluralism and a secular state that is neutral in matters of religion. However, distinguishing the roles of the secular power and of the spiritual and ecclesiastical sphere still matters today to avoid an improper intrusion from the other side. We know that, historically, the doctrine of the two kingdoms or, more specifically, regiments, led to various limitations and dangers, resulting in subservience to an authoritarian, totalitarian regime in Nazi Germany. However, in a context where there are clear claims to power by churches and their leaders, making a distinction between the spheres as Luther insisted acquires a new contemporaneity.

These five aspects – of being, of living, of persevering, of serving, and of being under two regiments – of the person as a citizen represent for me the nucleus of a theology in the tradition of the Reformation that offers itself today for being a diaconal church in the public sphere contributing toward the transformation of society.

---

[40] Martin Luther, 'Lectures on Romans', *Luther's Works,* vol. 25 (Missouri, Minn.; Concordia 2002), 260.

Bibliography

Assmann, Hugo, 'Teologia da Solidariedade e da Cidadania, ou seja: continuando a Teologia da Libertação' in *Crítica à lógica da exclusão*. São Paulo: Paulus, 1994.

Assmann, Hugo, 'Por uma teologia humanamente saudável: fragmentos de memória pessoal' in Luiz Carlos Susin (ed.), *O mar se abriu: trinta anos de teologia na América Latina*. São Paulo: Loyola, 2000.

Bonhoeffer, Dietrich, *Ethics*. London: SCM, 1955.

Butler, Judith, Jürgen Habermas, Jürgen, Charles Taylor and Cornel West, *The Power of Religion in the Public Sphere*. New York: Columbia University Press, 2011.

Corrêa, Darcísio, *A construção da cidadania: reflexões histórico-políticas* (Ijuí: Unijuí, 2006).

Corporación Latinobarómetro, *Informe 2017*. Buenos Aires: Latinobarómetro, 2017; available at: http://www.latinobarometro.org/latNewsShow.jsp, accessed June 1, 2018

De Gruchy, John and Steve De Gruchy, *The Church Struggle in South Africa. 25th Anniversary Edition*. London: SCM, 2004.

Dreher, Martin N., 'Fundamentalismus tötet' in Franz Gmainer-Pranzl and Eneida Jacobsen (eds.), Deslocamentos – *Verschiebungen theologischer Erkenntnis. Ein ökumenisches und interkulturelles Projekt*. Innsbruck/Wien: Tyrolia, 2016.

Freire, Paulo. *Pedagogy of the Oppressed*. 50th Anniversary Edition. Translated by Myra Bergman Ramos. New York: Bloomsbury, 2018.

Freire, Paulo, *Cultural Action for Freedom*. Cambridge, Mass.: Harvard Educational Review, 2000.

Freire, Paulo, 'O papel educativo das Igrejas na América Latina' in *Ação cultural para a liberdade e outros escritos*. 14th rev. ed., Rio de Janeiro: Paz e Terra, 2011.

Feldmeier, Reinhard and Hermann Spieckermann, *God of the Living: a Biblical Theology*, trans. Mark E. Biddle. Waco, Tx.: Baylor University Press, 2011.

Freston, Paul, *Evangelicals and Politics in Asia, Africa and Latin America*. Cambridge: Cambridge University Press, 2001.

Habermas, Jürgen, *The Theory of Communicative Action*. Two volumes, Boston, Mass.: Beacon Press, 1985.

Habermas, Jürgen, 'Faith and Knowledge. Peace Prize of the German Book Trade 2001 – Acceptance Speech'. Available at: https://www.friedenspreis-des-deutschen-buchhandels.de/sixcms/media.php/1290/2001%20Acceptance%20Speech%20 Juergen%20Habermas.pdf, accessed March 26, 2019.

Habermas, Jürgen, *Religion and Rationality: Essays on Reason, God, and Morality*. Cambridge, Mass.: MIT Press, 2002.

Habermas, Jürgen, *The Future of Human Nature*. Cambridge and Malden: Polity, 2003.

'Infinite Justice out – Enduring Freedom' on BBC website, posted September 25, 2001, http://news.bbc.co.uk/2/hi/americas/1563722.stm, last accessed March 24, 2018.

Heuser, Andreas (ed.), *Pastures of Plenty: Tracing Religio-Scapes of Prosperity Gospel in Africa and Beyond*. Frankfurt: Peter Lang, 2015.

Jacobsen, Eneida, *Theologie und politische Theorie. Kritische Annäherungen zwischen zeitgenössischen theologischen Strömungen und dem politischen Denken von Jürgen Habermas*. Übersetzt von Bruno Kern. Berlin: Peter Lang, 2018.

Jacobsen, Eneida, 'Deliberative public sphere: The rereading of Habermas's theory in Brazil and its significance for a public theology', *Missionalia* 43:5 (2015).

Le Bruyns, Clint, 'The Rebirth of Kairos Theology and its Implications for Public Theology and Citizenship in South Africa', *Missionalia* 43:3 (2015).

Luther, Martin, 'Lectures on Romans', *Luther's Works,* vol. 25. Missouri, Minn.; Concordia 2002.

Luther, Martin, 'On the Freedom of a Christian', *Luther's Works,* vol. 31, ed. Helmut T. Lehmann. Philadelphia, Pa.: Muhlenberg Press, 1962.

Moe-Lobeda, Cynthia, *Public Church: For the Life of the World.* Minneapolis, Minn.: Augsburg Fortress, 2004.

Pagnan, Rogério, 'Metade do país acha que "bandido bom é bandido morto", aponta pesquisa. Folha de São Paulo online', October 5, 2015, available at: http://www1.folha.uol.com.br/cotidiano/2015/10/1690176-metade-do-pais-acha-que-bandido-bom-e-bandido-morto-aponta-pesquisa.shtml, last accessed March 24, 2018.

Parlow, Mara Sandra, 'Fruto maduro não volta a verde: Promotoras Legais Populares – um estudo de caso', unpublished Master's Thesis. São Leopoldo: EST, 2000.

Reblin, Iuri Andréas, 'Waves of Liberation Theology: God non-science since Rubem Alves', *Protestantismo em Revista*, 27 (January-April 2012).

Sobrino, Jon, 'Teología em um Mundo Sufriente: la Teología de la Liberación como Intellectus Amoris', *Revista Latinoamericana de Teología* 5:15 (1988).

von Sinner, Rudolf, *The Churches and Democracy in Brazil: Towards a Public Theology Focused on Citizenship.* Eugene, Or.: Wipf & Stock, 2012.

von Sinner, Rudolf, 'Pentecostalism and Citizenship in Brazil: Between Escapism and Dominance'. *International Journal of Public Theology* 6:1 (March 2012).

von Sinner, Rudolf, 'Public Theology as a Theology of Citizenship' in Katie Day and Sebastian Kim (eds.), *Companion to Public Theology.* Leiden: Brill, 2017.

von Sinner, Rudolf and Euler R. Westphal, 'Lethal Violence, the Lack of Resonance and the Challenge of Forgiveness in Brazil', *International Journal of Public Theology* 12:1 (2018).

Stoffel, José Carlos. Stoffel, *Ecumenismo de justiça: reflexão e prática. CECA – uma entidade a serviço do movimento ecumênico.* São Lepoldo: FAAP/CECA/Oikos, 2006.

The Church Responding to the Agenda 2030

Carlos E. Ham

The traditional development model of offering aid to 'developing' countries focusing on economic growth is being replaced by a new approach that integrates more dimensions. The UN Sustainable Development Goals (SDG) seek global answers to global challenges, and they invite not only governments but also civil society and faith-based actors to contribute to their realization. The SDG Agenda 2030 represents a new public platform for diaconal engagement. It challenges ecumenical *diakonia* to develop strategies for action, and of equipping local churches and other partners to assuming an active role in relation to the SDG agenda.[1]

Introduction

In this article I will start by introducing the United Nations' Sustainable Development Goals and I will suggest how the Faith Based Organizations (FBOs) in general and the churches in particular can creatively respond to them. In the various examples I will focus on and refer to some SDGs in relation to the diaconal mission of the Latin American churches as well as drawing some concluding remarks.

The article will make reference particularly to the mainline historical Protestant churches in Latin America, much of them with strong ecumenical vision and solid social commitment. It will argue how the Agenda 2030 can be instrumental to carry out its diaconal mission, principally at the congregation level, in order to support and accompany those in need. It will also state the importance for the churches to value more intentionally ancestral indigenous knowledge of the region, which challenges the Western paradigms of sustainable development highlighted in this Agenda.

Diakonia is faith in action;[2] it has been understood traditionally as a sensible service implemented by the churches by word and deeds, inspired by the gospel

---

[1] Various, *Called To Transformative Action. Ecumenical Diakonia (Unpublished Working Paper)* (WCC, Geneva, 2018).

[2] Carlos Ham, *Empowering Diakonia: A Model for Service and Transformation in the Ecumenical Movement and Local Congregations*, PhD Thesis – Free University of Amsterdam (Amsterdam, Netherlands, 2015), 7.

of Jesus Christ and in response to the needs of people.[3] *Diakonia* is an essential part of the mission of the church,[4] which is "called and sent to serve".[5]

The Sustainable Development Goals[6]

Having as background the Millennium Development Goals, on September 25, 2015, world leaders adopted a set of new global objectives to eradicate poverty, protect the planet and ensure prosperity for all as part of a new sustainable development agenda, called the Sustainable Development Goals (SDGs). Each of the 17 objectives has a total of 169 specific goals that must be achieved in the next 15 years. In order to reach these goals, everyone has to do their part: governments, the non-state sector and civil society in general, including FBOs, churches and ecumenical organizations as part of them.

---

[3] Teresa Joan White, "*Diakonia*" in *Dictionary of the Ecumenical Movement*, ed. by Nicholas Lossky et al, 2nd. edn. (Geneva: WCC Publications, 2002), accessed September 15, 2013, www.oikoumene.org, 305.

[4] In the ecumenical movement we find various definitions of *church*. In general terms, when I refer to the *church* or *churches* in this article, I am pointing to "The Church, as a community called into being through baptism and led by the Holy Spirit… As a diaconal community, the church is called to live out its Christian witness both at local and larger as well as personal and corporate levels. This is to be reflected in all the different expressions of being Church: in worship and proclamation, in practices of hospitality and visitation, in public witness and advocacy…" – WCC, "Theological Perspectives on *Diakonia* in the Twenty First Century. Document Adopted at the World Council of Churches Conference on Theology of *Diakonia*, 2012" in *Resource Book WCC 10th Assembly, Busan 2013* (Geneva: WCC Publications, 2013), pp. 2-3.

[5] WCC, *The Nature and Mission of the Church. Faith and Order Paper No. 198* (Geneva, 2005), http://www.oikoumene.org/fileadmin/files/wcc-main/documents/p2/FO2005_198_en.pdf, 6.

[6] https://undocs.org/en/A/69/L.85.

The Church Responding to the Agenda 2030

Even when we have to admit that the SDGs can be a "double edged sword", with their strength and weaknesses, as I will underline shortly, especially in relation to their concept of 'sustainable development', they are presented to us, to a large extent, from a Western worldview. However, I believe they help the FBOs not only to answer 'what' we intend to achieve as we serve the people in need, and ***what*** transformation we want to accomplish to leave a better and more sustainable world for our descendants, but also *how* to achieve it. In other words, they help us to consider what practical interdisciplinary methodologies to use to enable more effectively our social practice.

The SDGs can challenge the churches and provide the necessary instruments to help them to be consistent as they try to bridge words and deeds; as they try to relate their ecclesial reality to their respective social, cultural, political and economic realities; and finally, to connect their spirituality with their quest for holistic transformation, seeking peace, justice and hope.[7]

The Rev Dr Olav Fykse Tveit, General Secretary of the World Council of Churches, has referred to the emblematic example of the new outreach and interest in engagement of the UN on this topic. He has alluded to a presentation by Dr David Nabarro, the UN Secretary of the 2030 Agenda for Sustainable Development, who emphasized seven characteristic roles of religious communities and faith-based development and humanitarian organizations that he considered distinctive and significant in advancing the Sustainable Development Agenda:[8]

1. Promoting the inclusion of different groups;
2. Offering peaceful channels for conflict resolution;
3. Upholding the human rights of the most vulnerable;
4. Reminding political leaders of their duty to enable all people to realize their rights;
5. Helping ensure that investment takes place in communities, with people at the local level making those investments with their own resources;
6. Mobilizing people everywhere, especially young people;
7. Sharing expertise on how to deliver services to those who are hardest to reach.[9]

---

[7] Hansueli Meier, *Report (in Spanish) Workshop on Faith Based Organizations (FBOs) Organized by the Community of Cooperation 'Bread for All' (Switzerland), Held at the Evangelical Theological Seminary in Matanzas, Cuba, September 11-15, 2018* (Matanzas, Cuba, 2018), 10.

[8] This presentation by Dr David Nabarro was made in a meeting of senior leaders of the ACT (Action by Churches Together) Alliance, the Anglican Alliance, Caritas Internationalis and the Lutheran World Federation, convened by the WCC on February 8, 2016.

[9] Olav Fykse Tveit, *The Role of Religion in Sustainable Development and Peace. Lecture at the Gathering 'Partners for Change: Religions and the 2030 Agenda for*

However, Olav Fykse Tveit stressed that reality is more complex, recognizing that religions are sometimes more part of the problem than of the solution. He further pointed out that:

> religion plays an important – even a central role – in people's lives, attitudes and practices, and therefore also in development. Religion informs people's understandings of what constitutes a 'good life', their hope, their self-esteem and belief in their own dignity and rights, their inspiration for asserting their dignity and rights, and their resilience in times of crisis. Therefore, religions *must* be considered in development and in humanitarian response... Religions orient the lives and important decisions of many families and communities on a strong base in values. With their holistic world views, religions continue to challenge the development of economic and political sub-systems that dominate societies and undermine and fragment life in community...[10]

The WCC has reflected on how its programmatic work relates with the SDGs.[11] Interestingly enough, for its *Diakonia* and Training program (the area that concerns us in this article) only four intersections with the SDGs were identified, namely: (1) Eradicate poverty in all its forms throughout the world; (2) End hunger, achieve food security and better nutrition, and promote sustainable agriculture; (3) Guarantee a healthy life and promote well-being for all ages; and (17) Strengthen the means of execution and rekindle the global alliance for sustainable development. However, precisely because of the holistic, contextual and interdisciplinary nature of *diakonia*, I believe that in practical terms the 17 SDGs have "something to say" in the relationship with this ministry, and therefore it would be interesting to analyze all of them with "diaconal lenses".

When it comes to Latin America, in general terms, the mainline Protestant churches in the region show a solid and profound biblical-theological understanding of their diaconal mission but do not know how to proceed, in practical terms. In our theological seminaries in the continent, where we train the new pastors and lay leaders to serve in the churches, we take very seriously exegesis and hermeneutics of the biblical text, but we need to build better

---

Sustainable Development (Berlin, Germany, 2016), p. 3. Paper presented the gathering on the 'Role of Religion in Sustainable Development and Peace', Berlin, February 2016.

[10] Fykse Tveit, 4.

[11] On October 5, 2015, a group of WCC staff and collaborators participated in a workshop in Geneva, Switzerland, to discuss the intersections of their programmatic work with the SDGs as a whole. The objective was to analyze how the different areas of the WCC work are related to the SDGs, to define a strategic commitment, and to design mechanisms to guarantee consistency (including communication and commitment with the member churches) in the work of the WCC in relation with the SDGs. I find this methodology of interrelating the churches' diaconal plans with the SDGs as a relevant way to respond creatively to the Agenda 2030.

capacity on how to interpret the context where we are called by God to serve. Precisely here is where the SDGs can prove to be helpful.

In this regard, some examples can be mentioned on how churches, ecumenical organizations and theological institutions in the region have benefitted by this discussion. Just to mention some examples, at the *Emmanuel Centre* in *Colonia Valdense*, Uruguay, we participated in a very fruitful debate on 'The SDGs: Towards a New Reading of the Diaconal Mission in Latin America'. Other organizations and institutions, like the Ecumenical Regional Center for Advisory and Service (CREAS) in Buenos Aires, Argentina and the Reformed University (CUR) in Barranquilla, Colombia have also profited by this consideration. Another effective example is the *Cuban School of Diakonia* facilitated by the Evangelical Seminary of Theology in Matanzas, together with the Martin Luther King Center in Havana and the Cuban Council of Churches. This School is designed as a theoretical-practical training space in the field of *diakonia*, focusing on the following goals:

1. Deepen the biblical-theological and ecumenical formation as a foundation for *diakonia*.
2. Provide tools for personal and group work in the field of ecclesial service.
3. Strengthen the capacities and abilities of the participants for diaconal ministry.
4. Foster a space for meeting and exchange of experience among the participants.
5. Promote the knowledge and application of the UN Sustainable Development Goals (SDGs).

I will try in the next section to underline just five examples, more intentionally related to the understanding and practice of *diakonia*, mainly from a Latin American perspective:

The SDGs and the Diaconal Mission in Latin America

SDG1 – Eradicate Poverty

One of the trends that concerns us in our continent is the shifting of progressive governments to more conservative ones that introduce neo-liberal economies (Brazil, Argentina, Ecuador), which is already posing great challenges to the diaconal action of the churches, since poverty is increasing as the result of privatization or other non-popular measures. A few days ago, for example, we heard on the radio that "poverty already strikes one in three Argentinians". We see the images on TV where there are large demonstrations of people taking to the streets to demand justice. It seems that the slogan of liberation theology of the "preferential option for the poor" went out of fashion and not necessarily because there are no more poor people. How does this reality challenge our diaconal work today?

This SDG aims to eradicate poverty in all its forms everywhere, with an emphasis on social protection for the poor and vulnerable, increased access to basic services, and support for people affected by extreme weather-related events and other economic, social and environmental disasters and crises.

From a critical point of view, it can be said that the focus of the SDG agenda is too broad, with many goals and objectives. When addressing issues like this one of poverty (or "impoverishment" as the Latin American theologians of liberation would say), it lacks an approach that analyzes root causes and questions of the prevailing political and economic models.

This is where the prophetic *diakonia* makes an important contribution in trying to make a critical analysis of the causes, asking why poverty originates. As the Brazilian Roman-Catholic Archbishop Dom Hélder Cámara (1909-1999) once said: "When I feed the poor, they call me a saint, but when I ask why are they poor, they call me a communist." People who work in *diakonia* must be well informed about the 'diabolic' mechanisms in today's world that marginalize people and cause new forms of poverty and exclusion in order to be able to respond to the challenges of justice and human dignity.

SDG5 – Gender Equality and Empower Women and Girls

Indeed, the empowerment of women and girls is crucial. Nevertheless, quite often it is limited to this sector of the population, and the SDGs are no exception. However, from a diaconal perspective – and this is a contribution from the WCC 2012 Colombo conference on theology of *diakonia* – one of the challenges is to help facilitate an empowerment process so that those who are considered "objects" of our service can actually become "subjects", agents, actors of their own transformation.[12]

The Brazilian liberation educator Paulo Freire's understanding of empowerment can help to critically observe some obviously false ideas of the term, at least in three aspects, which I find useful for our work, particularly when it is implicitly related to emancipation. First, for him, empowerment is not about giving power to a powerless person from a paternalistic and individualist point of view; rather, it consists of helping to activate the potential creativity of the persons. Second, and related to the first, empowerment is a social and political act, in relation to the other, to the community; and finally, it binds together *conscience* with the notion of freedom, enabling dignity and capacity to transform situations of injustice; since for him, it is impossible to be free without going through a process of *conscientization*.[13]

---

[12] WCC, 'Theological Perspectives on *Diakonia* in the Twenty First Century. Document Adopted at the World Council of Churches Conference on Theology of *Diakonia*, 2012', 1-2.

[13] Pedrinho Guareschi, 'Article Empoderamento', *Dicionário Paulo Freire* (Brasil: Editora Auténtica, 2008), 148.

Thus, the treatment of the issue of power, which, in my opinion, is not addressed in the due critical depth in the SDGs, is of crucial importance. We are often proud that the center of gravity of Christianity has been shifted to the global South, but the control of power that marks the destiny of our world remains in the North. And, of course, this power asymmetry in the field of cooperation is also present in the relationships between the churches.

In this sense, a good illustration to better understand the notion of empowerment applied to practice can be taken from the book *The Gospel of Power-Service*, written by Clodovis Boff, in which we find an interesting perspective on how the concept of power is related to *diakonia*. He notes that "For Jesus, power is, in its concrete reality, lost. It needs to be evangelized, converted and saved... Jesus' proposal is the *metanoia* of power. It has to be rescued. It has to be converted from power-domination to power-service. In short, power needs to be transformed, revolutionized internally, and not only within the Church, but at the level of society. All power (religious and political) must become service. It is really 'the revolution of power'".[14]

SDG13 – Climate Change, SDG14 – Conserve Oceans, SDG15 – Protect Terrestrial Ecosystems

A relevant document to address the environmental issues of today is Pope Francis' 'Encyclical Letter Laudato Si'.[15] It is indeed crucial to study it in depth for the churches in general (not only the Roman-Catholic) to respond to this issue of humankind survival. As Guillermo Kerber notes, "The encyclical implies a turning point in the Social Teaching of the Church by including ecological destruction and its expressions as one of its core concerns. Affirming several times, the interconnectedness between the cry of the earth and the cry of the poor, the pope takes up liberation eco-theology affirmations."[16] He goes on to say that "... concrete actions at the personal, community, national and international levels are urgently needed to implement the 'ecological conversion' called by Pope Francis".[17] The SDGs in general and the number 13 in particular, dealing with climate change, can help the churches in the 'ecological conversion' process, which as all conversion should render its fruits.

Already more applied to our continental reality, Alberto César Croce emphasizes,

---

[14] Clodovis Boff, *El Evangelio Del Poder-Servicio* (Bogotá, Colombia: Confederación Latinoamericana de Religiosos – CLAR, 1985), 51.

[15] Pope Francis, 'Encyclical Letter Laudato Si' of the Holy Father Francis on Care for Our Common Home', 2015, 184, http://w2.vatican.va/content/francesco/en/encyclicals/documents/papa-francesco_20150524_enciclica-laudato-si.html.

[16] Guillermo Kerber, 'Ecumenical Background and Reactions to Laudato Si'', *EATOT*, XXXIX (2016), 9.

[17] Kerber, 9.

> From Latin America and the Caribbean, we have a fundamental asset, as is the knowledge and wisdom of our native peoples, which is not an archaic or museum knowledge, but a vivid consciousness of millions of people who live in this region. We have been trying to articulate this knowledge around the concept of 'Sumak Kawsay' or 'Buen Vivir' ('good living'). Basically, affirming that we are not interested in reaching the type of development that the countries of the North or the Center propose us. However, this also generates immense contradictions, especially in regard to the 'exploitation' of our natural resources. In a world where Latin America and the Caribbean were left the place to continue being a supplier of raw materials, this being still the main exportable resource that our countries have, it is very difficult to find alternatives to the 'extractivist' (of extraction) model imposed on us as the engine of our own development.[18]

Certainly, this ancestral philosophy and spirituality, of the interdependence between human beings and nature, is an important alternative to the Western development paradigm that our indigenous population offers to this crucial issue of preserving the "integrity of creation". As Arnhild Leer-Helgesen emphasizes, "indigenous knowledge in relation to nature is an important resource in the approach to sustainable development."[19]

From the Latin American point of view, Croce adds that "For us, there is no 'development' that does not embrace everyone, including the *Mother Earth*, of which we know ourselves are part of. Any proposal that does not contemplate this perspective, for us cannot be understood as a solution, but as a trap. The mandate of the Andean peoples of 'Do not lie, do not steal and not be lazy' seems to be as simple as it is necessary in the midst of the evils that afflict us..."[20] So, a very relevant contribution of the churches in this regard is to enable the building capacities of the indigenous and local institutions and the participation of the impoverished people by expressing their needs and involving them in solutions. Even when they find themselves in a state of seemingly financial powerlessness, from the perspective of development conceived by the West, nevertheless, they have an intrinsic power to change their desperate situation to one of dignity and self-realization.[21]

Ecumenical *diakonia*, therefore, is called to play a significant role within this Agenda, both in political advocacy and grassroots work. Its distinction as work carried out by the churches puts it in a privileged position in the

---

[18] Alberto César Croce, 'Un Desarrollo Para América Latina y El Caribe: Nuestra Propia Perspectiva', *América Latina En Movimiento – ALAI (Agencia Latinoamericana de Información)*, 2016, 3.

[19] Arnhild Leer-Helgesen, *Sustainable Development Goals: Rethinking Diakonia and Transforming Our World* (Stavanger, Norway, 2017).

[20] César Croce, 3.

[21] Carlos Ham, 'Empowerment Towards Development, an Interreligious Approach. Paper Presented at the International Conference on Religions, Values, Ethics and Development. Nanjing, China, December 11-14, 2016' (Nanjing, 2016), 4.

mobilization of the same and other people of faith, promoting the commitment for climate justice, which affects impoverished people in the first place.

Concerning this environmental SDG, "the notion *Environmental Citizenship*" promoted by AIPRAL (Latin American Alliance of Presbyterian and Reformed Churches) can be helpful. They say that it,

> could be the subject of a new Paradigm of Development. Citizenship is a process that revalues the content of socio-political relationships between individuals and groups, in the perspective of building a new social covenant for a nascent society, in which the environment is a basic factor to guarantee the survival of society itself. This implies a recovery of the theological and earthly concept of the *oikos* of God, our 'Common House' (Is 65, 17-25). This *Environmental Oikological Citizenship* encourages the generation of a citizen with new perspectives and responsibilities with the rest of society and the Planet. An *Environmental Citizen* is someone who organizes and participates in the direction of his/her own life and community from a framework of ethical values and a 'Common House' worldview. The *Environmental Citizen* acquire a communitarian local, regional and national political power and a capacity for collective change. An *Environmental Citizen* is a person committed to a profound change of mentality, concepts and values regarding the Environment and Climate change.[22]

SDG16 – Promote Peaceful Societies, Justice and Inclusiveness

This Objective calls for "promoting peaceful and inclusive societies for sustainable development, access to justice for all and creating effective, responsible and inclusive institutions at all levels". Without just peace, stability, human rights and effective governance, based on the rule of law, we cannot wait for the achievement of sustainable development. How can the churches respond to this?

The ecumenical movement – globally and not least in Latin America and the Caribbean – has a long history of work and the defence of peace and justice in the world. We can cite the struggle against the Apartheid regime in South Africa, the celebration of the Decade to Overcome Violence (2001-2010), the celebration in 2011 in Kingston, Jamaica of the great Ecumenical International Convocation for Peace.

Closer to us, how can we forget all the work that was done to do justice and to save lives during the terrible period of military dictatorships in Latin America in the 1980s? Just to mention one example, we remember the project 'Never Again' in Brazil, Chile and Argentina, aimed at preventing the atrocities that were committed from repeating themselves. Here, again, prophetic *diakonia*, especially at the global level, played a very important role

[22] Darío Barolín, *An AIPRAL Guide to Reflect and Act on the Environmental Issues in Latin America Linking Scientific Knowledge with the Spiritual and Social Life of the Churches in Harmony with the UN 2030 Sustainable Development Goals* (ODS), 108-109.

in the advocacy and work for peace and justice. It is not by chance that in a survey that was conducted following the workshop held in Geneva, mentioned earlier about the WCC's programmatic intersections with the SDGs, that the WCC's working structure refers mainly to peace issues and justice as the most characteristic, since it represents 47.6% of the work it does.

As its secretary general puts it well, "In the best of cases, communities and religious leaders have raised their voices in the context of economic injustice and rampant inequality, the misuse of political power, the ugly face of racism or of violence against women and children. The WCC has been calling for respect for human rights, the rule of law as well as respect for international law. These are essential to our vision of a just peace, a *Shalom*, which includes development and hope."[23]

We should also mention here in this section the relevant role that the whole process of the World Social Forum has played, as an alternative (viable?) to the World Economic Forum, which emerged in Porto Alegre in 2001, with its conviction that, indeed, "Another world is possible!". This Forum, in which the ecumenical movement has participated since its inception, adding its perspective of Christian faith has grouped diverse social movements beyond Latin America, has been celebrated in other regions of the world, and was an inspiration to hold the WCC 2006 Assembly in Porto Alegre.

SDG17 – Strengthen the Implementation Networks

As we stated earlier, the growing recognition of the role of religion in development represents a viable opportunity for the diaconal mission of FBOs. Of the world population, 85% belongs to a community of faith; in many cases, faith is transcendental in its daily life, it is its motivation and commitment when it dedicates itself to the struggle for a better future. For social engagement and service agents it represents a unique possibility to create alliances with people of faith and with religious communities, affirming their hopes and common action for the benefit of Creation. In addition, the identity and competence of these agents is affirmed, based on their faith, which is an added value that produces energy, synergy and motivation for the commitment to save lives and fight for justice.

For this reason, it is necessary not only for diaconal agents to strengthen their service capacity and review their objectives and strategies, for which, again, we find the SDGs very useful, but to carry out the work through the creation of cooperation networks. For this, strategies must be designed according to their distinctive role of faith. Various encounters that we hold in our region remind us of the relevance of South-South dialogue in a general sense and among churches in particular, but even more so to involve other religions. I am convinced that to achieve sustainable development in the region and globally, we are called to share our resources (not only financial – as

---

23 Fykse Tveit, 4.

highlighted in the 1980s around the 1987 El Escorial on the *Ecumenical Sharing of Resources*) – for the mutual benefit and especially of the most vulnerable and marginalized.

Among the resources we can share (and in fact share) are knowledge, wisdom (which includes the ancestral) and experiences, relationships, mutual empowerment, training, spirituality of commitment, etc. As we emphasized above, the SDGs are an opportunity to connect our diaconal efforts with the broader world, beyond FBOs to create more inclusive networks of discernment and common action. These networks have to include the voices of marginalized, impoverished people, socially excluded people, "the least of these", those who "are not worth" anything to the market and yet are empowered as agents of change and transformation toward the values of God's kingdom.

Conclusion

As churches – a relevant sector of the FBOs – we need to profit responsibly from the fact that among the governments, academe and social practitioners, there is an increasing awareness that the Sustainable Development Goals, to be reached in 2030, would be more difficult to be attained without benefiting from the positive contributions of various religions.[24] As it was noted in a Forum organized in Geneva to strategize, relating the ecumenical movement with the SDGs, "Clearly the 2030 Agenda presents both huge opportunities and challenges not only for states, but for everyone as we strive to change the world through co-operating in new ways for achieving sustainable development in its three dimensions – economic, social and environmental – and in a balanced and integrated manner".[25] It is, therefore, a convening space to hold each other accountable and to create a better integrated synergy on a common agenda that seeks not only to "leave no one behind" but also the abundance of life that God intends for all Creation. In this gathering the following "*Principles for Engaging in External Partnerships with government and secular agencies on Religion and Development*" were submitted:

a. Enter partnerships as *proactive agenda setters* for initiatives that keep people and their rights at the center, contribute to building a public space that is just for all and sustainable development that preserves the integrity of creation for current and future generations.

---

[24] Carlos Ham, 'Empowerment Towards Development, an Interreligious Approach. Paper Presented at the International Conference on Religions, Values, Ethics and Development. Nanjing, China, December 11-14, 2016' (Nanjing, 2016), 5.

[25] Various, *Transforming Our World: The 2030 Agenda for Sustainable Development. Working Paper Prepared for the Ecumenical Strategic Forum, Geneva, Switzerland, October 3-7, 2017* (Geneva, 2017), 1.

b. Expect mutual *transparency and accountability*, where expectations are articulated clearly, and "red lines" for unacceptable behaviour are discussed openly through ongoing and honest dialogue. Early consultation and ongoing sharing of information are important to increase basic levels of trust.
c. Build partnerships that promote *equality* and *mutual respect* between FBOs and other partners, irrespective of their size, status or power. All parts should respect each other's mandates, obligations and independence and recognize each other's constraints and commitments. Mutual respect must not preclude either part from engaging in constructive dissent.
d. Build *capacity* of those best placed to do development work and expect to see principles of subsidiarity practiced in our partnerships (i.e. *localization/contextualization*).
e. Contribute to *mutual language and learning* on religion and development in our partnerships. The diversity among religious actors and contexts creates possibilities and challenges which require multi-lingual ability. We see there is need to strengthen both religious and development literacy on both sides of the partnership.
f. Promote *interfaith cooperation* based on common concerns and values and the need to reach out to all actors.
g. Seek partnerships that *allow for funding to theological formation* on important issues requiring moral discernment for our time.[26]

As the WCC general secretary has stated: "Churches and other religious communities are not engaged in humanitarian response and development *because* of the SDGs (or the MDGs), but because of their fundamental faith commitments to respecting human dignity, to serving the community, to protecting creation, and to witnessing to the divine. The faith that is our fundamental point of reference is expressed and brought into action in many ways: in confidence and trust in God, in the content of doctrine, in the teaching of the tradition, in a commitment to serve and share, in embodying a community of faith and practice, in common witness in words and deeds."[27] Communities of faith can help contextualize development objectives, to empower people by their direct and continuous participation in the places where they live. An important task now is to equip the churches and diaconal agents at the national and local level to participate in the SDG process. There will also be a need to revise the theological curricula to include a better understanding of the diaconal mandate of the churches, of what this means in the political social context of today's world.

---

[26] Various, *Ecumenical Engagement on Religion and Development. Working Paper Prepared for the Ecumenical Strategic Forum, Geneva, Switzerland, October 3-7, 2017* (Geneva, 2017), 2-3.
[27] Fykse Tveit, 6.

In the preamble to the UN document that introduces the SDGs, the following is expressed with great optimism: "As we embark on this journey together, we promise that no one will be left behind." In biblical-theological terms this would be what we call achieving *koinonia*, which is the ultimate goal of God's mission that marks the presence of the church in the world. *Diakonia*, therefore, is not an end in itself, but rather an instrument used by God, along with others, to serve in the proclamation of God's reign of "justice, peace and joy in the Holy Spirit" (Rom. 14, 17), an inclusive and just community, an oikos, a home in which all creation is included, and can enjoy the fullness of the life that God, in Jesus Christ and by the Holy Spirit, intends for all Creation!

Bibliography

Barolín, Darío, *An AIPRAL Guide to Reflect and Act on the Environmental Issues in Latin America Linking Scientific Knowledge with the Spiritual and Social Life of the Churches in Harmony with the UN 2030 Sustainable Development Goals (ODS)*.

Boff, Clodovis, *El Evangelio Del Poder-Servicio* (Bogotá, Colombia: Confederación Latinoamericana de Religiosos – CLAR, 1985).

César Croce, Alberto, 'Un Desarrollo Para América Latina y El Caribe: Nuestra Propia Perspectiva', *América Latina En Movimiento – ALAI (Agencia Latinoamericana de Información)*, 2016.

Fykse Tveit, Olav, *The Role of Religion in Sustainable Development and Peace. Lecture at the Gathering 'Partners for Change: Religions and the 2030 Agenda for Sustainable Development* (Berlin, Germany, 2016).

Guareschi, Pedrinho, 'Article Empoderamento', *Dicionário Paulo Freire* (Brasil: Editora Auténtica, 2008).

Ham, Carlos, *Empowering Diakonia: A Model for Service and Transformation in the Ecumenical Movement and Local Congregations*, PhD Thesis – Free University of Amsterdam (Amsterdam, Netherlands, 2015).

———, 'Empowerment Towards Development, an Interreligious Approach. Paper Presented at the International Conference on Religions, Values, Ethics and Development. Nanjing, China, December 11-14, 2016' (Nanjing, 2016).

Kerber, Guillermo, 'Ecumenical Background and Reactions to Laudato Si'', *EATOT*, XXXIX (2016).

Leer-Helgesen, Arnhild, *Sustainable Development Goals: Rethinking Diakonia and Transforming Our World* (Stavanger, Norway, 2017).

Meier, Hansueli, *Report (in Spanish) Workshop on Faith Based Organizations (FBOs) Organized by the Community of Cooperation 'Bread for All' (Switzerland), Held at the Evangelical Theological Seminary in Matanzas, Cuba, September 11-15, 2018* (Matanzas, Cuba, 2018).

Pope Francis, 'Encyclical Letter Laudato Si' of the Holy Father Francis on Care for Our Common Home', 2015, p. 184, http://w2.vatican.va/content/francesco/en/encyclicals /documents/papa-francesco_20150524_enciclica-laudato-si.html.

Various, *Called To Transformative Action. Ecumenical Diakonia (Unpublished Working Paper)* (WCC, Geneva, 2018).

———, *Ecumenical Engagement on Religion and Development. Working Paper Prepared for the Ecumenical Strategic Forum, Geneva, Switzerland, October 3-7,*

2017 (Geneva, 2017).
———, *Transforming Our World: The 2030 Agenda for Sustainable Development. Working Paper Prepared for the Ecumenical Strategic Forum, Geneva, Switzerland, October 3-7, 2017* (Geneva, 2017).
WCC, *The Nature and Mission of the Church. Faith and Order Paper No. 198* (Geneva, 2005), http://www.oikoumene.org/fileadmin/files/wcc-main/documents/p2/FO2005_198_en.pdf.
———, 'Theological Perspectives on *Diakonia* in the Twenty First Century. Document Adopted at the World Council of Churches Conference on Theology of *Diakonia*, 2012' in *Resource Book WCC 10th Assembly, Busan 2013* (Geneva: WCC Publications, 2013).
White, Teresa Joan, '*Diakonia*' in *Dictionary of the Ecumenical Movement*, ed. by Nicholas Lossky et al, 2nd. (Geneva, Switzerland: WCC Publications, 2002), www.oikoumene.org.

Part 3

Contextual Reflections on the Diaconal Church

Diakonia as Asset-based Action and the Role of the Congregation

Zo Ramiandra Rakotoarison

'Mrs. Charline volunteered to sensitise people to protect the environment by teaching handicrafts made from used plastic bags.'[1] Mrs Charline is from a Lutheran congregation in the North South of Madagascar, in the city of Mahajanga. Her asset was her creativity and care for the environment. Her congregation offered, not only for her and other people, a space to share and increase their talents but also an opportunity to decrease used plastic bags in their town, granted a university student a good grade, and provided other people with a new financial source.

The term 'asset' stems from economics vocabulary, later to be used in the social and *diakonia* world. Asset used in an action context is referred to as an approach. In the diaconal sphere, while asset is a more preferable approach than the word needs, rights might be its company. An action is asset-based when it starts with what is present and not look for what is missing or hindering. In general, this kind of action emphasizes and values elements, which in other approaches are missed or undervalued. In this paper, the Use Your Talents approach is also viewed as an asset-based action. The first part of this article will introduce the Use Your Talents project: its history, its characteristics and its strength. The second part will account for ways talents are identified and activated. The ideas in these two sections were mainly drawn from the life and experiences of church in Madagascar. Before we conclude this paper, we will give some examples of congregational use of talents from various countries and denominations in Africa.

Introducing the Use Your Talents Project

In the Dictionary of the Ecumenical Movement, *diakonia* is defined as "responsible service of the gospel by deeds and by words performed by Christians in response to the needs of people".[2] This, in my understanding,

---

[1] Charline Norohanta Razanamampionona, 'Report on beautiful handbags made of re-used plastic bags' in *Use Your Talents – the congregation as primary development agent*. Sigurd Haus (Oslo, Digni, 2017), 120-121.

[2] Teresa J. White, '*Diakonia*' in *Dictionary of the Ecumenical Movement* (Geneva, World Council of Churches and the Wm. Eerdmans, 2002), https://www.oikoumene.

shows the ground of the 'service' and its owner: the gospel and God. Christians are the 'agents' who execute and perform the service not only because of God the 'sender' but also in response to what they see around them, in people's lives and their contexts. With Use Your Talents, church members are the agents in their local communities.

The History

Use Your Talents is a project or an approach to development work that started in FLM[3] (the Malagasy Lutheran Church) in 2008. Madagascar is among the Least Developed Countries on the United Nations list.[4] Poverty, says Andriambonimihanta, the country coordinator for Use Your Talents Madagascar, is so 'obvious' that the church was looking for ways to respond to it through the use of talents.[5] The construction of this approach was built upon the development policy of FLM formulated in 2004 that emphasizes the idea of exalting the local power and work. Through its theologians, the church also worked on and formulated its theology of development on biblical narratives. This theology implies that all believers have a social responsibility to share their God-given 'talents': Jesus and all his blessings for the world's well-being. Use Your Talents teaches Christians that development is theirs: the conception, decision, resources and action are grounded in the church to reach out to the community and society; that they are both responsible before God and people.

FLM then put in place a development structure in keeping with the church's traditional structure[6] that is interconnected. As the concept of Use Your Talents was decided by the national decision body of the church, a project at national level was created to promote and teach the concept to the whole church. Few full-time staff working at national level developed the concept and disseminated it in collaboration with the main persons responsible in the development department structure.

In addition to Norwegian Mission Society, FLM's partner, other Norwegian missions and their church partners in Africa were attracted by the Use Your Talents idea. Following a workshop in 2012, Use Your Talents expanded and included these countries and churches with their partners and in 2013 became a

---

org/en/resources/documents/wcc-programmes/justice-*diakonia*-and-responsibility-for-creation/*diakonia*.

[3] FLM stands for Fiangonana Loterana Malagasy.

[4] United Nations, LDCs at a Glance, 2017, https://www.un.org/development/desa/dpad/least-developed-country-category/ldcs-at-a-glance.html.

[5] Antoine Andriambonimihanta, 'The development of "Use Your Talents" in Madagascar' in *Use Your Talents – the congregation as primary development agent.* Sigurd Haus (Oslo, Digni, 2017), 26.

[6] The smallest unit in the church is the home church and local congregation, one or two congregations form a parish, two or several parishes make a district. Two or several districts bring about a synod. FLM now has 25 synods. The church's associations/departments follow the same organization.

capacity-building project named Use Your Talents Knowledge Development Project. The aim of this knowledge project is an exchange of experiences and improvement of the Use Your Talents approach.

The Characteristics

This is a project or an approach to development that says that the church and its members as God's people have a treasure, 'talents', thus they have to be the first in the world to offer and act to better the life of those around them. The former President of FLM argues that the spirit of Use Your Talents is faith, that people inquire solution in the Bible when faced with difficulties.[7] Biblical interpretation within the Use Your Talents concept affirms that each person is given talents for their own and other people's good; that well-being would only happen if each person uses their talents for themselves and others. This concept is based on the Christians' mission and humans' identity, and the church/congregation is the place where this idea is nurtured.

Use Your Talents also got its inspiration from the ways FLM church was and is engaging itself with its community. The church organizes development activities through various structures: committees, associations and groups. Once the church approved the activities, the community of believers support and implement the work in collaboration with the local community and society. Use Your Talents is also a way to look positively on needs/problems and considers it a step to grow and develop. The United Nations Development Program in the Sustainable Development Goals describes development work as ending poverty, protecting the planet, and ensuring peace and prosperity. With Use Your Talents, development means the local community and nation's well-being that includes physical, mental and spiritual health and wholeness; existence of economic resource (stable and sufficient?); food production, which the former FLM's President describes as 'like survival', a view Campfens affirms[8] (healthy and enough?); educated and informed people to become responsible citizen (autonomous, self-confident?); and environment protection.

Use Your Talents works mainly with volunteers, not professional workers. In Madagascar particularly, Use Your Talents as approach to development is a teaching/concept and a way of working of the church, not an organization outside of the church. Use Your Talents has its foundation and roots in the liturgy and identity of the church. It does not depend on a personal/individual idea/conviction. It is the church's policy and strategy. It is implemented and conveyed within the church structure. Development work starts with what people have and are determined to do. The church members and people in the community who know they have talents increase them and enjoy the privilege

---

[7] Modeste Rakoto Endor, Foreword in *Use Your Talents – the congregation as primary development agent.* Sigurd Haus (Oslo, Digni, 2017), 8

[8] Hubert Campfens, *Community Development around the World. Practice, Theory, Research, Training.* (University of Toronto Press, 1997).

of knowing that they have gifts and a special mandate from God. They are also surprised to discover that they have many more talents and possibilities at their disposal than they thought. Those who experienced Use Your Talents called it an eye/mind-opener.

The Strengths

Based on the conviction that the church is rich, gifted with talents, although living in a poor context, Christians trust, are committed and fascinated by the idea. The concept takes the church into dignifying individuals and community, valuing local resources and expertise, and aiming at the well-being of individuals, community and nation – and ultimately the world. It affirms that Christians possess inherently the means to implement various good works. Gunderson and Cochrane first introduced the idea of asset within religion in relation to health.[9] They called them Religious Health Assets or RHAs. They presented two kinds of assets: tangible and intangible with its outcomes. They explain that tangible assets refer, for instance, to visible resources, and intangible to features such as ceremonies and blessing. In Use Your Talents, talents also include visible components like skills and relationship, and intangible constituents such as blessings and willingness. Like Gunderson and Cochrane with health issues, Use Your Talents proponents also 'advocate a shift of language from focusing on deficits to' talents concerning welfare in general. Use Your Talents affirms that God gives each person a talent; that each has strength and resources to thrive for one's wellbeing. Use Your Talents is against dependency. It is not about a project with external funding and expertise, needs or rights. Putting too much emphasis on talents and no concerns about problems may present a problem though. Problems are part of people's lives and context. If one wants to be effective, one has to consider the context and take seriously into account people's concerns.[10]

The second power of Use Your Talents is its framework. It is integrated in the church's structure that serves as a support and a vertical link to action. This structure is at work for the church/Christians to carry out the gospel and to commit to the wellbeing of all. It also has a horizontal link with the local community. The fact that Use Your Talents is knitted in the church structure ensures its stability and sustainability; it does not depend on a person. Taking into consideration that committees decide what action to implement, however, makes the work complicated and limits creativity. Yet, I suppose this way of working is a safeguard against going astray from the church's values and ways.

---

[9] Gary R. Gunderson and James R. Cochrane, *Religion and the Health of the Public: shifting the Paradigm* (N.Y, Palgrave Macmillan, 2012), 56.

[10] Timothy F. Lull, 'On being a Lutheran. Reflections on church, theology, and faith', *Lutheran Voices* (Minneapolis, Augsburg Fortress, 2006); Robert Linthicum, *Transforming Power. Biblical Strategies for Making a Difference in Your Community* (Illinois, InterVarsity Press, 2003).

It is still in the process of improving its methods, which may be both considered a strength and a weakness as it is open to new ways for improvement. To some extent, the fact that Use Your Talents is a top-down project weakens it as ownership depends on the moment when Christians convinced about the idea embrace it as theirs.

Its third force is its methods. Use Your Talents is a participative, self-help and independent action. Its way of working is summed up in 'the use of talents of Christians and people in the local community'. Use Your Talents gives importance both to action and talents and grassroots initiatives. The work focuses and depends on assets within the community. People are encouraged to voluntarily use their talents by participating, providing materials, ideas, physical energy, time and finance in the activities of the church. Some people with the same talents form a group, discuss and decide what they will do. A handful of dynamic persons stand out as field agents or volunteers. They serve as key people who learn, implement and share their particular knowledge. They play the role as models, mentors and leaders 'motivating and activating others'. It appears to some degree, however, that these people are the only ones who discern and know the community's problems and come to offer help or show how to do things in a better way; a unilateral action, not a community finding solutions together. A personification of the concept to some figures would be detrimental to Use Your Talents, because it risks the disappearance or fading out of the idea with that person.

With the project at national level and the international innovation project, people from different places and countries visit families in one congregation. They stay with the family for a certain time, watch how they live, talk with and learn from them. This network of sharing of experience and learning is also strong but not sustainable as it is dependent on external finances.

But who defines what talents one has and who decides when one uses them? We will try to answer these questions in the next section.

How to Identify and Activate Assets in Use Your Talents

The following ways of identifying and activating talents come from experiences of FLM.

Christian Teaching

The core of Use Your Talents is God and his kingdom.[11] Through Use Your Talents, the church teaches that God gave Christians possessions whether they are mental, physical and material, and these belong to God's kingdom and are meant to be used for it. Above that, God impartially gives human beings

[11] Fabien Lotera, Jean de Dieu Rafalimanana and Jean Claude, 'Talents in first century mediterranean community', Sigurd Haus, *Use Your Talents – the congregation as primary development agent* (Oslo, Digni, 2017), 44-51.

dignity independent of their social status.[12] Gunderson and Cochrane argued that qualifying congregations 'as deliverers of social services, builders of social capital, mobilizers of political constituencies or even producers of culture' distorted their portrayal. They value instead the congregations' spiritual contribution and their role in nurturing and committing people to their faith. Their resolution that RHAs 'cannot be understood without the human agency that moves them from being at rest into something useful' seems to agree with Use Your Talents. With the latter, burying the gift would not benefit the giver nor the one entrusted. This means that the talents/assets would be of no value without people using them. The more Christians use their talents, the more they bless themselves and others around them and God. Even a child can be a volunteer and be God's witness.[13] Thus, Christians became aware of their talents through the church's teachings. One decides to use their talents when one is convinced about God's dignifying word and mission/call.

Individual and Group Awareness

The congregation identifies individuals, family, church and communities' talents first through census. Each family fills or helps to complete a form, which contains the basic information about each family member's status, address, date of baptism, position/membership in the congregation's associations and daily occupation. The form's content depends on the aim of the congregation.

The parish pastor or the development coordinator, or the field agents also identify talents through home visits and individual meetings. During these visits and meetings, the visitors help their hosts to identify their talents and encourage them to use their talents for their own wellbeing and others. With the national and international workshops, those who visit families ask a pre-established set of questions and their exchange help both visitors and hosts to identify the family's talents.

Groups also help individuals identify talents. The Use Your Talents project in Madagascar started using the asset-mapping method of Snow[14] in 2015. This method gathers people in groups, who discuss and encourage one another to think and name their talents as well as those of the others in the group and the church. In Madagascar, one will not dare to say in public what is their special skills for fear of being proud, and this method to some degree helps to overcome that fear. When asked about their talents, often individuals used to

---

[12] Kjell Nordstokke, 'Mapping Out and Mobilising Diaconal Assets' in Stephanie Dietrich, Knud Jørgensen, Kari K. Korslien and Kjell Nordstokke (eds.), *Diakonia as Christian Social Practice. An Introduction* (Oxford, Regnum Books International, 2014), 224.

[13] Sigurd Haus, *Use Your Talents – the congregation as primary development agent* (Oslo, Digni, 2017), 61, 133.

[14] Luther K. Snow, *The Power of Asset Mapping: How Your Congregation Can Act on Its Gifts* (Alban Institute, 2004).

point to their current occupation. Yet, talents include both visible components like skills and relationships, and imperceptible constituents such as blessings and willingness.[15] After learning that God gave each person talents and discovering one's and the community's talents through individual consciousness and other people's help, how may individuals and the community activate their talents?

The Call

The church/individuals activate their talents through various calls. For example, the church may call for volunteers for its activities during the time of announcement within the church service. It also happens that church leaders encourage and call particular persons for specific actions. The church also encourages the grouping of individuals with the same talents or occupation. This group then discusses and decides what they will do together and who will do what, when and where. This group would also discuss their resources and their needs to the church committee if necessary. If there are needs for volunteers or materials, the church will call for other people to get involved or to give. Sometimes, one would only know that they have a certain talent while using it.

Thus, identification and activation of talents relate to each person's response to the church's teaching, encouragement and needs. We will see in the following section experiences from different church and countries.

Examples of Use Your Talents in the Congregations

To illustrate the above presentation, I chose three ways congregations use their talents: as a model and innovator, as a facilitator and as a collaborator. Within the complexity of the Use Your Talents approach, these examples do not represent all experiences in different congregations and countries.

The Congregation, a Model and Innovator

Many people in Africa are experiencing poverty in their lives, families and society, which also affects the congregation's finance. In the story of the Chikwizo community in Zimbabwe, the local community expresses their wish to change their situation and to find a way out.[16] Generally, they rely on external support to meet their needs and the pastor shared in their struggle. The congregation discussed the matter and decided to work on a chicken-breeding project using a new technique. A group was created and families worked together to ensure the norm in the breeding. As a result, the pastor reports that

---

[15] Haus, Use Your Talents, 43, 145.

[16] Margaret Macheca, 'Report on the breeding of bushveld road runners in Chikwizo community', Sigurd Haus, *Use Your Talents – the congregation as primary development agent* (Oslo, Digni, 2017), 122-127.

although the work is in progress, there are encouraging signs that the project is alleviating poverty. In addition, the pastor noticed spiritual growth and increased financial contribution and church membership. Andriambonimihanta states that 'when they (Christians) realise that the work is theirs, they do everything themselves'.[17] Christians are not simple executives; they own the work and invest in it.

The Congregation, a Collaborator

Some contributors of the Use Your Talents book mention that with this approach, the congregation partners with the local people, NGOs and authorities in development work. For instance, with the report on road renovation, all villagers in the district of Vondrozo Madagascar made hundreds of kilometers of road accessible by car, though they are not all Christians. Usually, people in the community not only benefitted from the work but are also called to participate, engage themselves and use their talents in the work. This means in my understanding that all people in the community also contribute to God's kingdom and have talents.

The Congregation, a Place for all Possibilities

In Kenya, with Tinuane, a self-help micro-credit project, the church is working to create 'opportunities for women to actively participate in economic development'.[18] The church assisted women to make savings, be entrepreneurial and improve their lives, which resulted in them 'gaining voice and bargaining powers'. Through this project, some women put in groups find a place for communal sharing, learning and praying.[19] Their group became a home of mutual care.

In other cases, Use Your Talents offers opportunities for people to volunteer, learn, give, and be part of other people's struggles and success.[20]

You may find other experiences in the book *Use Your Talents – the congregation as primary development agent.*

Conclusion

In this paper, we presented the Use Your Talents approach as a diaconal asset-based action in development work, in responses to people's needs, starting with

[17] Andriambonimihanta, *The Development*, 27.

[18] Grace Auma, 'How women can use their talents – experience from Tuinuane savings groups', Sigurd Haus, *Use Your Talents – the congregation as primary development agent* (Oslo, Digni, 2017), 78-80.

[19] Jonah Kitur, 'Tinuane saving groups: Impact on FPFK congregations', Sigurd Haus, *Use Your Talents – the congregation as primary development agent* (Oslo, Digni, 2017), 85.

[20] Sigurd Haus, *Use Your Talents – the congregation as primary development agent* (Oslo, Digni, 2017), 32-41, 53-61.

the congregations', Christians' and local communities' assets. We saw that congregations contribute in the life and welfare of the local community using its talents. We tried to demonstrate that congregations have a firm basis of capacity and strength available for the community. We also showed the sustainable aspect of Use Your Talents and the congregation's place and role in the welfare of the society through this approach.

Bibliography

Campfens, Hubert, *Community Development around the World. Practice, Theory, Research, Training*. University of Toronto Press, 1997.

Gunderson, G. and Cochrane J. R., *Religion and the Health of the Public: Shifting the Paradigm*. N.Y: Palgrave Macmillan, 2012.

Haus, Sigurd, *Use Your Talents – the Congregation as Primary Development Agent*. Oslo: Digni, 2017.

Linthicum, Robert, *Transforming Power. Biblical Strategies for Making a Difference in Your Community*. Illinois: InterVarsity Press, 2003.

Lull, Timothy F., *On Being a Lutheran. Reflections on Church, Theology, and Faith*. Lutheran voices. Minneapolis: Augsburg Fortress, 2006.

Nordstokke, Kjell, 'Mapping Out and Mobilising Diaconal Assets' in *Diakonia as Christian Social Practice. An Introduction*. Ed. Stephanie Dietrich, Knud Jørgensen, Kari K. Korslien and Kjell Nordstokke, Oxford: Regnum Books International, 2014.

Snow, Luther K., *The Power of Asset Mapping: How Your Congregation Can Act on Its Gifts*. Alban Institute, 2004.

United Nations, *LDCs at a Glance*, 2017, https://www.un.org/development/desa/dpad/least-developed-country-category/ldcs-at-a-glance.html.

White, Teresa J., 'Diakonia' in *Dictionary of the Ecumenical Movement*. Geneva: World Council of Churches and the Wm. Eerdmans, 2002, https://www.oikoumene.org/en/resources/documents/wcc-programmes/justice-diakonia-and-responsibility-for-creation/diakonia.

New Paradigms of Leadership in the Church: Leadership as Empowerment?

Beatrice Juma

> A good objective of leadership is to help those who are doing poorly to do well and those who are doing better to do even better. (Jim Rohn)[1]

Introduction

Leadership is a crucial and widely discussed topic where change has been experienced both in the corporate world and religious circles. Empowerment, which is one of the three core aspects of *diakonia*, has increasingly been engaged in the new ways of leadership in business and public sectors as well as in the church. Scholars in *diakonia* have defined empowerment in different ways; this article adopts the definition from Carlos Ham, which is also closely related to the findings in the study presented later in the article. In his words, Carlos defines empowerment as:

> …a dynamic process that enables and inspires, that enhances people's skills and self-confidence; it is a movement by which persons are liberated, to take back and develop the power within, in order to unlock their immense potential and boost their skills, self-confidence and self-assertion….[2]

In the above definition, the source of power is not from outside the person being empowered but within them. The process of empowerment therefore seeks to unlock that power by helping the people involved to discover it and use it. In the field of *diakonia*, scholars emphasize recognizing and integrating *diakonia* in church, thus the church is not church without *diakonia.*[3] Paula Gooder defines a diaconal church as 'a church of disciples, a church which treasures, nurtures, inspires, and challenges all Christians to follow Christ

---

[1] Jim Rohn, 'Servant leadership: Putting your team first and yourself second' in *Mind Tools: Essential skills for an excellent carrier* (December 9, 2017).

[2] Carlos Ham, 'Empowering *diakonia*: A perspective from the world council of churches' in Dietrich Stephanie, Jørgensen Knud, Korslien Karsrud Kari and Nordstokke Kjell (eds.), *Diakonia as Christian Social Practice: An Introduction.* (Oxford: Regnum, 2014).

[3] Kjell Nordstokke, *Liberating Diakonia* (Trondheim: tapir akademisk forlag, 2011), 13.

every day in their lives.'[4] He puts emphasis on the believers: a diaconal church should focus on recognizing and empowering the believers to grow as disciples of Jesus and take part in the church's mission. It seeks to serve the whole person, to empower and grow the person, to prepare and enable them to reach out and serve others. The church exists for a purpose, which should be realized through its vision. Gooder summarizes the vision of the church as one whose focus is:

> …learning together, on the recognition of the gifts offered to all, on mission and, perhaps most importantly, on being a diaconal church which seeks to serve not only the community of the kingdom but also the whole humanity.[5]

This agrees with Jesus' statement in the great commission in Matthew 28:18-20 that the good news should reach out to all humanity. Kari Jordheim points out that through *diakonia*, there is a connection between the church and the community, thus the role of the church in extending the kingdom of God outside the four walls.[6] The diaconal church needs a leadership that aligns itself with this vision and mission and endeavors to employ leadership styles that seek to empower instead of disempower believers. This article reflects on leadership in the diaconal church, and focuses on the role of leaders in fulfilling the mission of a diaconal church through empowerment. The article attempts to respond to the questions: *How can church leadership contribute in creating and attaining a diaconal church? Which leadership styles are appropriate and which roles do the leaders play to empower the church to fulfill her mission?*

The first part of the article discusses research conducted in Kenya on two Methodist congregations on the topic: Use of talents: a way to transform and develop communities in Kenya through congregations. The study sought to describe how two specific congregations in the Methodist Church in Kenya in Kisumu circuit developed church projects through empowering members to use their talents and local resources. This research revealed among other things that church leadership plays a role in either empowering church members to use their talents or the opposite, depending on the leadership approach engaged. The second part of the article briefly discusses Servant leadership as a biblical leadership paradigm with emphasis on empowerment. This article does not analyze "The use of talents" approach; instead it focuses on the role and place of leadership in empowering the congregation to use their talents. Another

---

[4] Paula Gooder, 'Towards a diaconal church: some reflections on the New Testament material' in Clark David, *The Diaconal Church, Beyond the Mould of Christendom* (Epworth, 2008), 99.

[5] Gooder, 'Towards a diaconal church', 99.

[6] Kari Jordheim, 'Bridge-building and go-between: The role of the deacon in church and society' in Dietrich Stephanie, Jørgensen Knud, Korslien Karsrud Kari and Nordstokke Kjell (eds.), *Diakonia as Christian Social Practice: An Introduction* (Oxford: Regnum, 2014), 187.

article in this book analyzes "The use of talents" as an asset-based development approach.

Use of Talents: A Way to Transform and Develop Communities in Kenya through Congregations

The Methodist Church in Kenya (MCK) is one among denominations in Kenya where Christianity was introduced through missionaries. Church buildings and community development projects were built and supported through external funding. Some congregations and projects still flourished after the funding was withdrawn; others were left struggling, partly because of the dependency syndrome mind-set. This research focused on how local congregations can enhance community development that is based on local assets as an alternative way without depending on external aid. The research did not intend to disapprove traditional development approaches, but it attempted to address the dependency syndrome mind-set in church members through creating awareness and encouraging the use of talents and local resources to transform communities.[7] The research question explored was: How can the Methodist church in Kenya, Kisumu circuit create awareness and encourage use of talents to transform and develop their local community?

The study took place in two congregations: an urban congregation, St. Mark; and a rural congregation, Bumula. The congregations were selected because they both had experiences of projects developed through external funding and projects accomplished using local assets. The research involved three projects: a private school and rental houses from St. Mark, and a church building in Bumula. St. Mark Methodist School was initiated by a priest who sought a donor to help build the first part of it, approximately in 1995.[8]

Neither the donor nor St. Mark congregation continued building the school for a long time. After 17 years St. Mark congregation under a new leadership decided to continue building the school using local resources. The second project was the rental houses that the congregation at St. Mark initiated and mobilized local resources to build. Both projects were built out of the need to generate income, to pay the workers and other budget demands. The third project under study was a church building in Bumula, which was started through a brick-making project.[9] Members gathered every Saturday at the church compound and made bricks. When the bricks were ready, some were sold to buy cement and other building material, and the rest were used for building.

---

[7] Beatrice Johansson, *The Use of Talents: A way to transform and develop communities in Kenya through local congregations* (Master thesis, VID vitenskapelige Høgskole, Oslo, 2017).

[8] Johansson, *The Use of Talents*, 42.

[9] Johansson, *The Use of Talents*, 50.

In the study, the building was divided into three phases. The first phase started in the year 2000, laying the foundation, and later building the walls through the bricks project. The second phase, roofing, was done through funding from an American mission team that came to Kenya for a trip. After the second phase, there was a period of conflict in Bumula, partly because of the funding, which led to stagnation of the project. The majority of the members left the congregation to join other churches while others stayed at home and the priest lost the job. The third phase involved a new priest, who decided together with the few members left in the congregation to go back to the brick-making project and continued building the church structure. Through the brick-making project, the former members of the congregation got motivated to return and finish the church project.

The use of talents approach is based on the principle that every community has local assets that can enable development to take place. "Use of Talents" is a biblical approach developed from the parable of the Talents in Matthew 25:14-30. The Use of Talents approach started in Malagasy Lutheran Church as a development approach in the year 2004-2005, but picked up later in 2008. The approach intended to motivate and support the church members to use their talents to build a better Madagascar, thus the question, "What can we do with what we have here and now?[10] In the study, the words "Use of Talents" were used alternatively with "Use of local assets". Through this research, the role and place of leadership in a diaconal church will be revealed as the leaders interact with the members in the initiation and implementation of the projects.

Methods

The study borrowed a lot from action research (AR) strategy, although it was not entirely an action research study. AR deals with practical problems and purposes to cause change in the way of doing things. It also actively includes participants in the study, which happens in cycles, and the knowledge gained therein is applied during the study.[11] The purpose is to empower the participants, including them in the process of research through participation, which enables them to find better ways of solving their daily challenges. The researcher once worked as a priest in both congregations and was involved in the projects under study. As a member of Kisumu circuit from Bumula congregation, the researcher was still directly involved in the continuation of the projects after leaving the circuit and by the time of the study.

The research employed both an unstructured observation method and semi-structured interviews. The researcher visited the congregations to learn and

[10] Sigurd Haus, *Use Your Talents: the congregation as primary development agent Stavanger* (Stavanger: Senter for Intekulturell Kommunikasjon, 2016), 11.

[11] Martin Densombe, *The Good Research Guide: for small-scale social research projects*, 5th edition (Glasgow: Bell & Bain Ltd, 2014), 123.

interact with members working on the ongoing projects. A total of 20 participants took part in the study: 15 were interviewed in two separate focus groups from the 2 congregations. Individual interviews were conducted with five people, including the senior church leaders. The interviews took place in December 2016.[12] There were two main theme areas that guided the study. The first was asset mapping and mobilization, and the second was empowerment. The interview guide, findings and discussion of findings were all guided by the two themes. Three different theories were used in the study, but only relevant concepts from the theories were employed. The dependency theory was applied to understand more about the dependency syndrome mind-set in church members, while empowerment theory and *diakonia* theory were used to understand more about empowerment and the use of talents approach. The following is a presentation of the analyzed data from the study.

Asset Mapping and Mobilization

Asset mapping is a process in which individuals or groups engage to identify different assets in a given setting. Luther Snow presents a four-step process in asset mapping with groups. The process involves participants identifying assets, connecting different assets that can work together, identifying assets the participants feel comfortable to work with, and the group reflecting on the whole process.[13] During the focus group interviews, participants were engaged in a short session where they were asked to identify assets in their community. Since some of the participants were semi-literate, the four steps were not strictly followed. The main idea was to help participants to recognize different resources they had as individuals, groups and community. The assets were listed following Snow's six different categories: physical, economical, individual, associations, institutions and social capital assets.[14]

Asset Mapping Creates Awareness about Available Resources

Stephanie Dietrich observes that all human beings, regardless of who they are in society, are endorsed from creation with talents, abilities and capabilities.[15] On the contrary, it is possible for people to fail to realize this God-given potential unless and until they are empowered and enabled to recognize them. At the end of the process, participants were excited as they commended the process. It was clear that asset mapping was an eye-opener to participants who realized that they had more resources than they ever thought. The asset

[12] Johansson, *The Use of Talents*, 28.

[13] Luther Snow, *The Power of Asset Mapping* (Virginia: The Alban Institute, 2004), 40.

[14] Snow, *The Power of Asset Mapping*, 5.

[15] Dietrich, 'Reflections on core aspect of Diaconal Theory' in Dietrich Stephanie, Jørgensen Knud, Korslien Karsrud Kari and Nordstokke Kjell (eds.), *Diakonia as Christian Social Practice: An Introduction* (Oxford: Regnum, 2014).

mapping process also revealed that church leadership can help and guide members into looking within their churches and communities to find solutions to some of the challenges they are facing. Congregations through leaders can be instrumental in equipping members with how to recognize and mobilize their assets, and this will also impact the community. However, one participant argued that local resources are not sufficient to meet the needs of the community: he added that communities still need external support to supplement local assets.

Initiation and Mobilization of the Church Projects

The researcher sought to know how the projects under study were initiated and mobilized, as well as those who were involved in the process. The findings revealed that all the three projects were initiated and mobilized by the help of leaders, especially priests. However, there was a big difference in how different leaders shared the vision of the projects with the members. Participants pointed out that it matters a lot the way the vision is communicated from the leader at the beginning of the whole process of initiating and mobilizing a project. If the leader imposes the vision exclusively without engaging members' ideas, members feel excluded and left out. All the three projects in the study were initiated to solve a certain need in the congregation. The school and rental houses at St. Mark were both initiated to help the congregation generate income. The church structure at Bumula was started because of increased membership, thus the need for a bigger and better building. The researcher learnt from the participants that church leaders should not give solutions; instead they should motivate, encourage and empower members to find solutions to the needs. Responding to the question of why the St. Mark school project stagnated for too long, one participant expressed his disappointment, saying:

> … the members were not involved in initiating this project and even later on the running of the project, many things were kept in secret and members knew only a little about the project. That made the people not to own the project because they did not feel attached to it, thus lack of ownership….[16]

This suggested that leaders in church should allow space for members to share in the vision, to own and contribute in finding solutions to their needs or challenges. Leaders should not use their authority to dictate what should be done; instead they should give opportunity to members to collectively come up with a solution. Bryant Myers argues that the present approach of social analysis empowers the community so that its members who understand the history and social structure and context of their communities can actively take part in the analysis process. Unlike the traditional analysis in development, the

[16] Johansson, *The Use of Talents*, 43.

task should be left to the community members as a way of empowering them for action.[17] The researcher used the process of asset mapping to help participants realize the possibilities they had in using the local resources to solve their needs. Only one participant expressed that it did not matter who initiated the project: members had a responsibility to embrace what was given to them and take care of it because it was meant to benefit them.

Missing Diaconal Work, Missing Church in the Community?

The study revealed that both congregations had limited knowledge about diaconal assets and there was no diaconal work done by the congregations in the community. Both congregations concentrated on meeting their needs and thought they did not have enough resources to reach out to the needs in the community. Leaders can use the asset-mapping process to create awareness in congregations about the diaconal assets and how the church can mobilize them for social work. Kjell Nordstokke's article *Mapping out and Mobilising Diaconal Assets* identifies diaconal assets as those assets found within the church to be used for social work, classified into tangible and intangible assets.[18] Tangible assets include: church programmes for social work, institutions and buildings, people's abilities, economic support, and publications that communicate about *diakonia*. Intangible assets include: bible narratives and personalities in history, rites and rituals, value systems in the communities, the sense of belonging and inclusiveness. In addition, intangible assets consist of the commitment of religious institutions to human wellbeing, religious leaders' moral authority in communities, the role of being pioneers in social change, promoting the rights of the vulnerable such as the disabled and children, and promoting the role of women.

On the St. Mark church compound, there were three different projects that in fact are diaconal assets to the congregation. The school at St. Mark whose purpose is to generate income for the congregation can be a means to assist children from poor families who could not afford to pay fees. There are also two humanitarian organizations: Kisumu Action Disability Development Network (KADDET) and Life in Abundance, which have rented space and built offices to organize their activities to serve the community. Both these organizations do not belong to St. Mark congregation, but their presence on the church compound is an opportunity that the congregation could use to learn more and network to reach out and serve the community. The brick-making project at Bumula could also be an opportunity for the congregation to challenge people in the community who are idle and those who think they have no resources to make their lives better.

---

[17] Bryant Myers, *Walking with the Poor: Principles and practices of transformational development* (Maryknoll, NY: Orbis Books, 2016), 248-249.

[18] Nordstokke, *Liberating diakonia*, 217.

Empowerment

In the study, empowerment was the second theme. The researcher employed empowerment theory from the development area of study to discuss the ability of every community to start development using local assets. The theory recognized that people are a major asset: their abilities, talents and other local resources can make a big difference. This research revealed that empowerment started with asset mapping. Involving participants in this process helped them to discover on their own the resources and talents they had as individuals, the church and the community. When leaders give room to members to be part of this process, the members get empowered to know they are trusted and expected to contribute to their community.

The research findings revealed that empowerment starts from what is already available in people. As indicated earlier, the source of power is not from outside the person being empowered but within them. It was interesting to see how the participants got excited and energized when they discovered how much resources they had. The power was already within them but it required someone to help point to that power. In empowerment, church leaders are instrumental in creating processes or spaces to motivate people to see their potential. Unfortunately, churches have experienced the opposite when leaders, whether consciously or unconsciously, deny people the opportunity to discover their potential. In addition to the questions about who initiated the projects, the researcher also sought to understand who and how the members and leaders in both congregations were involved in the projects and what were their experiences.

Participation and Voluntary Work are Key to Empowerment

Empowerment comes through participation and voluntary work. Participants from both congregations in the study shared their different experiences between projects funded by donors and those funded through local resources. Through observation, the donor-funded projects were nice looking and well-finished compared to the latter. In terms of time, it took shorter time with external funding to complete the projects while those implemented using local resources took longer to finish. However, participants confessed that it was almost impossible to learn anything from projects funded by donors, members were hardly involved in any way and they did not have a story to tell. On the other hand, participants from MCK Bumula narrated how they initiated a brick-making project to start building the new church structure and how St. Mark members initiated a rental house project. They shared their positive experiences and challenges they encountered throughout the process. It was clear that members volunteered and participated more when they did not have external funding, and this was a better way to learn and get empowered. Participation and use of talents also increased ownership of the projects' sustainability.[19] Ownership was emphasized as a crucial motivator in accomplishing the projects. Sometimes the priest who shared the vision of a certain project can get transferred to another circuit before the completion of the project, which can be a challenge to the congregation to complete the project. Participants explained that when members own the project, it is easier to overcome challenges and finish the project than when they do not own it.

Participants also shared about the growth experienced through their involvement. They learnt lessons in the process of working together and discovered where to improve in the next project. The interviews in the St. Mark focus group brought back memories for the participants, who expressed how they had overcome the fear of impossibility after accomplishing the rental house project. This was a small congregation that was afraid to start the rental house project because they were few. One participant summarized his experience saying: *"We felt we have grown but we also feel we need to grow more. We are now energized, we can now think of building another house and even do it in a better way."*[20]

In both congregations, participants had experienced both good and bad leadership. Some leaders were praised for being at the forefront in initiating and mobilizing projects, including members in the vision for projects, sacrificing themselves to give their resources, and serving the congregations selflessly. However, some leaders imposed visions on the congregations and did not allow members to be part of the decision-making process. Others misused money meant to be used for projects, which in turn ruined the trust of members and stagnated the projects. The research also revealed members' overdependence on leaders. All the three projects and others not in this study were initiated and mobilized by priests. This is a weakness observed in the study and it reveals the need for empowerment. When members over-depend on the leaders it depicts lack of empowerment either in the leaders or members or both parties. At the end of the study, the researcher suggested that "The use of talents" approach should begin by empowering church leaders to be servant leaders, who will in turn empower the members to serve and share in God's mission.

Biblical Leadership Model – Servant Leadership

In the Bible, leadership is portrayed to mean service/*diakonia*.[21] Different words are used to refer to servant in the New Testament. The word *diakonos* was used to refer to a servant or waiter with emphasis on serving one another,

[19] Johansson, *The Use of Talents*, 37-58.
[20] Johansson, *The Use of Talents*, 72.
[21] Knud Jørgensen, *Equipping Christian Leadership for Service in Church and Society* (Oxford: Regnum, 2012), 23-24.

as in the case of widows in Acts 6. Another word is *doulos*, which means a slave, emphasizing the relations between a servant and a master. In John 13: 4-15, Jesus overturns the roles of a master and his juniors when he the master and teacher washes his disciples' feet. He challenges them to go out and serve each other in the same way. *Huperetes* is another word that refers to a slave chained to his bench with a duty to row the ship across the sea. The word is used to emphasize the task of leaders as servants under authority in 1 Corinthians 4:1. The word *leitourgos* has emphasis on a leader in an organization, thus a leader should act for the good of everybody under their leadership. In addition, *diakoneo* was used to mean different things, among them to refer to the ecclesiastical office of a deacon.[22] Deacons were well known as servants, so leadership is servantship. Jesus emphasizes to his disciples that the greatest among them was a servant in Luke 22:27.

In these scriptures, a few characteristics of Jesus' model of leadership can be identified. The aspect of putting others first is visible. Jesus brought out the aspect of humility using the example of a child in Mark 9:33-37. The idea of humility can easily be confused for weakness, but Jesus confirms that he is the Lord and servant at the same time. He said to the disciples in John 13:13-14, 'You call me "teacher" and "Lord". And this is right because that is what I am.' This statement reveals that Jesus was conscious of his power and authority and confirmed to the disciples that he was powerful, yet he humbled himself to serve them.

Servant leadership entails taking part in the *missio dei*, which involves the Trine God, thus the Father sends the Son, and the Son sends the Spirit who sends the church. Jesus was sent by God to bring good news of God's kingdom to the suffering world. He declared his mission in Luke 4:18, to reach out to the poor, to those struggling spiritually, to the blind, to those who have been treated unfairly, he announced a new reign, a transformation. Servant leaders should be occupied with this mission of changing the communities, societies and the environment, to enable a foretaste of God's kingdom on earth.[23]

Knud Jørgensen emphasizes the caring role of a leader as a shepherd illustrated in John 21.16.[24] God has bestowed leaders with the responsibility of feeding, protecting and guiding, among other duties. Andrew Clarke expresses the same sentiments when he asserts that Pauline epistles reveal two metaphors used alongside church leadership: the body and the household.[25] Church leadership includes 'ensuring that due honour and recognition are given to the

---

[22] Ikenye, Ndung'u John Brown, *Modelling Servant-Leaders for Africa: Lessons From St. Paul* (Eldoret: Zapf Chancery Publishers, 2010), 77.

[23] David Verlingieri, 'Servantship', www. academia.edu/people/search/servantship, accessed January 20, 2018, 9.

[24] Jørgensen, *Equipping Christian Leadership for Service in Church and Society*, 27.

[25] Andrew Clarke (ed.), *A Pauline Theology of Church Leadership* (London: T&T Clark, 2008), 182.

weak, vulnerable and marginalized, and that all members of the body are fulfilling their God-appointed task and contribution to the body of Christ.'[26] Paul also uses the metaphor of the household in leadership to refer to the task of teaching. In the house-church, the head was the overseer and was responsible for teaching members of the household. The two tools for leadership presented by Paul were teaching and persuasion.[27]

In the spirit of the priesthood of all believers, leaders have a duty to train and equip more people to take part in the ministry. This can be achieved through Theological Education by Extension (TEE), bible schools and seminars.[28]

Robert Greenleaf, who is the author of servant leadership, brings out the difference between one who is 'a servant first' and one who is 'a leader first'. In his words:

> The servant leader is a servant first. It begins with the natural feeling that one wants to serve. Then conscious choice brings one to aspire to lead. The best test is: do those served grow as persons: do they, while being served, become healthier, wiser, freer, more autonomous, more likely themselves to become servants? And, what is the effect on the least privileged in society; will they benefit, or, at least, not be further deprived?[29]

The questions point to the empowerment aspect of the leader, one who desires to make others better as he leads. Servant leadership literature points out the sharp contrasts in the use of authority of the leader. In traditional autocratic leadership, the leader always at the top owns all the power; the difference with servant leadership is the social aspect and responsibility.[30] In servant leadership power is shared, the needs of others come first and the leader is willing to help people to bring out their best.[31] Ten characteristics define servant leaders: listening, empathy, healing, awareness, persuasion, conceptualization, foresight, stewardship, commitment to growth of the people, and building community.[32]

In church leadership research, servant leadership model is now widely discussed by scholars, who also point out the difference between servant leadership as practiced in management versus biblical servant leadership. Vhumazi Magenzi states these differences:

---

[26] Clarke, *A Pauline Theology of Church Leadership*.
[27] Clarke, *A Pauline Theology of Church Leadership*.
[28] Jørgensen, *Equipping Christian Leadership for Service in Church and Society*, 26.
[29] Spears, *Character and Servant Leadership*, 26.
[30] Magenzi, 'God-image of Servant King as powerful but vulnerable and serving', 6.
[31] Robert Greenleaf, Center for Leadership, www.greenleaf.org, accessed January 10, 2018.
[32] Spears, Character and servant leadership: Ten characteristics of effective, caring leaders, 27-28.

> Biblical servant leadership is different in five areas, reference, guiding principles, motivation, agent and goal. The reference point is Jesus as King and servant, the guiding principles are drawn from the normative source – scriptures; motivation is the realization of God's kingdom on earth; agent refers to the embodiment of the biblically desired leadership by human leaders; and the goal is faith development. This framework of servant leadership suggests that the locus and context of biblical leadership is the church, although the reach is both to the faith community and to the larger community.[33]

Biblical servant leadership refers to Jesus as the model of a good leader, thus the essence of this leadership is to follow Jesus Christ.

Conclusion

The first part of this article has tried to show that dealing with the challenge of dependency syndrome mind-set requires the right leadership to empower church members to realize the local resources at their disposal. The research revealed that when church members were given room to be involved in the projects, they got empowered and enabled to use their talents. As a result, they were able to take part in the projects of the church and the church's mission.

Church leaders can either enable or hinder empowerment depending on their use of authority. Through asset mapping, it is possible to guide people to realize and recognize the God-given potential and the local assets that can be used in church and community. Participation and voluntary work is one way of empowering people. The second part of the article reflected on the biblical servant leadership model, which revealed that service is key to leadership as stipulated in the Bible. Jesus himself is the model of a servant leader and expects that all church leaders follow his example. Servant leadership exemplifies the model of leadership in the diaconal church. The researcher recommends that church leaders should be empowered to practice servant leadership.

Bibliography

Clarke, Andrew (ed.), *A Pauline Theology of Church leadership* (London: T&T Clark, 2008).

Dietrich, Stephanie, 'Reflections on core aspect of Diaconal Theory' in Dietrich Stephanie, Knud Jorgensen, Kari Karsrud Korslien and Nordstokke (eds.), *Diakonia as Christian Social Practice: An Introduction* (Oxford: Regnum, 2014).

Eldebo, Runer, 'The Complexity of Church Leadership' in Harald Askeland and Per Hansson (eds.), *The Second International Conference on Church Leadership* (Uppsala: Sweden, September 15-16, 2005).

[33] Magenzi, 'God-image of Servant King as powerful but vulnerable and serving', 6.

Fretheim, Kjetil, 'Church Leadership and Congregational Change' in Harald Askeland, Ulla Schmidt (eds.), *Church Reform and Leadership of Change* (Oregon: Pickwick, 2015).

Gooder, Paula, 'Towards a diaconal church: some reflections on the New Testament material' in Clark David, *The Diaconal Church, Beyond the Mould of Christendom* (Epworth, 2008).

Ham, Carlos, 'Empowering *diakonia*: A perspective from the world council of churches' in Dietrich Stephanie, Knud Jorgensen, Kari Karsrud Korslien and Nordstokke (eds.), *Diakonia as Christian Social Practice: An Introduction* (Oxford: Regnum, 2014).

Haus, Sigurd, *Use Your Talents: The Congregation as Primary Development Agent* (Stavanger: Senter for Intekulturell Kommunikasjon, 2016).

Ikenye, Ndung'u John Brown, *Modelling Servant-Leaders for Africa: Lessons from St. Paul* (Eldoret: Zapf Chancery, 2010).

Jørgensen, Knud, *Equipping Christian Leadership for Service in Church and Society* (Oxford: Regnum, 2012).

Jørgensen, Knud, 'Equipping for service: *Diakonia* and capacity building' in Dietrich Stephanie, Knud Jorgensen, Kari Karsrud Korslien and Nordstokke (eds.), *Diakonia as Christian Social Practice: An introduction* (Oxford: Regnum, 2014).

Magenzi, Vhumazi, 'God-image of Servant King as powerful but vulnerable and serving: Towards transforming African leadership at an intersection of African kingship and biblical kingship to servant leadership' in *HTS Telogogiese Studies/Theological Studies*, 71, nov.2015 (accessed January 4, 2018).

Myers, Bryant, *Walking with the poor: Principles and practices of transformational development* (Maryknoll, NY: Orbis Books, 2016).

Nordstokke, Kjell, *Liberating Diakonia* (Trondheim: tapir akademisk forlag, 2011).

Patte, Daniel (ed.), *The Cambridge Dictionary of Christianity* (New York: Cambridge University, 2010).

Snow, Luther, *The Power of Asset Mapping* (Virginia: The Alban institute, 2004).

Spears, Larry C. 'Character and servant leadership: Ten characteristics of effective, caring leaders' in *The Journal of Virtues and Leadership*, Vol 1 (2010).

Rethinking Ecclesiology in a Diaconal Way in the Anglican Church in Malawi

Jeromy Limbani Juttah

Introduction

The Anglican Church in Malawi is part of the Church of the Province of Central Africa encompassing the countries of Malawi, Zambia, Zimbabwe and Botswana. The province is also part of the worldwide Anglican Communion. The church owes its beginning to the work of Universities Mission to Central Africa in the second half of the 1800s. The connections to the Western world and the historical developments are reflected in the ecclesiological trends and action of the Malawi church. The ecclesiological stance therefore contributes greatly to the path taken by the church in its action at every political turn. Malawi is one of the countries where the Church has played a fundamental role in both social and political contexts. This is true since the missionary age, throughout the colonial period to the present. With its roots in the Western domain, the Malawi Church has reflected an ecclesiology that reveals much of ecclesial heritage of the time. However, the link between the social practice of the Church and *diakonia* is faint. Despite the growing Western interest in *diakonia* during the past decades, little has been done to present a diaconal reflection on the mission and ministry of the Church aside from the Western reflections or reflective of the heritage of colonialism.

This article will explore and discuss how the church in Malawi can reflect on its nature and purpose from a diaconal perspective. This will be done in three stages: first, I will give a general view of Anglican Ecclesiology; second, I will present a brief Malawian history and the functionality of the Church in Malawi, and the third stage will concern understanding ecclesiology from a diaconal perspective. Studies on *diakonia* have only sparingly been part and parcel of the Malawian theological literature (with the exception of Master Theses presented at universities across the world by Malawian students). As such, the literature referred to is at most Western, and the Malawian literature used on ecclesiology is not directly diaconal. The approach is critical to the current practice and presents empirical material that highlights the perception in view of ecclesiology in the Anglican Church in Malawi, while the data of the Church in general is derived from desk research.

General Anglican Ecclesiology

The Hannover report of the Anglican-Lutheran International Commission defines *diakonia* as:

> …ministry of service, outreach, humility and concern for human needs that finds its source in Jesus "…the agent and image of the one who sent him, acting and forgiving with his Father's own power, mediating the Father's will to the world".[1]

This places the diaconal function within the theology of the nature and being of the Church, such that one can talk of an ecclesiology from a diaconal perspective. Anglican ecclesial theology recognizes the need for structures that help to order the life of the church. The church is a community that is in the world. By the act of baptism, God calls into being the members who form the ecclesial reality. This is based on the biblical image of the church as the body of Christ.[2] The baptismal community expresses its life through liturgy and the sacraments, service for one another and services in the community at large. All members of this community are naturally involved in ministry in their life situation. The understanding is that through baptism, members of the ecclesial community engage in ministry. Since ministry in Anglican ecclesiology is threefold, baptism then enables the believers to be part of ministry of priesthood, of episcope, and of *diakonia*.

> The whole community of the baptized is called to proclaim the good news of God in Jesus Christ, to administer the sacraments, and to care for the people of God. The whole community of the baptized is called to preserve faith, order, discipline, and unity. And the whole community of the baptized is called to be agents of God's mercy, healing, and justice in the church and the world.[3]

All the baptized participate in the ministries of bishop, deacon and priest. The church ordains some within the community through the sacrament of ordination in order to represent the community of believers in their ministry and mirror the priesthood of all.[4] In keeping with this concept, Anglican ministry exercises the threefold ordained ministry of deacons, priests and bishops. Ordained ministry is "service of leadership".[5] It is leadership in the sense that the ordained function as missional pioneers for the corporate body of Christ. Deacons enable others also to serve; priests function to make the

---

[1] The Hanover Report*: The Diaconate as Ecumenical Opportunity* (London, UK: Anglican Communion Publications, 1996), paragraph 10.

[2] A.E. McGrath, *Christian Theology: An Introduction* (Oxford: Blackwell, 1994).

[3] The Iona Report: *The Diaconate in the Anglican church of Canada*, the general Synod of the Anglican Church of Canada, 2016: 16.

[4] P. Avis, T*he Anglican Understanding of the Church* (New Edition). (London: SPCK, 2013).

[5]Weil, Liturgy for Living (New York: Seabury Press, 1979), 286.

priesthood of all believers possible; and bishops exercise responsible oversight over all such ministries. The ecclesial functionality rests on the ministerial functionality of the office bearers. The diaconate is an essential office in the life of the church. It reminds the church of its servant character and call to service. While all the believers by their baptism are called to feed the hungry, offer drink to the thirsty, welcome the stranger, clothe the naked, care for the sick and visit those in prison (Matt 25:31-46), deacons are specially charged with the task to be models, enablers, leaders and motivators for all the faithful. They are meant to reveal the presence of Christ among the needy and helpless and reveal this to all the people of God.[6] Deacons being part of the ecclesial functionality means that we cannot build an ecclesiology without the diaconal calling of the church, hence a diaconal ecclesiology.

Introduction to Malawi and the Church

Malawi in General

Malawi is a small landlocked country of 118,484 square kilometres, 20 percent of which is water, located in southeast Central Africa, west and north of Mozambique, east of Zambia and south of Tanzania. Eighty percent of the population lives in rural areas where the main means of living is rain-fed agriculture. Malawi's population is 13,077,160 people; 82.7% are Christians, 13% are Muslims, 1.9 % other religions and 2.5 % non-religious. Women represent 51.4% of the total population (Malawi National Statistics 2008). The country is divided into three administrative regions: north, center and south. Christianity in Malawi is a combination of Catholics, Protestants and African churches. Catholics are less than Protestants in number. Protestants are further grouped in the following: Presbyterians, Baptist, Pentecostal, Evangelical, Apostolic and Methodist, just to mention a few. The Church of Central African Presbyterian (CCAP) in Malawi has the highest population of the Protestant.

Brief History of Malawi

Malawi was colonized by Great Britain from 1891 until July 1964 when she got her independence and gained republic status in 1966, under the leadership of Ngwazi Dr H. Kamuzu Banda, who ruled the country autocratically from 1964 to 1994 with the Malawi Congress Party (MCP). He led a repressive regime, having a strong personal interest in policy and engaging closely with a capable civil service. Banda's government delivered a rapid economic growth; the economic and political he used could be described as 'unsustainable'.[7]

---

[6] O. Plater (Rev. Ed.), *Many Servants: An Introduction to Deacons* (Cambridge: Cowley Publications, 2004), 111.

[7] Chirwa and Dorward, *Malawi: Political, Policy, Livelihoods, and Market Background,* Oxford Scholarship Online: January 2014.

There was also no meaningful regard for welfare policies in his policies. He and his party played down the existence of chronic poverty, leading to growing suffering and discontent. He was ousted and in 1994, when the country adopted a multi-party system of government whose first president was Dr. Bakili Muluzi. Muluzi led the country up to 2004 under the United Democratic Front (UDF) party. Muluzi's era reveals serious macro-economic mismanagement, resulting in rampant inflation, worrisome falls in the value of the Malawi currency, as well as a weakening of government capacity. Social protection and welfare services crumbled and poverty levels increased.[8]

Bingu Wa Muntharika, Muluzi's handpicked candidate, succeeded him following the 2004 elections. Mutharika's policies led to government success in improving macro-economic management. However, Mutharika also shared Banda's autocratic tendencies. His second term saw increasing concerns about corruption and patronage within his government. Following his sudden death in 2012, his vice Joyce Banda, who by then had also formed her Peoples Party (PP), took over the presidency to finish his term, which ended in 2014. Joyce Banda lost the elections to Bingu's brother, Peter Mutharika, in 2014. Peter's term claims to have made economic gains despite facing challenges of donor apathy and severe weather. However, increasing prices on the market and a heavily taxed system has led to an increase in poverty and suffering of the people. Throughout the period presented above, the church continued to be a great partner to the government in development, through provision of services like health, agriculture and education among others. The period also reveals that the church was either passive and tolerant of oppression of the masses or active and critical to the regime.[9] The question then is, why did the church, for instance during Banda's regime, tolerate the status quo? This no doubt was based on a particular ecclesiological view.

General Church Functionality in Malawi

The Church has been present in Malawi's history since the missionary era in the 1900s. The social role or involvement of the Church in social political activities has always been there. However, the article questions whether this can be connected to the diaconal image and discusses the need for a diaconal ecclesial image of the Church.

Kenneth Ross, formerly a professor at University of Malawi's Chancellor College, has documented the development of Christianity in Malawi. He traces the social impact of the Christian witness and how social issues – gender, for instance – have been affected by the presence of Christianity. Clearly such questions provide an arena for discussing issues that relate to the social-

---

[8] *Ibid.*

[9] P. Gundani, *Church-State Relations in South Africa, Zambia and Malawi in Light of the Fall of the Berlin Wall* (October 1989), HTS Teologiese Studies/Theological Studies 74 (1), 4852. https://doi.org/ 10.4102/hts.v74i1.485.

economic relevance of the Christian witness. Ross highlights a Roman Catholic Bishops' letter to the State, which contributed to the political changes in Malawi between 1992 and 1994, changes that culminated in the dawn of multiparty democracy. In the letter the bishops highlighted the role of the church in the social arena and the need for the church to communicate its view of human life and of the society. The reason for this view is ecclesiological in nature based on the understanding that the church 'exists in the world…', citing Pope Paul the VI, who stated that the church did not mean to restrict her action only to the religious field, but rather she is to take into account the issues pertaining to man's temporal situations.[10] Ross provides a historical understanding of the development of Christianity in Malawi and shows that the nature of the church has always had social action as part of its self-consciousness. This is ecclesiological in perspective since one cannot talk of the being of the church while excluding the social dimension.

Billy Gama[11] presents three models of ecclesial reflections in relation to the church's involvement in the socio-political matters. He argues Malawian theologians portray theologies of separation, identification, prophetic and transformational. Each of these theological models describes how the proponents view and interpret ecclesiology. Theologies of separation argue that the Church be separated from the worldly issues like participation in socio-political matters. This model encourages the believers to accept the hardships that rise out of the world order, and that they concentrate on their need to conform to the will of God. Romans 12:2 and Hebrews 11: 25 are used as biblical verses in support of the above. In identification theologies, the church is said to identify itself with the secular, arguing that both Joseph and Daniel in the OT took positions in the secular system and assisted the welfare of the people, believers and non-believers alike. Transformational and prophetic models argue that the Church is a watchdog and challenge the enslaving systems of the world. Building on the models of the liberation stories in the OT and the call of Jesus as one to liberate the poor, these models argue that the church is called to be an instrument of the transformation as part of its service and mission in the world. These analyses bring out images of the Church that the Malawian community shares.

In another publication, Kenneth Ross[12] carried out research to see the main emphases in sermons of mainstream Christianity in Malawi. Among the themes that he considered were mission and evangelism, incarnation and social renewal. Among these, social renewal was not popular in the sermons. The

---

[10] K. Ross, *Christianity in Malawi: A Source Book* (Kachere: Zomba, 1995), 205.

[11] Billy Gama, *The Relationship between the State and the Church: A Theologically Based Investigation into the Social Doctrine of the Church in Malawi*, Master Thesis, University of Fort Hare.

[12] K. Ross, *Gospel Ferment in Malawi: Theological Essays* (Gweru: Mambo Press, 1995)

results portray that in the minds of the preachers, practical Christianity was not highly regarded. Ross agrees that there was little attention given to family life or society as a whole for instance, as part of the preachers' image of the Church.[13]

Malawi Anglicanism and Ecclesiology

From an Anglican perspective there is a lack of literature from Malawian Anglican writers that reflect theologically on the Church. The Anglican view of ecclesiology given here is based on two main texts: one by James Tengatenga, former bishop of the Anglican Church in Malawi, and another by Henry M'baya, a minister in the Church, but resident in South Africa. Tengatenga in one of his works has dedicated a whole chapter to discussion on ecclesiology from a Malawian perspective. Tengatenga states that the church's involvement in socio-political matters as well as its failure to get involved makes a statement on what it means to be church. The question then is how the church perceives that involvement in society and state, and if it is to be understood as part of its character. This is an ecclesiological statement and it begs for an evaluation of the church's self-understanding and self-identity, which must trigger its external behavior. I believe that the practice seems to have been that the church acts first, then reflects on her action, and mostly the reflection is left with those who are able to theologize. At the very beginning of the action, can we talk of the motivation of the action being the church's ecclesiological self-consciousness? Or is the action simply out of circumstances and without a deliberate self-understanding in the background? The ecclesiology of the church cannot in anyway be one that isolates itself from the world in which it is placed.[14] The question then is how the church perceives that involvement in society and state, and if it is to be understood as part of its character. This is an ecclesiological statement and it begs for an evaluation of the church's self-understanding and self-identity, which must trigger its external behavior.

The Anglican involvement in the society and the state from the beginning of the missionary task in Malawi as Tengatenga highlights was one that tended to preserve the order of the day. The church sought to maintain order by collaborating with the colonial establishment of the time, basically because of the connections of the missionaries with the British colonizers. This self-identity resonated with an ecclesiology that allowed for the collaboration without considering the human condition that culminated in suffering under the injustices that the colonial rule caused. Tengatenga argues that the early

---

[13] Ross, 1995b, 84.

[14] J. Tengatenga, *Church, State and Society in Malawi: The Anglican Case*. Zomba MW, Kachere Series, 2006.

Anglican ecclesiology in Malawi can be interpreted as Erastian.[15] Most of this period is counted from the early missionary tasks until the independence and the democratization process in the country. The semblance that can be deducted from the Anglican position in relation to its political environment and some strokes in the history of the early church begs for the need to briefly look at the historical church position in relation to its environment. How did the early church understand itself in relation to the world, in this case represented by a political relation? It is understood that the Jesus dispensation portrays a tension similar to that of the Old Testament; in the religious establishment one is aware of the presence of civil rule but acknowledges the sovereignty of the rule of God. The early church was passively resistant to political power but understood that political power was an entity under the sovereignty of God.[16]

Dramatic change occurs when the church rises to political and civil involvement with the coming of Emperor Constantine. Tremendous growth of power among the religious leaders occurs – a situation that compromises the critical distance witnessed in the early church and the Old Testament. This, however, does not imply the failure by the Church to render services to humanity. It does not imply the loss of diaconal identity of the church. My argument here is that this model affects the ecclesial outlook. With change in the historical events of the church's circumstances comes change in the ecclesial theology. It can also be argued to bring about changes in the diaconal identity. Thus, constructing an ecclesial profile of the Anglican Church in Malawi can be said to depend on the historical landscape over a certain stretch of time.

Henry Mbaya states that the ecclesiology of the Anglican Church in Malawi and Central Africa as a whole was derived from that of the ecclesial views of the West following its origin from English-based missionaries in the name of Universities Mission to Central Africa (UMCA) and Society for the Propagation of the Gospel (SPG). This background leads to the church's view of bishops being that of the Anglo-Saxony, which in turn influenced the ecclesiology of the Church. The church is first an institution, and then viewed as a community, which according to Mbaya is because "traditionally the Anglican Church in Central and Southern Africa has been too closely identified with the sacramental role of the episcopate, and by extension the priesthood".[17] Mbaya's observations imply an institutional ecclesiology. Tengatenga points out that the Anglican Church in Malawi is institutionally governed, with the

---

[15] Doctrine that the state is superior to the church in ecclesiastical matters, see Tengatenga, *Church, State and Society in Malawi: The Anglican Case*. Zomba MW, Kachere Series, 2006.

[16] See Tengatenga 2006, Webber 1986.

[17] Henry Mbaya, 'Church as Mbumba and Bishop as Nkhoswe: Anglican Ecclesiology and Missiological Imperatives in Central Africa' in *Journal of Anglican Studies Vol. 14(2)*, 183.

ordained taking higher hierarchical positions above the laity. What this polity means is that the ordained and especially the bishops are the chief theologians, teachers and spokespersons of the church. What this means for me is that much of the church's action and ecclesiology is based on that of the bishops as the chief pastors. This questions whether the bishop's view of things is the layman's view of things.

This question can be observed in Tengatenga's findings, in which understanding of what church is among the laity was limited as compared to that of the clergy. In the research Tengatenga carried out, in which respondents were answering the question 'what is Church?', the clergy presented a communal understanding of the church, dwelling on the meal of the communion, the Eucharist, while there was lack of clarity and resonance with regard to communal view of ecclesiology among the laity.[18] However, the theology that reflects the identity of the Church and its placement in the world was missing from the responses. Despite the gaps, Tengatenga's work points to a kind of ecclesiology that reaches the diaconal realm, although the language of *diakonia* and the connection to the ministry of deacons are not found in his work. The ecclesiology he reflects can to an extent be described as diaconal. It is aware of the call that the church answers not only to the faithful but also to the world at large, offering service to one another and to the world.

What has been presented here shows that the church in Malawi has serious connections to the colonial heritage with regard to its ecclesiology. Perhaps this as well as consideration of the African own hierarchical heritage has resulted in a leadership that is top-bottom. As a result, there is little understanding of the ecclesial basis and purpose of the church's action by those in the pew. The people at the grassroots are not aware of the theological grounding of what the leaders are doing on behalf of the Church. Furthermore, the descriptions highlight the lack of diaconal reflections in the ecclesiology of Malawi Christianity. There is a conspicuous gap of the diaconal presence in the functionality of the Church seen mainly through the absence of the mention of deacons in the theoretical and practical exercise of the ecclesial perceptions. This then calls for the need for the Church in Malawi to reconsider its stand with regard to ecclesiology, especially toward a diaconal perspective.

Masters Research Findings

In June 2016 I presented a master thesis on 'the role, identity of deacons and the practice of diaconal ministry in the Anglican Church in Malawi. How is the deacon's ministry understood and how does this affect the practice of diaconal ministry in the Anglican Church in Malawi?' This empirical study established that despite there being structures of *diakonia* in the church, there are gaps in relating these structures and programs to the ministry of deacons, as well as

[18] James Tengatenga, 2006.

relating them to the nature and purpose of the church. The research discovered that there is a dichotomous view of the diaconal structures and the spiritual life of the church.

The study indicated that deacons are commonly understood as servants, assistants to priests and bishops, as well as priests-in-the-making. As servants they are expected to offer and submit to humble service, in a menial and servile sense, which in the end diminishes their importance and authority. The study revealed that viewing deacons as being assistants and priests-in-the-making results in obscurity of their office, as they do not fully serve in the capacity. Their office is confused with that of priests, mainly because deacons in the Church are mostly transitional. The one year or less during which they serve as deacons is spent instead on preparation for the next office, which limits the chances of cultivating their diaconal understanding and practice. This means the transitional diaconate in part contributes to a distorted picture of the diaconate. In terms of their roles the research found that deacons are charged with liturgical and pastoral roles. In addition, deacons may carry out social responsibilities but this is not obvious in practice. The research found that the practice of the liturgical and social roles of deacons are all limited due to the menial and servile conception of their being servants.

The study also revealed a detachment of the deacons from some aspects of *diakonia* like the social and developmental. Although the church has diaconal structures beyond the liturgical or pastoral, deacons' participation in those structures is lacking. Further, these diaconal works are detached from the main call and mission of the church, especially among the lay respondents. Despite having health structures, education structures and other care institutions, respondents, especially lay and some ordained, could not articulate how these are connected to the purpose and being and call of the church. This implies not only a lacking in the diaconal theory that could engender a holistic ecclesial picture but also lack of translation of the available theory into practice. As was shown, the deacons' ordination especially indicates a holistic picture, which is not translated into the mission perspective and practice of the deacons. This in part is a result of the conception of the diaconate that the church in Malawi as well as its clergy has. A saying that "once a deacon always a deacon"[19], an aspect that underlines the indelible nature of the diaconal calling, can also mean that one's diaconal picture influences their view and practice of their mission. This illustrates that a diaconal ecclesiology is far from being a strong concern in the theology of the Church and more so in the praxis of the Church. Generally, the images are torn between realization of the Church's role within the community and ones that want to limit the Church to spiritual matters that exclude its role from the world. Consequently, the church's practice of diaconal ministry is defined by its diaconal view.

---

[19] H. Foshee (1975). *Now that You are a Deacon*. USA, Broadman Press.

From a contextual perspective, the paper had drawn out the influence of the European culture under the colonial imperative together with the influence of the African hierarchical trends on the inferior perception of the deacons' position. This has further been perpetuated by the concept and practice of transitional deaconate, which owes to lack of a diaconal tradition that can have a lasting ecclesiological impression on the Church. Not only that but also the limitation that deacons have when it comes to the functions that they play. Deacons' tasks are limited to liturgy because it is understood as a period of training and not necessarily that they are in mission and an established office. This causative is also linked to the view of deacons as priests in training, aiming at the higher offices of Priesthood and Bishop. In the end, this view affects the concept of Church, as it presents an ecclesiology that is not diaconal, while as the diaconal theory argues, the ecclesiological question brings the sense of diaconal practice, especially when viewed in light of the nature and purpose of Church.

The paper instead argues that there are resources that the church may build on. For instance, the dichotomous view of life, which is a product of the European cultural influence, may be countered by the African cultural strengths, for instance the unified sense of the physical and the spiritual worlds. The contextual approach is vital in helping the church to realize a well-rooted sense and practice of mission, which in the end can make the diaconal practice meaningful. These findings, seen within the ecclesial, diaconal and contextual theories, shows that the Anglican Church in Malawi has a task to reconsider the position of the deacons, which is a question of the ecclesiology.

Rethinking Ecclesiology from a Diaconal Perspective

I conducted a seminar on *diakonia* and diaconal ministry from August 2017 to August 2018, which included priests, deacons and the laity from the Anglican dioceses in Malawi. It was clear from the seminars that deacons did not put themselves within the ecclesial profile of the Church. The laymen on their part did not regard the diaconate and diaconal ministry as an office that meant much within the ecclesiological framework of the Church. This poverty in theory was reflected in the poverty in praxis, although it did not mean lack of actions of charity within the Church. There are many programs that the Anglican Church undertakes in the country, from schools and hospitals; agriculture and relief programs in times of emergencies, such as the devastating floods and droughts Malawi has experienced since 2014, to environmental rehabilitation and management. Not only that but also Malawi has contributed greatly to the leadership of the country through education programs[20]. In all such programs

[20] C.M. Pauw, *Mission and Church in Malawi*: *The History of the Nkhoma Synod of the Church of Central Africa Presbyterian, 1989-1962*. Diss. University of Stellenbosch, 1980.

the lay faithful participate, while for the deacons the participation is almost zero. What does it say to the ecclesial reality? First, as already stated earlier, the missing piece is the diaconal perspective. Second, even for the participating laity, the motivation is not necessarily ministry but rather employment.

Furthermore, despite the claim that the Church has been part and parcel of Malawi's development, the colonial structures are still conspicuously present in the country. For instance, the hospitals that belong to the Anglican Church are the ones that exist with not many new structures raised. Some commentators have stated that the church from the missionary era had a hand in the underdevelopment of the country.[21] It can also be said of the church after colonialism. Part of the reasons for this is the ecclesiological views of the time, which either encourage or limit the action of the church toward human development.[22] This questions the church's purpose for its actions and is the basis for my arguments that the Church in Malawi must reconsider its theology from a diaconal perspective. But what will this take?

My view of a diaconal ecclesiology is that it is an ecclesiology that places itself within the world, witnessing to Christ and representing Christ in communion with God and with mankind. This means there has to be not only a sacramental view of ecclesiology but also action-based ecclesiology. The five marks of Mission in Anglicanism state that the baptized are called to proclaim the Good News of the Kingdom; to teach, baptize and nurture new believers; to respond to human need by loving service; to transform unjust structures of society; to challenge violence of every kind and pursue peace and reconciliation; and finally to strive to safeguard the integrity of creation, and sustain and renew the life of the earth.[23] These marks cannot be summarized as diaconal in nature. The church therefore needs to be holistic in its self-identity and practice. However, to achieve these some steps may need to be taken:

- I argue that the diaconate has to be restored to its nature in the New Testament and the early Church so that it can act as a visible exemplification of the Church's understanding and practice of diaconal ministry, and especially to create an ecclesiology with a diaconal identity.
- The Church needs to evaluate its instructional emphasis, and building on existing structures of communality in the African philosophy seek to propound a communal ecclesiology that is incorporative of all the structures as opposed to overemphasis on institutional hierarchies that in the end obfuscate the other aspects of mission and ministry in the ecclesiology as pointed out earlier. The Church will need to build

[21] McCracken, *Underdevelopment in Malawi, the Missionary Contribution*, African Affairs Vol. 76, No. 303 (April 1977), pp. 195-209.

[22] Billy Gama, *The Relationship between the state and the Church: A Theologically Based Investigation into the Social Doctrine of the Church in Malawi*, 2006.

[23] http://www.anglicancommunion.org/mission/marks-of-mission.aspx.

transformational and prophetic engagement within its ecclesiology[24] because I am of the view that among the models of ecclesiology in Malawi, these two models represent Christ more than the others. Tengatenga argued that the church's involvement in the world is to be that of a prophetic nature, an ecclesiology of prophetic engagement.

- Furthermore, since the Anglican ecclesiology calls for others being representatives of the Church, exercising mission within and with the faithful, Malawian bishops will need to find ways in which the theology of the Church is not only 'their theology' but also rather they need to find ways in which the faithful are aware of the theology of the Church that they bring to the public. In such a way the layman will not be left behind but ably articulate the theological explication of the actions of the Church.

These observations can lead to a church and an ecclesiology that is holistic and that can be described as diaconal in nature, especially when considered from the perspective of roles and involvement of deacons and as well as present a '*diakonia* oriented praxis', based on the diaconal ecclesiology perspective. Not only that but also this will enhance the quality and extent of the church's social action. For instance, if the diaconal ecclesiology is carried in the lives of the believers at all times, it will reflect in what they do both within and without the church, as part of their obedience to the will of God. Finally, if the church in Malawi reflects on its self-identity aside from a missionary identity, it will result in developing strong roots, and instill a sense of ownership, which can go a long way in enhancing the life and praxis of the church. All this directly connects to the need for a diaconal identity, based on the context of Malawi.

Conclusion

Much more could be said but the observations above show that the church cannot truly describe itself without the diaconal calling. The diaconal functionality is observed in the diaconal services that can be observed from the Old Testament and the New Testament. The fact that the Church in Malawi has sought to take part in various ways in the socio-political activities shows that the self-understanding of the church cannot avoid its participation in the practical matters of humanity and creation as a whole; in other words, an ecclesiology that is diaconal. However, various factors observed may have hampered a clear articulation and practice of this conception. There is a need, therefore, to rethink ecclesiology in a diaconal way.

---

[24] James Tengatenga 2006; Billy Gama 2006.

Bibliography

Avis, P., (2013) *the Anglican Understanding of the Church* (New Edition). London, SPCK.

Chung, P. S., (2010) 'Engaging God's mission and diakonia in the life of public spheres: Justification and economic justice' in *Dialog: A Journal of Theology*, 49(2).

Cranfield, C E B (1966), 'Diakonia in the New Testament' in Parker & McCord: 37-48.

Delkeskamp-Hayes, C., (2009) Diakonia, the state, and ecumenical collaboration: Theological pitfalls. *Christian Bioethics* 1-26, 16, 18. http://www.anglicancommunion.org/mission/marks-of-mission.aspx.

Chirwa E. & Dorward A., *Malawi: Political, Policy, Livelihoods, and Market Background,* Oxford Scholarship Online: January 2014.

Gama, Billy (2006), The Relationship between the state and the Church: A Theologically Based Investigation into the Social Doctrine of the Church in Malawi, *Master Thesis, University of Fort Hare.*

Kim, A. E., (2000): Korean religious culture and its affinity to Christianity: The rise of Protestant Christianity in South Korea. *Sociology of Religion* 61(2).

Latvus K., (2008): The paradigm challenged a new analysis of the origin of Diakonia. *Studia Theological*, 62, 145.

Mbaya, H., (2016). Church as Mbumba and Bishop as Nkhoswe: Anglican Ecclesiology and Missiological Imperatives in Central Africa, *Journal of Anglican Studies Vol. 14(2) 172–191doi:10.1017/S1740355316000140.*

McGrath, A.E., (1994). *Christian Theology: An Introduction*. Oxford: Blackwell.

Pauw, C. M., *Mission and Church in Malawi*: *The History of the Nkhoma Synod of the Church of Central Africa Presbyterian, 1989-1962.* Diss. University of Stellenbosch, 1980.

Plater, O., (Rev. Ed.). (2004) *Many Servants: An Introduction to deacons*. Cambridge, Cowley Publications.

Ross, K, R., (1995). *Gospel Ferment in Malawi: Theological Essays*. Mambo Press, Gweru.

Ross, K. (1995)., *Christianity in Malawi: A Source Book*. Kachere, Zomba: 205.

Ross, K. R., (ed.) (1996). *God, People and Power in Malawi: Democratization in Theological Perspective*. Christian Literature Association in Malawi (CLAIM), Zomba.

Stephen, M., (2000). *A New Mission Agenda: Dialogue, Diakonia and Discipling.* Delhi: ISPCK.

Tengatenga J., (2006): *Church, State and Society in Malawi: The Anglican Case*. Zomba MW, Kachere Series.

The Hanover Report, (1996). *The Diaconate as Ecumenical Opportunity* (London, UK: Anglican Communion Publications), paragraph 10.

The Iona Report, (2016). *The Diaconate in the Anglican Church of Canada*, the general Synod of the Anglican Church of Canada, 16.

Weil, L. (2016). *Liturgy for Living*. New York: Seabury Press.

Diakonia: An Ecumenical Perspective

Olav Fykse Tveit

In the face of the many and perilous tests that humanity faces today, the activism and advocacy of Christian churches around the world have never been as vital or relevant as they now are. In that light, I would like to reflect on the crucial concept of *diakonia,* that is, the service of the church in the world, and how it relates to the current work of the World Council of Churches (WCC) and the Pilgrimage of Justice and Peace.

The WCC is an ecumenical fellowship of churches founded in 1948 that today brings together 350 Protestant, Orthodox, Anglican and other churches representing more than 560 million Christians in more than 120 countries. I do not presume to speak for other churches or church-related organizations, let alone the billions of believers from other religious traditions and spiritualities. But our long experience of ecumenical and interfaith dialogue and cooperation encourages me to think that many of my remarks will resonate with partners across the world of faith.

In this chapter I cannot hope to address the mountainous challenges that we encounter today in our world and in our work as churches. But I hope we can at least shed some light on the important and exciting ways the churches' work in the world is being conceived. So I will address, first, the theological underpinnings of *diakonia*; second, our efforts to integrate the classic quest for Christian unity with the mandate to realize the reign of God in justice and peace; third, seeing *diakonia* in light of the pilgrimage; fourth, the changed context for *diakonia* today, especially recent and widespread respect for the role of religion in human life and development; and finally, our fundamental commitment to a diaconal spirituality guided by a realistic hope for the human future.

Shared Faith in the God of Life

When the World Council of Churches met for its First Assembly in Amsterdam 1948, the same year the United Nations adopted the Universal Declaration of Human Rights (the United Nations officially came into existence on October 24, 1945), the assembly said that "we are committed to stay together". When the 10th Assembly of the WCC met in Busan, Republic of Korea, in 2013, we said, "We are committed to move together."[1] These messages are two sides of the same call and commitment. We can only move together as churches when we are united in our faith in the God of life, who created all to live in fellowship and who calls the church to be a sign and foretaste of the unity of all life and humankind: one God and one humanity.

From its earliest days, we learn in Acts, the communities formed by the followers of Jesus were intent on mutual aid and on helping the sick, the poor and the oppressed. As Christians we are, by the grace of God, liberated to join hands, to be enabled to give glory to God, as a just and inclusive fellowship in Christ, in spite of and with all our differences. In Christ there is no condemnation but a new fellowship of hope for us and the whole of creation (Romans 8). We make this visible as we respond to our calling to serve one another; and we give the days of our lives and our resources as a holy sacrifice for others, as Christ did, to be transformed and to transform the world. "I appeal to you therefore, brothers and sisters, by the mercy of God, to present your bodies as a living sacrifice, holy and acceptable to God, which is your spiritual worship. Do not be conformed to this world, but be transformed by the renewing of your minds, so that you may discern what is the will of God – what is good and acceptable and perfect" (Rom. 12:1-2). Therefore, we are called "to receive one another, as Christ has received us" (Rom. 15:7.)

We can stay in this given fellowship together only if this is an active and proactive life together, willing to venture into new landscapes, to go out of the comfort zones of the churches and our families and friendships, to live in the world as it is and to be with our fellow human beings as they are, as we struggle for justice and peace and share the joy of life together.

Therefore, the churches and the one ecumenical movement cannot say that we are going to stay together, and that we are going to move together, without saying that we are going to act together. From the start, this orientation to action has been a hallmark of the one ecumenical movement.[2] What, in the immediate post-War period, focused on inter-church aid and refugee resettlement, has blossomed across the decades and continents to encompass global work in development, disaster relief, health initiatives, and much, much more.

---

[1] See the message of the 10th Assembly at: https://www.oikoumene.org/en/resources /documents/assembly/2013-busan/adopted-documents-statements/message-of-the-wcc-10th-assembly.

[2] A brief history by Teresa Joan White of the concept of *diakonia*, from the *Dictionary of the Ecumenical Movement*, 2nd ed. (Geneva: WCC Publications, 2002), can be found at: https://www.oikoumene.org/en/resources/documents/wcc-programmes/justice-*diakonia*-and-responsibility-for-creation/*diakonia*.

Walking, Working and Praying Together

As a fellowship of churches we are moving together in faith, with a purpose and shared values, in service to one humanity, ready to encounter God in the needs of others. That work is *diakonia*. As with any work we human beings undertake together, be it in the name of the churches or not, our service is not perfect. None of us or our institutions are perfect. That is also one significant meaning of the image of our Pilgrimage of Justice and Peace.[3] It is a movement for people who recognize that we are in need of change and sometimes even in need of conversion, called to move on or to change our direction. Nevertheless, in spite of our shortcomings and even given our best intentions, we do want and dare to take steps forward together that can be identified as contributions to this pilgrimage, this journey in faith together, joining hands together. We believe that God leads us into life, into the places and realities and times where we should be; where we can focus on something beyond ourselves and our internal issues. We need to help one another to be on the move forward together, on a Pilgrimage of Justice and Peace: for the sake of those who need it the most.

Diakonia in Light of the Pilgrimage

I believe God is now calling us to one ecumenical movement in this Pilgrimage of Justice and Peace through:

A Renewed Commitment

The biblical word for the service to which we are called is *diakonia*. This word, and the language we have connected to it, is a common basis for what we do as the WCC with our member churches, specialized ministries, with the ACT Alliance, and with a broad range of international agencies. Since the last assembly, we have had occasion to engage in protracted reflection on the call to ecumenical and international *diakonia*, on our service together; and we continue to reframe and renew our engagement in light of these inspiring and encouraging reflections. This important and ongoing work, in draft form:

- Takes into account the longstanding experiences of diaconal practice and reflection within the ecumenical movement, in particular by the WCC and the Lutheran World Federation;
- Considers the specific contribution of professional diaconal agencies in their role as members of the ACT Alliance;
- Responds to relevant social and political issues in today's world that challenge churches and related agencies in their diaconal action;

---

[3] See the invitation, from the WCC's central committee, to the Pilgrimage of Justice and Peace: https://www.oikoumene.org/en/resources/documents/central-committee/geneva-2014/an-invitation-to-the-pilgrimage-of-justice-and-peace.

- Provides theological insight that underscores the Trinitarian and ecclesiological founding of *diakonia* and that can orient churches and related agencies in their diaconal practices; and
- Proposes concrete steps to be taken in order to strengthen the diaconal capacity of the churches in cooperation with their ecumenical partners.

In this ongoing reflection on ecumenical diaconal ministry we aim to address both the theological and practical dimensions of our work together, especially in light of the vastly changed geopolitical, social and ecclesial landscape in which we engage today, and particularly across confessional, geographical and other lines.

Marks of our Service

The service we are called to offer is, broadly speaking, pastoral care, which is approaching our task as a community of faith, sharing the values and the potential of our faith in the triune God. This is a holistic approach, through which we acknowledge all dimensions of our human life as relevant and significant for the church. We are serving as church, as members of the church, in which all are called to offer the priestly sacrifice to honor God through ministry for others. The assets already present in all churches and local Christian communities, of communication, care, creativity and commitments, need to be affirmed and strengthened through what we can do in our work together. *Diakonia* is for everyone, not just the professionals.

Prophetic

Our service together must be public and prophetic. We need to be willing and able to analyze, to name and to address what we are convinced is wrong or does not nurture or carry the values of God's kingdom. *Diakonia* today embraces advocacy and public witness.

Accountability

This implies that we need to be self-critical, as well as accountable to one another and thereby to God. This call to, and practice of, being mutually accountable for what we do, what we have as resources within our communities and countries, is a way forward, not backward. We should be mutually accountable in order to be on our way, on our pilgrimage forward, into solutions, giving our contributions when and where we have something to contribute.[4] Being prophetic means being part of the life that is moving forward, not dwelling and remaining with the past and the mistakes of the past.

---

[4] See my work on this concept: Olav Fykse Tveit, *The Truth We Owe Each Other: Mutual Accountability in the Ecumenical Movement* (Geneva: WCC Publications, 2016); and recently, "What Does Mutual Accountability Mean?" at: https://www.oikoumene.org/en/press-centre/news/tveit-what-does-mutual-accountability-mean.

When we discuss development, for example, it is as the way forward, making changes together that bring hope in terms of justice and peace. The *diakonia* we are promoting is honoring, protecting and promoting the rights of every human being.

Care for Each Other – and the Earth

The service we are called to offer is not limited to the human family in a strict sense. The climate changes we are experiencing, acknowledging slowly, too slowly, as results of human activity, are affecting the most vulnerable because they are destructive to nature, in which we all live.

Radically Inclusive

The *diakonia* of today requires that we act together with all people of good will, but also that we maintain a sense of serving the whole of creation. The day before the summit of global leaders on climate change, just before the historic meeting of COP 21 in Paris, we gathered together with leaders of all faith communities to affirm our common commitment. Christian service is never and can never be an excluding or exclusive form of "solidarity". Our pilgrimage for justice and peace moves as we become part of the wider peoples' movements in which we now mobilize, in all parts of the world.

Building Community and Just Peace

Our service to the world must be dedicated to bringing both justice and peace, to focus on how these are interrelated in every challenge we face today, as they are interrelated in the kingdom of God. The dramatic deterioration of security in today's many conflicts, for example, has a lot to do with ignorance in many local and national contexts of how to develop a just and sustainable community. We understand also that religion can serve as a source or as a way to fuel conflicts. There is no service to God that can be identified as a holy war. We must continue to build and focus on the just peace that is needed, even when security needs to be properly addressed. More than ever, it is time to work with and ally with other peoples and leaders of faith who support a peaceful coexistence and visions for peaceful political solutions of conflicts. Service to all, regardless of faith, is and must be a sign of our commitment to serve the God of life who is the creator of all and who cares for all, and for all creation.

Professionalism in Christian Service

There must also be a professional dimension to our service. We need to use all the qualifications and competences available. Part of our professionalism is to acknowledge and to cooperate with people who have different backgrounds and different roles in a community, whether they have formal education or not. On the other hand, it is also particularly relevant for our Christian service to develop the relevant skills and competences through offering education, training and capacity-building. The WCC is working on how we bring ecumenical formation, which is a concept that includes both theological education and abilities to be a part of and lead processes of ecumenical *diakonia*, to the fore. I am honored to work with many, and I would also say many who are younger than I, who offer different professional capacities to our ecumenical *diakonia* from many of our member churches and partnering organizations.

The Indispensable Role of Younger Generations

A growing portion of the world's population consists of younger people, children and youth.[5] In many countries of the world they represent an actual majority. They are particularly in need of respect for their rights, to a safe environment, to education and to protection from abuse or violence. They very often represent the strongest sense of justice and the most committed and creative voices for peace. However, they are often not properly offered their rights, particularly not the girls; neither are they given their space to contribute to the work for justice and peace, not in the church nor in their societies in general. They are not only the future of the church but they are also the church and contribute to the service of the church today.

The Critical Role of Religion

Today, in so many ways, we find a new and indeed radically altered context for the church's service in the world. In part because of our work in the pilgrimage, and in part because of the monumental geopolitical changes and growing peril of the contemporary world, our perspectives on *diakonia* have changed, grown and broadened. One key factor in the shape and scale of ecumenical *diakonia* is renewed appreciation for the role of religion.

Today we find, and I wish to underline the historical significance of, a new engagement with religion by international agencies, the United Nations and governments. A literature review undertaken by DanChurchAid noted that as recently as 2000 the sociologist Kurt Allan ver Beek – after comprehensive research in development literature – concluded that "religion seems to be a *development taboo*".[6] Neither development academics nor development practitioners took an interest in the role of religion in development. On the contrary, they seemed consciously to avoid the subject – from a secular

[5] Presently, 42 percent of the world's population is under 25 years of age, according to the World Bank: http://blogs.worldbank.org/opendata/chart-how-worlds-youth-population-changing.

[6] See Joergen Thomsen, "From Rejection to Recognition: How does Religion Contribute to Rights-Based and Sustainable Development?", *Ecumenical Review* 68:4 (2016): 414-22.

perception that religion was at best irrelevant for societal development and at worst an obstacle to the advancement of social development and human rights.

Today, thankfully, religion is no longer a "taboo" in political science and development literature. There has been a noticeable *discourse change*. The earlier understanding that "religion will gradually disappear when economic growth and modernization/globalization spread" now gives way to a growing recognition that religion plays an important – even a central – role in peoples' lives, attitudes and practices, and therefore also in development. Religion informs peoples' understanding of what constitutes a "good life", their hopes, their self-esteem and belief in their own dignity and rights, their inspiration for asserting their dignity and rights, and their resilience in times of crisis. Therefore, religion *must* be considered in development and humanitarian response.

Indeed, in practically all parts of the world religion is very much alive, and that it is not limited to the function of coping with moments of uncertainty and crisis in one's private life, but remains a key factor shaping life in community.[7]

Religions orient the lives and important decisions of many families and communities on a strong base of values. With their holistic world views, religions continue to challenge the development of economic and political subsystems that dominate societies and undermine and fragment life in community. At their best, religious communities and religious leaders have raised their voices in the context of economic injustice and rampant inequality, the misuse of political power, the ugly face of racism or of violence against women and children. From the start, the WCC has been calling for respect for human rights, the rule of law as well as respect for international law. These are all essential for our vision of a just peace, a *shalom/salam*, that includes development and hope.

Levels of Interreligious Cooperation

Religious pluralism and multi-religious societies have become – self-evidently – an ever more significant reality in the context of globalization, migration and massive flows of refugees. Yet with a shared commitment to the flourishing of communities and nature, religious leaders *are* able to cooperate across faith boundaries to demonstrate care for creation, justice, reconciliation and peace. At the WCC, we have experienced this again and again in our interreligious relationships, in such instances as these:

- interfaith cooperation at COP 21 in Paris – a common witness of religious leaders addressing climate change;
- hope for young people in Egypt in cooperation with Al Azhar and the Coptic Orthodox Church;

---

[7] See the dozen contributions to the topic "Religion and Development" in Dietrich Werner and Corrie van der Ven (eds.), *Ecumenical Review* 68:4 (2016).

- action against violence and for reconciliation of communities in Nigeria; and
- interfaith coalitions for gender justice.

In our experience, practical cooperation on the basis of shared values, concerns and goals is the best hermeneutical tool toward common understanding and mutual recognition. They are capacities so urgently needed in the face of religiously inspired violence and justification of terrorism based on exclusion and denial of the dignity of the other. And there is still a vast unexplored terrain for such cooperation in addressing shared human development concerns.

In the leading development-policy approach today – the Rights-Based Approach (RBA) – development practitioners aim for change at different levels – at the levels of policies, of practices and of beliefs, values and ideas. Some may fear that engagement with religion and religious actors could undermine the rights-based approach. On the contrary, a fuller understanding of religion's role will help complete the picture. Hitherto, development actors have generally engaged mostly with the two top levels (policies and practices) and avoided engaging with the foundational level of "beliefs, values and ideas", even if this is probably the most important level for sustainable change.[8]

An example is the promotion of more equal gender relationships between women and men (SDG 5) – or, in our terminology, a *Just Community of Women and Men*. Good policies and recognized practices may bring us a long way. But only when men begin to see themselves differently and women internalize their equality and claim their God-given dignity is the change sustainable. And the primary source of *social capital* to drive – or obstruct – this change is very often in the communities of faith and the precepts they teach.

Whether in the context of advancing gender equality, of promoting human rights and inclusion, or of addressing extremist violence, the fact that the role of religion may be ambiguous simply serves to underline that *religion is never irrelevant for development*, if the change we desire is to be sustainable.

Global Goals, Local Communities

The shift in discourse toward greater recognition of religion's role in development processes coincides with the shift in the United Nations from technical, limited Millennium Development Goals (MDGs) to the *holistic, integrated and universal agenda of the Sustainable Development Goals* (SDGs).[9] The convergence of these two trends holds great potential, yet they

---

[8] See the discussion of "Rights-Based Development from a Faith-Based Perspective" in the work of ACT Alliance: https://actalliance.eu/resources-post/rights-based-development-from-a-faith-based-perspective/.

[9] Further information at: https://www.un.org/sustainabledevelopment/sustainable-development-goals.

also challenge us as churches, faith communities and faith-based organizations to find our proper means and methods of engagement with this framework.

We welcome and appreciate, at this practical level, the new recognition and appreciation by governments, bilateral donors, multilateral organizations and the entire international development community of the critical role of religion and religious actors in human and sustainable development, in humanitarian response, and in the search for peace in our conflict-torn world.

In this regard, let me be clear: churches and other religious communities are not engaged in humanitarian response and development *because* of the SDGs (or, formerly, the MDGs), but because of their fundamental faith commitments to respecting human dignity, to serving the community, to protecting creation and to witnessing to the divine. The faith that is our fundamental point of reference is expressed and brought into action in many ways: in confidence and trust in God, in the content of doctrine, in the teaching of the tradition, in a commitment to serve and share, in embodying a community of faith and practice, and in common witness in words and deeds.

As communities of faith, our relevance to this discourse goes far beyond the common recognition that faith-based organizations or FBOs "run high-quality clinics and schools and are present in the remotest corners". Local religious authorities and institutions are fully part of their communities. They are, in almost all development contexts, the *key sources of social capital for sustainable change, transformation and hope*. The contributions to promoting the 2030 Agenda made by agencies – whether intergovernmental, governmental, international NGOs or FBOs for that matter – may be, and undoubtedly will be, very valuable. But if the social capital of local religious authorities and institutions is not engaged, I fear that sustainable change and transformation will elude us.

Speaking for the WCC, its member churches and our ecumenical partner organizations – and I am sure for many other partners from other faith traditions – we have worked hard to integrate into our programmatic plans the 2030 Agenda for Sustainable Development and its holistic approach to framing the challenges we collectively face and the goals and indicators to guide our responses. We welcome, for example, the inclusion of SDG 16 to promote peaceful and inclusive societies for sustainable development. But we are also laboring hard in other areas, and we are grateful for identification of climate change, women's equality and rights, children's rights and protections, resolution of protracted crises, human rights for all and "leaving no one behind" as "golden threads" in the SDG agenda. We are open to joining in collective efforts for these purposes, especially through national and local action. Together with our international ecumenical partners in the ACT Alliance, Anglican Alliance, Caritas Internationalist and Lutheran World Federation, and with many other partners inspired by faith, we will continue to accompany and support local churches and faith communities in their engagement with the SDG framework.

A Diaconal Spirituality

The last point I would like to make about ecumenical *diakonia* is what I have already touched on in different ways, namely, that this larger movement and engagement by the ecumenical churches stems from faith, is fueled by hope and is animated by love. In fact, the fellowship we enjoy as Christians is itself a form and movement of love. In that perspective, *diakonia* is not some application or afterthought of faith, but the concrete, loving engagement that transforms us into authentic disciples of Jesus.

Historically and today, the concept and practice of pilgrimage has served as a meaningful, even life-changing dimension of personal life, occasioning the maturing and the spiritual growth of each person. This is indeed of the highest relevance and makes the perspective of pilgrimage relevant in all contexts. But through ecumenical *diakonia* that dares to cross confessional and religious and geographical and ideological divides, we see that our pilgrimage is also inherently, deeply social, communal and relational. The growth and the maturity we need as human beings of today and tomorrow, and particularly the spiritual growth we need, must be developed in our deeper understanding of how we are connected, how we build relations to one another, and how we best can be enabled to achieve something together for the sake of God's world.

Finally, and most importantly, let me stress that the characteristic message and contribution of religion must be hope. *Hope is a defining and indispensable quality of faith.* From a specifically Christian perspective, the church's role in society must be based on a faith that has a prophetic, critical approach aimed at transformation and hope, not marked by fatalism, indifference, devaluation or demonization of others, but by love. In our understanding, faith is intrinsically linked to and only properly understood under the criterion of love. Moreover, true hope is never only for me and my own community; it is anchored in a transformational event that has universal implications, the coming of Jesus Christ and the advent of God's reign. Accordingly, I believe that if it is not a hope for all, it is not a real hope, and it is not a genuinely Christian hope. A necessary condition for hope is that it expresses itself in love for others, whoever and wherever they are.

I believe and affirm that with this narrative of faith, hope and love in our hearts and minds, the transformations envisaged in our diaconal work – for people, planet and prosperity – are possible, and can be achieved through a whole society engagement fully inclusive of the religious reality.

Salvation and Healing in a Diaconal Church

+ Luis Antonio G. Cardinal Tagle[1]

The renewal brought about by the Second Vatican Council to the Catholic Church has led to a rethinking or re-imagining of the Church as a Servant or Diaconal Church, one significant sign of which was the restoration of the permanent diaconate. This renewal was a product of many factors, among them a rediscovery of Biblical and Patristic sources, an openness to other Christian communities and non-Christian religions and a non-belligerent view of the world. We hear from the Pastoral Constitution on the Church in the Modern World (*Gaudium et spes*) 92 the following call to all Christians: "Let us take pains to pattern ourselves after the Gospel more exactly every day, and thus work as brothers [and sisters] in rendering service to the human family. For in Christ Jesus this family is called into the family of the children of God." The Church does not exist for itself but for the Kingdom of God and for the human family. In Christ the Head and in the animating Holy Spirit, the whole Christian community has a vocation to be a Servant or Diaconal Church.

In his encyclical *Deus caritas est* 25, Pope Benedict XVI affirms that the Church's nature is expressed in its three-fold responsibility of proclaiming the word of God (*martyria*), celebrating the sacraments (*leitourgia*) and exercising the service of charity (*diakonia*). The Pope enunciates a key principle: "These duties presuppose each other and are inseparable. For the Church, charity is not a kind of welfare activity that could equally well be left to others, but is a part of her nature, an indispensable expression of her very being." The mutual dependence of the three elements is exhibited in the life of the early Christian community depicted in Acts 2:42-45: "They devoted themselves to the teaching of the apostles and to the communal life, to the breaking of bread and to prayers…All who believed were together and had all things in common; they would sell their property and possessions and divide them among all, according to each one's need." *Diakonia* expresses and authenticates preaching and worship. In a true sense, the proclamation of the word and the celebration of the sacraments are also acts of service or ministry of the Church. Without service motivated by love, the ministry of the word and sacrament falls flat. Whoever claims to know God but does not keep the commandment to love one's neighbors is a liar. "Whoever keeps God's word, the love of God is truly

---

[1] Lecture given September 8, 2017, IDC Lourdes, France

perfected in him/her. This is the way we may know that we are in union with him: whoever claims to abide in him ought to live as he lived" (I John 2:4-6).

The diaconal or servant Church participates in the diaconal life of Jesus, the Lord and Master who is Servant. He understood his whole mission from the Father as service: "The Son of Man did not come to be served but to serve and to give his life as a ransom for many" (Mk 10:45). Offering his life on the cross for the salvation of humanity is his ultimate act of service. This was prefigured in the supper before he died, when he washed the feet of his disciples. His rank as teacher would traditionally have prevented him from doing the lowly task of a slave. This was dictated by the cultural and religious mores of the time. But he chose to be a servant in life and death to leave a testament to his disciples: "If I, the master and teacher, have washed your feet, you ought to wash one another's feet. I have given you a model to follow, so that as I have done for you, you should also do" (John 13: 14-15). Instead of seeking the seat of honor at the dinner table, one should take a wash basin and towel, like Jesus (cf. Luke 14:7-14). His disciples' humble service must not be tainted by the hypocrisy and grand display with which some scribes and Pharisees performed their good works: "The greatest among you must be your servant" (Matthew 23:11). Nor should the disciples behave like the rulers over the Gentiles who lorded it over others and made their own importance felt. "It shall not be so among you. Rather whoever wishes to be great among you will be your servant" (Mk 10:42-43). Humility or self-emptying love (*kenosis*) is the spirit of Jesus' diaconal or servant life (Philippians 2:5-11). Jesus who gave up his life found it in the greatness of being a servant in God's Kingdom. Servanthood is a descent, not an ascent to greatness as one author fittingly puts it.

How does a diaconal or servant Church serve salvation and healing in our time today? It must be noted that Jesus' service of the Kingdom of God came through preaching and healing. Healing was one of the signs that salvation has come. When Jesus sent his disciples on mission, he instructed them, "As you go, make this proclamation, 'The Kingdom of heaven is at hand.' Cure the sick, raise the dead, cleanse lepers, drive out demons" (Mt 10:7-8). Another basic insight from Vatican II can show us a path to understand the connection between salvation, healing and the Diaconal Church.

In the Dogmatic Constitution on the Church, *Lumen gentium* 1, the Council states, "By her relationship with Christ, the Church is a kind of sacrament of intimate union with Christ, and of the unity of all humankind, that is, she is a sign and an instrument of such union and unity." The Church, although a little flock, is a "lasting and sure seed of unity, hope and salvation for the whole human race" (LG 9). We can safely say that the Council connects salvation intimately with communion, our relationship with the Trinity and with humanity. The Church is not only a sign but also a servant or instrument of communion. What are the threats to communion? Isolation, division, alienation and aloneness are wounds to communion. The human family needs salvation from exclusion and disconnectedness and salvation for communion. The

Church serves by bringing to a humanity wounded by strife, rejection and violence, the healing and saving balm of communion. Of the many needs of humanity today, I believe that the exclusion and alienation of persons need urgent attention from a diaconal Church that is a sign of communion. In his book *Becoming Human*, Jean Vanier[2] poignantly describes the journey from exclusion to inclusion as a path to healing. Allow me to raise a few points for further reflection.

James Sweeney, CP observes that the prevailing culture

> takes the laissez-faire attitude that the individual reigns supreme and individuals can look after themselves" (*Faith in Culture*).[3] Even families suffer from a breakdown in relationships and communication. Individuals do not need others. Each one must look after oneself only. If you are poor, you have no one else to blame but yourself. Do not expect others to lift you up; do it yourself. Alienating individualism has acquired social forms in ethno-centrism, racism, nationalistic xenophobia, religious and racial discrimination, scapegoating, stigmatizing people who differ from us like the migrants, strangers, and the minority (Kristine Suna-Koro, "*The Sign of Unity and the Bond of Charity*"[4]; Fr. David Izuzquiza, SJ, "*Breaking Bread: Notes for a Political Theology of Migration*).[5]

The culture of individualism is one of the causes of the disappearance of human persons from our consciousness.

In the economic sphere of life, which impacts on the social, cultural and political spheres, we see economic growth that excludes the greater part of humanity and wounds creation. Philippine news agencies reported on January 17, 2017, the eve of the World Economic Forum in Davos, Switzerland, a significant finding of a study conducted by Oxfam, an anti-poverty organization. It revealed that in 2016, 8 persons in the world were as rich as half of the world or 3.6 billion people. This datum prompted the Executive Director of Oxfam to comment, "It is obscene for so much wealth to be held in the hands of so few when one in ten people survive on less than $2 a day." But what makes it more bothersome is when we realize that in 2015 or the year before, 62 persons were as rich as half of the world. Now they are reduced to 8. We do not deny that the most successful persons in the world are enterprising, driven, creative and "lucky". But we are still disturbed and should be disturbed at the thought that wealth generated with the help of many people and nations is not distributed justly. We need to ask if economic growth that excludes the bigger portion of humanity is genuine growth or legitimated injustice.

---

[2] Jean Vanier, *Becoming Human* (Mahwah, New Jersey: Paulist Press), 2008.

[3] James Sweeney, *Faith in Culture* (New Black Friars), 2013.

[4] Kristine Suna-Koro, *The Sign of Unity and the Bond of Charity: On the Eucharist as a "Taskmaster" in the Context of Global Migration* (Wiley Online Library), 2014.

[5] Barcelona, 2011.

We need self-critique or self-examination for a renewal of mentalities and attitudes that promote communion. We also need social structures that would allow room for the values of communion and solidarity to flourish. But let me emphasize the need for personal encounter with the people who are excluded, as stressed time and again by Pope Francis in *Evangelii Gaudium* and *Laudato si*. A diaconal Church needs to promote a culture of encounter, of recognition of human faces and persons. In personally meeting the excluded, seeing and touching their wounds the way Jesus asked Thomas to put his fingers into his wounds, we realize that the issue of exclusion is not only about statistics and numbers. They are human beings, not numbers. They are persons with feelings, dreams and dignity. They could be me or my parents or my siblings or my friends. Seeing the wounds of the excluded people confronts us with a choice: will I ignore them or will I stop, come close and carry them to healing like the Good Samaritan? I must promptly add that when we encounter the outcast, we should not come from a position of superiority, strength or importance. We come as neighbors, brothers and sisters willing to learn worthwhile lessons about communion and healing from them. The poor can impart to us the values that the prevailing system lacks. And we must do the healing encounter with wounded persons together, as a Church. All the baptized are asked to participate actively not only in worship and liturgy but also in the service of charity that heals. The leaders and pastors are not the only ones called to be servants of healing but also the whole community. The leaders must form, equip and encourage everyone to serve. Deacons, imaging Jesus the Servant, should inspire the faithful to serve humbly and so promote the healing of the human family and of creation.

I will end with some stories of human encounters.

October 2015, I visited a refugee camp in Idomeni, Greece, along the border with the Former Yugoslav Republic of Macedonia. You see, touch and smell human suffering and misery. People who came from Syria, Iraq, even Sudan had nothing with them except the clothing on their bodies and the most precious to them, namely their families. After helping in the distribution of food, medicines and clothing and conversing with some refugees, I talked with the lady supervising the relief effort. She was a local official of the town. I asked if it was part of her official duty to oversee the camp. She said it was volunteer work, not an obligation for her. Surprised that she chose to add more tasks on herself, I jokingly remarked, "Don't you have enough work to do that you embrace more?" She replied, "My ancestors were refugees too. I have refugee DNA. They are my brothers and sisters. I will not abandon them." Service, healing, communion have met.

My final story illustrates how the wounded could be agents of healing through communion. One day I went with a friend in his car to visit a place in the Metro-Manila area. On one of the roads we stopped when the traffic light turned red. Immediately vendors selling flowers, cookies, candies, etc.

streamed from the sidewalks to the vehicles. Our driver signaled to the vendors who had approached us that we were not buying anything. So, they moved on to the vehicles behind us. Suddenly, one of them, selling cookies, came back running to our car and waved at me while calling out "Cardinal! Cardinal!" The driver and my friend both signaled to him respectfully that we would not buy. But the vendor continued calling me and offering the cookies. Without asking permission from my friend who owned the car, I lowered the window and greeted the man. Our driver again politely told him that we were not buying anything. But the vendor said, "I am not selling it. I want to give it to the Cardinal as a gift." This poor man who needed every cent to live on was willing to give up his profit so he could give his bishop a simple gift. It was Valentine's Day. His cookies were the only gift I got that day. A new world erupted before my eyes, exhibiting the mighty power of the wounded to offer communion and healing. There is hope for the world where communion is restored.

Diakonia as Public Service and Public Witness

Rudelmar Bueno de Faria

Introduction

In this chapter I want to highlight the rapid, changing and complex state of the world, as well as the need for churches to rethink their way of being relevant today. I seek to identify elements of the changing world and potential situations and processes for prophetic and political engagement of churches and diaconal organizations in the public realm. Historically, churches have played a prophetic role in society, in some situations even shaping national and global political agendas and highlighting values of inclusion and human dignity in the public square. However, from my own experience, over the past few decades the prophetic voice of churches has been minimized to accommodate political agendas and different values perspectives, especially in times when people need it the most.

Learning and practicing *diakonia* for more than 25 years, I realize how the different dimensions of the diaconal work complement each other. As a practitioner at the national level, both in Brazil and El Salvador, I could connect my experience with the inexorable multidimensional scope of *diakonia*, when I started engaging with global organizations such as the Lutheran World Federation (LWF), the World Council of Churches (WCC) and the ACT Alliance (Action by Churches Together). On this journey, I realize the equal importance of *diakonia* as a public service, as well as a public witness.

Humanity is facing a challenging time. Values are being redefined based on the evolution of society and our understanding of the world. Churches and diaconal organizations have an enormous responsibility to respond to today′s time by upholding Jesus' teachings and deeds and embracing *diakonia* both as a public service and a public witness to respond to the challenges and threats that are undermining life and putting God's creation at risk. Likewise, it is imperative that the wider ecumenical movement come together to strategically set up a platform to leverage ecumenical *diakonia* as a motivational tool to jointly promote inclusion, leverage the gifts and expertise of the different churches, as well as to establish strategic partnerships with other religions and secular bilateral and multilateral organizations fighting for inclusion and the common good.

A Globalized World Amid Inequalities, Populism and Polarization

Globalization brought the world together, a process that evidently had many positive effects, while simultaneously causing new divisions, mainly between the rich and those living in poverty, those who are powerful and those who are powerless. One of the worrying effects of globalization is the way economic and political power are being exercised, emptying the role of local, national and international authorities and undermining their democratic legitimacy. In addition, transnational corporations do not have to give account for how they are acting and expanding their power.

It took some time for ordinary people in the communities and villages to realize how globalization and neoliberal policies impacted their daily lives. Cultural boundaries started to disappear, and technical innovation brought people closer through the virtual world. However, these interactions have not prevented the surge of extreme poverty, exclusion, hatred and fear. More than a billion men, women and children continue to be imprisoned by poverty, even though the world has made remarkable progress in reducing the number of people living in extreme poverty in the past two decades. Political, cultural, ethnic and religious tensions fuel terrible hostilities worldwide, increasing hatred and fear. Populist political leaders use divisive rhetoric to hold up support for their causes, often promoting division and polarization within and between families, communities, societies and countries, fueled by racist, xenophobic and homophobic extremism.

The local and global contexts within which churches are immersed are ever more volatile and uncertain, and the challenges we all face in promoting a world where we all live with dignity have become more complex. A long-term crisis of democracy linked with a distrust in democratic institutions, a decrease in traditional forms of political participation (elections, political party membership, etc.), disrespect to human rights and biased media are often the causes of insecurity and polarization. At the same time, this is exacerbated by crises linked to the economic situation of countries and with individuals' economic insecurities. Also, the space for civil society organizations, including churches, is further shrinking in local, national and multilateral arenas, and is affecting organizations and individual human rights defenders.

For many years, researchers, academics and policy makers have anticipated that modernization and globalization would lead to a secularized world, where religion would be less regarded in most of societies. Paradoxically, there is a renewed and growing recognition that religion in our world is an important factor in public life and all its social, economic and political aspects, and as such needs to be taken seriously, both in its negative and positive aspects.

A Change of Era?

In the Middle Age, religion was a determining factor for the future of humanity. In the modern or contemporary era, modernization, knowledge and technology brought a series of seemingly indisputable benefits to people (health, economy, social development, etc.), but at the same time, dark sides of modernity (atomic bombs, wars, environmental problems, psychological and moral hazards) produced a society of exclusion. Are we facing a change of era?

In every change of era paradigms, values and structures were challenged, often leading to conflicts. It seems that we are now living in a world without strong bonds and common values, where people are disregarded because of what they are and represent. Hedonism, disenchantment of the world,[1] and the loss of a generally agreed upon definition of human dignity, human nature and the resulting loss of value in human life are stronger than ever before. As result of a crisis of values, we now see a realignment of forces within our communities and societies, where even religious organizations, including churches, are associating themselves with people, institutions and values that sometimes further exclusion and undermine human dignity. On the other hand, we also see the same happening between groups that seek to promote an inclusive agenda, where human dignity and equality are central.

Some 40 years ago, the sociologist and theologian Peter L. Berger propagated the secularization theory. Later, he changed his opinion, recognizing that in most parts of the world, religions are flourishing. He concluded that to replace secularization theory – to explain religion in the modern world – we need the theory of pluralism. 'Modernity does not necessarily produce secularity. It necessarily produces pluralism, the coexistence in the same society of different worldviews and value systems.'[2]

More recently, the international community, especially the United Nations (UN) and some of its member states, realized that religious leaders and organizations play an essential role in political, social, cultural, economic and cultural realms. Churches and their diaconal institutions are at the front as service providers at community level. That led to the UN to create in 2009 an inter-agency task force to engage with faith-based organizations on issues related to development and advocacy. In August 2018 the UN created an Advisory Council of Faith-Based Organizations to help support the UN in coordinating more systematic outreach, interaction and engagement with faith-based entities, and enhancing focus on and knowledge around religious representation and dynamics.

---

[1] Max Weber, *The Protestant Ethic and the Spirit of Capitalism*, New Introduction and trans. by S. Kalberg, Blackwells Roxbury Publishing Company, Los Angeles, USA, 2002.

[2] Interview with Gordon College's Gregor Thuswaldner: http://thecresset.org/2014/Lent/Thuswaldner_L14.html.

It is undeniable that religions orient the lives and important decisions of many families and communities on a strong base of values. At their best, religious communities and religious leaders have raised their voices in the context of economic injustice and rampant inequality, the misuse of political power, the ugly face of racism or of violence against women and children, and religious hate speeches that could lead to atrocity crimes. At their worst, they have supported structures that undermine human dignity and human rights.

If a change of era is eminent, then this new era will be based on values. As Christians, we need to ensure that Jesus' teaching and deeds define our values and standing. Christian witness and service entails responding concertedly to the challenges posed by poverty, socio-economic inequalities and ecological destruction, thereby contributing to the realization of the sustainable development goals developed by the UN in 2015. The ethical and theological undergirding of these intertwined concerns strengthen the diaconal work of the churches, providing resources for community work, networking, sharing of ecumenical initiatives and developing national and international strategies for advocacy.

Diakonia as a Public Service

Diaconal organizations and religious leaders are in the front line of communities all over the world, and people look to them for leadership in the most difficult times. Globally, it is estimated that 80 percent of people identify themselves with a religious group.[3] It is a truism that faith communities are capable of unparalleled social mobilization, not to mention some form of moral standing.

The responses of Christian communities to serve whole communities in epidemics and health crisis are notable in history. They have responded to plague, leprosy, tuberculosis, smallpox and more recently HIV and AIDS and Ebola. Be it in the Byzantine monasteries of the Judean desert in the fourth and fifth century, sanitary cordons and quarantine stations in medieval Europe, leper colonies of Asia and Latin America in the 19th century, or hospices and home-based care services in Africa during the 20th and 21st centuries, the involvement of Christian communities have contributed to, and continues, controlling epidemics and the spread of diseases among communities.[4]

In my long diaconal career, I could realize that churches and diaconal organizations are among the first responders in emergency situations, as they live in and are part of the disaster-affected populations. My family and I are

[3] Pew Research Center's Forum on Religion & Public Life, *Global Religious Landscape*, December 2012.

[4] Manoj Kurian, Kenneth Ross, Jooseop Keum, Kyriaki Avtzi and Roderick Hewitt (eds.), *Ecumenical Missiology 1910–2012: Together Towards Life*, Regnum Edinburgh Centenary Series, Oxford: Regnum Press, 2016.

survivors of earthquakes and hurricanes in Central America, and our work together with several churches and church-related organizations was crucial to save lives, and provide refuge and community psychosocial support in a compassionate way. Because of this caring and human approach, all communities have created resilience and learnt how to support each other. Churches have convening capacities inherent in raising and working with a legion of people, which no other institution can afford worldwide. In times where the world is facing a complex humanitarian and development crisis, these capabilities cannot be underestimated. In the diaconal humanitarian response to the hurricane Mitch (1998) in Central America and the earthquakes (2001) in El Salvador, the participation of youth volunteers from different churches was fundamental to save lives and provide comfort within the first 12 hours after the disasters struck.

A study published by the World Health Organization (WHO) in the early part of the Millennium indicated that faith-based organizations (FBOs) provide an average of 30 to 40 percent of basic health care in the world.[5] This figure is expected to be much higher in contexts where conflicts and/or humanitarian emergencies are active (e.g. South Sudan, the Democratic Republic of Congo, Syria). In the most recent Ebola crisis in West Africa (2014), the WHO and WCC conducted a survey and identified that in Liberia and Sierra Leone, 46 percent and 30 percent, respectively, of overall health services were run by FBOs, not to mention the role of religious leader engagement to stop the spreading of the virus by calling followers to change their burial methods. Guinea had no national faith or NGO coordinating mechanism, but FBOs run some health clinics and programs.[6]

In most parts of the world, in addition to being health providers, churches contribute immensely to education and agriculture. For decades they have been operating schools and supporting agricultural projects around the world. But churches are not uniform or monolithic. There is significant variation in beliefs and practice, depending on the confession, the denomination and the local context. There are opposing approaches to issues such as sexual reproductive health and rights, gender equality and human sexuality, and those affected by them. These variations affect the ways churches do *diakonia*, and their respective role as a service provider.

In my diaconal experience I realized that the understanding of *diakonia* at a community level is easily understood, as it's based on practical work with a strong emphasis on solidary and community values. When we go to a wider

[5] Azza Karam (org), *Religion and Development Post 2015, Report of a Consultation between Donor Organizations, United Nations Development Agencies and Faith-Based Organizations*, UNFPA, New York, May 2014.

[6] Katherine Marshall, *Case Study Responding to the Ebola Epidemic in West Africa: What Role Does Religion Play?*, Berkley Center for Religion, Peace, and World Affairs, Georgetown University, 2016.

dimension, the concepts and understandings become more complex, especially when it reaches the ecumenical movement. The history of *diakonia* in the ecumenical movement has certainly not been without controversies, struggles and challenges. It has, nevertheless, always been the reflection, however limited, of the authentic desire of renewed discipleship on the part of Christians involved in *diakonia*, challenging and confronting the injustices, suffering and oppressions of the world. The embracing of development and sustainability theories also implied that church-related terms, such as *diakonia*, largely ceased to be used. Critics claimed that there would be no difference between church-based and secular agencies in implementing development projects, while others asked why there should be any difference if the objectives were achieved. In some contexts, the quality of the services provided by churches are recognized, mainly because of the Christian values associated to them.

Anyway, due to the current complexity of the world today, Churches are confronted to contextualize their diaconal commitment and define their unique role in shaping a different approach for their diaconal work. Christian leadership is fundamental to finding collective solutions and make a difference on how churches practice *diakonia*. They can help to localize development objectives, and to empower people for their direct and continuous participation in the places they live. They can do this on the base of social mobilization and two-way communication.

Questions related to justice and to the root causes of poverty influenced the diaconal work of church communities; if they in the past had presented their work as charity, and even as a humble service, they now underscore the importance of responding to burning social and political issues. As communities of faith, the relevance to this discourse goes far beyond the common recognition that churches 'run high quality clinics and schools and are present in the remotest corners'. Diaconal action is more and more claimed to be aimed at being rights-based, to promote human dignity and work for justice, peace and the integrity of creation.

Diakonia as Public Witness

The political role of religion and the Church during the Middle Age is undeniable, for the good and for the worse. Today, while churches and diaconal organizations are often recognized as important actors in humanitarian and development work, they are not necessarily seen as influencers of global political processes. The most emblematic example of prophetic and political engagement of churches in our time started in Latin America with the Theology of Liberation in the 70s and 80s.

At that time, churches had to seek support from the established powers and the economically powerful groups to carry out their task. However, they have made a big effort to end that situation and shake off the ambiguous protection offered by the upholders of the unjust order. The pastoral goal of setting up a 'new Christianity' brought about a political commitment by many Christians to create a more just society. They became more radical in their political stance. The increasingly more revolutionary political postures of Christian groups led the lay movements into conflict with the church hierarchy, opening the question of where they fit into the Church, and caused serious conscience problems for them. They called for radical changes in the Church's presence and activity. At that time, many priests and pastors were labeled 'subversives'. Many of them were monitored or sought by the police. Others were jailed, exiled or even assassinated by anticommunist groups. The Church rediscovered its prophetic role, and the theology of liberation has shaped the global political agenda and uplifted values of justice, inclusion and human dignity.[7] Diaconal institutions have been more political than before, addressing root causes of poverty and injustice while assisting the poorest communities and groups.

Likewise, the ecumenical movement played an important prophetic and political role in the world, for instance, in leading the anti-apartheid struggle in South Africa,[8] as well as other liberation struggles in Africa, Asia and Latin America. Nonetheless, based on my experience working in political (advocacy) *diakonia*, over the past few decades economic and political groups have been working to silence the prophetic voice of churches, in a time when the people needed it the most. In the context of polarization and populism, my perception is that local churches and the wider ecumenical movement have not been able to steer or lead processes to challenge unjust global policies and situations by remaining afraid of being labeled as leftists or socialists. Many of them have not been able to deal with critical human rights' issues to not upset or lose their members. Meanwhile, conservative forces that benefit from exclusion and discrimination celebrate the fact that churches and church leaders are relatively quiet.

Today's time urges Churches to rethink their ecclesiology, the way of being church today. Prophetic (or political) *diakonia*, understood as actions that denounce injustices (advocacy) and announce the Good News (actions), is more relevant and urgent than ever. This time also recognizes the role of religion in the public space, sometimes regarded as part of the problem, but always as part of the solution. Therefore, churches are expected to be relevant to the challenges humanity is facing today. For agents involved in development work, including diaconal organizations, this means a shift from exclusively traditional services to a comprehensive framework that also supports the struggle for justice. The face of poverty has changed; what is new is that large

[7] M. Gustavo Gutiérrez, *Notes for a Theology of Liberation*, Volume 31, issue 2, page(s) 243-261, Lima, Peru, May 1970.

[8] Graham A. Duncan and Anthony Egan, *The Ecumenical Struggle in South Africa: The Role of Ecumenical Movements and Organizations in Liberation Movements to 1965*, Volume 17, Issue 3, pp. 269-282, Ecclesiastical Law Society, Cambridge University, September 2015.

areas of poverty exist within middle-income countries. In many cases, growing poverty is a result of political mismanagement, corruption, warfare and climate change, and not because of lack of development.

Diakonia is thus expected both to be political and prophetic. It is political in the sense that it recognizes the political context in which it is embedded and develops forms of action that denounce injustice and supports processes toward a more just society. It is prophetic in the sense that it is inspired by the example of the Old Testament prophets and of Jesus who defended the dignity and the rights of the excluded, while announcing the values of God's reign, among which are justice and peace. In this journey, churches must be prepared to examine old narratives to assess whether their diaconal understanding is still relevant for the current religion and development discourse and the challenges humanity is facing. There is a crisis in the nation state as the key driver of development, and an increased expectation that new actors, including faith actors, fill the gap. At the same time, there is a lot of confusion about the role of religion in the public space. Churches have important work to do in promoting an agenda of being together with others in the public space, and shaping policies and customs that are inclusive and sustainable.

From my experience working in New York as the WCC Representative to the UN, I can say that for churches to come together in the public space requires that they transform the way they think and act to respect the dignity of our fellow human beings. It is imperative that churches revisit their theological interpretations and cultural practices that undermine human dignity. They should understand sustainable development promoting the God-given dignity of each person, which does not discriminate based on race, color, gender, language, religion, political or other opinion, national or social origin, property, birth or other status. It is about embracing the dignity of the whole human family.

The increasing recognition of the role of religion in development also represents an opportunity for *diakonia*, a unique possibility of building alliances with people of faith and with religious communities, affirming their hopes and distinct assets. In addition, it affirms the distinct identity and competence of the faith-based actors and adds energy to the commitment to save lives and struggle for justice. It also reminds *diakonia* of the calling to be agents of reconciliation and peace, in contexts where the 'politization' of religion and the 'religionization' of politics nurture mistrust among people and cause open conflicts. Churches and diaconal agents should take a leading role in establishing safe spaces for interfaith dialogue and interreligious platforms for promoting social justice and development.

Building Common Ground Between Faith and Rights

Long before the current human rights instruments were developed in the 20th century, there were religious communities that upheld human dignity and advocated for people who suffered from exclusion and discrimination. However, it is well known that some faith communities struggle to link their theological concepts of human dignity with international human rights standards and instruments. Again, based on my engagement in political *diakonia* at national and global level, one of the reasons for this struggle is related to the fact that there is not enough opportunity to get concrete information about and acquire knowledge of the important role of human rights as a legal framework and policy tool for upholding human dignity and expanding the agency and protection of people everywhere. We are aware that in many churches and Christian organizations there are still many obvious needs for increased dialogue, education, practical training and understanding of the intersection of faith and human rights.

In my understanding of *diakonia*, we keep faith and rights together. Prophetic *diakonia* implies to be faith and rights-based. But there is still the need for building bridges between 'people of faith' and 'human rights activists', because they do not always understand each other, they do not speak the same language. People of faith often speak about love, generosity and compassion, and not so much about legal frameworks, entitlements, duty bearers, rights holders, etc. But what does 'love' mean when it is not related to justice? And what does justice mean when it is not related to legal frameworks? Churches and the wider ecumenical movement should encourage this conversation, recognizing the deep and mutually enriching connections between *diakonia* and human rights.

Ecumenical Diakonia

The Ecumenical *Diakonia* document prepared by the World Council of Churches and ACT Alliance in 2017 indicates that throughout history, *diakonia* has been an integral part of the Church's mission, and that the understanding of ecumenical *diakonia* has deepened over the past few decades; in responding to challenges and critical questions, it has gained new insight and learned to articulate its role and mandate in new ways, and it has developed new organizational frameworks in order to be relevant and objective in today's socio-political reality.

Based on my diaconal experience, which started when I was working in the *Diakonia* Department of my Church in Brazil, then working for the LWF in Central America and Colombia, with the WCC in New York and more recently as the head of the ACT Alliance, I may say that *diakonia* is stronger and more effective when we work ecumenically. A diversified and vibrant ecumenical *diakonia* offers to the local and wider ecumenical movement a framework to promote diaconal intersectionality as the prophetic way forward. It can help to identify how intertwining systems of power impact those who are most marginalized in society, considering that the various aspects of humanity, such as class, race, sexual orientation, disability and gender, do not exist separately from each other but are complexly interwoven, and how diaconal action interacts in this equation.

The ecumenical movement should, however, find strategic ways to leverage the specific mandates and skills of diaconal institutions and churches to respond to the challenges of today's world. To respond to the physical and spiritual needs of those affected by disasters or conflicts, or to address unjust structures that are undermining life, the ecumenical movement needs to work closely together and establish close cooperation with other faiths. The competition and prominence of ecumenical structures and organizations cannot supersede the primary purpose of *diakonia*. Every organization has a distinctive role to play, and the combination of the coordinated actions are fundamental to serve those people and communities that are struggling to survive and uphold their dignity. As religions are not uniform, *diakonia* also has its variations. Churches and ecumenical institutions and organizations are required to make efforts to build on the diversity and the different approaches to respond to the needs and challenges of the world. The distinctiveness of the diaconal organizations has the potential to leverage the richness of our Christian faith, not to promote actions that are competing and divisive.

The ecumenical *diakonia* is an inherent testimony of faith and commitment to the principles Jesus Christ has taught us. It happens at the local, national, regional and global level, requiring that many ecumenical actors support this role. It is a concerted and intertwined effort that seeks to contribute to God's reign. The ecumenical movement is called to intentionally and truthfully work together to set up a platform to leverage ecumenical *diakonia* as a motivational tool to jointly promote inclusion, leverage the gifts and expertise of different churches, and to establish strategic partnerships with other religions and secular bilateral and multilateral organizations fighting for inclusion and the common good.

Partnerships

As already said, we are in a moment in time that require wide-ranging and strong partnerships to ensure just and inclusive societies. We live in the context of globalization, a complex dynamic that both supports and challenges human dignity. In my time working at the UN in New York, I have actively participated in global political processes, such as the 2030 Agenda for Sustainable Development, which is a platform for partnerships between faith actors and governmental, intergovernmental and civil society sectors.

Based on my experience, when entering into external partnerships, an overriding principle for churches and their diaconal institutions is to maintain the integrity of religious communities' mandate and mission, and to guard against instrumentalization. They should enter into partnerships as proactive agenda-setters for initiatives that keep people and their rights at the center, contribute to building a public space that is just for all and sustainable development that preserves the integrity of creation for current and future generations. In this process we should expect mutual transparency and accountability, where expectations are articulated clearly, and parameters for unacceptable behavior are discussed openly through ongoing and honest dialogue. We should build partnerships that promote equality and mutual respect between FBOs and other partners, irrespective of their size, status or power. All parts should respect each other's mandates, obligations and independence, and recognize each other's constraints and commitments. Mutual respect must not preclude either part from engaging in constructive dissent.

In this way, it is important to build the capacity of churches and communities to engage in development work and expect to see principles of subsidiarity practiced (i.e. localization/contextualization), but also to appreciate the mutual understanding of religion and development in our partnerships. The diversity among religious actors and contexts creates possibilities and challenges that require multilingual ability. There is a need to strengthen both religious and development literacy on both sides of the partnership. Local communities, churches and government actors often do not sufficiently share language and discourse on issues of mutual concern. Church communities need to bridge this gap by enabling effective communication and better understanding of their position vis-à-vis sustainable development concerns and human rights frameworks. Also, the priorities of church communities do not necessarily coincide with those of governments, especially with respect to timescales. For example, church communities often perceive their efforts as oriented toward long-term changes and improvements whereas government operations speeds are often dictated by short-term bureaucratic or political cycles.

We should also promote interfaith cooperation (diapraxis), based on common concerns and values and the need to reach out to all actors, including strengthening government compliance with human rights, especially where Freedom of Religion or Belief is under pressure. Interfaith collaboration counters identity politics and strengthens stability and social cohesion.

Diakonia and the Sustainable Development Goals (SDGs)

The world is changing in many ways, and so is the role of *diakonia*. When churches engage in *diakonia*, they engage by drawing from the mission of God, who is the God of life. The 2030 Agenda for Sustainable Development[9] provides a political and transformational framework to address many of the root causes of issues that are diminishing people's lives and damaging God's creation. None of the Sustainable Development Goals can be reached in isolation. From the perspective of ecumenical *diakonia*, the SDGs provide an

[9] https://sustainabledevelopment.un.org/post2015/transformingourworld.

important platform for action. It is a universal agenda that applies to all countries, it is integrated, it is indivisible and it is based on a clear set of borrowed principles, including Christian values. They were established with the purpose of engaging civil society and voluntary organizations, including faith communities, and of promoting active citizenship.

Churches, together with other ecumenical and other faith communities, have been engaged in the discourse on sustainable development and participated actively in the process of formulating the SDGs, and have joined in initiatives to lobby governments to address inequalities, governance, climate change, and conflict and fragility. Therefore, prophetic *diakonia* becomes a key part of any strategy for implementing the 2030 sustainable development agenda. Church communities can help to localize development objectives, to empower people for their direct and continuous participation in the places they live. They aim at empowering people to engage as active citizens, claiming economic and social rights. The SDGs serve as a relevant point of reference, especially when engaging in advocacy and public debate.

In working together as church communities, we owe it to each other to reflect critically on our own responses to changing landscapes, and to treasure the opportunity for mutual accountability. At the same time, it is vital that churches continue to engage in dialogue and cooperation with the international community. Churches must come together to provide hope. Particularly in the current landscape, hope must be the characteristic message of the Church. The advocacy of the church can only be based on a Christian faith that has a prophetic, critical approach that is aiming at transformation and hope; not marked by fatalism, by indifference or cynical words of devaluation of others, but by love.

Conclusion

Given the situation in the world today, where people's needs and available resources determine different roles, it is important to identify *diakonia* in this context. The realities of service provision, resource capacity and political presence have made it clear that being knowledgeable of the diaconal work of churches is necessary, if we are to take seriously the fundamental dimension of social development and social capital. Thus, some reflection on, among other factors, development partners in the world of religion, especially where community service provision has already been a reality for centuries, is essential, particularly as we consider the imperatives of future development agendas.

Transformation engages and changes all who are a part of social and developmental processes. In that manner, transformational *diakonia* helps to overcome helpers' syndromes, practices and relations that separate 'we' from 'they'. In the end, no person escapes vulnerability. We all need to be transformed, reconciled and empowered. For that reason, we are all in need of *diakonia*, first of God's *diakonia* as revealed in Jesus Christ, and then as mutual care and accompaniment of one another. Transformation is clearly a process, but at the same time, it envisions the achievement of certain goals, arriving at a new situation where human dignity is more respected with peace and justice for more people. Thus, transformation is closely related to what also may be defined as social change, progress or development.[10]

Churches and other faith communities play a critical role in peace building, promotion and education. Many churches and diaconal structures have vast experience in working in humanitarian response and engagement in action-oriented activities that encourage the understanding of values of a culture of peace, tolerance and non-violence within communities in many parts of the world. For churches, promoting peace requires different approaches, from preventive to proactive actions oriented to bring about positive and lasting change in the structures, systems and policies that perpetuate impoverishment and injustice, which lead toward conflict. Prophetic *diakonia* is then a key tool for promoting just peace. The world today is becoming more complex, and churches are increasingly facing new emerging challenges, which require that they look toward a prophetic way to conduct their mission. By addressing changes at the political and policy levels rather than by treating symptoms of social problems, prophetic *diakonia* work has the potential to affect many more lives than direct diaconal service alone.

Although churches and ecumenical organizations have significant experience in humanitarian, development and advocacy action, they will not make substantial changes in humanity if they work alone or in competition. Therefore, there is a need to intentionally work together to equip churches and ecumenical organizations to better understand the different dimensions of *diakonia* and create tools and strategies to support the ecumenical *diakonia* as the way forward. Prophetic, inclusive and value-based actions will determine the future of humanity. Prophetic *diakonia* compels churches to be at the side of those excluded and marginalized in society, those who do not have access to basic services and human rights. Churches and ecumenical organizations must avoid exclusion of migrants, ethnic minorities, social minorities, human rights defenders, people with different capacities, the elderly, women, LGBTIQ people, youth, etc. They must partner with other sectors and actors that seek to include everyone, in a great solidarity project based on human rights and ethical values inherent to the prophetic religious doctrines: all created in the image and likeness of God.

---

[10] Lutheran World Federation, *Diakonia in Context: Transformation and Practice of Diakonia*, p. 41f, LWG, Geneva, Switzerland, 2009.

Bibliography

Dietrich, Stephanie and Jorgensen, Knud and Korslien K. Kari (eds.), *Diakonia as Christian Social Practice, an introduction*, Regnum Books International, Oxford, UK, 2014.

Duncan A, Graham and Egan, Anthony, *The Ecumenical Struggle in South Africa: The Role of Ecumenical Movements and Organizations in Liberation Movements to 1965*, Volume 17, Issue 3, pp. 269-282, Ecclesiastical Law Society, Cambridge University, September 2015.

Gutiérrez, M. Gustavo, *Notes for a Theology of Liberation*, Volume 31, issue 2, pp. 243-261, Lima, Peru, May 1970.

Karam, Azza (org)., *Religion and Development Post 2015, Report of a Consultation between Donor Organizations, United Nations Development Agencies and Faith-Based Organizations*, UNFPA, New York, May 2014.

Kurian, Manoj and Ross, Kenneth, and Keum, Jooseop and Avtzi, Kyriaki, and Hewitt, Roderick (eds.), *Ecumenical Missiology 1910–2012: Together Towards Life*, Regnum Edinburgh Centenary Series, Oxford: Regnum Press, 2016.

Lutheran World Federation, *Diakonia in Context: Transformation and Practice of Diakonia*, p. 41f, LWG, Geneva, Switzerland, 2009.

Marshall, Katherine, *Case Study Responding to the Ebola Epidemic in West Africa: What role does religion play?* Berkley Center for Religion, Peace, and World Affairs, Georgetown University, 2016.

Nordstokke, Kjell, *Liberating Diakonia*, Tapir Akademisk Forlag, Trondheim, Norway, 2011.

Pew Research Center's Forum on Religion & Public Life, *Global Religious Landscape*, December 2012.

Weber, Max, *The Protestant Ethic and the Spirit of Capitalism,* New Introduction and trans. by S. Kalberg, Blackwells Roxbury Publishing Company, Los Angeles, USA, 2002.

World Bank Group, *Annual Report 2017, End Extreme Poverty – Boost Shared Prosperity*, Washington, USA, 2017.

World Council of Churches and ACT Alliance, *Ecumenical Diakonia*, Geneva, Switzerland, 2018.

Index

Editors and Contributors

Editors

Stephanie Dietrich, b. 1966. Professor diaconal studies, VID Specialized University, Oslo, Norway. Studied theology in Neuendettelsau and Erlangen, Germany, and in Oslo. Dr Theol from MF, Norwegian School of Theology, Religion and Society, in 1998 with 'Das schweigende Gebet: Zur fundamentaltheologischen Grundlage des Gebets in ökumenischem Blickwinckel' (Silent prayer: On the theological basis for understanding prayer in an ecumenical context). Teacher and PhD scholar at MF 1991-1998. 1998-2007 senior advisor on ecumenical theology with Church of Norway Council on Ecumenical and International Relations. For many years involved in national and international bi- and multilateral ecumenical dialogues and organizations. Member of the Joint Lutheran-Orthodox Commission since 2004. Member of presidency of CPCE (Community of Protestant Churches in Europe) 2006-2012. 2012-2016, convener of the Church of Norway Theological Committee. Since 2014, member of the WCC Faith and Order Commission. At VID Specialised University, she chairs the interdisciplinary research fellowship CODE (Diaconal Community Development). Has edited several books and published numerous articles on ecclesiology, *diakonia*, ecumenical theology and community development.

Knud Jørgensen, 1942-2018. MTh from University of Copenhagen, Ph.D. in Missiology, Fuller Theological Seminary. Journalist and theologian, served with Radio Voice of the Gospel, Addis Ababa, Ethiopia, the Lutheran World Federation, Geneva, the International Mass Media Institute, Kristiansand, Go out Centre, Hurdal, Norway, Norwegian Church Aid, the Mekane Yesus Seminary, Addis Ababa, and the mission foundation Areopagos. Dean of Tao Fong Shan, Hong Kong until 2010. Served as adjunct professor at the MF Norwegian School of Theology. Coordinated the Egede Institute. Published several books and articles on journalism, communication, leadership and mission, including 'Equipping for Service: Leadership in Church and Society' (Regnum 2012). One of the editors of the Regnum Edinburgh 2010 Series.

Kari Karsrud Korslien, b. 1958. Was until 2019 associate professor at VID Specialized University, Diakonhjemmet. Trained as a social worker and deacon, working as a researcher and lecturer in diaconal studies. Now serving as deacon in the Church of Norway, The *Diakonia* House, Gjøvik. Has contributed in editorial teams to various textbooks in Norwegian (2009, 2011) and English (2014, 2016) about professional practice, recognition and inclusive fellowship. Special areas are relation-based *diakonia*, voluntary work, exposure, cooperation and local community work. She has contributed to establish the Master Programmes in *Diakonia* and *Diakonia* and Christian Social Practice (2004, 2010) and lately Master in Community Development and Social Innovation with specialization in *Diakonia*, Community Development, and Christian Social Practice. In 2019 she undertook research on diaconal voluntary work in the Church of Norway.

Kjell Nordstokke, b. 1946. Professor emeritus at Diakonhjemmet University College in Oslo, Norway; studied theology in Stavanger and Oslo. Dr. Theol. from University of Oslo, 1990, with the thesis Council and Context in Leonardo Boff's Ecclesiology. The Rebirth of the Church among the Poor; Dr.h.c. from Escola Superior de Teologia (EST) in São Leopoldo, Brazil, 2017. He lived ten years in Brazil, serving as pastor with Evangelical Church of Lutheran Confession (1974-81) and as professor of theology at EST (1994-96). Since 1990 he has been employed at Diakonhjemmet in Oslo, mainly responsible for diaconal training and for developing *diakonia* as an academic discipline; 1998-2005, CEO of Diakonhjemmet Foundation; 2005-2009, Director of the Department for Mission and Development, Lutheran World Federation, in Geneva. Since 2009, lecturer in the Science of *Diakonia* at Diakonhjemmet (now VID). Has published books on *diakonia*, such as *Liberating Diakonia* (Tapir, 2011) and various articles, for instance "*Diakonia* in Context: Transformation, Reconciliation and Empowerment" in *Mission as Ministry of Reconciliation* (Regnum Books, 2013), and "Trinitarian Perspectives on *Diakonia*" in *Evangelism and Diakonia in Context* (Regnum Books, 2015), as well as in two former volumes in this *diakonia* series: *Diakonia as Christian Social Practice* (Regnum Books, 2014) and *Diakonia in a Gender Perspective* (Regnum Books, 2016).

Contributors

Tony Addy, b. 1946. University of Manchester, MA (Theol), University of St. Andrews (PG Dip). Ordained Minister, Community Minister, South Leeds (1971 – 1976), Executive Secretary, Division of Community Affairs, British & Irish Council of Churches (1976 – 1980), Director, William Temple Foundation (1980 – 1991), General Secretary, European Contact Group on Urban Industrial Mission & Work and Economy Network (1991 – 2004), Consultant on Globalisation, World Council of Churches (1998 – 2000), Head of International Education, Diaconia University of Applied Sciences, Finland (2005 – 2012), Chairperson, International Society for the Study and Research of Diaconia and Christian Social Practice (2012 – 2016), Member, editorial team, 'Diaconia, Journal for the Study and Research of Diaconia and Christian Social Practice' (2010 –), Head of Education, interdiac, Czech Republic (2008 –), Consultant, Lutheran World Federation process 'Re-forming Community *Diakonia* in Europe' (2012 –). Published on community development and local *diakonia*, work, economy, globalization and more recently on conviviality as a core concept for *diakonia*.

Jostein Ådna, b. 1955. Doctor theologiae from MF – Norwegian School of Theology, Religion and Society, Oslo, Norway, 1994. *Wissenschaftlicher Assistent* of Professor Dr. Dr.h.c. Peter Stuhlmacher at the University of Tübingen, Germany, 1988–93. Since 1993 teacher and researcher at the School of Mission and Theology, Stavanger, Norway (part of VID Specialized University since 2016), from 2000 as Professor of New Testament.

Rudelmar Bueno de Faria, b. 1963. PgD from EST on *Diakonia*, BS from UNISINOS on Administration and Foreign Trade and AdvDip from University of Geneva on International Humanitarian Law. General Secretary of the ACT Alliance. Served as the World Council of Churches Representative to the United Nations in New York (2014-2017) and worked for 18 years with the Lutheran World Federation's World Service, in different countries and capacities. Member of the United Nations Faith Advisory Council, UN Steering Committee to Prevent Incitement to Violence and the Humanitarian Encyclopedia of the Graduate Institute and University of Geneva. Published books, chapters and articles on religion and international affairs, sustainable development (Routledge 2018) and *diakonia*.

Maria Louise Munkholt Christensen, b. 1986. Studied Protestant Theology at Aarhus University, Denmark, and earned her PhD degree at the same university in 2015 (her dissertation will be published with the title *Relating through Prayer: Identity Formation in Early Christianity* (Frankfurt am Main: Peter Lang 2019 (forthcoming)). Since 2015 she has been a postdoc in the Research Centre "Education and Religion" at the University of Göttingen, Germany. In her current project she investigates late antique Christian texts that feature women as teachers. Since 2014, Munkholt Christensen is a member of the Faith and Order Commission.

Wanda Deifelt, b. 1963. BA from Escola Superior de Teologia (São Leopoldo, RS, Brazil), MTS from Garrett Seminary (Evanston, IL, USA) and PhD from Northwestern University (Evanston, IL, USA). Ordained Lutheran pastor and theologian, served as the first professor of the chair of feminist theology at Escola Superior de Teologia (now Faculdades EST, São Leopoldo) for 14 years. At EST also served as vice-president of the seminary, dean of graduate studies, and national coordinator of INATE (International Network of Advanced Theological Education). Visiting faculty at Emmanuel College (Toronto, Canada) and Gurukul (Chennai, India). Professor at Luther College (Decorah, IA, USA) since 2004. Publications in the areas of constructive and contextual theologies, embodiment, ecumenical and interreligious dialogue.

Rose Dowsett, b. 1943. BA (1965) from Bristol University, UK. Married to Dick, mother to three, grandmother to five. Staff worker with IVF, now UCCF

UK, 1966-69. Member of OMF International 1969 to present (though now retired). Served in Philippines 1969-77, Scotland to 1984, and then international role as conference speaker, Bible teacher and training minister. Lecturer in Church History and Missiology at Glasgow Bible College for 18 years. Author, editor and contributor to many multi-author volumes, commentaries, etc. Council and/or leadership roles for UCCF (IVCF UK), Interserve International, Evangelical Alliance UK, World Evangelical Alliance Mission Commission, Lausanne Theology Working Group, WCC Commission on World Mission and Evangelism, Edinburgh 2010, Scottish Evangelical Theology Society, and others. Member of West Glasgow New Church. Current research on China Inland Mission, OMF International and church (es) in South East Asia.

Carlos Emilio Ham (Rev. Dr.), b. 1956 in Cuba. He has been a pastor of the Presbyterian-Reformed Church in Cuba for more than 30 years and served as its General Secretary for 8 years (1993-2001). He was appointed President of the Student Christian Movement in Cuba in 1989, elected Co-President of the Caribbean Conference of Churches (CCC) in 1997 and elected Vice-President of the Caribbean and North America Council for Mission (CANACOM) in 2000. He joined the World Council of Churches' (WCC) staff in March 2001 as Program Executive for Evangelism, served as the Co-ordinator of the Mission and Ecumenical Formation Team and later as Programme Executive for *Diakonia* & Latin America-Caribbean until December 2013. In June 2015 he was installed as the Rector of the Matanzas Evangelical Theological Seminary and Pastor of the Presbyterian-Reformed Church *The Redeemer* in Versalles, Matanzas. He currently is part of the advisory team for the WCC's Program on *Vital and Sustainable Churches in Diakonia and Development*. He studied theology at the Matanzas Theological Seminary in Cuba and received his degree in 1984. In 1999 he obtained his Doctor of Ministry degree at the Austin Presbyterian Theological Seminary in Texas, USA, working on the project *The Homiletical Tripod: A Guide for Cuban Lay Preachers*. At this Seminary in Austin he also received in February 2011 a *Distinguished Service to the Church Award*. In November 2015, Ham completed his PhD in the area of Theology with the Free University of Amsterdam. The tittle of the thesis is '*Empowering Diakonia*: A Model for Service and Transformation in the Ecumenical Movement and Local Congregations'. He has published various books and articles on the topics mentioned above and has preached and/or lectured in the USA, Canada, Central America, South America, the Caribbean, Europe, Asia, the Middle East and the Pacific.

Beatrice Nekesa Juma, b. 1978. MTh, from MF Norwegian School of Theology, Master in *Diakonia* and Christian Social Practice from VID Specialized University, Oslo, Master in Arts and Leadership (MAL) from Pan Africa Christian University, Kenya. Ordained in the Methodist Church in Kenya (MCK), served as a Methodist minister (priest) since 2004, a Superintendent Minister (in charge of several Methodist congregations), a youth patron for Kilifi Synod (parish) in Kenya and adjunct lecturer in Kenya Methodist University, Mombasa Centre, Kenya (2007-2010).

Jeromy Limbani Juttah, b. 1981. MA, VID University, Priest in the Anglican Diocese of Northern Malawi. Worked as Assistant Parish Priest at St Marks Parish in Mzuzu (2008-2011); Registrar for Board for Theological Studies, Zomba Malawi (2012-2014) and Adjunct Lecturer at Leonard Kamungu Theological College Zomba Malawi (2011-present).

Nicolas Abou Mrad, b. 1970. Ph.D. in Biblical Studies, Friedrich Alexander Universitaet zu Erlangen – Nuernberg. Theologian, taught Biblical studies and ancient languages at the Saint John of Damascus Faculty of Theology, Lebanon. Member of the Biblical Federation in the Middle East, and one of the editors of the Arabic Contemporary Commentary of the Bible. Author of commentaries and articles on Old and New Testament themes.

Rodolfo Gaede Neto, b. 1951. Graduation, master's degree and doctorate in Theology, with emphasis in *diakonia*, attended the Faculdades EST, in São Leopoldo, Brazil. Pastoral ministry practiced in two parishes of the Evangelical Lutheran Confession Church in Brazil, in the State of Espírito Santo. District Pastor of the Southern Ecclesiastical District of Espírito Santo. Vice Synodal Pastor of the Synod Espírito Santo a Belém. Director of the Lutheran Diaconic Association, in the State of Espírito Santo, Brazil. Teaching in undergraduate and postgraduate studies in Theology since 2003 and coordination of the undergraduate course in Theology since 2007, at Faculdades EST, in São Leopoldo, Brazil.

Zo Ramiandra Rakotoarison, b. 1978. Master in *Diakonia* and Christian Social Practice from Diakonhjemmet Oslo, Bachelor in Geography from University of Antananarivo, Madagascar. Served as Program Leader Empower FLM, Assistant and Secretary for the Malagasy Lutheran Church, Madagascar until 2017; Communication assistant for the "Programme de Professionalisation de l'Agriculture" Antananarivo Madagascar 2000 – 2001. One of the contributors of the Regnum Edinburgh 2016 Series. Since October 2017, PhD research fellow at VID Specialised University, Oslo, working on a PhD project with the title "Faith-oriented and asset-based community development in a Malagasy context: a qualitative study of Use Your Talents capacity building project".

Luis Antonio "Chito" Gokim Tagle, b. 1957. He is the 32nd Archbishop of Manila. He has been Archbishop since December 12, 2011, and a cardinal since November 24, 2012. He also serves as President of Caritas International, a federation of Catholic relief, development and social service organizations, and of the Catholic Biblical Federation. Tagle has become involved in many social issues in the Philippines with emphasis on helping the poor while maintaining opposition against what he terms "practical atheism", abortion and contraception (equated with abortion in the Philippines). Dubbed as the "Asian Francis", Tagle is often characterized as a representative of the Church's progressive wing. He has criticized the Catholic Church for using "harsh words" to describe LGBT and divorced and remarried Catholics. He is also a proponent of allowing divorced and remarried Catholics to receive communion on a case-by-case basis. He generally prefers to be called by his nickname rather than by his clerical title. Aside from his native Filipino (Tagalog), he also speaks English and is fluent in Italian. He is also proficient in reading Spanish, French and Latin.

Olav Fykse Tveit, b. 1960. He is general secretary of the World Council of Churches, elected in August 2009, re-elected to a second term in July 2014. Led the International Ecumenical Peace Convocation (Kingston, Jamaica, 2011), the 10th Assembly of the WCC (Busan, Republic of Korea, 2013), and other conferences and consultations. Awarded doctorate in theology by MF, Norwegian School of Theology, Religion and Society in Oslo in 2002. His thesis reframed in *The Truth We Owe Each Other: Mutual Accountability in the Ecumenical Movement* (WCC Publications, 2016). Also author of *Christian Solidarity in the Cross of Christ* (WCC Publications, 2012). Prior service as general secretary of the Church of Norway Council on Ecumenical and International Relations (2002-09), a member of the Faith and Order Plenary Commission, co-chair of the Palestine Israel Ecumenical Forum core group, on the board of Norwegian Church Aid.

Rudolf von Sinner, b. 1967 in Basel/Switzerland, Dr. theol. habil., was from 2003-19 Professor of Systematic Theology, Ecumenism and Interreligious Dialogue at Faculdades EST in São Leopoldo, Rio Grande do Sul, Brazil, where he also served as Dean of Postgraduate Studies and Research (2007-19) and Director of the Ethics Institute (2014-19). In 2019, he moved to Curitiba to serve as Associate Professor of Systematic Theology at the Pontifical Catholic University of Paraná. Since 2013, he has been Professor extraordinary at Stellenbosch University. He holds a personal rated scholarship from the Brazilian National Council for Scientific and Technological Development and is a member of the National Committee on Respecting Religious Diversity of the Brazilian Ministry for Human Rights and Moderator of the World Council of Churches' Commission on Education and Ecumenical Formation, as well as an ordained minister of the Evangelical Church of the Lutheran Confession in Brazil. A prolific writer and frequent lecturer, his latest book in English is *The Churches and Democracy in Brazil: Towards a Public Theology Focused on Citizenship* (Wipf & Stock, 2012).